THE WORLD OF GEOFFREY KEATING

THE WORLD OF GEOFFREY KEATING

History, myth and religion in seventeenth-century Ireland

Bernadette Cunningham

FOUR COURTS PRESS

Set in 10 on 12 point Ehrhardt for
FOUR COURTS PRESS LTD
7 Malpas Stree, Dublin 8, Ireland
e-mail: info@four-courts-press.ie
http://www.four-courts-press.ie
and in North America
FOUR COURTS PRESS
c/o ISBS, 920 NE 58th Avenue, Suite 300, Portland, OR 97213-3786.

A catalogue record for this title
is available from the British Library.

ISBN 1–85182–533–9 hbk
ISBN 1–85182–806–0 pbk

Printed in Great Britain
by Antony Rowe Ltd, Chippenham, Wilts.

To my father and first history teacher, Seán Cunningham,
and to the memory of my mother, Úna Cunningham

Contents

LIST OF ILLUSTRATIONS   viii

LIST OF ABBREVIATIONS   ix

PREFACE   xiii

PREFACE TO PAPERBACK EDITION (2004)   xv

PART 1: THE AUTHOR'S WORLD AND WORK

1   Introduction: Geoffrey Keating and the Irish people   3

2   Family background and educational influences: Irish and European   17

3   Catholic teaching and social change in Munster   41

4   Scholarly networks and approaches to the historical record   59

5   Foreign writers and Irish readers: the wider world of print in *Foras Feasa ar Éirinn*   83

PART 2: AN IRISH CATHOLIC PERSPECTIVE ON THE PAST

6   Irishness and the recall of the past   105

7   Origin myths: people, language, place   122

8   Political and social hierarchies   141

9   The moral order   159

PART 3: SCRIBES, TRANSLATORS AND OTHER READERS

10   Catholic readers and translators of *Foras feasa ar Éirinn* in the seventeenth century   173

11   Catholic history; Protestant history: *Foras feasa ar Éirinn* in circulation, 1680-1740   201

12   Conclusion   226

BIBLIOGRAPHY   227

INDEX   251

List of illustrations

1   Inscription over west doorway of Tubbrid chapel, 1644. Sketch by G. du Noyer   15

2   Moorestown castle, County Tipperary, 1840. Sketch by G. du Noyer   21

3   Pierre de Besse, *Conceptions theologiques sur les quatres fin de l'homme* (Paris, 1622), frontispiece   51

4   'Heaven and hell'. Pierre de Besse, *Conceptions theologiques sur les quatres fin de l'homme* (Paris, 1622), p. 484   55

5   *Foras feasa ar Éirinn*. Closing page of preface, from a manuscript written 1641-6   71

6   Late seventeenth-century copy of the Catholic 'A defence' translation of *Foras feasa ar Éirinn* into English   107

7   Opening page of book 1 of Michael Kearney's 1635 translation of *Foras feasa ar Éirinn*. Scribe Domhnall Ó Suilleabháin, 1668   175

8   *Foras feasa ar Éirinn*. Interpolated(?) text on the theme of inauguration   179

9   Brian Bóroimhe, monarch of Ireland, frontispiece from Dermod O'Connor's 1723 English adaptation of *Foras feasa ar Éirinn*   219

List of abbreviations

ARÉ	*Annála ríoghachta Éireann: Annals of the Kingdom of Ireland by the Four Masters from the earliest period to the year 1616*, ed. and trans. John O'Donovan (7 vols, Dublin, 1851)
BL Cat. Ir. MSS	S.H. O'Grady and Robin Flower, *Catalogue of Irish manuscripts in the British Museum* (3 vols, London, 1926-53)
BL	British Library, London
Bodl.,	Bodleian Library, Oxford
Census Ire.,	*A census of Ireland, circa 1659* (Dublin, 1939)
Civil survey, i	R.C. Simington (ed.), *Civil survey, i, Tipperary* (Dublin, 1931)
Clanricarde	*Memoirs of the right honourable the Marquis of Clanricarde, lord deputy general of Ireland* (London, 1722)
Cronin, 'Printed sources'	Anne Cronin, 'Printed sources of Keating's *Foras feasa*', *Éigse*, iv (1943-4), 235-79
Cronin, Sources of Keating's *Foras feasa ar Éirinn*	Anne Cronin, Sources of Keating's *Foras feasa ar Éirinn* (M.A. thesis, UCD, 1933)
Cronin, 'Manuscript sources'	Anne Cronin, 'Sources of Keating's *Foras feasa ar Éirinn*: 2, manuscript sources' *Éigse*, v (1945-7), 122-35
DNB	*Dictionary of National Biography*
ESA	Geoffrey Keating, *Eochair-sgiath an Aifrinn: an explanatory defence of the Mass*, ed. Patrick O'Brien (Dublin, 1898).
FFÉ	Geoffrey Keating, *Foras feasa ar Éirinn: the history of Ireland*, ed. David Comyn and P.S. Dinneen (4 vols. London, ITS, 1902-14)
Fiants, Ire.,	*The Irish fiants of the Tudor sovereigns during the reigns of Henry VIII, Edward VI, Philip & Mary, and Elizabeth I* (4 vols, Dublin, 1994)
FLK	Franciscan Library, Killiney (now in UCD Archives)
GO	Genealogical Office
Hayes, *Mss sources*	R.J. Hayes, *Manuscript sources for the history of Irish civilisation* (11 vols, New York 1965); *First supplement* (3 vols, New York, 1979)

HMC	Historical Manuscripts Commission
IER	*Irish Ecclesiastical Record*
IMC	Irish Manuscripts Commission
ITS	Irish Texts Society
JRSAI	*Journal of the Royal Society of Antiquaries of Ireland*
LG	*Leabhar gabhála*
Maynooth	Russell Library, NUI/St Patrick's College, Maynooth
MSE	*Magnum speculum Exemplorum* (Douai, 1603, etc.)
NA	National Archives, Dublin
New Hist. Ire., iii	T.W. Moody, F.X. Martin and F.J. Byrne (eds), *A new history of Ireland, iii, early modern Ireland, 1534-1691* (Oxford, 1976)
New Hist. Ire., iv	T.W. Moody, W.F. Vaughan (eds), *A new history of Ireland, iv, eighteenth-century Ireland, 1691-1800* (Oxford, 1986)
New Hist. Ire., ix	T.W. Moody, F.X. Martin and F.J. Byrne (eds), *A new history of Ireland, ix, maps, genealogies, lists* (Oxford, 1984)
NLI Cat. Ir. MSS	Nessa Ní Sheaghdha et al., *Catalogue of Irish manuscripts in the National Library of Ireland* (Fasc.1-13, 1967-96)
NLI	National Library of Ireland
NLS	National Library of Scotland
NUI	National University of Ireland
Ó Bruadair, *Poems*	J.C. Mac Erlean (ed.), *Duanaire Dhaibhidh Uí Bhruadair: the poems of David Ó Bruadair* (3 vols, London, 1910-17)
PCT	*Pairlement Chloinne Tomáis*, ed. N.J.A. Williams (Dublin, 1981).
PRIA	*Proceedings of the Royal Irish Academy*
PRO	Public Record Office, London
QUB	Queen's University, Belfast
Rawl.	Rawlinson
RIA Cat. Ir. MSS	Thomas F. O'Rahilly, Kathleen Mulchrone, et al., *Catalogue of Irish manuscripts in the Royal Irish Academy* (Fasc. 1-28. Dublin, 1926-1970)
RR	*Réim ríoghraidhe*
TBB	Geoffrey Keating, *Trí bior-ghaoithe an bháis: the three shafts of death*, ed. Osborn Bergin (Dublin, 1931)
TCD	Trinity College, Dublin
UCC	University College, Cork, NUI Cork
UCD	University College, Dublin, NUI Dublin

'And when you and I talk about history, we don't mean what actually happened, do we?'

Penelope Lively, *Moon tiger*

Preface

The real Geoffrey Keating is more elusive than Shakespeare. No manuscript in his hand has been identified and none of his contemporaries mentions having met him. The most tangible links to the real person are a chalice bearing his name now in Waterford Museum and a plaque erected in his memory, by persons unknown, in 1644, and still visible in its original location over the entrance door to Cillín Chiaráin, in Tubbrid, County Tipperary. Most of the folklore about him cannot be traced back to the seventeenth-century but is drawn primarily from later published sources the accuracy of which cannot be tested. Although the historical Keating is no longer familiar, his writings have had an influence on Irish language and literature as significant as Shakespeare's role in relation to English. Less recognised, but no less influential, has been his role in shaping Irish people's perceptions of their own identity, their country, their history and their religion. All writers reflect the concerns, beliefs and values of the world in which they live. Keating's historical and theological writings are a guide to the issues and values that were important to him. By focussing on those writings and especially on the connections between his major historical work, *Foras Feasa ar Éirinn*, and the religious and social issues that dominate his theological texts, this study illuminates the interrelationships between religion and history in early modern Ireland.

Keating's interpretation of his world offered contemporaries and later readers a sense of Ireland, of Irishness, and of Catholicism that had wide appeal. His idea of Ireland as an ancient and worthy kingdom had enormous attractions for his contemporaries. Because he wrote about the past in accessible language and style, yet in a manner acceptable to scholars, using primary sources, his legacy has been very significant. His writing was an important channel through which older historical traditions preserved in early manuscripts and poetry were transmitted to later generations. Through the efforts of scribes, translators, publishers, editors, readers, teachers, preachers and storytellers, his ideas have been widely disseminated in ways that have never been explored or understood. This book examines these issues during the first century of the life of his works, from the 1620s to the 1730s, but also offers clues as to why his ideas still have resonance today.

Over the last century the name Seathrún Céitinn has become associated, in the minds of generations of Irish students, with textbooks for advanced study of Irish.

Those same students, and many thousands of others, have also been taught legend, myth and history in Irish schools without ever realising the extent of the influence of Keating's writings on this communal memory of the Irish Catholic past. This book offers an interpretation of the world of Geoffrey Keating that seeks to make intelligible to the inheritors of his legacy how their own perceptions of Ireland, as well as his, have been formed.

The research and writing of this book has been done over a number of years and could not have been undertaken without ongoing access to the collections of the National Library of Ireland. The evening opening of the National Library, in welcome contrast to all other significant Dublin repositories of Irish manuscripts, made my research possible. Its long-established policy of acquiring microfilms or photostats of manuscripts of Irish interest from other archives proved invaluable in making texts held in other institutions at home and abroad accessible to me. I have also relied on the facilities of the British Library, old and new, and made extensive use of the Bodleian and Taylorian Institution libraries during a year spent in Oxford and benefited greatly from the facilities offered. I am also grateful to the staff of other libraries and archives I have used including the Russell Library and John Paul II Library, Maynooth, Trinity College Dublin, the Royal Irish Academy, the Franciscan House of Studies, Killiney, Milltown Park Library, the Public Record Office of Northern Ireland, Queen's University Belfast, the Folger Shakespeare Library, Woodstock Theological Center Library at Georgetown University, Washington D.C., the National Library of Wales, Aberystwyth, John Rylands Library, Manchester, Chetham's Library, Manchester, Archbishop Robinson Library, Armagh, Marsh's Library, Dublin, and Boole Library, University College Cork. I am especially grateful to my former employers and colleagues at the Dublin Diocesan Library for allowing me leave of absence during the academic year 1996-7 which gave me time to research and write. The Warden and fellows of All Souls College, Oxford, unwittingly provided me with the opportunity for research by awarding my husband a visiting fellowship there. The hospitality of the Principal and fellows of Hertford College, Oxford, made the time spent in Oxford especially enjoyable. Many people provided me with assistance and encouragement including Toby Barnard, Nicholas Canny, Vincent Carey, Clare Carroll, Vincent Comerford, Tom Connors, Margaret Crawford, George Cunningham, Virginia Davis, Jackie Hill, John Kennedy, Colm Lennon, Brian Mac Cuarta, Joe McLaughlin, John MacLoughlin, Gerry Moran, Hiram Morgan, Kenneth Nicholls, Jane Ohlmeyer, Siobhán O'Rafferty and Katharine Simms. I am particularly grateful to William O'Sullivan for his interest and for giving me access to the unpublished papers of his late wife (Anne O'Sullivan, née Cronin) on Geoffrey Keating. Micheál Mac Craith and Nollaig Ó Muraíle each kindly read and commented on draft chapters of the book. Their corrections and thought-provoking suggestions are much appreciated; the remaining errors are my responsibility. The interest shown in this book by Michael Adams and the staff of Four Courts Press has contributed greatly to ensuring its eventual completion. My husband, Raymond Gillespie, turned most trips to archives into holidays (or was it the other way round?), provided a well-stocked library in what might otherwise be a normal house, consulted manuscripts on my behalf in the National Library of Scotland and the National Archives, Dublin, accompanied me on numerous trips to south Tipperary in search of Keating's roots and recognised the significance for Keating's ancestry of legal documents he happened to examine in the course of his own researches.

The illustrations on pages 15, 21, 71, 175, and 179 are reproduced by kind permission of the Officers of the Royal Irish Academy, pages 51 and 55 courtesy of the Bodleian Library, Oxford, and page 107 courtesy of the Council and Trustees, National Library of Ireland.

Preface to paperback edition (2004)

Since the original edition of this book was published in 2000 two categories of manuscripts which I used extensively have, of necessity, been transferred to new locations. The unpublished papers of the late Anne O'Sullivan (née Cronin), to which her late husband, William, had kindly given me access when they were in his care, are now among the O'Sullivan papers bequeathed to the Manuscripts Department, Trinity College, Dublin. The Gaelic manuscripts, 'A' series, from the Franciscan Library Killiney, which include the earliest extant copy of Keating's *Foras Feasa ar Éirinn*, were transferred to UCD Archives, University College Dublin, in November 2000.

I have availed of the opportunity afforded by the paperback edition to amend some small errors and to update the bibliography

BC

PART I
THE AUTHOR'S WORLD AND WORK

Introduction: Geoffrey Keating and the Irish people

I

Within a few years in the early 1630s Catholic Ireland produced two remarkable Irish prose works. The first was a long discourse on sin and repentance and the second was a narrative history of Ireland. Even more remarkable is that these apparently diverse works were written by the same man, Geoffrey Keating, a Catholic priest working in Tipperary. *Trí bior-ghaoithe an bháis* (Three shafts of death) is believed to have been in circulation by 1631 and *Foras feasa ar Éirinn* (Compendium of wisdom about Ireland) was probably completed by 1634. Although both works have been available in print in scholarly editions since the early twentieth century, these books have been mainly studied by scholars interested in their linguistic or literary merits, or occasionally by historians seeking a handy guide to early Ireland. The inter-relationships between these texts, and indeed the other writings of Geoffrey Keating, have been little explored.

The links between the central themes of Keating's writings, whether historical or religious, and the reality of the workings of society in seventeenth-century Ireland have not previously been analysed in any detail. Confining the study of Keating's writings to a mere paper-chase in search of the sources used, or discussing these texts simply as linguistic models or examples of baroque literary art, ignores their real significance. These works were the considered response of an educated Old English clergyman to his experiences on the Irish mission over more than twenty years in early Stuart Ireland. Thus, *Trí bior-ghaoithe an bháis*, although drawn mainly from European sermon literature, also incorporated the author's reflections and comments on the Irish situation in the first quarter of the seventeenth century. The concern with moral reform and with the preservation of social order, which were underlying themes of *Trí bior-ghaoithe an bháis*, were issues that concerned many Counter-Reformation clergy. Perennial problems of greed, dishonesty, self-indulgence, as expressed in theft, land-grabbing, illicit collusion with those in power, adultery and other misdemeanours, were portrayed as breaches of a contract between God and his people.[1] These lapses of the moral order were seen

1 *TBB*, ll. 3370-550.

3

as creating difficulties for the community of the faithful that could only be recti-
fied through moral reform, both personal and communal. Problems arising from a
marked increase in social mobility, which many of Keating's contemporaries commented on, were addressed in *Trí bior-ghaoithe an bháis* as part of Keating's vision
for a more moral society.[2]

This concern with the maintenance of order – theological, social, moral and
political – links the theological text of *Trí bior-ghaoithe an bháis* with the historical
narrative found in *Foras feasa*. It has not been sufficiently recognised that *Foras
feasa* is a highly polemical work, with strong religious overtones. It argues, for
instance, the case of the secular clergy against that of the regular clergy, a matter
of heated debate in Keating's own day. The blueprint for the institutional church
presented by Keating was an episcopal and parochial one, in which the hierarchical order would prevail.[3] This was paralleled by an understanding of the political
order in which the kingdom of Ireland was a harmonious commonwealth resting
on a contract between king and people, built on respect for the law.[4] Keating's historical writing presented layers of evidence from the past to support his view of
contemporary society.

History, myth, and religion are inextricably intertwined in all of the writings
examined here through which the world of Geoffrey Keating is explored. The first
part of this study (chapters 1-5) examines the social, cultural and theological background of Keating's writings. The second part (chapters 6-9) analyses his presentation of a coherent Irish Catholic perspective on the world through the medium
of history and theology. The final part (chapters 10-11) assesses the impact of his
work as it lived on among other Irish communities long after the author's familiar
world had virtually disappeared.

II

The cultural and intellectual world in which Keating's theological works took shape
are the focus of chapters 2-3. Both the sources of his theological ideas and his
motivations in framing them in a manner appropriate to Irish audiences are considered. While his theological ideas demonstrate the debt he owed to Counter-
Reformation teaching, the manner in which he communicated those doctrines to
Irish audiences reveals his understanding of the realities of the world in which he
lived. It was not a world in which there were clear divisions between religion and
secular affairs.

---

2 See ch. 3 and ch. 9. 3 Bernadette Cunningham, 'Seventeenth-century interpretations of the past: the
case of Geoffrey Keating', *Irish Historical Studies*, xxv, no. 98 (Nov. 1986), pp. 116-28. Cainneach Ó
Maonaigh, 'Scríbhneoirí Gaeilge Oird San Froinsias' in Benignus Millett and Anthony Lynch (eds), *Dún
Mhuire, Killiney, 1945-95, léann agus seanchas* (Dublin, 1995), pp. 37-56; Pádraig A. Breatnach, *Téamaí
taighde nua-Ghaeilge* (Maigh Nuad, 1997), ch. 4. 4 Bernadette Cunningham, 'Representations of king,
parliament and the Irish people in Geoffrey Keating's *Foras feasa ar Éirinn* and John Lynch's *Cambrensis
eversus* (1662)', in Jane Ohlmeyer (ed.), *Political thought in seventeenth-century Ireland* (Cambridge, 2000).

Keating sought to transform the Irish people he addressed from a social elite into a morally just community. Failure to reform, he warned, would result in extinction, as immoral lineages would be allowed to die out as divine punishment. This concern to establish social and moral order in a potentially disordered world depended for its success on fostering among that elite a sense of both their entitlements and their responsibilities. Thus, the relationship of the Irish people with God, and their relationship with their king are parallel themes. The need for an acceptable political order, to be achieved through a contract between king and people (chapter 8), which would result in harmonious social relationships was paralleled by a concern with the need for respect for the moral law, to overcome the burden of original sin and gain the eternal reward of paradise (chapter 9).

The ideas formulated by Geoffrey Keating were not developed solely within an Irish political and religious context. His earliest known prose work, a tract on the Mass called *Eochair-sgiath an Aifrinn*, bears the hallmarks of his seminary training under Counter-Reformation influence. It has, for instance, many similarities with the English language tract on the Mass published in 1611 by the Irish Jesuit, Henry Fitzsimon. The value of Keating's tract on the Mass for contemporaries lay in its simple presentation of core Tridentine teachings on the Mass in a form appropriate to Irish-speaking audiences. The lively refutation provided by *Eochair-sgiath an Aifrinn* of the ideas of Martin Luther and John Calvin, two key exponents of the doctrines of the Protestant Reformation, finds echoes later in Keating's criticism of hostile writers in the polemical preface to *Foras feasa*. His depiction of loyalty to the Mass as a clear indicator of fidelity to Catholicism, which lay at the core of *Eochair-sgiath*, had significant political implications for Irish Catholics in the reign of James I. Concern over the tenuous political and social status of elite Irish Catholics was very real to the communities addressed in Keating's theological tracts.

Through his writings Geoffrey Keating sought to interpret the Counter-Reformation for Irish readers, and these texts reveal to us his priorities. By considering what he chose to communicate we can understand what he judged to be appropriate concerns for a pastor working in Ireland. By looking at his method of communicating with his audience we can deduce the audience he had in mind and in this way we can gain insights into his understanding of the Irish Catholic community in the early seventeenth century (chapters 2-3).

While the influence of his continental education is immediately obvious in *Eochair-sgiath*, the experience of living and working in Europe affected Keating's thinking on many levels. Thus the example of Catholic histories of European nations would have encouraged Keating to write similarly about Ireland. He was motivated, in part, by the desire to prove that 'if only indeed they had given their proper estimate to the Irish, I know not why they should not put them in comparison with any nation in Europe in three things, namely in valour, in learning, and in being steadfast in the Catholic faith'.[5]

---

5 *FFÉ*, i, 76-9.

The context and traditions, Irish and European, from which Keating's historical writings derived are considered in chapters 4 and 5. His network of scholarly contacts, and the source materials to which he had access, provide the context within which to evaluate his historical method and achievement.

The writing of national history had received renewed impetus in a Europe dominated by religio-political rivalries. It should come as no surprise that in Keating's history of the Irish nation religious allegiances should have been more significant than ethnic identities in forming the author's ideas. The focus of *Foras feasa* was on the shared heritage of those Gaeil and Sean Ghaill (Old English) who were Catholic. It was a depiction of the origins of the people who now saw themselves as 'Éireannaigh'.[6] The motivation to study history was closely linked with the retrospective justification of current religious positions, and it will be seen that in this context the biblical framework of early history had a particular significance.

III

The story of Ireland was presented in the narrative of *Foras feasa* in a manner that allowed the various peoples of Ireland to be incorporated into a shared origin legend. From Keating's own perspective, the facilitation of a *rapprochement* between the Old English and the Gaelic Irish allowed him to assert that his personal sense of Irishness had an historical validity no less acceptable than that of the Gaelic population. The quest for historical legitimacy was important for the cultivation of cohesion among the Irish Catholic population which was seen as necessary to the preservation of political order in early Stuart Ireland (chapters 6-8).

The historical background of this vision of Ireland was drawn from a range of medieval texts ranging from Cormac Mac Airt's advice to his son to the origin myth contained in *Leabhar gabhála Éireann*. This latter text, probably first assembled in the eighth century, and now extant in its twelfth-century form, retained its popularity through successive generations because it was an historical framework that legitimised change. Keating's approach to this traditional interpretation of the past was consistent with that of his contemporaries. The Louvain Franciscan historians who were active at the same time were equally drawn to this framework of waves of invasions of peoples who were the ancestors of the Irish. Micheál Ó Cléirigh and his Franciscan associates produced a revised text of the *Leabhar gabhála* as well as compiling genealogies of saints and kings, and *Annála ríoghachta Éireann*, a history of the kingdom of Ireland in the form of annals.[7] While the form

---

6 Breandán Ó Buachalla, Preface to Geoffrey Keating, *Foras feasa ar Éirinn*, eds, David Comyn and P.S. Dinneen (4 vols, London, ITS, reprint, 1987); Cunningham, 'Seventeenth-century interpretations of the past'; D.R. Kelley, *Foundations of modern historical scholarship* (New York, 1970); for a discussion of the idea of 'Éireannach' see Breandán Ó Buachalla, *Aisling ghéar: na Stíobhartaigh agus an taos léinn, 1603-1788* (Baile Átha Cliath, 1996), pp. 73-80.   7 Bernadette Cunningham, 'The culture and ideology of Irish Franciscan historians at Louvain, 1607-1650', in Ciaran Brady (ed.), *Ideology and the historians: historical studies xvii*

of Keating's work was different from that of the Franciscans, essentially both were the product of an intermingling of a new Counter-Reformation Catholic ideology with a long established Irish tradition of historical scholarship.[8]

Later in the seventeenth century, some among the New English used the model of the *Leabhar gabhála* to create echoes of the present in the Irish past. When a Cheshire man, Peter Leycester, wrote a brief history of Ireland in the 1660s he referred to the same prehistoric migrations Keating had discussed, but called them 'plantations'.[9] Richard Bellings, the Old English historian of the Catholic Confederation, writing in the 1670s portrayed both the Old English and the native Irish as themselves 'colonyies'.[10] Michael Kearney, the Tipperary man who undertook an English translation of *Foras feasa* in 1635 also described new arrivals from the time of the Fir bolg forward as 'colonists'.[11] Earlier, the attorney general of Ireland, Sir John Davies, writing in 1612 had discussed the possibility of an accommodation between different groups of the Irish population in the context of the plantation of Ulster. He contrasted that scheme with earlier English plantations, asserting that the plan for Ulster was for

> a mixed plantation of British & Irish, that they might grow up together in one Nation ... and this truly is the Masterpiece, and most excellent part of the work of Reformation ... it will secure the peace of Ireland, assure it to the Crown of England for ever; and finally, make it a civil, and a rich, a mighty, and a flourishing Kingdom.[12]

Simultaneously, some Irish poets, writing in the early years of the reign of James I, gave their sanction to the idea of the Stuart kingdom of Ireland by drawing attention to the Milesian origin of James Stuart.[13]

There was a general restructuring of political and social allegiances in the aftermath of the 1603 treaty of Mellifont that concluded the Nine Years' War. The concern of all sections of Irish society after 1603 to attempt to find a workable political framework on which to build a new society, in the wake of the treaty of Mellifont, is a crucial part of the context of the writings of Geoffrey Keating. It

(Dublin, 1991), pp. 11-30; 223-27; *Genealogiae regum et sanctorum Hiberniae*, ed. Paul Walsh (Maynooth, 1918); *Leabhar gabhála: the book of conquests of Ireland, the recension of Micheál Ó Cléirigh, part 1*, ed. R.A.S. Macalister and John MacNeill (Dublin, 1916); *Annála ríoghachta Éireann: annals of the kingdom of Ireland by the Four Masters from the earliest period to 1616*, ed. & trans. John O'Donovan (7 vols, Dublin, 1851). **8** Breandán Ó Buachalla, '*Annála ríoghachta Éireann* agus *Foras feasa ar Éirinn*: an comhtheacs comhaimseartha', in *Studia Hibernica*, nos. 22-23 (1982-3), pp. 59-105. **9** Chester, Cheshire Record Office, DLT/B/2, ff. 262-8. See also George Ormerod, *History of Cheshire* (3 vols, 1882). **10** *History of the Irish Confederation and the war in Ireland*, ed. J.T. Gilbert (7 vols, Dublin, 1882) i, 2. **11** RIA, MS 24 G 16, preface. **12** Sir John Davies, *Discovery of the true causes why Ireland was never entirely subdued* (London, 1612), pp. 281-2. **13** Breandán Ó Buachalla, 'Na Stíobhartaigh agus an t-aos léinn: Cing Séamas', *PRIA*, lxxxiii, C (1983), pp. 81-134; 'James our true king: the ideology of Irish royalism in the seventeenth century', in D.G. Boyce, Robert Eccleshall, and Vincent Geoghegan (eds), *Political thought in Ireland since the seventeenth century* (London, 1993), pp. 7-35.

was necessary to provide an appropriate historical underpinning for the legitimacy of a Catholic political elite that would have sufficient moral authority to preserve the social order within the framework of the Stuart kingdom of Ireland. The cultivation of a shared belief in a particular historical mythology was part of the process of preserving social order at a time of political and social transformation (chapters 7-8).[14]

Keating's *Foras feasa*, focusing on the antiquity of the kingdom of Ireland, and integrating lineage, language and landscape to mould a new sense of Ireland and of Irishness (chapters 6-7) quickly became the agreed version of the Irish past for Catholics of his generation. Over time, it gained favour with all those for whom a sense of their own Irishness had political or cultural importance, regardless of their religious affiliation (chapter 11). The polemical preface to *Foras feasa*, with its emphasis on the dichotomy between authors who had denigrated Ireland and Keating's defence of Ireland's reputation, was designed to appeal to the reader's sense of Irishness. He criticised earlier writers who had provided inaccurate portrayals of Ireland, or had presented the Irish people in an unfavourable light. He accused hostile commentators of concentrating on the negative aspects of the lower orders rather than on the virtues of the Irish kings and nobility. He regarded even the palesman Richard Stanihurst as hostile because of his rejection of the Gaelic inheritance which Keating used as the core of his myth of the Irish past.[15]

For Keating, the establishment of appropriate links to the Irish historical past was the key to the cultivation of the idea of Irishness among the Old English community. He carefully reconstructed the story of an ancient kingdom of Ireland, moulding the narrative to suit his own social and religious agenda. The establishment of continuities from ancient to modern was achieved through the formulation of an appropriate myth of the Irish past. Keating's version combined the *Leabhar gabhála* framework and the genealogical record of the kings of Ireland derived from the *Réim ríoghraidhe* with traditional stories about the exploits of particular king heroes, to provide an historical narrative that appeared familiar and therefore authentic. For those Irish who were of Anglo-Norman ancestry, the narrative continued sufficiently far into the twelfth century to provide them with an honourable place in the story of the kingdom of Ireland. It linked the Old English Catholic community in Ireland directly into the Irish origin myth, thereby affirming their status in the modern Irish kingdom (chapter 8).

This account of the origins of the Irish kingdom and people formed the backdrop on which was superimposed a view of the Irish Church that was appropriate to the ambitions of Irish diocesan Catholic-Reformation clergy. By linking religion and history he conveyed to his elite Irish readers an understanding of Irish Catholicism that had meaning in their secular as well as in their spiritual lives. The

14 See R.R. Davies, 'Law and national identity in thirteenth-century Wales', in R.R. Davies, et al. (eds), *Welsh society and nationhood* (Cardiff, 1984), p. 52.   15 *FFÉ*, i, 4, 20, 30-42, iii, 350, 358-66; Colm Lennon, *Richard Stanihurst: the Dubliner, 1547-1618* (Dublin, 1981).

emphasis on traditions of piety, hospitality and generosity to the church which was integral to Keating's portrayal of early Irish civilisation, had a contemporary purpose. Drawing on the motifs of praise that were traditionally used in entries in the Irish annals, it constructed a vision of a Christian people bonded together by both moral and social obligations. It asserted the confidence of Irish Catholics in the future of their church and indicated the structures and role appropriate to that church in contemporary society.

IV

Keating appears to have heeded Cicero's warning to historians that those who 'did not embellish their facts' would be mere 'chroniclers and nothing more'.[16] It is evident from his theological writings, *Trí bior-ghaoithe an bháis* and *Eochair-sgiath an Aifrinn*, that Keating was a skilful preacher who had a good understanding of the power of story-telling in communicating fundamental truths to general audiences. That awareness of the communicative power of story underpinned the sophisticated combination of myth and history found in his historical writing also. While some elements of *Foras feasa* were soon dismissed by critics as 'fable',[17] the decision to include such stories had been a deliberate one. Myth and legend were not something peripheral to Keating's historical text. Traditional stories were intentionally incorporated into his historical framework of invasions and kings as part of the origin legend of the Irish people. The more elements of traditional lore that were knitted into Keating's reconstruction of the past, the more convincing would be his history as the 'true' history of the Irish people.

It has been argued that the real significance of Keating's history lay 'not in its historical accuracy, but rather in its capacity to capture the imagination, to feed an affective, an ideological rather than a scholarly interest in Irish antiquity'.[18] On one level, therefore, our concern is not to judge whether what he chose to write was 'true'. Rather it is to seek to understand why he wrote what he did, what values informed his work, what social and cultural circumstances allowed him to share his concerns with others, and what meaning his work had for the audiences he addressed.

The creation of a new myth about the Irish past gave the work a wide general appeal because it was an assertion of pride in being Irish. The Irish 'nation' as defined by *Foras feasa* was a kingdom. His definition of '*Éireannaigh*' was exclusive rather than inclusive in that Catholicism was a prerequisite. His portrayal of the '*Sean Ghaill*' as '*Éireannaigh*' was not innovative, but was comprehensively

---

16 Cicero, *De Oratore*, 2: 236-37 (II.xii.54) cited in Martine Watson Brownley, *Clarendon and the rhetoric of historical form* (Philadelphia, 1985), p. 4.   17 See John Colgan's annotations in FLK, MS A 14, and, from a very different perspective, Richard Cox's preface 'To the reader' in *Hibernia Anglicana* (London, 1689-90), i, which described *Foras feasa* as 'an ill-digested heap of very silly fictions'.   18 J. Th. Leerssen, *Mere Irish and fíor-Ghael* (2nd ed. Cork, 1996), p. 275.

argued through the medium of an historical narrative of an ancient and honourable kingdom.

   Although the Irish language was beginning to be replaced by English in certain
circumstances among the Irish elite by the 1620s, Keating chose Irish as the appropriate language for his history. In the context of language change, the language in
which *Foras feasa* was written gradually came to have an added significance for the
way in which its story of the Irish people was understood by its target audience.
This theme is discussed in chapters 6-8.

                                          V

The view of the world recorded for us by Geoffrey Keating was not just the view
of one man. His polished articulations of the history and the religious ethos of the
society in which he lived quickly became part of expressions of Irish cultural and
political identity in the seventeenth and eighteenth centuries. It is his historical
narrative that is best remembered. It was available first in manuscript form, then
by being absorbed into the work of other writers, and finally by the publication of
printed editions. Chapter 10 of this study evaluates how Keating's writings were
appropriated and transmitted among his fellow Irish Catholics in the seventeenth
century, while chapter 11 considers the later legacy down to the first appearance of
his history in print.

   Keating's history circulated in a range of scholarly environments. Among those
closest to home were members of the Ó Maolchonaire family of professional
scribes, in county Clare, especially Iollann[19] and Seán Ó Maolchonaire, the latter
being one of the most prolific scribes of Keating's works in the mid-seventeenth
century. Also involved at an early stage in the transcription of *Foras feasa* were
members of the Ó Duibhgeannáin family. Flaithrí Ó Duibhgeannáin had transcribed one version of the history in 1638.[20] By 1646, another of the same learned
family, Fearfeasa, was at work on another copy.[21] These early transcripts indicate
that *Foras feasa* found keen readers among the traditional scribal families and that
their work facilitated the dissemination of Keating's history. Their acceptance of
this innovative text suggests that they were sympathetic to its message and
accepted its treatment of the traditional Irish historical record as appropriate to the
needs of their time (chapter 4).

   The manuscript was also available, almost immediately, to the community of
Irish Franciscan scholars and very quickly found its way to the desks of the Irish
historians working at St Anthony's College, Louvain. Two very early copies of the
text now preserved in the Franciscan Library Killiney[22] were the work of
Franciscan scribes; one was partly written by Micheál Ó Cléirigh himself.[23] Pól Ó

19 RIA, MS 23 O 19.   20 BL., Egerton MS 107.   21 TCD, MS 1394.   22 FLK, MSS A 14; A 15.
23 The second scribe of FLK, MS A 14 has not been identified. Myles Dillon, et al. (eds), *Catalogue*

Colla, a Franciscan working in county Leitrim also made a transcript of the history in 1644.[24]

This scribal activity in Irish, which continued unabated in a variety of milieux down to the nineteenth century, represented but one dimension of the dissemination of the works of Geoffrey Keating. Copyists working with Latin and English translations of *Foras feasa* also found a steady interest in their work. Thus, although not fully available in print in the Irish language until the early twentieth century, the text of *Foras feasa* was accessible to those who sought it, and in a choice of languages. The divergent interests of the audiences who encountered *Foras feasa* in each of these three languages is explored in chapters 10-11. The interest in Keating's theological tracts seems frequently to have been ancillary to his status as a historian, and unlike the history, no translation into English has ever been published. Yet these texts too were valued by later generations of readers and scribes, and they, no less than the history, were multi-layered texts which were read and understood in a variety of ways by diverse audiences over many generations.

The extant manuscripts containing his various writings are one guide to the audiences Keating's writings may have reached. It is known that many of the manuscript copies of *Eochair-sgiath an Aifrinn* were made for, or were at one time owned by, priests.[25] We can be confident that the material contained in the tract influenced the way in which the Mass was understood in seventeenth-century Ireland and subsequently.

The prose works of Geoffrey Keating were transmitted over time through a range of networks to reach audiences whose responses to the author and his writings do not conform to any one neat pattern. An examination of the legacy of Geoffrey Keating involves not so much questions about the text itself as about its diverse audiences, those involved in the dissemination of the ideas it contained as scribes and translators and most commonly as readers. There was, even in the late seventeenth century, more than one legacy of Geoffrey Keating. His *Foras feasa* was valued by diverse communities of readers for a range of contrasting reasons.

The various mechanisms through which Keating's writings circulated among different textual communities in Ireland in the first century after they were written are considered in part three of this study. The way the prose works were transmitted in the seventeenth century in Irish in manuscript form by a range of scribes on behalf of their patrons was refocussed in the eighteenth century as the

of Irish manuscripts in the Franciscan Library, Killiney (Dublin, 1969), pp. 27-30. **24** Paris, Bib. Nat. Fonds Celtique MS 66 (NLI, microfilm P463). Pól Ó Colla was among those who had links with the Church of Ireland bishop and scholar James Ussher; see *The Book of Lecan: Leabhar Mór Mhic Fhir Bhisigh Leacain*, ed. Kathleen Mulchrone (Dublin, IMC fascimile, 1937), introduction. **25** Bernadette Cunningham, 'Geoffrey Keating's *Eochair-sgiath an Aifrinn* and the Catholic Reformation in Ireland', in. W.J. Sheils and Diana Wood (eds), *The churches, Ireland, and the Irish: studies in church history, xxv* (Oxford, 1989), pp. 133-43. Manuscript copies of *Eochair-sgiath an Aifrinn* commissioned or owned by priests include RIA, MS 23 C 14 (1752); 23 L 25 (1697-8); 23 N 18 (1701-2); BL, Egerton MS 181 (1709); Egerton MS 189 (1658); Maynooth, MS B 7 (1675); Maynooth, O'Curry MS C 14; UCC, Fermoy Gaelic MS 24, etc.

motivations of both scribes and patrons changed. While traditional mechanisms of scribal transmission in Irish proved appropriate to cater for the demand that existed for Keating's theological tracts, the case of *Foras feasa* proved immensely more complex.

It was already apparent in the mid-1630s that scribal transmission in the Irish language was not adequate to cater for the needs of all those who desired to have access to Keating's *Foras feasa*. The work of translators and adaptors of the history reveals much about contemporary and later responses to the work. It illustrates the way the text was read and responded to, not least because most translators, including Michael Kearney and John Lynch, added their own introductions to the history outlining their views on the significance of the author and his work.

In addition to the various translations there were historians and polemicists who based their own narratives of Irish history very closely on Keating's text. Prominent among such work was Peter Walsh's *Prospect of the state of Ireland* (1682), Thomas Harte's manuscript history of the kingdom of Ireland (late 1680s), and Hugh MacCurtin's *Brief discourse in vindication of the antiquity of Ireland* (1717), published in reply to Sir Richard Cox's *Hibernia Anglicana*. Even writers such as Cox, hostile to the views contained in *Foras feasa*, did not ignore the work, despite their reluctance to credit it as authentic history.[26]

The appropriation of Keating's myth-history of Catholic Ireland by Protestant readers in the eighteenth century is explored in the final section of this book. By the early eighteenth century, when *Foras feasa* became available in print in an English language version as translated and adapted by Dermod O'Connor (1723), the publication was aimed primarily at an Irish Protestant readership. That *Foras feasa* could be so readily adapted to meet the needs of new categories of readers was its guarantee of lasting popularity. Over the centuries different audiences read the text in new ways as dictated by the political and social circumstances of their own time (chapter 11).

The availability of a version of Keating's history in print in English allowed much wider public access to the text than previously. Through the nineteenth century cheaper editions of *Foras feasa* derived from O'Connor's version were issued by a variety of publishers, not least the successful Dublin Catholic publisher James Duffy. The first scholar to attempt a new translation in the nineteenth century was the Fenian leader John O'Mahony whose text was published in New York in 1857. His introduction outlined the Fenian perspective on Keating's work, and provides evidence of the power of Keating's polemical preface to influence later thinking:

> If it be the mark of a partisan to be thoroughly Irish in heart and soul, to
> love men of Irish name and blood more than men of any other, to abhor

---

26 Charles O'Conor, *Dissertations on the history of Ireland* (1766), p. x, appears to have followed Cox in regarding *Foras feasa* as 'a most injudicious collection'; Nollaig Ó Muraíle, *The celebrated antiquary: Dubhaltach Mac Fhirbhisigh (c.1600-71)* (Maynooth, 1996), p. 310.

the destroyers of his nation and kinsmen, who are also the desolators of his own paternal hearth, with a hatred that neither time nor distance can mitigate, then this is the work of a most undoubted partisan. ... neither has he in any one particular swerved from the truth of history as he has understood it.[27]

While O'Mahony's interpretation of *Foras feasa* echoed through the Irish literary and cultural revival of the early twentieth century, O'Connor's version of the text in English had met the needs of both Catholic and Protestant readers for a century and a half before that. While some scholars protested vigorously that the translation was seriously flawed, its popularity was unaffected. Nineteenth-century scribes continued also to make copies of the Irish language text of Keating's history, a practice which came to an end only when the full text was published in Irish and English by the Irish Texts Society, beginning in 1902.

VI

By the late nineteenth century Keating's reputation was such that his writings were among the first selected for attention by enthusiasts working for the revival of the Irish language. Thus his modern reputation rests primarily on his perceived status as the founding father of the Irish language in its modern form. Generations of students, down to the present day, have studied the language using extracts from Keating's prose works. Robert Atkinson's 1890 edition of *Trí bior-ghaoithe an bháis*, as part of the Royal Irish Academy's 'Irish Manuscript Series' was very influential because it was then 'the only considerable body of classical modern Irish accessible to students'.[28] It was replaced in 1931 by a new edition prepared by Osborn Bergin. A shorter text, *Selections from Keating's Three shafts of death*, edited by F.W. O'Connell, was issued in 1910, again intended for the student market. Osborn Bergin's *Sgéalaigheacht Chéitinn: stories from Keating's history of Ireland*, was first issued in 1909, proved immediately popular, and is still in print. Bergin had a dual purpose in his selection:

> First, from a linguistic point of view it would familiarise readers of modern Irish with the beautifully clear yet thoroughly idiomatic form of the literary language which was the common property of the Gaelic race in Ireland and Scotland three hundred years ago. In the second place, it would form an easy introduction to that part of our native literature which has been cultivated with most success – the romantic tales.[29]

27 Geoffrey Keating, *The history of Ireland from the earliest period to the English invasion*, transl. John O'Mahony (New York, 1857), p. 11.   28 Geoffrey Keating, *Trí bior-ghaoithe an bháis*, ed. Osborn Bergin (2nd ed. Dublin, 1931), p. v.   29 Osborn Bergin (ed.), *Sgéalaigheacht Chéitinn: stories from Keating's history of Ireland* (3rd ed. Dublin, 1930), p. iii.

Bergin's textbook edition is largely responsible for the extent to which readers of Irish today have a general familiarity with the work of Geoffrey Keating. At the time these textbooks were first issued, the interest in the revival of the Irish language, as exemplified by Keating's works, was being actively pursued by a variety of cultural groups. In the early years of the twentieth century, branches of Conradh na Gaeilge were named after him. His history was among the first texts issued by the Irish Texts Society.[30] David Comyn, editor of the first volume in the Irish Texts Society edition, dedicated his work to Douglas Hyde, president of Conradh na Gaeilge, 'in recognition of our long friendship as fellow-workers for the same good old cause'.[31] The 'cause' was the revival of the Irish language and, for many, Keating was its symbolic personification.

VII

Writing in 1939, Paul Walsh, a scholar who had devoted much of his life to the study of the Irish manuscript tradition, commented in pessimistic mood:

> Strange to say, scarcely anything in known traditionally of Keating in the parish of his birth and the scene of his missionary labours. What with cinema and radio and 'scuse me dances, there will be less known about the good man in the future.[32]

While it is true that much of the local lore concerning Keating is derived from printed sources compiled long after his death, his scholarly work is still a source of pride in the area of his birth. In the townland of Burgess, in south county Tipperary, a plaque was erected on Burgess bridge in 1990 by the local community, in memory of the neighbourhood's famous son, Dr Geoffrey Keating, Catholic priest, historian, and poet.[33] A short distance away, in this still rural area, the ruined walls of the church known as 'Cillín Chiaráin' at Tubbrid stand in the shadow of a larger, disused, nineteenth-century Church of Ireland church. On the west gable of this simple rectangular structure, over the arched doorway, there is another commemorative plaque, erected in 1644, bearing a Latin inscription.

> *Orate pro animabus Patris Eugenii Duhy vicarii de Tybrad et Domini Doctoris Galfridii Keating huius sacelli fundatorum necnon et pro omnibus aliis tam sacerdotibus quam laicis quorum corpora in eodem iacent Sacello, Anno Domini 1644.* (Pray for the souls of Father Eoghan O'Duffy vicar of Tubbrid and Dr Geoffrey Keating the founders of this chapel, as likewise for all others, clergy as well as laity whose bodies rest in the same chapel, AD 1644).

---

30 Pádraigín Riggs, 'The beginnings of the Society', in Pádraig Ó Riain (ed.), *Irish Texts Society: the first hundred years* (London, ITS, 1998), pp. 30-2.   31 *FFÉ*, i, dedication.   32 Paul Walsh, 'Review of Patrick Power, *Waterford and Lismore*', *Irish Book Lover*, xxvi (1938-9), p. 43.   33 The plaque was unveiled by the archbishop of Cashel, Dr Thomas Morris. See below ch. 2 for Keating's probable connections with Moorestown Keating.

1 Inscription over west doorway of Tubbrid chapel, 1644. RIA, G. du Noyer,
Antiquarian sketches, vol. 7 (1865), f. 100

That such an inscription was erected in the mid-seventeenth century, presumably
by individuals who had personal memories of the two Catholic priests it commemorated, suggests that Geoffrey Keating was particularly renowned in his own
time, and that his career had earned him widespread respect and admiration. The

fact that his reputation survived, so that he was still being commemorated by his local community in the late twentieth century, suggests that Geoffrey Keating's life's work was of lasting value. This study is an exploration of that work, of the world from which Keating drew his inspiration, and of the nature of his contribution to Irish culture and society both in his own day and among subsequent generations.

Before the significance of his various writings can be evaluated within the context in which they were produced and disseminated, it is necessary to trace Geoffrey Keating's intellectual journeys from the place where he himself began, among his family living in the valley of the River Suir in that small part of the ancient territory of Decies that now lies in the County of Tipperary.

2

Family background and educational influences: Irish and European

I

The river Suir, rising in the north of County Tipperary in the province of Munster, flows southwards through Thurles and Holy Cross before reaching the town of Cahir, which nestles in the shadow of the Galtee mountains. From there the river flows on to Ardfinnan and Newcastle, where it widens, turns northwards for some miles and then curves eastwards skirting the Comeragh mountains, as it passes through the towns of Clonmel and Carrick before meeting the sea at the port of Waterford. The lower Suir valley, south and east of Cahir, stretching from Ardfinnan to Carrick, was one of the most densely populated regions of Tipperary in the seventeenth century.[1] In that part of the Suir valley designated as the barony of Iffa and Offa, the town of Cahir, with its weekly market on Thursdays and an annual three-day fair commencing on 15 May[2] together with Ardfinnan, a settlement which was ecclesiastical in origin, were the largest centres of population.

The area lay on the south-western periphery of the area of influence of the Butlers of Ormond. It adjoined land that had traditionally been in the hands of the Fitzgeralds, earls of Desmond, but which had been included in the plantation of Munster in the closing decades of the sixteenth century. The barony of Iffa and Offa itself lay just outside the region directly affected by the Munster plantation. To the west lay the White Knight's territory of Clangibbon, and that of the Mac Briens in Aherlow. The Suir valley region enjoyed considerable prosperity in the sixteenth century, in spite of the disruption sporadically caused by local rivalries, particularly between the Butlers of Dunboyne and the Butlers of Cahir.

In the barony of Iffa and Offa itself, the barons of Cahir, a cadet branch of the Butlers of Ormond, were the largest landholders and the area was loosely under

---

1 William Smyth, 'Property, patronage and population: reconstructing the human geography of mid-seventeenth century County Tipperary', in William Nolan (ed.), *Tipperary: history and society* (Dublin, 1985), p. 106. 2 Patrick Power, *The placenames of Decies* (2nd ed., Cork, 1952), p. 297; Bodl., Carte MS 62, f. 171; *Calendar of state papers, Ireland, 1611-14*, p. 513.

their overlordship.[3] Cahir Castle, a Butler stronghold, stood out as one of the most imposing structures in the region. In 1647 it was described by Colonel Thomas Pigott as 'the strongest castle I know in the kingdom'.[4] In Keating's youth, the baron of Cahir was Theobald Butler and, together with his wife Mary Cusack, he enjoyed a reputation as a patron of poets and historians. Thus, for example, the anonymous poem '*Triall gach éinfhir gu cúirt Teabóid*',[5] expressly praised Theobald Butler's patronage of learning, and concluded with five stanzas in praise of his wife, Mary Cusack. The poet placed Theobald Butler on a par with the great names of the Gaelic nobility, O'Neill, O'Brien and McCarthy on the basis of his generous patronage of poetry and seanchas. The poem, in the form of a *crosántacht*, contains many historical allusions that are obscure to the modern reader, although it is noteworthy that some of them are illuminated by passages in Keating's *Foras feasa*, which suggests that both the poet and Geoffrey Keating were drawing on a common source of historical knowledge.[6]

The extent of the possible links between the Butlers of Cahir, the Keating family, and other local landholders is worth exploring in some detail. The Civil Survey conducted by commissioners in 1654, inquiring into landholding and land quality in the Suir valley region, recorded, amongst other matters, the names of the proprietors of land in the barony of Iffa and Offa in 1640. The evidence recorded by the surveyors, relying on local residents for their information, shows a pattern of long established families, other than the Butlers, having substantial holdings of land, 'inherited from their ancestors'.[7] A commonly occurring name in ten neighbouring parishes in the rich arable lands south and east of Cahir was the Anglo-Norman surname of Keating. The Keatings were proprietors of more than 10 per cent of the land that lay in ten parishes in the immediate vicinity of Cahir. The centre of Keating landownership in the region was at Nicholastown, in the parish of Derrygrath. In 1640 Richard Keating of Nicholastown was 'proprietor in fee by descent from his ancestors' of a substantial holding of 777 acres of land.[8] In 1654, following the wars of the 1640s, the lands at Nicholastown were recorded as containing a castle, the walls of a house within a bawn, a thatched house with a chimney and some cabins. There was an orchard and ash trees had been planted, indicating that it was a region that had seen some improvement.[9] The proprietors in the parish recorded in the 1659 census all bore the surname Keating. In 1659, Nicholastown was the largest population settlement in the parish of Derrygrath.[10]

3 R.C. Simington (ed.), *The civil survey, A.D. 1654-1656, county of Tipperary, i, eastern and southern baronies* (Dublin, IMC, 1931), pp. 257-384. See also W.F. Butler, 'An Irish legend of the origins of the Barons of Cahir', *JRSAI*, lv (1925), pp. 6-14.   4 Power, *Placenames of Decies*, p. 296.   5 James Carney (ed.), *Poems on the Butlers* (Dublin, 1945), poem 6, pp. 20-30.   6 See Carney (ed.), *Poems on the Butlers*, pp. 112-15.   7 *Civil survey*, i, pp. 306-76.   8 *Civil survey*, i, pp. 316-17.   9 W.P. Burke, 'Geoffry Keating', *Jnl of Waterford and South East Ireland Archaeological Society*, i, no. 4 (1895), pp. 173-82, illus., p. 173. The castle was described by Burke in 1895 as having the bawn still enclosed, 'the flanking towers and curtain walls, with their sentry-walks, recesses and embrasures, are in excellent preservation'.   10 Seamus Pender (ed.), *A census of Ireland, 1659* (Dublin, 1939), p. 311.

Adjoining Nicholastown was the land known as Garryroe, held by Morish Keating of Loghloghry, an area which also seems to have been a relatively well populated and developed area in 1640. Indeed, these two individuals, Morish and Richard, held lands not just in the heartland of Keating territory in the parish of Derrygrath, but also in the neighbouring parishes of Tullaghmelan, Ballybecan and Ardfinnan, Ballyclerahan, Rochestown and Cahir. Some of the land had been inherited, some had been purchased, while still more land was held in mortgage from other individuals with Old English surnames, including Prendergast, Power, Mocler, English, and Butler. Each of the Keatings who held land in the barony of Iffa and Offa in 1640 was described as 'Irish papist', and 'gentleman', except for Richard Keating of Nicholastown who was designated 'Esquire'.[11]

Only one Protestant was recorded as holding land in any of the ten parishes in which there were proprietors bearing the surname Keating. He was Robert Cox of Bruff, County Limerick, to whom three persons surnamed Keating had mortgaged some land before 1640.[12] In 1659, the only significant concentration of persons described as 'English' in the barony of Iffa and Offa was in the town of Cahir (16 per cent). Just two of the seventy-four persons (3 per cent) enumerated in the parish of Derrygrath were described as English.[13]

Some seventeenth-century legal documents have come to light which provide important circumstantial evidence as to the precise family to which Geoffrey Keating belonged.[14] An undated, post-1641, chancery bill citing the evidence of Nicholas Maguon of Loghloghry, County Tipperary, records details of the lands inherited by the seven male heirs of James fitz Edmund Keating.[15] After the death of James, his sons, John, Richard, Geoffrey, Edmund, Walter, Nicholas and Thomas, each inherited portions of land in accordance with the custom of gavelkind.[16] The lands in question were quite extensive and included 'divers castles and lands' in Moorestown, Knocklought, Kilmurray, Waterstown and Corlis[e], in the parishes of Inislounaght and Derrygrath, in the barony of Iffa and Offa. The portion alloted to the eldest son and his heir was Moorestown (also known as Ballynamoney), so that this family can most conveniently be described as the Keatings of Moorestown.

A plausible case can be made that the Geoffrey Keating mentioned in this Chancery bill, the third son of James fitz Edmund Keating of Moorestown, is our priest author. The two elder sons, John and Richard, along with Richard son of John, can be identified in 1640 as significant landholders in Moorestown and Kil-

11 *Civil survey*, i, pp. 257-376.   12 *Civil survey*, i, pp. 311, 317, 361. The mortgaged lands included Moorestown Keating.   13 *Census Ire.*, p. 311.   14 The evidence relating to the immediate family connections of one Geoffrey Keating of Moorestown, County Tipperary, was found by Raymond Gillespie among the seventeenth-century Chancery bills in the National Archives, Dublin.   15 NA, Chancery bills, G 351.   16 The details came to the attention of the courts because of a later dispute over the inheritance of the eldest son, John, and his eldest son, Richard, who pre-deceased him, and his grandson, John son of Richard. This eldest son of an eldest son sought to overturn the gavelkind arrangement and claim all the lands of his great-grandfather, James fitz Edmund Keating, as his own. NA, Chancery bills, G 351.

ballynamoney and adjoining lands.[17] It is particularly noteworthy that the third and
fourth sons, Geoffrey and Edmund, who together inherited 113 acres of arable
land at Corlise and Kilmurray just south of Moorestown,[18] had promptly conveyed
their interest to Michael White, a merchant in nearby Clonmel. The disposal of
their share of their father's lands strongly suggests they were not destined to make
their living from the land. That Geoffrey and his younger brother, Edmund, might
have already left to train as priests is one likely explanation for not retaining the
lands they inherited.

While this new evidence linking Geoffrey Keating with the Moorestown branch
of the family is very significant, his association with the parish of Tubbrid is
equally important. The parish lies south of Cahir and immediately west of the cluster of small parishes which formed the centre of Keating proprietorship. All of the
land in the parish of Tubbrid was in Catholic hands in 1640, much of it held
directly by the Butlers, barons of Cahir. The largest centre of population in the
parish was at Rehill, a manorial centre that had been incorporated into the Cahir
Butler estate before the seventeenth century. In 1640 it contained a mill, house and
bawn, two thatched houses and some cabins, and it was at Rehill that the manor
court met.[19] A significant proportion of land in the parish of Tubbrid was held by
members of the Meic Craith kin group, and they were the proprietors of the lands
of Burgess.[20] Theirs was one of the few Gaelic surnames among landed proprietors
in the district. Their occupation of land in this locality was very probably associated with their role as poets to the Butlers. The evidence of surviving poems to the
Butlers reveals that Meic Craith poets enjoyed Butler patronage in the late sixteenth and early seventeenth centuries.[21] In particular, they enjoyed a share of the
patronage of Theobald Butler, who was lord of Cahir from 1566 to 1596, and for
whom a *duanaire* was compiled.[22] Such cultural links were one of the elements of
the trappings of Gaelic lordship adopted by the barons of Cahir, even while guarding the rights and privileges derived from their Norman origins.[23] Thomas
O'Sullevane, writing in 1722, stated that 'Dr Keating was born towards the end of
Queen Elizabeth's reign, in the county of Tipperary, ten miles to the south-west
of Clonmel, near a village call'd Burgess, where a seminary or school for Irish
poetry had been kept for a considerable time'.[24] This statement, which is the
source of the modern tradition that Geoffrey Keating was born at Burgess, does
not actually pinpoint Burgess as the precise place of his birth. O'Sullevane continued: 'As his parents (who were of good reputation, and in warm circumstances)

17 *Civil survey*, i, pp. 311, 317-18. 18 *Civil survey*, i, p. 317. 19 *Census Ire.*; *Civil survey*, i; Smyth,
'Property, patronage and population', p. 114. 20 *Civil survey*, i, pp. 363-70. 21 Carney (ed.), *Poems
on the Butlers*, pp. xvi-xvii. 22 RIA, MS 23 F 21; Carney (ed.), *Poems on the Butlers*, pp. xiv-xv. 23
Carney (ed.), *Poems on the Butlers*, p. ix. 24 *Memoirs of the Right Honourable the Marquis of Clanricarde
… to which is prefix'd a dissertation, wherein some passages of these Memoirs are illustrated. With a digression containing several curious observations concerning the antiquities of Ireland* (London, 1722), pp. cxxv-
cxxvi. The relevant portions of the preface are reprinted in Brian Ó Cuív (ed.), 'An eighteenth-century
account of Keating and his *Foras Feasa ar Éirinn*', *Éigse*, ix (1958), pp. 263-9.

2 Moorestown castle, County Tipperary, 1840. Sketch by G. du Noyer. RIA, Ordnance Survey drawings, MS 12 T 2, no 87

design'd him for the service of the Church they took care to give him early education, such as that part of the country could best afford'.[25] There seems no way of verifying O'Sullevane's claims, but the suggestion that Geoffrey Keating's parents were 'in warm circumstances', together with the fact that he had access to the necessary financial support for a university education abroad, implies that they were among the better off in the locality. This conclusion is compatible with the evidence for his being the third son of James fitz Edmund Keating of Moorestown.

A long-standing association with the Mac Craith family may explain Geoffrey Keating's access to an early education which provided him with the professional knowledge of the Irish language and its oral and written literature so evident from his writings. Such an association would provide a link to Burgess, since the lands of that townland were held by the Meic Craith. O'Sullevane records that Keating,

> being often in company with the masters and scholars of the said seminary [of Irish poetry], by conversation and use, he attain'd to a competent skill

25 *Clanricarde*, p. cxxvi; Ó Cuív, 'Eighteenth-century account', p. 267.

in the dialect, and strains peculiar to that profession: Hereof there are many instances; and among the rest two elegant poems, viz. an elegy upon the death of the Lord Desies, and a burlesque poem in praise of a servant of his own, nam'd Symon, whom he compares with the ancient heroes.[26]

The Meic Craith were known as historians or preservers of the *seanchas* (historical lore) as well as being poets, and it appears that they were indeed associated with a school of *seanchas* at Burgess. Such schools were concerned with genealogy, placelore, mythology, history, law, language and grammar. Students were also trained in the use of Irish and Latin manuscripts. The Meic Craith of Ballylomasey in Tubbrid parish who were contemporaries of Keating included Eoghan mac Donnchadha Meic Craith and Flann mac Eoghain Meic Craith. These two men were named along with others of their kin group and seven men bearing the surname Keating in a long list of followers of James Butler, brother of the lord baron of Cahir, who had obtained a pardon in 1601. The pardon was linked to their having gone into rebellion and the terms required them to submit to the authority of the English provincial administration in Munster.[27] The episode is interesting for the evidence it provides of close interconnections between the Mac Craith and Keating families as well as for the detail it reveals of the relationship between the Butlers of Cahir and the lesser families of the area. Like the Keatings, the Meic Craith held land in this part of south Tipperary 'by descent from their ancestors'. Given that both family groups lived in close proximity and were of comparable social standing, it is likely that there were marriage links underpinning the social contacts between the families. The identity of Geoffrey Keating's mother is not known, but it is most likely that she came from a family of similar status to the Keatings in the locality.[28]

The Mac Craith poets and historians would have relied for patronage on the local elite, who commissioned commemorative pieces as occasion demanded and they were among those who composed poetry not just for the Butlers of Cahir but for Thomas Butler, earl of Ormond, also.[29] A late sixteenth-century vellum manuscript *duanaire*[30] containing poetry in praise of the Butlers reveals that Eoghan mac Donnchadh Maoil Meic Craith of Burgess along with Domhnall Mac an Bhaird, Giolla Iosa Ó Dálaigh and Giolla Brighde Mac Bruaideadha had enjoyed the patronage of Theobald Butler, baron of Cahir.[31] Genealogies were also the responsibility of these families who were keepers of the *seanchas*, and the genealogical materials preserved in the Mac Bruaideadha compilation now known as the *Leabhar Muimhneach* would have been well known to the Mac Craith historians.

---

26 *Clanricarde*, p. cxxvi. (No extant copy of this poem has been located.)   27 *Fiants Ire., Eliz*, 6495.
28 *Civil survey*, i. Kenneth Nicholls' (unpublished) suggestion that Keating's mother was a McGrath is eminently plausible, but no supporting documentary evidence has been found.   29 On the role of the bardic poet see James Carney, *The Irish bardic poet* (Dublin, 1967); Pádraig Breatnach, 'The chief's poet', *PRIA*, lxxxiii, C (1983), pp. 33-79.   30 RIA, MS 23 F 21.   31 Carney (ed.), *Poems on the Butlers*, pp. xvi-xvii.

Such information was processed in new ways also and in the 1630s Hugh Oge Magrath supplied a detailed pedigree of the Butlers of Shanballyduff, County Tipperary, to the office of the Ulster King at Arms, the body authorised to regulate the assumption of heraldic arms. He had compiled the relevant genealogies from manuscript sources using 'the new and old books of his ancestors written in the Irish language'.[32]

Although the Keatings were not a traditional bardic family, it is clear that Geoffrey was skilled in the use of the Irish language as taught by the cultural elite who practised the art of poetry and who preserved the historical record. O'Sullevane's 1722 account of his life notes that when he left his home area he spent his time 'mostly at the abodes of the poets, with whom he had contracted a friendship in his youth'.[33] Contact with either the Meic Craith or their patrons, the Butlers of Cahir, might have allowed Keating socialise with other learned families such as Mac Bruaideadha, Ó Dálaigh, Mac Aodhagáin and Mac Eochagáin. There is evidence that Keating himself acted as poet propagandist on occasion for the Butlers, barons of Cahir in the 1620s. Poems ascribed to Geoffrey Keating include a lament for Thomas Butler, baron of Cahir, who died in 1627. The poem of 32 stanzas '*Is uaigneach duit, a phuirt na bpríomh-fhlaith*' describes the lonely state of Cahir castle after the death of the baron. Among those mentioned as having suffered from this loss are a clergyman who used to spend time in the castle studying the Bible.[34] This presumably refers to a chaplain to the Butlers; there is a distinct possibility that it may even refer to Keating himself. Further Butler connections are suggested by other poetic compositions. '*Uch is truagh mo ghuais ón ghleo-bhroid*', a lament on the death of James Butler of Knocktopher, composed before 1620, is sometimes attributed to Keating.[35] A connection with the Butlers, barons of Dunboyne, is also likely. '*Mór antrom inse Banbha*', a poem on the death of Thomas and John Butler, sons of the third Baron Dunboyne, is attributed to Keating,[36] as is '*Druididh suas, a chuaine an chaointe*' which lamented the death of Éamonn Fionn mac Piarais Butler, who died on 17 March 1640.[37] Keating is also credited with having composed '*A Bhanbha bhog-omh dhona dhuaibhseach*', on the illness of Edmund, third baron of Dunboyne, but in all three cases the link with Keating is made only by a late scribe, Micheál Ó Longáin, and cannot be verified from contemporary sources.[38] A link with the Butlers of Dunboyne could have

---

32 NLI, GO, MS 159, f. 55, cited by K.W. Nicholls, 'The Irish genealogies: their value and defects', *Irish Genealogist*, v, no. 2 (1975), p. 256. See also Terence Francis McCarthy, Ulster Office, 1552-1800, M.A. thesis, QUB, 1983. 33 *Clanricarde*, p. cxxix. 34 Eóin Mac Giolla Eáin (ed.), *Dánta, amhráin is caointe Sheathrúin Chéitinn* (Dublin, 1900), poem 17, esp. ll. 1545-9. 35 BL, Egerton MS 97, f. 156. 36 Mac Giolla Eáin (ed.), *Dánta*, poem 14; for further discussion of this poem see Breandán Ó Buachalla, 'Cúlra is tábhacht an dáin *A leabhráin ainmnighthear d'Aodh*', *Celtica*, xxi (1990), pp. 410-13. 37 Mac Giolla Eáin (ed.), *Dánta*, poem 12; The attribution to Keating is made by the mid-eighteenth century scribe Micheál Ó Longáin, RIA, MS 23 N 15, p. 1354; RIA, MS 23 G 24, p. 687; however, this poem is also attributed to Pádraigín Haicéad, see Máire Ní Cheallacháin (ed.), *Filíocht Phádraigín Haicéad* (Baile Átha Cliath, 1962), poem 30. 38 Mac Giolla Eáin (ed.), *Dánta*, poem 17. These poems are not considered in detail because the attribution to Keating is highly dubious.

brought Keating into contact with Michael Kearney of Ballylusky, servant to Margaret Butler, dowager Baroness Dunboyne, until her death in 1636.[39] Michael Kearney translated *Foras feasa* in the 1630s, very soon after the Irish text was completed. The two men moved in similar social circles and were very probably personally acquainted.

These literary connections, if valid, suggest that the Butlers of Dunboyne and also the Butlers of Cahir may have acted as patrons of the scholar priest. Keating may well have been a visitor at both houses on occasion. O'Sullevane's assertion in 1722 concerning the manuscript of Keating's history of Ireland, *Foras feasa ar Éirinn*, that 'the original belongs to the Lord Baron of Cahir in Ireland',[40] also points to traditional knowledge of a patron – client relationship between Geoffrey Keating and the local prominent Old English lord.[41] Other poems reputedly composed by Keating include one to the Fitzgeralds of Decies. Such compositions, if the authorship is correctly ascribed, point to a slightly wider, but still local, patronage network.[42]

In addition to this elite patronage, which may have been only sporadic, Geoffrey Keating could also draw on the resources of his own kinship network. He lived for the greater part of his life in a locality where he had direct ties of kinship with propertied individuals. The extended family network of the Keatings of Moorestown would have formed Geoffrey's most significant set of social relationships in his early years. Those close bonds would have been temporarily disrupted during his sojourn on the continent, but on his return the parochial framework into which he presumably entered would have evolved within those same kinship networks around which secular society was organised.[43] The resources of that family network would have been drawn on to fund his continental education, and his subsequent life as a secular priest, in the early part of the seventeenth century.

Keating's understanding of the world of his youth would have been informed by the social networks of the locality in which he lived. His poem of farewell to that world gives an idea of what he valued from the Ireland of his youth. The poem '*Mo bheannacht leat, a scríbhinn*', written from France looking back on the Ireland he had left behind, while seeing Ireland through the haze of exile nonetheless provided an insight into the kind of place Keating regarded as home.[44]

The predominant images were concerned with the physical landscape of the island of Ireland, naming generic features, hills, lakes, rivers, woodland and harbours, rather than a specific locality. This landscape provided the backdrop for a

---

39 Donald Jackson, 'Michael Kearney of Ballylosky: Irish scribe and Butler servant', *Journal of the Butler Society*, ii, no. 1 (1980–81), pp. 84–5. 40 *Clanricarde*, p. cxviii; Ó Cuív (ed.), 'An eighteenth-century account', p. 264. 41 The location of this manuscript is not now known. 42 Ó Cuív (ed.), 'An eighteenth-century account' p. 267; A lament on the death of Seán Óg mac Gearailt, lord of Decies (died 1626) '*Lá da raghas ar maidin*' (Mac Giolla Eáin (ed.), *Dánta*, poem 9). 43 John Bossy, 'The Counter-Reformation and the people of Catholic Ireland, 1595-1641', in T.D. Williams (ed.), *Historical Studies, viii* (Dublin,1971), pp. 155–69; Canice Mooney, 'The Irish church in the sixteenth century', *IER*, 5th ser., xcix (1963), pp. 102–13. 44 Mac Giolla Eáin (ed.), *Dánta*, poem 2.

homeland peopled with nobility, clergy and scholars, an island of saints despite the troubles of its peoples, a homeland in which he has a particular affection for the clergy. In the poem he evoked the attractive landscape of hills and river valleys of the Keating homeland around Cahir. He also effectively gave voice to the perspective of one who had come from a comfortable social background, a world of patronage and learning, a social setting in which he was more likely to mix with the social elite than with the poor. Writing such a poem from his new location on the continent revealed how the experience of exile had heightened his appreciation of the land and people of the island of his birth.

II

From the last quarter of the sixteenth century, and throughout the seventeenth and eighteenth centuries, Irish Catholics who wished to provide a higher education for their sons usually sent them to universities and colleges in mainland Europe. Attending a university at home was not an option, since the university founded in Dublin in 1592 was firmly Protestant, indeed Puritan, in ethos.[45] From the late sixteenth century the traditional path to the universities of Oxford and Cambridge was no longer the first choice for those for whom Catholicism was important. Government policy dictated that the sons of the nobility would be educated in England where possible. In Keating's own neighbourhood the sons of the baron of Dunboyne and the nephew of the baron of Cahir were among those earmarked for such an upbringing in the second decade of the seventeenth century.[46] Those destined to become lawyers, whether Catholic or Protestant, were normally educated at London, spending time at one of the Inns of Court, perhaps preceded by a year or two at Oxford or Cambridge.[47] For others, particularly seminarians, mainland Europe was the destination of choice. While their Protestant fellow-countrymen remained in Dublin, attending the newly-established Trinity College, Irish Catholic students were to be found in all the main university towns of western Europe from Louvain in the north to Lisbon in the south.

The edict issued by King James I in 1605 forbidding 'all our subjects of Ireland to shelter or countenance any Jesuit, seminarist or other priest who will dare to remain in Ireland' made clear the official government position on the status of Catholic clergy.[48] The home environment which Keating and his fellow Munster seminarians left behind when they departed for Europe was one which had at least

---

45 Helga Robinson-Hammerstein, 'Archbishop Adam Loftus: the first provost of Trinity College, Dublin' in Helga Robinson-Hammerstein (ed.), *European universities in the age of Reformation and Counter Reformation* (Dublin, 1998), pp. 34-52. **46** *Calendar of state papers, Ireland, 1611-14*, pp. 459, 483. **47** Donal Cregan, 'The social and cultural background of an Counter-Reformation episcopate, 1618-60', in Art Cosgrove and Donal McCartney (eds), *Studies in Irish history presented to R. Dudley Edwards* (Dublin, 1979), pp. 85-117; NLI, MS 3111, ff. 77-8. **48** *Calendar of state papers, Ireland, 1603-06*, pp. 355-6.

occasionally given them an experience of the concept of persecution on grounds of religion, and this dimension of their experience was one that later generations chose to remember.[49] Other influences were at work also, and some of the poetry composed by Ulster poets who joined the Franciscan order emphasised more positive aspects of the decision to pursue learning overseas rather than continue with the traditional craft of their forefathers at home. Thus Giolla Brighde Ó hEoghusa in 'Slán agaibh, a fhir chumtha' gave his reasons for abandoning Gaelic poetry and joining a religious order:

> *Ní fuath d'ealadhain mh'aithreach*
> *tug fúm aigneadh athraightheach*
> *ná an ghlóir do-gheibthí dá cionn*
> *do neimhthní ó fhóir Éirionn.*
> *Gidh beag ar n-eólas ionnta,*
> *sduidéar leabhrán léighionnta*
> *iseadh ro chealg uaibhsi inn*
> *an cheard is uaisle aithnim.*

> (It is not hatred of my forefathers' art
> that has unsettled my mind;
> nor the fact that the honour which was once bestowed on it
> by the Irish race has disappeared.
> Though our knowledge of them is small,
> it is the study of learned books
> – the most noble profession known to me –
> that has enticed me away from you.)[50]

The precise destination chosen by any individual student depended on his contacts with others who were making the journey to Europe or who had done so in the recent past. Students from a particular locality were likely to follow the path of other students from that same neighbourhood. Ulster had established strong links with Spain and the Spanish Netherlands.[51] Catholic students leaving Ireland from northern ports tended to reinforce those traditional links between Ulster and the Spanish territories. In contrast, Munster and South-Leinster gentry who wished to have their sons educated abroad at Catholic universities would normally have arranged for their offspring to travel on ships departing from Cork, Waterford or Wexford. Those ships followed traditional trade routes and were usually destined for France. While Waterford had trading contacts with many continental as well as British ports, its links with France were particularly strong.[52] Among the more

---

49 Bernadette Cunningham and Raymond Gillespie, '"Persecution" in seventeenth-century Irish', *Éigse*, xxii (1987), pp. 21-8; John Lynch, *Cambrensis eversus*, ed. and trans. Matthew Kelly (3 vols, Dublin, 1848-51), iii, 101. 50 Cuthbert Mhag Craith (ed.), *Dán na mBrathar Mionúr* (2 vols, Dublin, 1967-80), poem 5. 51 J.J. Silke, *Ireland and Europe, 1559-1607* (Dundalk, 1966). 52 T.W. Moody, F.X. Martin,

important French destinations from ports on the south coast of Ireland were St Malo, Bordeaux, and the inland cities of Rheims and Paris.[53] If Bordeaux and Paris became two of the more significant centres for Irish seminarians from Munster in early seventeenth-century France, it was because these Catholic university towns were particularly accessible from Munster, through the ongoing trading connections of the merchant community.[54]

If, as appears likely, Keating's time on the continent commenced before 1600, there were few Irish colleges yet in existence to which he could have gone. The college at Bordeaux, with which he was later associated, was not founded until 1603, at which date Keating may well have completed his seminary training. Documentary evidence of Geoffrey Keating's time spent in continental seminaries as either student or teacher is sparse. The chance references which survive link him with Rheims and later with Bordeaux. Writing in 1624, Philip O'Sullivan Beare provides a list of Catholic priests and nuns working in Ireland and on the continent and includes '*Geofridus Ketinus Rhemis theologici doctoris insignibus honestatur*'.[55] This scrap of evidence suggests that Keating's degree of doctor of theology had been obtained at the University of Rheims. The university had strong English Catholic connections and was associated also with the English Jesuit college at Douai.

There had also been an Irish college at Douai from 1594, catering primarily for Old English students from the south and east of Ireland. Although detailed records of the early students there do not survive, it is known that Thomas Messingham, later rector of the Irish college in Paris, David Rothe, later bishop of Ossory, and Diarmuid Mac Carthy, founder of the Irish college at Bordeaux, were among those associated with it at the end of the sixteenth century. Whether or not Geoffrey Keating shared in their early seminary education, it is clear from his work and theirs that he shared their outlook on Ireland and on Catholicism. Their common interest in the Irish past and in the reputation of the 'Island of saints and scholars' was revealed in their writings. Thomas Messingham's best known work, the *Florilegium sanctorum, seu vitae et acta sanctorum Hiberniae*, published at Paris in 1624 was intended to present Ireland's Christian past in a favourable light to European readers. Its introduction has many striking similarities with the opening sections of *Foras feasa*.[56] Rothe's *Hibernia resurgens*, published in 1621 had argued in defence of the Irishness of the early Christian saints against the claims of the Scot Thomas Dempster. The political perspective of Rothe's *Analecta sacra*, published 1616-19, shared a common outlook with *Foras feasa* in its affirmation of Irish Catholic loyalty to their Stuart king.

and F.J. Byrne (eds), *A new History of Ireland, iii, early modern Ireland* (Oxford, 1976), 8. **53** Éamon Ó Ciosáin, 'Les Irlandais en Bretagne, 1603-1780: "invasion", accueil, integration', in Catherine Laurent and Helen Davis (eds), *Irland et Bretagne: vingt siècles d'histoire* (Rennes, 1993), pp. 153-66. **54** Silke, 'The Irish abroad, 1534-1691,' in *New Hist. Ire.*, iii, 587-633. **55** Philip O'Sullivan Beare, *Zoilomastix*, ed. T.J. O'Donnell (Dublin, IMC, 1960), p. 22. **56** See below, ch. 9.

Keating's theological writings provide evidence that he was influenced by a curriculum on the Jesuit model, such as would have been the norm for those associated with Rheims or Douai.[57] When the Irish college at Bordeaux was established
it too was supportive of the Jesuit ideals and its students attended a Jesuit-run university in that city. Keating's move to Bordeaux, presumably as a teacher of theology, after 1603 would have found him among men many of whom were drawn
from his home diocese of Lismore and Waterford and the neighbouring diocese of
Cork.[58] A very definite Munster bias is evident, for instance, in the list compiled
in 1618 of 208 individuals who had been associated with the Irish college at
Bordeaux since its foundation in 1603. Geoffrey Keating, who was described as a
doctor of theology from the diocese of Waterford, was one of those on the list,
which also included a significant number of Butlers, not least the son of the baron
of Dunboyne.[59] A bias in favour of Munster students persisted at Bordeaux into
the eighteenth century.[60]

Among the Irish students resident in the Irish College at Bordeaux in the early
years of the seventeenth century were a small number from the Waterford region
who were not training to be clergy. Thus '*Monsieur Maurice de la Roche, docteur en
medecine, Waterfordiensis*' (whose title indicates that he was from the diocese of
Waterford and in Bordeaux to pursue studies in medicine)[61] is probably the same
person as 'Morrish Roch of Killcomanbegg Doctor of Physick' noted in the Civil
Survey as being a proprietor of some land in county Tipperary in 1640. In that
year, it is recorded that Morrish Roche held 366 acres in the parish of Tubbrid in
County Tipperary in mortgage from Theobald Butler of Ruskagh.[62] Earlier, in
1627, the same man was involved in a land transaction with the Moorestown
Keatings.[63] Money he had earned from his medical pursuits may have enabled him
to acquire additional land by mortgage in the area. Given the likelihood of their
common link to the Bordeaux college, and the proximity of Roche's lands to
Tubbrid, it seems probable that Keating would have known him.

The Irish college at Bordeaux had been founded by Diarmuid MacCallaghan
MacCarthy, a priest from Muskerry. He had left Ireland in the late sixteenth century and spent time in Douai and Rome before choosing Bordeaux as the venue for
a new college. Bordeaux was both a university town and a cathedral town. Through
a combination of the patronage of Cardinal De Sourdis and the initiative of
MacCarthy, the college was established to accommodate Irish students attending

---

57 Diarmaid Ó Laoghaire, Príomh-fhoinseacha *Eochair-sgiath an Aifrinn*, MA thesis, UCD, 1939. There
is no copy of this thesis in the library of UCD, but the author's own copy, with his later annotations,
is in the Jesuit Library, Milltown Park, Dublin. I am grateful to Fergus O'Donoghue for facilitating my
access to this copy. The discussion of the printed sources of *ESA* presented here relies extensively on
the work of Ó Laoghaire.   58 The first group of Irish students to attend MacCarthy's foundation were
drawn mainly from his own diocese of Cork, but it was from the port of Waterford that they set sail
for Bordeaux; see T.J. Walsh, *The Irish continental college movement: the colleges at Bordeaux, Toulouse
and Lille* (Dublin, 1973), p. 91.   59 *Calendar of state papers, Ireland, 1615-25*, pp. 315-20.   60 Walsh,
Irish continental college movement, pp. 102-5.   61 *Calendar of state papers, Ireland, 1615-25*, p. 319.   62
Civil survey, i, p. 367.   63 NA, RC 5/22, pp. 160-9.

the Jesuit-controlled Madeleine University. The college itself housed seminarians destined to return to Munster as secular or diocesan clergy. Some of them may already have been ordained before leaving home and many would have spent just one or two years abroad.[64]

Writing about 1618 or 1619, an official of the Dublin government reported that he had seen a copy of the published list of people associated with the Irish college at Bordeaux, and noted:

> There are hundreds in the colleges whose names I saw the last Lent, from Waterford, Limerick, Clonmel, Cork, Galway, Kilkenny and Drogheda, and from the counties abroad throughout the realm, and I am sure that there is no worthy gent in all the realm, nor merchant, but have there some of their nearest kinsmen; but what in the p[ar]ticular is sent unto them is the portion there fathers do leave them, and some collections that yearly is taken up for them, and with this they live together with certain yearly pensions that is allowed unto the colleges by the kings and princes in whose dominions they are.[65]

The comments of observers reporting to the Dublin administration on the activities of the Irish in continental colleges, though hostile, were reasonably well informed. Thus the individual who commented on the 1618 Bordeaux list highlighted the fact that these were the sons of gentry and merchants, in other words, they were drawn from among the more affluent groups within Irish society. Brockliss and Ferté's statistical study of Irish students in early modern France has drawn attention to the comparatively wide spread of family names among Irish students in higher education in France, but this was more significant in the eighteenth century than the seventeenth.[66] The partially subsidised nature of education as provided in the seminaries may have opened the path of higher education to a broader cross section of Irish Catholic society than would otherwise be the case. Nonetheless, most students, while abroad, depended in part on the financial support of their own families.

The Irish colleges that were founded in a variety of locations in western Europe in the early seventeenth century provided vital support for students from Ireland pursuing higher education abroad. The colleges provided accommodation, and those students who were seminarians lived in a community environment where formation in faith, devotion and obedience were an intrinsic part of daily life. There was a daily routine of early rising, long periods of prayer and periods of silence. Attendance at daily Mass was the norm, frequent resort to the sacraments was

---

64 Although the official records of the college were destroyed at the time of the French Revolution, the story of its early years is recounted in Abbé Bertrand's *Histoire des seminaires de Bordeaux et de Bazas* (Bordeaux, 1894). 65 William Carrigan, *The history and antiquities of the diocese of Ossory* (4 vols, Dublin, 1905), i, 91, from TCD, MS 567. 66 L.W.B. Brockliss and P. Ferté, 'Irish clerics in France in the seventeenth and eighteenth centuries: a statistical study', *PRIA*, lxxxviii, C (1987), pp. 527-72.

encouraged. A Friday fast was observed, some colleges enforced a Wednesday fast also, and Lent would have been strictly observed.[67] Whereas students followed approved university courses in theology and philosophy outside the college, education more directly focused on their spiritual formation was pursued within the college. At Bordeaux, the students were read to at mealtimes, the material usually drawn from the Bible or lives of saints. The text read might be in a choice of languages, Latin, French, Irish or English, and college rules stipulated that no reader could ascend the rostrum without adequate skills in all four.[68] Catechetical instruction was provided for the younger students, with spiritual conferences for the more advanced students. Attendance at Sunday sermons within or outside the college was encouraged.[69] As will be seen below, it seems likely that Keating may well have attended some Sunday sermons in Bordeaux cathedral.

A 1621 list of the contents of the library of the Irish Franciscan college at Paris gives an indication of the choice of reading material available.[70] In addition to the tools of trade, in the form of a Bible, missal, breviary, martyrology, and the decrees of the Council of Trent, the collection included a range of devotional material. Thomas à Kempis' *Imitation of Christ*, the *Confessions* of Augustine, the spiritual writings of Bonaventure and of Luis de Granada, Francis de Sales' *Introduction to the devout life* (first published 1608), together with lives of saints, appear to have been the most frequently used devotional texts. The collection also included works of controversial theology by Bellarmine and Becanus, and the writings of Toletus. Different colleges had different emphases, and the secular college at Bordeaux would not have mirrored the Irish Franciscan college at Paris in every respect. Nevertheless the objective of forming clergy in line with the decrees of the reforming Council of Trent (1543-63) underpinned the ethos of each of the colleges.

It was not unusual for individual students to move between a number of different colleges and universities in the course of their studies. The length of time spent in pursuit of such studies varied from perhaps as little as six months to a period of perhaps six or seven years. Such matters depended in part on the resources available to individual students and colleges, and funding was a constant source of concern. Students worked to support themselves with stipends for saying Masses, and a variety of pastoral duties in the locality.

Bertrand recorded that among the activities undertaken by Irish students at Bordeaux was that of burying the dead. The chapel of St Eutrope which was assigned for the use of the Irish college had been the chapel of a pious sodality, the Tretzenna, whose work involved one of the corporal works of mercy – burying the dead. Thus grave-digging and the conduct of funerals in Bordeaux became part of the responsibility of the students at the Irish college, a function they apparently continued to perform until the end of the eighteenth century.[71] Faced with this

---

67 Cregan, 'Counter-Reformation episcopate'.   68 T.J. Walsh (ed.), 'Some records of the Irish College, Bordeaux' *Archivium Hibernicum*, xv (1950), p. 101.   69 Cregan, 'Counter-Reformation episcopate', p. 107.   70 Brendan Jennings (ed.), 'Miscellaneous documents, I, 1588-1634', *Archivium Hibernicum*, xii (1946), pp. 88-9.   71 Walsh, *Irish continental college movement*, p. 92.

task, or ministering to students whose task this was, it is perhaps not surprising that one of Geoffrey Keating's lengthy theological writings should be a meditation on death. It was a relatively straightforward task for a writer of Keating's ability to adapt material for Irish readers from some of the many published Counter-Reformation writings on death and repentance. The inspiration for actually embarking on the task may have come from the experience of having been part of the community of the Irish college at Bordeaux. The experience of observing funerals as conducted in Bordeaux would also have prompted comparison in the minds of Irish participants with the different traditions associated with funerals in seventeenth-century Ireland, and Keating later recorded funeral customs in Connacht that differed from those in the diocese of Waterford and Lismore.[72] This may be one instance of the vast multitude of ways in which his continental experience would have influenced the way in which Keating subsequently viewed his homeland, its customs, traditions and people.

III

The first-hand experience that Geoffrey Keating gained of Counter-Reformation ideas, during his years of study in France at the beginning of the seventeenth century, provided him with the primary impetus for his prose writings, both theological and historical. Building on the range of ideas and experiences which he had taken with him from his early life in Munster, he absorbed various elements of European Catholic thinking and subsequently adapted some of those ideas for his Irish readers.[73]

Clerical students who went from Ireland to the European mainland to attend university in the seventeenth century were exposed to a range of experiences and ideas that they would not have encountered at home. The significance of the reality of their receiving their training in theology and philosophy in a non-Irish environment should not be underestimated. First, there was the experience of being Irish in a foreign place. Individuals were thereby confronted with the altered perspective of temporary exile from which to look anew at their idea of Irishness. They found themselves living among Catholics whose ideas about the Christian faith and the institutional Church often differed from those that had been encountered in Ireland. University training in philosophy and in theology introduced them to European intellectual traditions that were not part of the experience of most lay people at home. For Keating, the confluence of two sets of experiences, an Irish upbringing and family connections, and a continental education, prompted the intellectual explorations that find expresssion in his writings.

That Geoffrey Keating's earliest substantial work in prose should be a handbook in Irish on the Mass, encapsulating current Catholic teaching, is easy to

---

72 *TBB*, ll. 5717-20.   73 For context see Cregan, 'Counter-Reformation episcopate'.

understand. The education of a Catholic priest in accordance with the guidelines laid down at the Council of Trent would have placed particular emphasis on the Mass. Theological tracts explaining the Catholic Church's teaching on the Mass had been produced in a variety of vernacular languages in the years after the Council of Trent, and Keating's *Eochair-sgiath an Aifrinn* is best understood in that context.[74] Following Lutheran and Calvinist criticisms, and in particular the denial that the Mass was a sacrifice, or that transubstantiation occurred, Catholic tracts on the Mass had been produced from the 1520s. When the Council of Trent met at intervals between 1546 and 1562, the doctrines associated with the Mass were dealt with at various stages. The Council dealt separately with the issues of the sacrament and the Real Presence, communion and the canon of the Mass, and finally the Mass as sacrifice. This arbitrary division of themes, prompted by a debate to which the Tridentine discussions were a response, was retained with little alteration in most tracts on the Mass drawing on the Tridentine deliberations, and Keating's work conformed to this pattern.[75] While the tract was derivative of continental sources, *Eochair-sgiath an Aifrinn* was the result of Keating's own selection and rearrangement of material on the mass and confession drawn from a variety of sources, particularly Francis Suarez, Robert Bellarmine and William Durand. It is possible that Keating originally wrote the work in Latin as a university thesis and subsequently translated it into the vernacular for use in an Irish pastoral context.

There was a strongly controversial element in the way Keating approached his tract on the Mass. He prefaced his work by claiming that the arguments of Martin Luther and John Calvin were not worth refuting, but since he deemed them to have transgressed the bounds of truth and light, being the principal antagonists who challenged Catholic teaching on the Mass, he felt moved to defend the position of the Catholic Church.[76] In this *Eochair-sgiath an Aifrinn* was heavily influenced by the continental preoccupation with denigrating Protestant authors and the academic model of the disputation. It reads more like the work of a seminarian immersed in the topical Catholic literature of the day rather than the composition of a pastor thoroughly familiar with the particular concerns of the Catholic clergy and laity within Ireland.

IV

Diarmaid Ó Laoghaire, writing in 1939, identified a range of Latin publications, well known in early seventeenth-century Europe, that were key sources of Keating's tract on the Mass.[77] Two texts provided the main inspiration: Francisco de Suarez, *Defensio fidei Catholicae adversus Anglicanae sectae errores*,[78] and Robert

74 Cunningham, 'Geoffrey Keating's *Eochair sgiath an Aifrinn*', pp. 133-43.   75 Josef A. Jungmann, *The Mass, an historical, theological and pastoral survey* (Collegeville, 1976), pp. 83-7.   76 *ESA*, p. 19.   77 Ó Laoghaire, Príomh-fhoinseacha.   78 Coimbra, 1613 etc. Francisco de Suarez (1548-1617) was a Spanish Jesuit theologian, best known for his philosophical treatise *Disputatae metaphysicae* (1597) and

Bellarmine, *Disputationes de controversiis Christianae fidei adversus huius temporis haereticos*.[79] Suarez's book was an orthodox work, prefaced with an array of appropriate episcopal approbations and statements that it was free from doctrinal error. Robert Bellarmine (1542-1621) was also a Jesuit, and his *Disputationes de controversiis Christianae fidei* offered a clear and systematic defence of Catholic doctrine. The influences of these two sources on Keating's tract is particularly noticeable where the debate on the Mass is presented as a refutation of heretical arguments. Keating's use of the writings of these authors was not unusual. Other writings by of these influential Jesuits were well known not just to Irish clergy but to the educated laity also. Their appeal may have been enhanced by the relevance to Irish Catholics of the political arguments they expounded.[80]

Bellarmine's was the earlier of the two works, and Suarez himself used Bellarmine as a source for his writings so that it is not always certain which of the two authors Keating drew his material from. Much of the general information on Catholic doctrine on the Mass would have been available to seminarians from other sources, noteably through the writings of Martin Becanus.[81] His *Compendium manualis controversarium* was the text through which the works of a variety of authors were mediated to seminarians. It is probable, too, that some material inserted by Keating may have been drawn from memory but nevertheless Keating appears to have used Bellarmine and Suarez extensively. Keating probably had access to the full text of the Suarez treatise since he cites material from sections other than those directly concerned with the Mass. The preface and first chapter of *Eochair-sgiath an Aifrinn* were drawn from Bellarmine's *Disputationes*,[82] and the first volume of Suarez, *Defensio fide Catholicae*. Here Keating outlined the three conditions of the true Church: unity, catholicity and holiness, and gave his reasons for writing about the Mass. He illustrated, by reference to the writings of the early church fathers, notably St Ambrose, St Augustine, Bede, St Anselm, Pope Leo I, Pope Gregory and others, that the Mass originated at the time of the Apostles and had continued in existence since that time. He discussed the essential elements of the sacrament of the Eucharist: the blessing of the bread and wine, offering bread and wine to the Almighty Father, and receiving the body and blood of Christ under the form of bread and wine. Keating reaffirmed that only a priest had authority to say Mass.

Keating's second and third chapters were devoted to proving that the Mass was a sacrifice and relied mainly on the third volume of Bellarmine's *Disputationes*, entitled 'De sacramento eucharistiae'.[83] Suarez's *Defensio fide Catholicae* was also used.[84] Keating distinguished between three different types of sacrifice: the figurative sac-

his *De legibus* (1612) on the principles of natural and international law. **79** Ingoldstedt, 1568-9; Venetia, 1596; Paris, 1608 etc. **80** Cregan, 'Counter-Reformation episcopate', pp. 111-14. **81** Ó Laoghaire, Príomh-fhoinseacha, p. 31. The prevalence of Becanus's handbook of controversial theology in seminary and clerical libraries suggests that it was known to many generations of Irish clergy. Cregan, 'Counter-Reformation episcopate', p. 114. **82** Specifically ii book 3, *De Ecclesia militante*; iii, book 4, *De notis Ecclesiae*; and i, *De Romano Pontifice*, books 1 and 2. (Ó Laoghaire, Príomh-fhoinseacha, ch. 1). **83** Bellarmine, *Disputationes*, iii, especially books 5 and 6 entitled 'De Missa'. **84** Book 2, ch. 1-6.

rifice of the death of Abel in the Old Testament, the sacrifice of Christ on the cross, and the sacramental sacrifice of the Mass. He asserted that the Mass was a sacrifice under this last sacramental form and not, as he claimed the heretic stated, under the second form.

The sources for the fourth chapter of *Eochair-sgiath an Aifrinn*, on the etymology of the Latin word *'Missa'*, have not been identified. The topic gave rise to problems for Keating for there was no obvious link between the Irish word for Mass, *'Aifreann'* and the Latin *'Missa'*.[85] He concluded somewhat lamely that it was not particularly strange that there were different words for the Mass in different languages, as *Liturgia* in Greek, *Aifreann* in Irish, and *Mass* in English.

Keating's descriptions, in chapter five, of the priest's vestments worn at Mass correspond to material found in the *Summa casuum sive instructio sacerdotum* of Francis Toletus (Toledo).[86] The guidelines on appropriate locations and frequency for hearing and saying Mass are also from Toletus.[87] Editions of Toletus's book were available in many languages in Keating's time, but if he encountered this work in the seminary he probably used a Latin version.

Keating's sixth chapter explained the liturgical content of the opening section of the Mass and was drawn principally from William Durand's *Rationale Divinorum Officiorum*.[88] This was a standard textbook on ritual, first published in the mid-fifteenth century and still valued long after Keating's time.[89] Its descriptive indices contained forty-three separate entries for *Missa/Missae*, etc., so that it was a relatively easy task for Keating to find appropriate material. Durand commenced each chapter with an outline summary of the main points, and biblical references were given in italics in the margin. Numerous extracts from this source were rearranged for use in *Eochair-sgiath an Aifrinn*, usually summarised rather than translated in full.[90] Thus the seventh chapter of *Eochair-sgiath an Aifrinn*, the first of four on the Canon of the mass, combines material from Suarez and Bellarmine with the work of Durand.[91] Much of the detail on the canon of the Mass presented in chapters seven, eight, ten and sixteen of *Eochair-sgiath an Aifrinn* can be found in Durand.[92] In this instance Keating may have been working from lecture notes drawn from a full printed text.[93]

---

85 The Latin source Keating was evidently translating here might possibly have been his own work. 86 *ESA*, ch. 5. Toletus, *Summa casuum sive instructio Sacerdotum* (Lyons, 1599 etc.). See Ó Laoghaire, Príomh-fhoinseacha, pp. 60-6, for detailed references to sources of specific extracts from Toletus. 87 *ESA*, ch. 18. Toletus is not named in the text of *ESA* but is cited by name as the source of the appendix to *ESA*, pp. 122-4. 88 G. Durantus, *Rationale Divinorum Officiorum* (Mainz, 1459; Ulm, 1473; Venetia, 1572; Antwerp, 1614 etc.). 89 There is a copy of the 1559 edition in the National Library of Ireland. For a modern edition of the first six books see A. Davril and T.M. Thibodeau (eds), *Guillelmi Duranti, Rationale Divinorum officiorum, i-vi* (2 vols, Turnholt, 1995-8). 90 Ó Laoghaire, Príomh-fhoinseacha, pp. 47-58. 91 Keating's seventh chapter uses Bellarmine's *Disputationes*, ii, book 2, *De (Reliquiis) et imaginibus Sanctorum*, as well as Suarez, *Defensio fide Catholicae*, book 2, chs 11 to 14, and Durand, *Rationale Divinorum Officiorum*. 92 *Rationale Divinorum officiorum*, book 4. 93 The reference to Sergius on the Agnus Dei found in *ESA* corresponds to the last sentence of book 4, ch. 52 of *Rationale Divinorum Officiorum* (198v), *'Sergius Papa primus constituit Agnus Dei inter communionem ter*

The discussion on the Real Presence (chapter nine of *Eochair-sgiath an Aifrinn*) contains material found in the third volume of Bellarmine's *Disputationes*.[94] Chapters eleven and twelve of *Eochair-sgiath an Aifrinn*, on the need for confession, also draw on this source. The discussion on purgatory in chapter seventeen likewise draws on Bellarmine and Suarez.[95] It may have been because these source texts ranged far more widely than just a discussion on the Mass that Keating was prompted to digress into a consideration of confession and purgatory. The writings of all of these authors formed the basis of the theology taught in Catholic seminaries in the early seventeenth century. Keating's work, in turn, was an important mechanism for the transmission of these core texts to Irish audiences.

Preacher's handbooks of more general interest were also used by Keating. In particular, the compilation of *exempla* published at Douai in 1603, and regularly reissued, entitled the *Magnum speculum exemplorum*, was Keating's source for nineteen moral tales recounted in *Eochair-sgiath an Aifrinn*.[96] This was a standard preacher's handbook of moral tales, and material from it was adapted for Irish audiences by the Louvain Franciscans as well as by Keating.[97] Thus when Keating required material on the topic of confession, for example, the *Magnum speculum exemplorum* provided him with over thirty stories to select from. When using stories from this source, Keating sometimes described it as *Sgáthán na sompladha*[98] (Mirror of examples), other times he simply described his material as *sompladh*[99] without naming his source. Though all of the stories thus cited are printed in *Magnum speculum exemplorum*, Keating's prose versions are not direct translations and he may on occasion have been retelling them from memory.[100] Keating drew on further *exempla* from this source for *Trí bior-ghaoithe an bháis*. He sometimes added to the stories as given in the *Magnum speculum exemplorum*, and sometimes shortened them. Thus the story from Cesarius about the woman beekeeper whose bees made a church and altar in the hive[101] had a closing sentence by Keating not found in his source '*agus níor cealgadh aonduine do'n chuideachtain leo ag teacht nó ag imtheacht dóibh*'.[102] Elsewhere, his rendering of '*daemones venientes*' was not a direct translation. '*Go dtáinig sluagh do airmhighthe de dheamhnaibh isteach*' is the storyteller's reworking of the sparce Latin of his source.[103]

a clero et populo decantari' but Keiting supplies a date for Sergius not found in Durand. Keating's selection of this historical point, rather than the theological and scriptural material which forms the bulk of the chapter 'De Agnus Dei' may have been influenced by his studies of church history.   **94** The section entitled 'De Sacramento Eucharistiae', books 1-4.   **95** Bellarmine, *Disputationes*, ii, books 1 and 2, and Suarez, *Defensio fidei Catholicae*, book 2, ch. 15.   **96** Ó Laoghaire, Príomh-fhoinseacha, pp. 69-114.   **97** Aodh Mac Aingil, *Scáthán Shacramuinte na hAithridhe*, ed. Canice Mooney (Dublin, 1952).   **98** *ESA*, pp. 88, 112, 115.   **99** *ESA*, pp. 64, 67.   **100** A revised version in which the material was reorganised by theme rather than by source compilation was available by 1607 but the way individual exempla from the *Magnum speculum exemplorum* are cited by Keating suggests that he had consulted one of the earliest editions, either that published in 1603 or 1605. (A copy dated 1607 (in the British Library) is the earliest one I have identified in the revised format. The 1603 and 1605 editions I consulted are in the Bodleian Library, Oxford.)   **101** *ESA*, p. 62; F.C. Tubach, *Index exemplorum: a handbook of medieval religious tales* (Helsinki, 1969), no. 2663; *Scala coeli* (1480), sub 'Corpus Christi', *MSE*, Eucharistia, exemplum V.   **102** *ESA*, p. 62; Ó Laoghaire, Príomh-fhoinseacha, p. 108.   **103** *ESA*, p.

Pádraig Ó Fiannachta has suggested that one of the earliest scribes to make copies of *Eochair-sgiath an Aifrinn*, Seán Ó Maolchonaire,[104] consulted a printed edition of the *Magnum speculum exemplorum* to revise Keating's text, inserting the original Latin version of four of the stories, and providing an alternative Irish translation to that which Keating had originally given. In one instance the Irish translation supplied by the scribe was borrowed from Aodh Mac Aingil's *Scáthán shacramuinte na haithridhe*, but in other instances Ó Maolchonaire made his own translations.[105] These variations in the manuscript tradition indicate that the *Magnum speculum exemplorum*, together with the other theological texts on which *Eochair-sgiath an Aifrinn* was based, may have been in circulation among the more learned of the laity in Ireland, and were not restricted to continentally-educated clergy.

When using *exempla* Keating occasionally cited the *Scala coeli*[106] as his source. This publication, dating from 1480, was a forerunner of *Magnum speculum exemplorum*. It likewise served for generations as a preacher's handbook of moral tales. The compiler of *Magnum speculum exemplorum* acknowledged *Scala coeli* as the source of some of his exempla, and it appears likely that Keating's references to *Scala coeli* were derived through *Magnum speculum exemplorum*. Among the material he used was the story of a child at Mass who saw Jesus, then saw the priest swallowing Jesus, and ran away lest the priest would next eat him.[107] The story of the woman beekeeper and the church made of honey, already mentioned, was attributed by Keating to Caesarius Book 9, chapter 8. This reference is found in both *Scala coeli* and *Magnum speculum exemplorum*.[108] Another story for which Keating used *Scala coeli* as his source concerned a woman who had concealed a sin for eleven years.[109] Dragons, snakes and other horrors appeared until she confessed. The story is indeed found under the heading 'Confessio' in the 1480 edition *Scala coeli*. However, the same story was reissued from that source and features as *distinctio 9 exemplum 31* of the first edition of the *Magnum speculum exemplorum*. In later editions it was *exemplum 22* in the 'Confessio' category. In this instance Keating's reference is vague enough for any of the editions of these works to have been his source.

Two of the *exempla* used by Keating in *Eochair-sgiath an Aifrinn* are not found in *Magnum speculum exemplorum*.[110] They appear, however, in a similar handbook of exempla, the *Promptuarium exemplorum*.[111] Other stories used by Keating in

---

88; Ó Laoghaire, *Príomh-fhoinseacha*, p. 105.   **104** NLI, MS G 49.   **105** Pádraig Ó Fiannachta, 'Scéalta ón *Magnum Speculum Exemplorum*', *IER*, 5th ser, xcix, no. 3 (1963), 177–84. A manuscript entitled '*Scáthán na Sompladha*' preserved in fragmentary condition in the Cork diocesan library, now located in Cork University Library, may be relevant here. In this text, the headings of chapters agree with those cited in Mac Aingil, *Scáthán* and references are to books and chapters. See *BL Cat.Ir. MSS*, ii, 569. It would appear that this is not the work Keating has in mind when he refers to '*Scáthán na Sompladha*' since Keating's references to exempla as given in *ESA* are to distinctions as in *MSE* and not to chapters.   **106** Johannes Gobius, *Scala coeli* (Ulm, 1480).   **107** *ESA*, pp. 62–3, Tubach, *Index exemplorum*, no. 1001. The story was stated by Keating to have come from the *Scala coeli*.   **108** *ESA*, p. 62, Tubach, *Index exemplorum*, no. 2662.   **109** *ESA*, p. 80.   **110** *ESA*, pp. 102, 114.   **111** Ó Laoghaire, *Príomh-fhoinseacha*, p. 109; *Eucharistia Exemplum xxi, and Sermo xlviii*. This compilation was pub-

Eochair-sgiath an Aifrinn provide evidence that he was familiar with the contents of the *Legenda aurea* (golden legend) of Jacobus de Voragine.[112] It is possible that Keating encountered this material through an intermediate source. This medieval compilation would have been readily available in European libraries and the stories would have been in general circulation. When retelling stories from the golden legend not included in compilations such as the *Magnum speculum exemplorum*, Keating did not rigidly adhere to his source. Thus, for instance, the story Keating related about St Anthony was told of St Martin in the golden legend.[113] Keating's error seems to have arisen from the fact that the story about St Martin ultimately derived from the Chronicle of Antonius. Keating may have misheard or misread the story, or he may have heard a variant version. The part of the story in which God told Ambrose about the altar where St Martin was buried, not in a dream but an apparation, may have been Keating's own invention.[114] Another story told by Keating in *Eochair-sgiath an Aifrinn* concerned St Dominic.[115] This was also drawn from the golden legend,[116] but Keating's version was shorter than the Latin source. Yet another story in *Eochair-sgiath an Aifrinn* from this source related to St Mark, the evangelist.[117]

The use of all these medieval sources in Keating's tract on the Mass means that we can view his prose text, at least in part, as a continuation of a medieval preaching tradition. Keating combined material from these traditional sources with more orthodox Counter-Reformation literature, to produce a medley of ideas and stories which he deemed appropriate for use among Catholic readers in Ireland. The text was not necessarily perceived as innovative, but the language and style of its presentation ensured its impact.

These traditional homiletic devices were combined with a reliance on biblical sources in a manner that helped distinguish Counter-Reformation writing and preaching from that which had gone before. Keating's use of scriptural references is interesting. When the scriptural references in the text of *Eochair-sgiath an Aifrinn* (as printed) are compared with the Vulgate, it becomes apparent that his quotations and references are sometimes wrong.[118] He probably quoted many scriptural passages from memory. A consciousness of scriptures as a memorised rather than a printed text would explain his lack of precision. Indeed, the practice of giving biblical quotations by citing chapter but not verse was the norm for Catholic writers. It was the style used by influential writers such as Suarez and Pierre de Besse.

---

lished in a folio edition in 1492, twelve years after the date of the *Scala coeli*, and was the work of Ioannes Herolt.   112 Jacobus de Voragine, *The Golden legend: readings on the saints*, translated by William Granger Ryan (2 vols, Princeton, 1993).   113 *ESA*, p. 64; de Voragine, *Golden legend*, ii, pp. 292-300. Golden legend under St Martin: '*Eadem die cum beatus Ambrosius*'.   114 Ó Laoghaire, Príomh-fhoinseacha, p. v.   115 *ESA*, p. 58.   116 '*In eadem ecclesia (i.e. S. Sixti) dum fratres circiter xl maner-ent*'.   117 *ESA*, p. 99; Jacobus de Voraigne, *Golden legend*, 'Saint Mark, evangelist', i, 242-8.   118 Some examples of incorrect references in *ESA* include: Deuteronomy 7, *recte* Deuteronomy 17:12 (*ESA*, p. 56); IV Kings 8, *recte* IV Kings 19:34 (*ESA*, p. 53); Psalm 18, *recte* Psalm 16:15 (*ESA*, p. 108); Psalm 118, *recte* Psalm 113:17 (*ESA*, p. 110); Proverbs 20, *recte* Proverbs 5:22 (*ESA*, p. 76). See full details in Ó Laoghaire, Príomh-fhoinseacha, pp. 115-16.

While we cannot be sure than some of the inaccurate references are not the work of careless scribes, the extent of the errors (and the fact that the text was copied and recopied without those errors being corrected) suggests that *Eochair-sgiath an Aifrinn* was compiled and circulated in an environment where the precision of scriptural citations was not usually regarded as important.

Of more substance is the fact that the wording of many of the extracts of Scripture quoted in *Eochair-sgiath an Aifrinn* is rendered inaccurately. This applies to both Old Testament and New Testament passages. Examples include the passages from III Kings, 19: 6,7, '*Respexit, et ecce ad caput suum subcinericius panis, et vas aquae: comedit ergo, et bibit, et rursum obdormivit*'. '*An bhfaice (ar an t-aingeal) láimh réd' cheann an toirtin fá luaith aráin? Éirigh (ar sé) agus ith nidh dhe, is fada an ród atá romhad*',[119] and Psalm 18, 5 '*In omnem terram exivit sonus eorum, et in fines orbis terrae verba eorum.*': '*Rachaidh (ar sé) a bhfoghair anns an uile thalamh, agus rachaidh a mbriathra i gcríochaibh cruinne na talmhan.*'[120] Significantly Keating's gloss on this particular passage, 'Their voice will go out to all the earth and their words to the end of the world' makes the point that it was 'words' and not 'writings' that were prophecied by David. It therefore involved not just Scripture but word of mouth, or tradition: '*comhradh béil d'a ngoirtear sean-chuimhne sinnsear.*' This emphasis on tradition accorded with Catholic teaching and was an major issue of theological controversy between Christian denominations.

Among the inaccurate New Testament quotations in *Eochair-sgiath an Aifrinn* is Matthew 24:27. '*Tiocfaith (ar sé) amhail soinnean ar an aird anoir*' is his rendering of '*Sicut enim fulgur exit ab oriente, et paret usque in occidentem: ita erit et adventus Filii hominis*'. This quotation is evidently derived second hand from Thomas Aquinas, though Keating's wording differs slightly.[121] Again, Luke 1:35: '*An gein do rugadh uaibh-se (ar sé) is ó'n Spiorad Naomh atá sé*',[122] is an inaccurate rendering of the Vulgate text: '*Et respondens angelus dixit ei: Spiritus sanctus superverveniet in te, et virtus Altissimi obumbrabit tibi.*' In each of these instances, the inclusion of the colloquial '*ar sé*' ['said he'] is reminiscent of oral rhetoric.

Nicholas Williams has identified examples among Keating's scriptural quotations in *Eochair-sgiath an Aifrinn* which appear to derived from the 1602 translation by William Daniel [Ó Domhnaill] of the New Testament into Irish.[123] However, he also notes that Keating's quotations are often inaccurate, and that, while he appears to have had the language of the 1602 translation in mind, he was evidently working from memory.[124]

Despite his somewhat cavalier attitute to scriptural quotations, and his rejection of Protestant privileging of scripture and consequent disregard for tradition, it is

---

119 *ESA*, p. 98. 120 *ESA*, p. 15. 121 Thomas Aquinas, *Summa Theol.* II, Q. LXXXIV, Art 3. (The printed text of *ESA* (p. 42), incorrectly gives Matt 14 as the reference.) 122 *ESA*, p. 66. 123 *Tiomna Nuadh ar dTighearna agvs ar Slanaightheora Iosa Críosd, ar na tarruing gu firinneach as Gréigis go gáoidheilg re hUilliam Ó Domhnuill* ... (Baile Átha Cliath, 1602) [STC 2958]; Nicholas Williams, *I bprionta i leabhar: na Protastúin agus prós na Gaeilge, 1567-1724* (Dublin, 1986), pp. 130-1. 124 Williams, *I bprionta i leabhar*, pp. 130-1.

nonetheless clear that the Bible was regarded by Keating as the essential underpinning of all his arguments. There are almost 300 specific references to scriptural passages in *Eochair-sgiath an Aifrinn*, which number far exceeds the quantity of material drawn from any other source.

V

While a range of medieval continental preaching handbooks were used by Keating, the *Flores* of Thomas Hibernicus was not. This suggests that the source compilations available to Keating when writing *Eochair-sgiath an Aifrinn* were continental rather than Irish, and reinforces the view that the text was probably originally put together while he lived abroad. Nevertheless the polemical introductory chapter was not without its particular relevance to the political circumstances in which Catholicism functioned in early seventeenth-century Ireland. Without mentioning Ireland specifically, Keating drew a distinction between ecclesiastical and secular authority, denied by the proponents of the established church in Ireland, but supported, in Keating's view, by the biblical authority indicated in '*Reddite quae sunt Caesaris, Caesari; et quae sunt Dei, Deo*' ('Render unto Caesar that which is Caesar's and to God that which is God's').[125] Keating presented the Mass to his Irish readers as the central tenet of Catholicism as contrasted with Protestantism. He regarded devotion to the Mass as a touchstone of loyalty, regarding those who were not loyal to the Mass as heretics.[126] This was echoed in his other theological tract, *Trí bior-ghaoithe an bháis*, when he warned Catholics against any outward conformity to Protestantism for the sake of a quiet life.[127] The way in which Keating (and Henry Fitzsimon's similar and roughly contemporary work in English) presented the Mass as central to Catholicism drew attention to these writers' awareness of the fact that they were defining Catholicism for Irish audiences. Their discourses emphasised the centrality of the Eucharist in that definition.[128]

A concern to promote practical piety was an important outcome of the Tridentine recommendation on seminary education for Catholic clergy. Religious writing in the vernacular, designed to encourage devotion, was widely disseminated throughout much of western Europe.[129] In the Irish language, it was the work of the Franciscans, particularly those associated with the Irish college of St Anthony at Louvain, who led the way in utilising the print medium for the dissemination of devotional texts in the vernacular.[130] Their first catechisms designed for use with Irish speakers were produced before the end of the sixteenth century, although the first to become available in print appeared in 1611, the work of a poet turned

125 A quotation highlighted by Suarez, *Defensio*, book 3, ch. 4, p. 237.   126 *ESA*, pp. 16-17.   127 *TBB*, l. 3549.   128 Henry Fitzsimon, *The justification and exposition of the divine sacrifice of the Mass* ([Douai], 1611). A fascimile edition has been published in English Recusant Literature Series, 108 (1972).   129 Terence C. Cave, *Devotional poetry in France, c.1570-1613* (Cambridge, 1969), pp. 1-57. 130 Cunningham 'The culture and ideology of Irish Franciscan historians' pp. 11-30, 222-7.

preacher, Bonaventura Ó hEodhasa.[131] Longer devotional treatises by Hugh Mac Caughwell (Aodh Mac Aingil) and Florence Conry (Flaithrí Ó Maolchonaire) were also published. Mac Aingil's *Scáthán Shacramuinte na hAithridhe* (A mirror to the sacrament of penance) and Ó Maolchonaire's *Desiderius* were compilations adapted from the literature of the European Counter-Reformation. Geoffrey Keating's theological writings had much in common with the work of the Franciscan writers, and although his texts were not disseminated in printed form, they went into circulation in Ireland nonetheless. *Eochair-sgiath an Aifrinn* summarised Counter-Reformation doctrine on the Mass for Irish audiences, making it available in the vernacular in attractive language. It drew on the intellectual resources of the Catholic Reformation and acted as an important means of transmitting the doctrines promulgated at the Council of Trent to Irish audiences.

The manuscript tradition suggests that *Eochair-sgiath an Aifrinn* long fulfilled a role as a handbook for the clergy and provided material for many a sermon.[132] It would have served as a useful handbook for clergy who had not themselves received a prolonged seminary education. It was also probably intended to be read by some of the laity. Though written for the minority of Irish Catholics who could read and could afford access to such texts, Keating's tract on the Mass eventually did help mould popular attitudes to the Mass and confession, as nurtured through the sermons of clergy who encountered the text. There is evidence that the stories survived in folklore down to the nineteenth century, though its more immediate impact on seventeenth-century audiences is difficult to discern. For later generations, it provided ample confirmation that Keating had been a fearless advocate of the core values of Counter-Reformation Catholicism, and contributed in no small way to people's eagerness to remember this scholar priest.[133]

---

131 Brian Ó Cuív, 'Flaithrí Ó Maolchonaire's catechism of christian doctrine', *Celtica*, i (1950), pp. 161-98; Bonabhentura Ó hEodhasa, *An Teagasg Críosdaidhe* [Antwerp, 1611], ed. Fearghal Mac Raghnaill (Dublin, 1976).   132 For manuscript copies of the text owned by clergy see above p. 11, n. 25; see also Cainneach Ó Maonaigh (ed.), *Seanmónta Chúige Uladh* (Baile Átha Cliath, 1965), pp. xv, 14.   133 Helena Concannon, *The Blessed Eucharist in Irish history* (Dublin, 1932), p. xxii. In this context it is not surprising that the set of priest's vestments from 'penal times' preserved in the ecclesiastical museum at St Patrick's College, Maynooth, are reputed to be those of Geoffrey Keating.

3

Catholic teaching and social change in Munster

I

Keating's purpose in going to Europe had been to prepare for a career in the diocesan priesthood in Ireland. After a number of years abroad he returned home. Apart from his writings, there is little direct evidence of his activities in Ireland. He was working as a priest in Munster by 1613, and probably spent most of his life in the diocese of Lismore, until his death which took place not later than 1644.

Clergy educated in continental seminaries, who had been immersed for a number of years in the Counter-Reformation ethos of the academic urban communities in French university towns, faced many challenges on their return to rural districts in Ireland. In the opening decades of the seventeenth century, secular clergy returning to Ireland had to operate without the support of a stable diocesan structure headed by a bishop or parishes to which priests had clearly defined appointments. There was no shortage of priests. By the second decade of the seventeenth century the province of Munster was well served with priests in proportion to its population. Tipperary was reported as having nineteen secular clergy together with five Jesuits in 1613.[1] Government observers were particularly concerned about the activities of Catholic clergy in the liberties of Tipperary, describing the area as 'the usual rendezvous of priests and Jesuits and other ill-affected persons'.[2]

One of the earliest references to Geoffrey Keating working as a priest in the region comes in 1613 where a Dr Keating features in a list of 'sundry priests and friars' in county Tipperary.[3] Two years later one of six named priests recorded in the 1615 visitation in the diocese of Lismore was 'Father Jeffry Keating, a preacher and a Jesuit, resorting to all parts of this diocese'.[4] Additional information is supplied for some of the other clergy of Lismore, detailing the houses of the gentry with whom they resided. That Keating's name was not associated with a specific

1 Evelyn Bolster, *A history of the diocese of Cork from the Reformation to the penal era* (Cork, 1982), pp. 150-1; TCD, MS 567, ff. 32-5. 2 *Calendar of the Carew manuscripts preserved in the archiepiscopal library at Lambeth, 1603-24*, p. 377. 3 TCD, MS 567, ff. 32-5. 4 *Liber regalis visitationis*, 1615 (BL, Add. MS 19,836), p. 283 (NLI, microfilm P509). (Cited inaccurately in Mac Giolla Eáin (ed.), *Dánta*, p. 4.)

parish at this point is partly explained by the lack of a coherent, functioning parish system. Formal hierarchical ecclesiastical structures in the diocese were negligible when Keating first returned there. Although James White had been active as vicar apostolic in Lismore and Waterford from 1600 to 1610[5] it was not until 1629 that a Catholic bishop was appointed to the diocese. In that year Patrick Comerford, having returned from the Irish college at Bordeaux, took charge there and remained as bishop until his death in 1652.

Much of Comerford's correspondence with Irish clergy in Europe survives, and while lamenting the state of the country he recorded that 'as yet we see no great persecution since the peace was proclaimed, although we may not presume much upon this little toleration'.[6] The threat of persecution was not the only difficulty being encountered. The ongoing rivalry between secular and regular clergy was probably just as disruptive as persecution. The competing interests of secular, or diocesan clergy, on the one hand, and members of religious orders, or regulars, on the other was a serious complicating factor in the organisation of the Catholic church in early seventeenth-century Ireland.[7] The religious orders functioned outside the jurisdiction of the episcopal authorities, and in some areas their activities tended to undermine attempts to establish a workable parochial structure under episcopal control. In particular, if regular clergy functioning out of revived monastic institutions conducted baptisms, marriages and funerals the income necessary for the support of a diocesan clergy was seriously undermined. As bishop of Waterford, Comerford, complained

> of the jealousies betwixt the regulars and prelates in this kingdom I am very loath, and would wish with all my hart they were ended after a good and legal manner, assuring you that they hinder much the conversion of souls, and bring to a contempt all ecclesiasticals.[8]

Comerford was more embroiled in the secular-regular rivalry than most. Although a member of the Augustinian order, he sided with the secular clergy. As a result, he found himself alienated and it was reported in 1631 that 'there are not two houses in this whole city [Waterford] where he is sure of a meal, because the seculars themselves deplore his opposition to the religious'.[9]

Few clergy could have been unaware of the dispute, and Geoffrey Keating made no secret of his preference for the claims of the secular clergy and the parochial system of ecclesiastical organisation as a means of maintaining order within the Catholic Church.[10] He accepted the ecclesiastical norms of Tridentine

5 T.W. Moody, F.X. Martin, F.J. Byrne (eds), *A new history of Ireland, ix, maps, genealogies, lists* (Oxford, 1984), 369.   6 HMC, *Report on Franciscan manuscripts preserved at the Convent, Merchant's Quay, Dublin* (Dublin, 1906) p. 38.   7 Aidan Clarke, 'Colonial identity in early seventeenth-century Ireland' in T.W. Moody (ed.), *Nationality and the pursuit of national independence: historical studies xi* (Belfast, 1978), pp. 57-71.   8 HMC, *Franciscan*, p. 39.   9 Ibid., pp. 46-50.   10 *FFÉ*, iii, 298-306, 356.

Catholicism as being an appropriate model for Ireland and through his writings he provided an historical justification for his views.[11]

Keating's account of the twelfth-century reform of the Irish church as ratified at the synod of Rathbreasail emphasised the establishment of a diocesan structure for Ireland, thereby providing the historical underpinning for the preferred church structures. The synod of Kells in 1152 at which the four archbishoprics of Armagh, Cashel, Dublin and Tuam had been ratified was presented as part of the closing narrative of Keating's *Foras feasa* in a manner that suggested that this diocesan structure for the island was an integral part of the origin myth of Catholic Ireland.[12]

From Keating's perspective it would appear that much progress had already been made in Munster by the 1620s towards the establishment of workable church structures relevant to the needs of the community to which he ministered. In his *Trí bior-ghaoithe an bháis* Keating reminded his readers that God wanted sinners to repent and that the populace could not excuse themselves on the basis of ignorance of God's law. He specifically asserted that the law of God was being widely broadcast and announced to Christians in general.[13] Such comments imply that the Catholic church in 1620s Ireland was much more than just a mission church.[14] Keating's view was that the populace were already educated in the faith, faced threats from officialdom in the exercise of that faith, but were expected to understand that adherence to the practice of their faith openly in the face of adversity and even persecution was the responsibility and duty of Christians.[15] Suffering was something to be endured, not evaded, because it was the will of God.[16] Keating was confident, in his writings, that he was addressing audiences of the upper social levels already well versed in the doctrines of Catholicism. They may have needed reminding of their duty to God, of the need to give priority to their obligations as Catholics above the attractions of secular ambition but, in his opinion, their familiarity with Catholic doctrines was not in doubt. His role in relation to this educated Catholic community was to remind them of their moral obligations and to warn them of the consequences of their neglect of God's law.

II

The surviving evidence suggests that Geoffrey Keating may have preached in a variety of areas in the diocese and that he had a considerable reputation as a preacher.[17] It seems certain that the wealthier members of the local elite were among his congregation. The silver chalice bearing the inscription '*Dominus*

---

11 Cunningham, 'Seventeenth-century interpretations of the past', pp. 116-28. See also Patrick J. Corish, *The Catholic community in the seventeenth and eighteenth centuries* (Dublin, 1981). 12 *FFÉ*, iii, 312, 356. 13 *TBB*, ll. 3388-9. 14 See Corish, *Catholic community*. 15 Bernadette Cunningham and Raymond Gillespie, '"Persecution" in seventeenth-century Irish', *Éigse*, xxii (1987), pp. 15-20. 16 *TBB*, ll. 5299-423. 17 BL, Add. MS 19,836, p. 283; *Clanricarde*, pp. cxxvi-cxxix.

Galfridus Keatinge Sacerd[os] Sacrae Theologiae Doctor me fiere fecit, 23 February 1634',[18] must have been paid for by a benefactor. Parishioners who could afford to erect the plaque inscribed to his memory in Tubbrid in 1644 must also have had some surplus income. The story told by O'Sullevane of Keating having offended Elinor Laffan, the wife of Squire Mocler, whether true or not, also places him in the context of ministering to the elite of society.[19] Squire Mocler, alluded to by O'Sullevane in 1722, was a member of the local gentry, presumably one of the Moclers of Moclerstowne, in the parish of Ballycleraghan, close to Moorestown Keating. Like the Keatings the Moclers were a long-established family in the district, although the evidence of the Civil Survey suggests that the principal Mocler proprietors had also been through a period of economic difficulty. Jeffrey Mocler of Moclerstowne had mortgaged some of his land to others before 1640, and most of the land he retained was described by the Civil Survey commissioners as being 'without improvement'.[20] Nearby, Henry Mocler of Ballycurrene, in the parish of Inishlounaght, whose lands adjoined Moorestown Keating, had mortgaged his lands to one Richard Keating.[21] These people, then, bonded together through economic ties, and long established family links with the locality, all described in 1640 as 'Irish papists', are identifiable members of the Catholic community to whom Geoffrey Keating would most likely have ministered.

Given the relatively comfortable social background of those families who could afford to have a son educated on the continent as a priest, it is fair to assume that the social status of those clergy who returned to Ireland from European colleges would have been high. The fact that he was one of only six out of 208 individuals associated with Bordeaux before 1618 who held the degree of doctor of theology[22] would have placed Keating among the clerical elite in the region. His educational achievements marked him out as unusual, and might have resulted in him choosing, or being chosen, to minister to the better educated sector of the community. We do not know with whom he lived but the likelihood that he would have been chaplain to a gentry family and lived in their Tipperary household is high.[23] While he had a definite link with Tubbrid, the evidence of the commemorative plaque erected there in 1644 does not actually state that he was parish priest there and the chapel of St Ciaran in Tubbrid may have been a chantry chapel rather than a parish church.

The internal evidence of Keating's writings tends to point to Keating having ministered mainly to the gentry. The spiritual and moral challenges of the rich rather than the poor tend to take priority in *Trí bior-ghaoithe an bháis*. For instance,

18 Burke, 'Geoffry Keating', p. 179; Patrick Power, *Waterford and Lismore: a compendious history of the united dioceses* (Cork, 1937), p. 280. The chalice was still in use in Cappoquin in 1895, but the idea that it provides evidence of a link between Geoffrey Keating and that parish is mistaken. In the twentieth century the chalice was removed to Waterford cathedral for safe keeping and in 1999 was placed on display in the new Waterford museum. I am grateful to the Very Rev William Ryan for confirming the current location of the chalice. 19 *Clanricarde*, pp. cxxvi-vii. 20 *Civil survey*, i, p. 214. 21 Ibid., i, p. 312. 22 *Calendar of state papers, Ireland, 1615-25*, pp. 315-20. 23 For Keating's probable links with the Butlers of Dunboyne see ch. 2.

the four things he listed that a person lost when reaching death were worldly honour, bodily luxuries, wealth, and companions.[24] He addressed readers whom he assumed had access to other reading materials then in circulation in Ireland. He assumed his readers would make wills, or act as executors for wills, and that they aspired to having their children educated at university.[25] He was well aware of the points of contention within his community. He knew that his audience included people who had acquired property at the expense of others. These people were portrayed as being like their ancestors before them, stealing from their neighbours and friends, extracting wealth through the partiality of bribed judges and secret trickery. It was a world which the Munster author of the early seventeenth-century satirical tract, *Pairlement Chloinne Tomáis*, would have recognised immediately.[26] Keating condemned those people as guilty of the sin of greed, and warned them that God would avenge their wrongs. 'Take care not to be the one on whom the hand of God will descend', he declared.[27] He may even have had in mind some of his own kinsmen and neighbours, those who were acquiring land by mortgage or purchase.

In a time of economic change opportunities arose for some individuals to advance on the social ladder, an advancement often achieved at the expense of others for whom the changed economic circumstances had meant declining fortunes.[28] The consequent readjustments to new-found social positions gave rise to tensions in society, and in these circumstances it appears that Keating's sympathies would have been with the old order rather than the *nouveau riche*.

Warning his readers that God would punish the sin of adultery, Keating cited named examples from six elite Munster and Leinster families, three native Irish and three Old English, who had been reduced to extreme poverty or left without heirs because of their sins.[29] Keating's use of such examples, which he said he felt able to mention because the cases were already so well known locally, indicates that he believed these examples drawn from the upper echelons of society would be particularly persuasive for his readers. That he could cite the example of such influential members of society suffering Divine punishment strengthened his moral argument.

Reminding his readers of their need for moral reform so that the awfulness of death could be averted, he described how death disrupted the social order.[30] Death did not discriminate according to status, he warned, but rather killed the lord as often as the soldier, the son with the father, the daughter with the mother, the rich with the poor. Death would leave land without a lord, a father without an heir, an orphan without a father.[31] Sin, which led to death of the soul, likewise resulted in usurpation of the right order of society. Thus, he argued, moral reform was necessary for society to work harmoniously.

---

24 *TBB*, book 1, ch. 3. **25** *TBB*, ll. 5103-92. **26** Marc Caball, '*Pairlement Chloinne Thomáis* i, a reassessment', *Éigse*, xxvii (1993), pp. 47-57; *TBB*, ll. 3546-47. See below ch. 8. **27** *TBB*, ll. 5388-443. **28** *TBB*, ll. 2000-22. See Raymond Gillespie, *The transformation of the Irish economy, 1550-1700* (Dundalk, 1991) for the economic conditions in Ireland in the early seventeenth century. **29** *TBB*, ll. 5424-507. **30** *TBB*, book 1, ch. 4. **31** Ibid., ch. 4, sect. 12.

Keating's seminary training and theological education would have prepared him to provide a range of services to his congregation, though given the difference between his educational experience and theirs, there was bound to be some distance between his expectations and theirs. The promotion of new religious ideas, or the adaptation of old ones was not achieved by any form of mass propaganda. Rather, new ideas were first shared in the context of personal links between the academically trained clergy and their circle of family and friends.[32] Priests operating in any area of Munster in the early seventeenth century relied primarily on the support and hospitality of relatives and other local patrons who provided the accommodation and sustenance necessary for them to carry out their duties.[33] The Mass was more likely to be celebrated in private houses than in the more formal setting of a parish church.[34] Private chapels of the gentry could come near the norm within which Keating functioned. The chaplain to Lady Frances Butler (wife of Richard Butler of Kilcash, brother to the earl of Ormond), commented on the private chapel she maintained. The Carmelite priest, Paul of St Ubald, praised 'the orderly composition of your chapel with those devout pictures of the altar, decent vestments, fine and clean altar clothes'.[35]

Keating's tract on the Mass was intended as a handbook for clergy on the orthodox celebration of the Mass. It should perhaps be regarded as a blueprint for, rather than an actual reflection of, the way the Mass was celebrated and perceived among his contemporaries in Munster. Religious life in early seventeenth-century Ireland did not only, or even primarily, focus on the priest and the mass. In the immediate neighbourhood of the Tubbrid chapel with which Geoffrey Keating was associated, there was, for example a holy well dedicated to St Ciarán. In the nearby parish of Cahir there was Tobar Íosa, associated with the influential Cahir abbey, a thirteenth-century Augustinian foundation that had been dissolved in 1540.[36] The well was known as a place of devotion where 'rounds' were made in accordance with long-established tradition, and may well have been the reason why Bishop Comerford tried to regain authority over the abbey at Cahir.[37] In the townland of Grangemore, also in the parish of Cahir, was St Patrick's stone with its associated stories of a visit by the Apostle of Ireland to the immediate neighbourhood.[38] Such features in the landscape were not ignored by Counter Reformation clergy but were utilised to integrate Tridentine teachings into the traditional belief of the people of a given locality.[39] Nearby, in the parish of Inislounaght was the renowned St

---

32 See Christopher Haigh, *Reformation and resistance in Tudor Lancashire* (Cambridge, 1975), pp. 163-70. 33 For a detailed list of such benefactors in Kilkenny at this time see Carrigan, *Ossory*, i, pp. 81-3, drawn from TCD, MS 567; no comparable detail for Lismore and Waterford seems to have survived. 34 Bossy, 'The Counter-Reformation and the people of Catholic Ireland, 1596-1641', pp. 155-69. 35 Paul of St Ubald, *The soul's delight* (Antwerp, 1654), sig. A2, A2v. 36 Aubrey Gwynn and Neville Hadcock, *Medieval religious houses: Ireland* (London, 1970), pp. 153, 162. 37 Power, *Placenames of Decies*, 298; G. Nuttall Smith, 'Holy well and antiquities near Cahir, Co. Tipperary', *JRSAI*, xxix (1899), pp. 258-9. On Comerford's involvement, see HMC, *Franciscan*, p. 38. 38 Power, *Placenames of Decies*, p. 300. 39 For the example of St Patrick see Bernadette Cunningham and Raymond

Patrick's Well. This well, alluded to in a life of St Declan, recorded by the Franciscan Mícheál Ó Cléirigh during Keating's lifetime, was another locus of the holy in the local landscape.[40] A little further afield, but still an entirely feasible pilgrimage destination for the people of south Tipperary was the Cistercian abbey of Holy Cross. There, in the early seventeenth century, the possession of a relic of the True Cross facilitated the Cistercians in re-establishing themselves as a group with significant pastoral appeal, not just in the immediate locality, but drawing visitors from many parts of southern Ireland. People came in search of cures from misfortune and disease, as well as for spiritual sustenance, they came on their own behalf and to intercede on behalf of others unable to travel.[41] All of these foci of devotion, some of considerable antiquity and often with associated stories which showed them as particularly significant points of access to divine power, continued to have appeal among the laity, and were not always under the immediate control of the clergy.[42] There were therefore a variety of means of access to the holy available to the people to whom Keating ministered in Munster.[43]

Formal parochial structures were also taking shape or being restored. In Tubbrid, the walls still standing are evidence of the church that existed there in the early seventeenth century, and, given the expression of appreciation in stone still visible on the gable wall, there seems little doubt that Keating, like his predecessor O'Duffy, had won a lasting place in the hearts of the people of the locality, through his work as a priest. They were probably also aware of his reputation for scholarship, and his renown as a preacher.

III

Keating's writings and sermons were one of the channels through which the ideas of Tridentine Catholicism he had encountered in France were communicated to Munster audiences.[44] His style of preaching probably conformed to the Jesuit norms that he would have known in Rheims and Bordeaux, and which was experienced by Munster congregations through the Jesuit missions of the early years of the seventeenth century. Barnabas Kearney, one of the Jesuits active in Munster in the opening decade of the seventeenth century was author of a collection of sermons for the Sundays of the year published in 1622.[45] Kearney's text, like

Gillespie, '"The most adaptable of saints": the cult of St Patrick in the seventeenth century', *Archivium Hibernicum*, xlix (1995), pp. 82-104. **40** Power, *Placenames of Decies*, p. 263; Patrick Power (ed.), *Life of St Declan of Ardmore ... and life of St Mochuda of Lismore* (London, ITS, 1916). **41** Raymond Gillespie and Bernadette Cunningham, 'Holy Cross Abbey and the Counter-Reformation in Tipperary', *Tipperary Historical Jnl* (1991), pp. 171-80. **42** Raymond Gillespie, *Devoted people: belief and religion in early modern Ireland* (Manchester, 1997), pp. 84-92. **43** Ibid., pp. 63-102. **44** Corish, *Catholic community*, pp. 40-2. **45** Barnabas Kearney, *Heliotrophium sive consiones tam de festis quam de dominicis quae in solari totius anni circulo occurrunt* (Lyons, 1622). For Kearney's pastoral activities in Munster see Edmund Hogan (ed.), *Ibernia Ignatiana, seu Ibernorum Societatis Jesu patrum monumenta collecta, 1540-1607* (Dublin, 1880), pp. 172-90; 216-20.

Keating's theological writings, drew on Jesuit style of preaching for its form and content. It presented, in the style of Counter-Reformation discourse, the kind of teachings that Kearney communicated to congregations in Munster, exhorting repentance and promoting Mass and confession.[46] The descriptions of Jesuit missions in Munster in the opening years of the seventeenth century provide some clues as to how such material was received by the congregation. It was recorded that Fr Wale's preaching in Carrick-on-Suir in 1604 had evoked sobs and moans from the congregation. In another instance, the congregation were so terrified by the sermon on hell delivered by a Jesuit preacher that goods that had been stolen were returned after the sermon.[47] Given the similarity of subject matter and style found in the theological writings of these two Munster preachers, the Jesuit Barnabas Kearney and Keating, the secular priest, we can assume that their preaching styles would have been similar also. Whereas Kearney's published work was in Latin, and must have been designed principally for use among the clergy, Keating's vernacular tract would have been more accessible to the laity. Both Kearney and Keating were drawing on a medieval preaching tradition which had been adapted to communicate the doctrines of Counter-Reformation Catholicism.[48]

Trí bior-ghaoithe an bháis provides ample evidence of the range of European teachings that Keating thought appropriate to Irish audiences. In a theological tract of some 120,000 words, divided into three books, he provided a compendium of tried and tested materials, in a form that made them accessible to Irish audiences.[49] The 'three shafts of death' theme was used as the framework of the first book only and was only briefly referred to subsequently. Book one took as its basic scriptural text Hebrews 9:27, '*Statutum est hominibus semel mori*' (it is our human lot to die), and the central idea was that there are three kinds of death. These were initially defined as '*bás céadfadhach, bás nadúrtha & bás spioradálta*' (death of the senses, natural death, and spiritual death),[50] and the elaboration explained these as signifying first physical death, secondly the soul of reason being separated from the body, and thirdly the separation of the soul from the Grace of God. A second set of definitions was then added: '*bás nádúrtha, bás na coire & bás na péine*' (natural death, death in sin, and the death of eternal suffering).[51] Keating had these two variants in mind for the meaning of 'three shafts' thereafter. Readers were encouraged to think of death constantly, so as to conquer pride, gluttony, lust and others of the seven deadly sins.[52] Readers were reminded that death did not just come at the end, it shadowed the boat of life every day.[53]

The second book of *Trí bior-ghaoithe an bháis* focussed on the theme of original sin, taking as its primary biblical text Romans 5:12 'Through one man sin

46 Hogan (ed.), *Ibernia Ignatiana*, pp. 135-7.   **47** J.J. Corboy, The Jesuit mission to Ireland, 1596-1626. M.A. thesis, UCD, 1941, citing Hogan (ed.), *Ibernia Ignatiana*, pp. 158, 164, and Edmund Hogan, *Distinguished Irishmen of the sixteenth century* (London, 1894), pp. 432-4.   **48** On the general context of this sermon literature see Peter Bayley, *French pulpit oratory, 1598-1650* (Cambridge, 1980).   **49** Book three is almost three times as long as either one of the first two books.   **50** *TBB*, ll. 978-91.   **51** *TBB*, ll. 984-5.   **52** *TBB*, ll. 368-520.   **53** *TBB*, ll. 2349-408.

entered the world and through sin death', and the first six chapters dealt with various aspects of the sin of Adam. So as to overcome original sin, the reader was encouraged to prepare for death by living a better life so as to look forward to death like an exile coming home.[54] The latter part of book two contained a miscellany of stories on the theme of exile and journeying, imprisonment and shipwreck, the impermanence of life and the unpredictability of death. A final chapter on purgatory ended abruptly with a contrived return to the theme of original sin and a repetition of the inaccurate opening scriptural quotation.

The third and final book of *Trí bior-ghaoithe an bháis* resumed the discussion of purgatory. Five chapters discussed the fate of those in purgatory and the responsibilities of the living members of the communion of saints. Chapter six began with a treatment of the untimeliness of the death of the young. It then treated at length of three categories of sin which Keating deemed of particular relevance for Irish readers: the spilling of blood treacherously, the oppression of the church, and adultery. The last was given the most attention. Funerals and mourning were dealt with in chapters seven to nine, while chapters ten to twelve described the pain of hell and outlined why it was important for people to be informed about hell. The last nine chapters of book three concentrated on various miscellaneous aspects of sin and the road to repentance, with progressively lengthier and more discursive treatment of the topic.

Essentially a communicator and teacher rather than an innovator, Keating did not enter into debate on the latest theological controversies. It seems fair to place Keating's *Trí bior-ghaoithe an bháis* in the tradition of a Jesuit-influenced revival of texts in the *ars morendi* mould on the transitoriness of life, a trend promoted by the founder of the Society of Jesus, Ignatius Loyola, himself.[55] Sermons on death and the pains of hell and on the need for repentance were no novelty for either Irish or European audiences. The preacher's duty, according to the medieval Franciscan rule, was 'to preach of the vices and virtues, the penalties of hell and the glory of heaven' and to do so effectively maintaining the hearer's attention.[56] Audiences liked some originality in the treatment of old themes. They also liked brevity, lack of monotony, entertainment, instruction, adherence to scripture, and conformity to the listener's own beliefs.[57]

There was little innovative theology in *Trí bior-ghaoithe an bháis*, and little that would have failed to conform to the religious beliefs of Keating's readers. His discussion of sin was conducted within the framework of the traditional doctrine of the seven deadly sins, rather than the ten commandments. Whereas his Franciscan contemporary Aodh Mac Aingil used the ten commandments as the framework for his examination of conscience in *Scáthán Shacramuinte an haithridhe*,[58] Keating

---

54 *TBB*, l. 2737. **55** Tadhg Ó Dushláine, *An Eoraip agus litríocht na Gaeilge: 1600-1650* (Baile Átha Cliath, 1987), p. 19. **56** H. Leith Spencer, *English preaching in the late middle ages* (Oxford, 1993), p. 93, citing S. Wenzel, *Verses in sermons, Fasciculus Morum and its middle English poems* (Cambridge, Mass, 1978), pp. 9-10. **57** Leith Spencer, *English preaching*, p. 107. **58** Louvain, 1618, ed. Canice Mooney (Dublin, 1952), pp. 94-104. I am grateful to Micheál Mac Craith for drawing my attention to this detail.

opted for a more conservative methodology. The use of the ten commandments as a catechetical tool, on the model of the *Catechism of the Council of Trent*, would have been innovative in an Irish context. On the other hand, he could have been confident that his readers were already familiar with the moral framework shaped around the seven deadly sins.[59] All of the seven deadly sins had a strong social aspect, and the traditional doctrine conveyed the idea of sin as offence against the community as well as being a turning away from God, an aspect emphasised by Keating. The material was presented in a literary style which drew people to the message. *Trí bior-ghaoithe an bháis* was attractive because it presented well-known teachings in familiar language in a persuasive style. It communicated doctrines about life and death that people believed they needed to hear. It summarised the doctrines Keating believed to be crucial to the maintenance of moral order in this world and as a means to ultimate salvation.

IV

In selecting material for inclusion in *Trí bior-ghaoithe an bháis* Keating combined material drawn from contemporary publications by Catholic authors whose works were in circulation on the continent with older texts that had been the staple of medieval preaching. Although the way in which the materials were combined to form the finished work was Keating's own creation, there were few original ideas in the text. The stories he retold would have been familiar to both Irish and continental audiences. As in his writing on the mass, he inserted numerous *exempla* drawn from the *Magnum speculum exemplorum*. Indeed the latter part of the third book of *Trí bior-ghaoithe an bháis* is little more than a miscellany of pre-Reformation preaching materials on the general theme of sin and repentance.

Osborn Bergin's suggestion that the fourteenth-century *Flores* of Thomas Hibernicus might have been the source for many of Keating's stories from the Church fathers has proved incorrect. Although the version of the *Flores* issued in 1622 contains a 15-page section on death,[60] few of Keating's references in *Trí bior-ghaoithe* actually correspond with the contents of this particular source. For instance, Keating's quotations from Jerome on death do not include such apt items as '*Memento mortis tuae, et non peccabis*', or '*Qui se quotidie recordatur esse moriturum, contemnit praesentia et ad futura festinat*'.[61] Of the five references to Seneca in *Trí bior-ghaoithe*, two can be found in the *Flores*,[62] but the other three are not included in the section of the *Flores* on death.[63] Nevertheless, like all preachers, Keating did

59 See below ch. 9 on the moral order. John Bossy, 'Moral arithmetic: seven sins into ten commandments', in Edmund Leites (ed.), *Conscience and casuistry in early modern Europe* (Cambridge, 1988), pp. 213-34.   60 [Thomas Hibernicus] *Flores Bibliorum, sive loci communes omnium fere materiarum ex veteri et novo testamento excerpti* (1622 edition), 'Mors', pp. 640-54.   61 *Flores Bibliorum* (1622 ed.) p. 642.   62 *TBB*, ll. 834-38, 2367-77, and *Flores* (1622 ed.) pp. 648 and 650.   63 *TBB*, ll. 4605-16; 6987-94; 9360-6.

3 'Death' frontispiece from Pierre de Besse, *Conceptions theologiques sur les quatres fin de l'homme*. (Paris, 1622)

rely in part on similar theological compendia, most notably the *Magnum speculum exemplorum*, the same source of moral tales which he used in *Eochair-sgiath an Aifrinn*. While such compendia of exempla were invaluable to the preacher or devotional writer seeking to enliven his sermon or tract with memorable stories that contained a suitable moral, they did not contain ready-made sermons. A writer or preacher who used these sources for illustrative material to enliven a sermon still had to construct the argument of the sermon itself.

Published sermon collections were also readily available, such works becoming an important element of religious publication in early seventeenth-century Europe. One study of this literature has identified over 300 published theological collections of sermons or meditations issued in France alone in the first half of the seventeenth century.[64] In many instances, renowned preachers published their sermons in a modified form as printed meditations. Although the closeness of the relationship between the sermon as delivered and the text that was subsequently published varied considerably, the link between printed meditations and oral sermons was significant. Geoffrey Keating's theological writings are no exception and the influence of the sermon genre on his *Trí bior-ghaoithe* is such that we can be confident that he must have used this same material as the basis of many of the sermons he preached in the diocese of Lismore.

Keating's *Trí bior-ghaoithe* was directly influenced by contemporary French sermon literature.[65] The published sermon of Pierre de Besse for the fifteenth Sunday after Pentecost, in *Conceptions theologiques sur tous les dimanches de l'annee*, begins by identifying the three kinds of death: '*celle du corps qui est naturelle, celle de l'ame qui est spirituelle, et la troisieme celle de la damnation qui est eternelle*'.[66] While the core of the sermon concentrates on the first of the three kinds of death, there are close and significant parallels between the work of Besse and Keating on this theme.

Part of book two of *Trí bior-ghaoithe an bháis*, which treats of original sin, has strong parallels with another French sermon, published by Besse in a collection entitled *Conceptions theologiques sur les quatres fins de l'homme*.[67] Again, a significant number of the scriptural quotations cited by Besse were used in Keating's discussion on original sin, and the interpretation of Scripture is very similar in both works.[68] In addition to the scriptural quotations, Besse's vague reference to a philosophical proverb, '*actus et potentia eiusdem sunt ordinis*' was echoed by Keating '*is

---

64 Bayley, *French pulpit oratory*.   65 Ó Dúshlaine, *An Eoraip agus litríocht na Gaeilge*, pp. 50–60; Bernadette Cunningham, 'The sources of *Trí bior-ghaoithe an bháis*: another French sermon', *Éigse*, xxxi (1999), pp. 73–8.   66 Pierre de Besse, *Conceptions theologiques sur tous les dimanches de l'annee* (2 vols, Paris, 1624), i, pp. 617–18.   67 Originally published in 1606 and issued in a revised edition in Paris, 1622; Cunningham, 'Sources of *Trí bior-ghaoithe an bháis*', pp. 73–8.   68 I Kings 1 (Besse, *Quatre fins*, p. 71; *TBB*, line 2421); Genesis 2:17 (Besse, *Quatre fins*, p. 73, *TBB*, ll. 2437–8); Romans 5 (Besse, *Quatre fins*, p. 76; *TBB*, ll. 2538–9); Ecclesiastes 7:30 (Besse, *Quatre fins*, p. 79; *TBB*, ll. 2998–3000); Psalm 48 (Besse, *Quatre fins*, pp. 82–3, *TBB*, ll. 3435–40); Daniel 1–4 (Besse, *Quatre fins*, p. 83; *TBB*, ll. 3460–9).

ionann ord don ghníomh agus do chumus re déanamh an ghníomha', and he also repeated Besse's citations from Augustine and Gregory.[69]

These parallels do not necessarily imply that Keating consulted the published sermons of Pierre de Besse.[70] He may simply have heard and taken notes on occasional sermons, perhaps even in the cathedral at Bordeaux. Besse's theological writings, like Keating's, were intended as preachers' handbooks, and his material may well have been used as the basis of sermons by other French clergy in the years after first publication in 1606.

Even in the discussion on original sin, Keating's text also contained substantial sections not found in Besse's sermons, so that he was not dependent solely on Besse's work. Rather, *Trí bior-ghaoithe an bháis* was the work of a writer who adopted the style, and occasionally the detailed content, of contemporary sermons in a skillful and confident manner, moulding the material into a form appropriate for Irish readers.

V

As already seen in the case of *Eochair-sgiath an Aifrinn*, Keating's respect for the authority of scripture is apparent throughout his writings. *Trí bior-ghaoithe* contains approximately 750 scriptural references. The rhetorical style of the first book consists largely of sequences of scriptural quotations very briefly elucidated in an explanatory sentence. There is little in-depth biblical criticism. Instead, a variety of short passages of scripture are cited in quick succession with Keating relying for effect on their cumulative impact rather than any detailed interpretation. Such an approach was a standard preaching technique among Keating's contemporaries in western Europe.[71] Thus for example in chapter nine of the third book of *Trí bior-ghaoithe*, Keating introduced a discussion of lamenting the dead by distinguishing between moderate and immoderate lamentation. He began with a quotation from the Letter to Romans, *'flete cum flentibus'* (*'déanaidh caoi le lucht an chaointe'*). The message was then repeated in his own words: *'Dá chor i gcéill gurab somholta caoi mheasardha do dhéanamh i ndiaidh na marbh'* (indicating that moderate grieving for the dead is commendable). Keating then cited brief quotations from Ecclesiasticus 22, Jeremiah 9, Genesis 13, II Kings 13, John 11, an unreferenced mention of Mary Magdalen at Christ's sepulchre, and four general references to the lamentation of saints Ambrose, Bernard, Martin and Dominic, without any analytical comment. He allowed the sequence of biblical and hagiographical examples to speak for themselves. A discussion of the legitimate reasons for moderate lamentation when a righteous persons died then followed, with further supporting citations

---

69 Besse, *Quatre fins*, p. 73; *TBB*, ll. 2514-15; Besse, *Quatre fins*, p. 88; *TBB*, ll. 3400-7; Besse, *Quatre fins*, p. 86; *TBB*, ll. 3386-98.   70 For further discussion see Cunningham, 'Sources of *Trí bior-ghaoithe an bháis*'.   71 Bayley, *French pulpit oratory*, pp. 77-85.

from the Bible and church Fathers. A single sentence conclusion reiterated the inappropriateness for Christians of excessive pagan-style lamentation.[72]

While biblical quotations such as Leviticus 19:28 were presented as a literal instruction, others such as Luke 8:52 were subjected to a slightly more sophisticated treatment. This gospel passage was introduced as containing the words of Christ, and the original setting in which the words were spoken was explained. Keating advised his readers that the quotation was to be interpreted allegorically to mean that people are destined to awaken in the resurrection, just as the daughter was destined to awaken from her sleep.[73] In choosing between literal and allegorical interpretations, Keating was guided by the method of the authors from whom he derived his material. The writings of Suarez, Bellarmine, Durand, de Besse and other intermediary authors did not just supply Keating with source references, they also influenced his method of interpreting those sources.

                                          VI

In addition to scripture Keating relied on the authority of the early church Fathers. Their authority was enhanced in his eyes by their having been alive closer to the time of Christ. He cited almost fifty references to the writings of St Augustine. Next in importance in the hierarchy of Keating's citations came St Gregory, St Bernard and St Jerome. The witness of St Thomas Aquinas, St Ambrose, St Basil and St John Chrysostom was also called on, each of them being mentioned on at least four occasions.

The view of life and death constructed by St Augustine and his followers in particular had a formative influence on Keating's imaginative universe. Augustine focussed on people's personal relationship with God, and stressed inner truth, inner experience, and introspection.[74] His pessimistic perspective on original sin found strong echoes in the middle book of *Trí bior-ghaoithe an bháis*. His emphasis on Adam's personal responsibility for the divine punishment he suffered was noted.[75] Quotations from Augustine featured most prominently in the third book of *Trí bior-ghaoithe* where the individual's personal struggle to resist his own faults and to follow the path of Christ was highlighted.[76] Again, Augustine's image of God as physician, administering unpleasant medicine to the patient when necessary, was interpreted allegorically, Keating presenting Christ as the physician of the soul.[77] Keating advised that people should welcome adversity as a necessary antidote to an undisciplined life. Above all, Augustine insisted that the education of the laity in the doctrines of Christianity should be firmly linked to the interpretation of scripture. Both scripture and theology, he believed, would

---

72 *TBB*, ll. 5811-74. 73 *TBB*, ll. 5875-96. 74 Henry Phillips, *Church and culture in seventeenth-century France* (Cambridge, 1997), ch. 4. 75 *TBB*, ll. 3400-42. 76 *TBB*, ll. 8020-43. 77 *TBB*, ll. 8212-25.

4 'Heaven and hell' from Pierre de Besse,
Conceptions theologiques sur les quatres fin de l'homme. (Paris, 1622), p. 484

lead the person towards love of God and love of neighbour, and it was the
preacher's duty to convey this idea. The preacher's objective was a moral rather
than an intellectual one,[78] and this philosophy underlay all of Keating's theological writings.

Alongside Augustine, the teachings of St Thomas Aquinas (c.1225–74) had an
equally significant influence on Keating's view of man's place in the universe.
Although pithy Thomist quotations were curiously absent from Keating's writings,
elements of Thomist doctrine were nonetheless inherent in *Trí bior-ghaoithe an
bháis*. Thomas Aquinas' enunciation of Christian thought, building on Aristotelian
philosophy informed much of the teaching in Jesuit schools through the first half
of the seventeenth century, and it is not surprising that his influence can be dis-
cerned in Keating's thought.[79]

Keating's explanation of death as derived from original sin drew on Aquinas's
insight into the pre-existing state of original righteousness as described in the
Summa theologica.[80]

> ... *gurab subháilce í do bronnadh d'Adhamh, dá dtiocfadh an réasún do ghial-
> ladh do Dhia, an toil don réasún, mothughadh na gcéadfadh don toil, umhla na
> mbeathadhach mbrúideamhail don duine, agus snadhmadh na hanma ris an
> gcorp do bheith dosgaoilte*.[81] ([Before original sin], there existed a state of
> grace which was a gift from God to Adam, whereby if he would yield
> reason to God, and will to reason, and senses to will, obedience of brutish
> senses to the person, then the union of the soul with the body would be
> indissoluble.)

That Keating did not quote directly from Thomas Aquinas may mean that he was
not using a printed text. It is significant that in spite of this he gave six lengthy
expositions of ideas drawn from Aquinas. Each was a substantive point rather than
simply quotations selected at random. Their incorporation into Keating's analytical discussions indicates that he had absorbed and been influenced by some of the
central ideas of Thomism. It also indicated that he considered that Thomas
Aquinas would have been highly regarded by his readers. It is of interest to note
that Pierre de Besse used Aquinas in a similar way, referring to his ideas but not
quoting phrases directly.

References to Thomas Aquinas found in Keating's *Eochair-sgiath an Aifrinn*,
are given in a similarly vague manner, and are sometimes inaccurate.[82] Here too,

78 Bayley, *French pulpit oratory*, pp. 40–3.   79 See also Phillips, *Church and culture in seventeenth-century
France*, ch. 4.   80 Aquinas, *Summa theologica*, q. 94 art. 1.   81 *TBB*, ll. 2882–6.   82 Diarmuid Ó
Laoghaire has identified ten passages in *Eochair-sgiath* derived from the writings of Thomas Aquinas, some
attributed, others not. (Príomh-fhoinseacha, pp. 42–6.) In one instance, Keating's reference was incorrect.
In another instance, details given in *Eochair-sgiath* citing the authority of St Thomas Aquinas, on four ways
in which a substance can be changed, are not found in the writings of Aquinas in the manner presented
by Keating. Aquinas' work contains similar, but different, statements from those atttributed to him by

it seems likely that Keating did not consult a printed text. It is more likely that he was working from secondary accounts, perhaps encountered in sermons or lectures. It is clear, nonetheless, that Keating had absorbed an appreciation of Thomas Aquinas's teachings and wished to share that understanding with a wide audience.

Citations from other Fathers of the church in Keating's theological writings are relatively sparse. Diarmaid Ó Laoghaire concluded that Keating's references to authors such as Gregory the Great, Bede and Eusebius in *Eochair-sgiath an Aifrinn* were usually derived from secondary sources. They were little more than decorative trimmings designed to enhance the overall effect of his theological arguments. It is evidently unnecessary to assume that Keating, any more than any of his contemporaries, necessarily consulted complete texts of the writings of all the authors he cited. The majority of the references to the church Fathers in *Eochair-sgiath an Aifrinn* and *Trí bior-ghaoithe an bháis* indicate nothing more than that Keating recognised their reputation as authoritative authors on church doctrine and that he expected his readers and listeners to share his respect for those scholarly churchmen whose reputation was enhanced by their having lived and worked close to the time of Christ.

VII

Keating's scholarly apparatus was merely a means to an end. The biblical and patristic quotations, together with the miscellaneous moral tales, provided material for sermons on key issues of Catholic doctrine, in the vernacular. If we look beyond the technical characteristics of his text we find his prior belief that there was an important message to be conveyed about salvation and the cultivation of Christian moral and social values. The message at the core of *Trí bior-ghaoithe an bháis* was not that Augustine, Aquinas, or even the Bible were important, rather it was that people needed to come to terms with the reality of death and thereby understand the meaning of life. It taught that Christian life involved both social and moral obligations to live according to the word of God and the doctrines of the Church. Whether that understanding primarily came from the teaching of Augustine, from the Jesuit revival of the *ars morendi* tradition, or from the reality of life as a priest ministering to people who were ultimately facing death, would not have concerned the audience Keating was addressing. They were presented with articulate homiletic discussions in their own language by a preacher for whom heaven and hell were almost as tangible as earthly existence.

Readers, and listeners, were left in little doubt of the code of behaviour they had a duty to observe if they were to gain access to the means of salvation. Keating had not simply confined himself to basic Christian teachings. Rather, he

---

Keating. *ESA*, p. 63; Ó Laoghaire, Príomh-fhoinseacha, p. 46a (extra page inserted by author in revision of MA thesis).

had spelt out clearly, as a preacher would, the specific shortcomings, both personal and communal, he had observed among his own community. The Irish Catholic community addressed by Keating through *Trí bior-ghaoithe an bháis* was a people whose sufferings were God's punishment for their own and their ancestors' misdemeanours.[83] They had duties and responsibilites towards the community in which they lived. If they supported the right moral order, they would live in harmony with their creator and be worthy of a place in the Kingdom of God for all eternity.

83 See also Ó Buachalla, *Aisling ghéar*, p. 35.

4

Scholarly networks and approaches to the historical record

I

When Keating returned to the land of his youth, and took up his duties as a priest, his interest in Irish historical scholarship had not diminished. In the later years of his life he devoted much of his energy to compiling a history of Ireland drawn from Gaelic manuscript sources. His *Foras feasa ar Éirinn*, which told the story of Ireland and her people from Creation to the coming of the Normans in the twelfth century, proved to be by far the most influential of his works. It was in circulation in manuscript by 1635[1] and since the extant manuscripts all cite a page reference to a book first printed in 1633,[2] the year 1634 is usually given as the date when *Foras feasa* was completed. Some manuscripts specify 1629 as the date of completion of Keating's history, but even the earliest of these '1629' texts, Fairfax MS 29 in the Bodleian library, transcribed in 1643/4, contains the page reference to the 1633 publication. While it is clear from this that 1629 was not the date of completion of the versions now extant, it is certainly possible that earlier forms of the history, perhaps lacking the preface and some other passages, had gone into limited circulation in the late 1620s. However, no such preliminary draft is now known to survive.

It is difficult to judge whether there is any truth in the folklore which tells of Keating, following an outspoken sermon, having been forced to abandon his parochial duties and go into hiding in the glen of Aherlow where he wrote his history.[3] The story, like most of what passes for information about the life and person of Keating, seems to owe its origin to the sometimes mischevious comments of

---

1 RIA, MS 24 G 16 contains a translation of FFÉ by Michael Kearney commenced in 1635. See below, ch. 10. 2 *FFÉ*, i, 48. Although this page reference to Meredith Hanmer's *Chronicle of Ireland* (published in an edition by Sir James Ware in 1633) occurs in Keating's preface, Keating refers to Hanmer's work through his history, which indicates that 'Keating's work did not assume its final form earlier than 1633', see *FFÉ*, iv, 327. 3 Although the later folklore portrays the glen of Aherlow as a place of exile the valley is clearly visible from, and within a day's walking distance of, the Keating castle at Moorestown. One nineteenth-century tradition of a cave 'where Father Keating remained for three days without food, when Cromwell's soldiers were hunting him', must have originated late enough for the local community to have forgotten that Keating and Cromwell were not contemporaries (Mac Giolla Eáin (ed.), *Dánta*, p. 4).

Thomas O'Sullevane published anonymously in 1722.[4] He asserted that Keating spent two years travelling in disguise, spending much of his time in the company of poets and, 'meeting with good store of old books and manuscripts, to divert his thoughts he would now and then look over some and copy out what he took a fancy for'.[5] It is difficult to reconcile this story with Keating's considerable scholarly achievement. O'Sullevane, writing just prior to the publication of O'Connor's English translation of *Foras feasa*, had his own reasons for seeking to underestimate if not discredit Keating's work.[6]

Whatever about the truth, or otherwise, of the glen of Aherlow tradition, it seems likely that by the 1620s Keating had resumed contact with people active in the sphere of Irish historical scholarship whom he had known in his youth. Through such contacts, a range of valuable Irish historical manuscript sources could have become accessible to him. Some valuable texts like the copy of the Psalter of Cashel that had been in local ownership in south Tipperary in the 1590s may have gone to new owners, but even it was not yet beyond reach.[7] The Butlers of Cahir were still in a position to offer patronage, and members of the Mac Craith family were still actively pursuing their scholarly craft as keepers of the *seanchas*. Keating's poems on members of the Butler family compiled in the late 1620s are evidence of his association with a likely source of scholarly patronage.[8]

It seems likely that Keating was also in a position to benefit from links with learned families slightly further afield. The interest shown by the Ó Maolchonaire family of scribes in Clare in his history, after its completion, could be explained by its favourable depiction of the O'Briens, but may well have been a continuation of a scholarly link between Keating and the Ó Maolchonaire family that predated the completion of his history.[9] A case can also be made for a probably collaboration between Keating and Conall Mac Eochagáin. As will be seen, historians like Conall Mac Eochagáin may have been Keating's source for some of the manuscript material consulted. It is also true that both Dubhaltach Mac Fhirbhisigh, best known as a compiler of genealogies, and Micheál Ó Cléirigh, chief of the Four Masters, were part of the same cultural circle as Keating at this time, using some of the same manuscripts in their researches. There is no evidence, however, that they ever met in person.

While detailed evidence concerning Keating's scholarly contacts is unavailable, and none of his contemporaries mention having actually met him, it is nonetheless clear that his researches necessitated extensive access to manuscripts in the hands of learned families. *Foras feasa* could not have been undertaken without the active support and encouragement of the scholarly families who were still the custodians of many Gaelic manuscripts.

The best guides we now have to the network of scholarly contacts on which Keating relied when compiling his history are the extant manuscripts that contain

4 *Clanricarde*, pp. cxxviii–cxxix.   5 Ibid., p. cxxix.   6 Ibid., pp. cxxiv–cxxv.   7 Anne and William O'Sullivan, 'Three notes on Laud Misc. 610 (or the Book of Pottlerath)', *Celtica*, ix (1971), pp. 135-51. 8 Mac Giolla Eáin (ed.), *Dánta*, poems 6, 14 and 18.   9 For discussion of Keating's links with specific manuscripts associated with the Ó Maolchonaire family (BL, Egerton MS 1782, BL, Add. MS 30,512, and Bodl., Laud Misc. 610) see below, ch. 10.

the materials he cited. Though some of the materials on whose authority Keating relied cannot now be traced, others can still be identified. One of the manuscripts Keating valued most highly was a composite work known as the Psalter of Cashel (*Saltair Chaisil*) a Munster manuscript. It was among the first great Irish manuscript miscellanies and is usually dated to *c.*AD 1000. This early text can no longer be traced but the compilers of the fifteenth-century manuscript now known as Laud Misc. 610 in the Bodleian library had access to the Psalter of Cashel.[10]

Laud Misc. 610 was begun for James Butler, fourth earl of Ormond, 'the White Earl', sometime after 1411, but was written mostly in the mid-1450s for Edmund Mac Richard Butler. The manuscript was in the house of Cosnamhach Mac Flannchadha at Lios in Mhetha in 1591. This location is probably to be identified as Lissava near Cahir, and the four sons of Cosnamhach were among the followers of James Butler, brother of Lord Cahir, in 1600. Others of his followers included two Mac Craith poets and several Keatings from near Cahir.[11] Geoffrey Keating's awareness of the manuscript's special reputation, owing to the extreme antiquity of the original Psalter of Cashel, is probably best explained by his links with the Meic Craith and the Butlers. Another possible link also existed. In 1619 David Rothe, Catholic bishop of Ossory, described for James Ussher, Church of Ireland archbishop of Armagh, an abstract of the Psalter of Cashel which he had seen. He was writing from memory, stating that he did not currently have the book to hand, but also stating that he expected again to be at the location where the manuscript was kept.[12] On the back of the letter Ussher named the owners of some manuscripts including '(Edmund's brother) for Psalter Cassell (which his friende hath)'. If this Edmund was related to the Butlers of Cahir, it is possible that the 'friend' who had the text containing the Psalter of Cashel would have been known to Keating also. Later, Ussher referred to the Psalter of Cashel as 'your book' when addressing Rothe, indicating that David Rothe had more ready access to this manuscript.[13] Keating might have had access to any such manuscript that was available to Rothe, though no direct evidence of contact between the two men survives.[14]

---

10 In an early sixteenth-century library list of the earl of Kildare, the '*Saltir Casshill*' is the first item listed among his Irish books. It is not certain whether this is now Laud Misc. 610. See Pádraig Ó Riain, 'The Psalter of Cashel: a preliminary list of contents', *Éigse*, xxiii (1989), pp. 107-31. 11 O'Sullivan, 'Three notes on Laud Misc. 610', pp. 135-6, 146; *Fiants Ire.*, Eliz, 6495. 12 Rothe to Ussher, 5 June 1619, TCD, MS 568, p. 165, printed in William O'Sullivan, 'Correspondence of David Rothe and James Ussher, 1619-23', *Collectanea Hibernica*, nos. 36-7 (1994/5), pp. 19-20. 13 O'Sullivan, 'Correspondence of Rothe and Ussher', p. 34. 14 Ussher, Rothe, and Keating were all part of the one scholarly movement of Christian humanism, interested in the past as the foundation of the Christian present. Keating occasionally referred directly to Ussher's work. *FFÉ*, iii, 4-6, 300. It appears that the version of the *Psalter of Cashel* seen by Ussher, through Sir George Carew (before 1617), differed in detail from the copy subsequently used by Ussher. This means that more than one copy was in circulation among Keating's contemporaries. It also seems very probable that Micheál Ó Cléirigh made another copy, later used by John Colgan, though the copy used by Colgan is not now known to survive. O'Sullivan, 'Three notes on Laud Misc. 610', pp. 146-7. O'Sullivan, 'Correspondence of Rothe and Ussher', p. 11. Ó Riain, 'Psalter of Cashel: a preliminary list of contents'.

The evidence of Laud Misc. 610 indicates that the Psalter of Cashel contained the corpus of secular genealogies, saints' pedigrees, the *Leabhar Breatnach*, a version of the *Dinnsheanchas*, *Félire Oengusso*, 'divers ancient rhymes of Colum-Cille, Cormack O'Cullenan and others', and *Acallam na Senórach*.[15] According to Pádraig Ó Riain, Keating probably used the Psalter of Cashel for four texts, the secular genealogies, the *Leabhar Breatnach*, a poem on the kings of Scotland and possibly for a Munster recension of the *Leabhar gabhála*.[16]

The Psalter of Cashel was apparently regarded with particular respect by the literati down to the seventeenth century. Conall Mac Eochagáin, writing in 1627, described its special features. Unlike Keating and others who attributed it to Cormac mac Cuileannáin, Mac Eochagáin attributed its compilation to Brian Bóroimhc, who

> assembled together all the nobility of the kingdom as well spiritual as temporal to Cashel in Munster and caused them to compose a book containing all the inhabitants, events and septs that lived in this land from the first peopling, inhabitation and discovery thereof after the creation of the world until that present, which book they caused to be called by the name of the psalter of Cashel, signed it with his own hands together with the hands of all the bishops and prelates of the kingdom, caused several copies thereof to be given to the kings of the provinces, with straight charge, that there should be no credit given to any other chronicles thenceforth, but should be held as false, disannulled and quite forbidden for ever. Since which time there were many septs in the kingdom that lived by it, and whose profession was to chronicle and keep in memory the state of the kingdom as well for the past present and to come.[17]

Evidently, Mac Eochagáin shared Keating's particularly high regard for the Psalter of Cashel as a record of the ancient history of the kingdom of Ireland. In addition to the major sources drawn from a version of the Psalter of Cashel itself, Keating also frequently cited a poem entitled '*Fuaras i Saltair Chaisil*'. This historical poem, common in the later manuscript tradition and apparently popularised by Keating's use of it, purported to tell the story of the first peoples to take possession of Ireland. It apparently dated from the fifteenth century, but used the reference to the supposedly tenth-century Psalter to bolster its claims to be authoritative history. This suggests that the Psalter of Cashel had a place of special importance among the historical records of Munster. However, the historical material in the poem

---

15 O'Sullivan, 'Three notes on Laud Misc. 610', p. 137. Myles Dillon, 'Laud Misc. 610', *Celtica*, v (1960), pp. 64-76. 16 Ó Riain, 'The Psalter of Cashel: a provisional list of contents' p. 124. It is probable that Keating was using a fuller text of the Psalter than what is now extant. 17 *Annals of Clonmacnoise from the earliest period to A.D. 1408, translated into English by Conell Mageoghegan, A.D. 1627*, ed. Denis Murphy (Dublin, 1896), pp. 7-8. The Psalter of Cashel was also used by the Connacht genealogist Dubhaltach Mac Fhirbhisigh in the late 1640s. Ó Muraíle, *Celebrated antiquary*, p. 174.

cannot all have been drawn from the tenth-century version of the Psalter, since the poem refers to the coming of the Normans in the twelfth century.[18]

'Fuaras i Saltair Chaisil' is evidence that the authority of the ancient written record was greatly valued by the fifteenth century, and there is a sense in which Keating's own history was the prose successor of such poems.[19] The approach to the historical record revealed in the attitude of both Keating and Conall Mac Eochagáin to the Psalter of Cashel, permeates the poetic writings of their contemporaries also. The antagonists in the poetic dispute of the 1620s usually known as *Iomarbhágh na bhfileadh* (Contention of the bards) were clear in their attitude to what constituted the historical record. Tadhg mac Dáire Meic Bhruaideadha defended his case by asserting 'I accept nothing – I must not – except according to clear books',[20] and insisted that every claim he made was 'in some song or book'.[21] When defending a specific point, he noted 'let him who would challenge me rub it out from the books'.[22] Although they were on opposite sides in the *Iomarbhágh*, Aodh Ó Domhnaill essentially agreed with Tadhg mac Dáire's attitude to the historical record. 'Not all Banba's poets nor all the dead and all the living however great their lore could refute the books of Éire.'[23] Ó Domhnaill then offered an extensive list of those books that could be consulted.[24] The list is quite similar to the list of the 'chief books' which Keating itemised as containing authoritative records of the history of Ireland still to be seen. Neither the poet nor the historian, however, actually claimed to have personally consulted these texts, which in Keating's case were itemised as *Leabhar Arda Macha, Saltair Chaisil, Leabhar na hUachongmhála, Leabhar Chluana hEidhneach Fionntain, Saltair na rann, Leabhar Ghlinne-dá-loch, Leabhar na gceart, Uidhir Chiaráin, Leabhar Buidhe Moling* and *Leabhar Dubh Molaga.*[25]

---

18 Ó Riain, 'The Psalter of Cashel, a provisional list of contents'; the poem is found in RIA, MS D iv 2, f. 1v, a fifteenth-century manuscript, which may be the only extant copy early enough to have been seen by Keating.   19 Keating used material from this poem in sections 4-5 of *FFÉ*, i, to supplement the narrative outline he derived from *LG*. For example, in his description of the invasions of Ireland before the flood he included the coming of the Daughters of Cain from *'Fuaras i Saltair Chaisil'* (Anne Cronin, 'Sources of Keating's *Foras feasa ar Éirinn*, 2: manuscript sources', *Éigse*, v (1945-7), p. 125). Keating likewise included invasions after the flood that are not now found in any extant recension of *LG*, e.g. the coming of Adhna son of Bioth. Where Keating deviates in this way from his principal source in *LG* it was usually in deference to a verse source (Cronin, 'Manuscript sources' p. 129). Thus, for instance, in describing the lakes that burst forth in Ireland, Keating's account differed from all the versions of *LG* in saying that Loch mBreunainn was the name of the lake that covered Magh nAsail in the territory of Uí Nialláin in Ulster. In this instance he selected information from the poem *'Adhamh athair, surith ar slógh'* in preference to the *LG* account (*FFÉ*, i, 176; Cronin, 'Manuscript sources', p. 129).   20 Lambert McKenna (ed.), *Iomarbhágh na bhfileadh: the contention of the bards* (2 vols, London, ITS, 1918), poem 18, verse 86.   21 McKenna (ed.), *Iomarbhágh*, poem 21, verse 7.   22 Ibid., poem 21, verse 9.   23 Ibid., poem 15, verse 8.   24 Ibid., poem 15, verses 9-13.   25 *FFÉ*, i, 78-80. Keating gave a slightly different list of such materials near the beginning of the second book of his history, *FFÉ*, iii, 32.*'Leabhar Ard Macha, Psaltair Chaisil, Leabhar Glinne dá Loch, Leabhar na hUa Chongmhála, Leabhar Chluana Mic Nóis, Leabhar Fionntain Chluana hEidhneach, Leabhar Buidhe Moling, is Leabhar Dubh Molaga'.* The *Book of Clonmacnoise* on this list corresponds to *Uidhir Chiaráin* in the earlier list, while the two items omitted in this instance are *Saltair na Rann* and *Leabhar na gCeart*.

Keating went on to assert 'there was a summary of the records in all these books in the Psalter of Tara', but he did not claim that the Psalter of Tara was extant in his own day.[26] Keating's understanding of the Psalter of Tara differed from the other manuscripts he listed in that he believed it to be a text revised every three years and containing the decisions of kings and their advisers assembled at Tara for the purpose of governing the country. This was an understanding of the historical record that placed a premium on the written word and perceived laws as written documents, subject to revision. Though probably in fact non-existent, the idea of the text of a 'Psalter of Tara' was reconstructed by Keating in accordance with the standards and perspective of a literate community. This conscious valuing of the written word was a manifestation of the need that existed for a written history of Ireland based on a wide range of the manuscript sources known to be available.

The very act of naming these ancient manuscripts was intended by Keating as a substantiation of the truth of his history. Historical claims commanded greater respect when the authority of such venerable sources could be invoked.[27] The poets in contention over the relative merits of the descendants of Éibhear and Éireamhón in *Iomarbhágh na bhfileadh* shared Keating's interest in the books containing the historical record. They happily invoked the Book of the Dun Cow (*Leabhar ha hUidhre*)[28] 'the ancient books of annals' [29] and even the apparently fictitious 'Psalter of Tara' itself.[30] In frustration at the claims of his opponent, Lughaidh Ó Cléirigh asserted 'I thought that at least the Book of Invasion was truthful when saying those words'.[31]

Keating was merely summarising common knowledge when he itemised some of the more important of the contents of those books of *seanchas* as *Leabhar gabhála, Leabhar na gcúigeadh, Réim ríoghraidhe, Leabhar na nAos, Leabhar comhaimseardhachta, Leabhar dinnsheanchuis, Leabhar bainseanchuis, Cóir anmann, Uraicheapt, Amhra Choluimcille.*[32] He also drew the attention of readers of history to other available histories that were not in those principal books, but which could also be consulted. He named some examples, *Cath Mhuighe Muccraimhe, Forbhais Droma Dámhghaire, Oidhidh na gCuradh, Cath Chrionna, Cath Fionnchoradh, Cath Ruis na Riogh, Cath Mhuighe Léana, Cath Mhuighe Rath, Cath Mhuighe Tualaing.*[33] The picture he portrayed therefore was of a wealth of manuscript materials on which the historian of Ireland, or the interested general reader, could draw. These were no idle claims. There were far more stories available to him than he could incorporate in his summary of the history of Ireland from earliest times to the late

---

26 *FFÉ*, iii, 32. For similar approach by John Lynch, in his *Cambrensis eversus* (1662), see Ó Muraíle, *Celebrated antiquary*, p. 230.   27 Ó Riain, 'The Psalter of Cashel, a preliminary list of contents', p. 108. 28 i.e. *Lebor na hUidre: book of the Dun cow*, ed. R.I. Best and O.J. Bergin (Dublin, 1929). McKenna (ed.), *Iomarbhágh*, poem 6, verse 8.   29 McKenna (ed.), *Iomarbhágh*, poem 6, verse 185.   30 Ibid., poem 15, verse 54.   31 Ibid., poem 6, verse 14.   32 *FFÉ*, i, 80.   33 Ibid.; Some of these same materials were alluded to by Lughaidh Ó Cléirigh who advised his opponent, for instance, to consult his *Battle of Muccroimhe* if in doubt about a point at issue, McKenna (ed.), *Iomarbhágh*, poem 6, verse 41.

twelfth century.[34] There was, however, a need for a text such as *Foras feasa* to make such material more accessible to the general reader. Robert Mac Arthur, in a poem which discusses the nature and authenticity of the historical record, made specific mention of the fact that even specialists had difficulties in reading (and thus interpreting) the 'ancient books'.[35]

II

The two major Irish language sources used in *Foras feasa ar Éireann* were *Leabhar gabhála Éireann* (Book of the taking of Ireland), and *Flaithusa Éireann* or *Réim ríoghraidhe Éireann* (Succession of kings of Ireland). They provided not just a wide range of source information but also the framework for his historical narrative. He expanded the material from these sources by reference to various poems and tales from among those manuscript authorities he listed as being available. The framework of the pre-Christian story of Ireland contained in Book one of *Foras feasa* is drawn primarily from *Leabhar gabhála*. This medieval text, of which the earliest extant rescensions are dated to the late eleventh or early twelfth century, probably first took shape about AD 800. It traced the history of the peopling of Ireland from creation down to the coming of the Clann Mhíleadh to Ireland. It told the story of a series of invasions, or waves of settlement of Ireland, by Ceasair, Parthalón, Neimheadh, the Fir bolg, Tuatha Dé Danann, and ultimately by the Sons of Míl, whose origins are traced back through Spain to Egypt, and ultimately Scythia.

The sequence of invasions and most of the illustrative poems in *Foras feasa* were derived from this source, although Keating used supplementary material not found in *Leabhar gabhála*.[36] It appears that Keating was drawing on at least two separate versions of *Leabhar gabhála*. These have been classified by Van Hamel as Recensions B and C, with Keating giving priority to C.[37] Anne Cronin demonstrated that a combination of the versions of *Leabhar gabhála* found in the Book of Lecan contained all the material used by Keating.[38] However, the exact manuscript

---

34 *FFÉ*, ii, 220. **35** McKenna (ed.), *Iomarbhágh*, poem 16, verse 76. **36** Anne Cronin examined the extant recensions in search of the manuscript Keating might have used, focussing particularly on the composite manuscripts now known as the Book of Leinster, the Book of Ballymote, and the Book of Lecan. No one of these manuscripts, in the form they survive today, corresponds precisely to Keating's source, and it appears that no version of *Leabhar gabhála* now extant seems to contain all the material Keating used. It also seems likely that he used more than one text of this work (Cronin, 'Manuscript sources', pp. 122-23). Keating's contemporary, Micheál Ó Cléirigh likewise used an exemplar for his version of *LG* that cannot now be positively identified, a version that was very similar, but apparently not identitical, to that used by Keating (Cronin, 'Manuscript sources'). For discussion of the copy of *LG* used by Dubhaltach Mac Fhirbhisigh see Ó Muráile, *Celebrated antiquary*, pp. 45, 58 (n.50). **37** A.G. Van Hamel, 'On Lebor Gabála' *Zeitschrift für Celtische Philologie*, i (1914), pp. 97-197. Anne Cronin, Sources of Keating's *Foras feasa ar Éirinn*, M.A. thesis, UCD, 1933 (RIA, MS 23 P 2: = Book of Lecan, 'Lec 2', ff. 264r-304r); also similar to that in the Book of Ballymote and the Book of Fermoy; Ó Riain, 'The Psalter of Cashel, a preliminary list of contents'. **38** RIA, MS 23 P 2. *The Book of Lecan (Leabhar Mór Mhic FhirBhisigh*

of *Leabhar gabhála* used by Keating as a source cannot be positively identified with any one text of *Leabhar gabhála* now extant.[39]

Keating was not simply turning *Leabhar gabhála* into a straightforward prose narrative. He was creating a new synthesis of that account and adding material from external poetic sources. Where inconsistencies emerged, he gave priority to the verse.[40] This appears to contrast with the attitude to the sources expressed by contributors to the 'Contention of the bards'. In one of the poems composed as part of the Contention, Lughaidh Ó Cléirigh asserted the value of the manuscript sources of early Irish history.

> *Mór dár seanchas ar gach taoibh,*
> *nach faghthar i rosg ná i laoidh,*
> *ar laoidh féin ní faghthar dath*
> *gan leabhar glan dá chumhdach.*

> (Much of our ancient history everywhere
> is not contained in Rosg or poem,
> and even a poem is not convincing
> unless it has an exact book to support it.)[41]

Similarly, he argued that

> *Dán órdha ní hé do ní,*
> *cosnamh gach cúise a-deirthí,*
> *as taosga i dtealaigh na bhFionn,*
> *acht leabhair aosda Éirionn.*

> (It is not a gilded poem
> which best defends the cause you plead
> in the land of the fair ones,
> but rather the ancient books of Eire.)[42]

The poets in the contention also made regular reference to the *Réim ríoghraidhe*, or *Flaithiusa Éireann*, which recorded the names of kings of Ireland from the set-

---

Lecáin), facsimile edition with introduction by Kathleen Mulchrone (Dublin, 1937). Not all of the analysis has been published, but is to be found in Cronin, Sources of Keating's *Foras feasa ar Éirinn*. I am very grateful to William O'Sullivan for generously facilitating my consultation of his late wife's (Anne O'Sulllivan, neé Cronin) unpublished research. **39** Copies of the Book of Lecan, then owned by James Ussher, were still being made in the 1630s, and it is possible that Keating may have had access to a modern manuscript derived from it. If this was the case, his most likely source was Conall Mac Eochagáin who had the manuscript on loan from James Ussher in 1634 and perhaps earlier (King's Inns, Gaelic MS 4, p. 54). An eighteenth-century copy of *FFÉ* (King's Inns, Gaelic MS 4, continued from NLI, MS G 994) notes that the poem '*Dá mhac déag do chídh ó Chas*' was taken from the copy of the *Book of Lecan* written by Conall Mac Eochagáin in 1634, having been originally written for Giolla Iosa Mac Fhirbisigh in 1418 (King's Inns, Gaelic MS 4, p. 54). **40** Cronin, 'Manuscript sources', p. 129, lines 5-10. **41** McKenna (ed.), *Iomarbhágh*, poem 6, verse 13. **42** Ibid., poem 7, verse 12.

tling of the sons of Míl in Ireland, with a further continuation detailing the kings of Ireland after the coming of Patrick down to the twelfth century.[43] While the poets argued about the detail, Keating simply used the framework of the *Réim ríoghraidhe* as the outline for the narrative history of the kings of Ireland found in the latter part of *Foras feasa* book one and most of book two.[44] In addition to the name of the king, the *Réim ríoghraidhe* gave some genealogical details, but little other information apart from the length of the reign and the manner of each king's death.[45] Thus *Réim ríoghraidhe* was a much sparcer source than *Leabhar gabhála* had been for the earlier period, and wherever possible Keating augmented his narrative of the kings of Ireland from other available sources.

Keating cited the *Réim ríoghraidhe* by name on five occasions, once to make amendments to the length of the reign of some of the pagan kings noted therein.[46] The synchronisms which were compiled as an appendix to *Foras feasa* incorporated Keating's own version of the *Réim ríoghraidhe* – which he described as such in the text of his history.[47] But his debt to this source was more fundamental. Its outline history of the kingdom of Ireland formed the basis of the Ireland of his historical imagination.[48] That the *Réim ríoghraidhe* was still cited by the poets and was reworked by other seventeenth-century scholars including Micheál Ó Cléirigh and Dubhaltach Mac Fhirbhisigh,[49] as well as by Keating, confirms the centrality of kingship to mid-seventeenth-century perceptions of the Irish historical past.

Keating supplemented his information on the kings of Ireland derived from *Réim ríoghraidhe* by using a genealogical collection, earlier versions of which existed in a variety of early composite manuscripts.[50] Two versions of this text have been edited by M.A. O'Brien, in *Corpus genealogiarum Hiberniae*,[51] but Keating's source appears to have been more detailed. As in the case of the other materials in the first book of *Foras feasa*, Keating's genealogical information follows the versions found in the Book of Lecan and the Book of Ballymote more closely than other early manuscripts.[52]

---

43 Book of Leinster 14b-26b; also Book of Ballymote. 44 From *FFÉ*, ii, 106, to *FFÉ*, iii, end. 45 Versions of Réim ríoghraidhe were extant in a range of early composite manuscripts including Book of Leinster, Laud Misc. 610, Rawl. B 502, Book of Lecan and Book of Ballymote, the version used by Keating being closest to that in the Book of Lecan (Cronin, Sources of Keating's *Foras feasa ar Éirinn*). 46 *FFÉ*, i, 82. 47 *FFÉ*, i, 111. 48 Anne Cronin's unpublished study of Keating's use of Réim ríoghraidhe shows that as was the case with *LG* Keating evidently used two recensions such as those found in Book of Lecan, ff. 10-22 (Lec I) and Book of Lecan, ff. 264-302 (Lec II). She again makes the suggestion that Keating was working from a text that had already combined these two sources (Cronin, Sources of Keating's *Foras Feasa ar Éirinn*, p. 41). In contrast with *LG*, where Ó Cléirigh and Keating used a similar source, this is not so in the case of Réim ríoghraidhe, and Cronin suggests that Ó Cléirigh's source for Réim ríoghraidhe was close to that found in the Book of Leinster (Cronin, Sources of Keating's *Foras Feasa ar Éirinn*, pp. 44-45). 49 Ó Muraíle, *Celebrated antiquary*, p. 166. 50 Early texts include those in the Book of Leinster, Bodl., Rawl B 502, the Book of Ballymote and the Book of Lecan. 51 M.A. O'Brien (ed.), *Corpus Genealogiarum Hiberniae*, i (Dublin, 1962); the texts used in this edition are Bodl., Rawl. B 502 and the Book of Leinster. 52 Cronin, Sources of Keating's *Foras feasa ar Éirinn*, pp. 47-8. Cronin suggested that the sources named by Keating as the *Leabhar na gCuigeadh* (Book of the provinces) and *Leabhar na nAos* (Book of tribes; *FFÉ*, i, 80), probably covered all the material in the genealogical tract used to supplement the outline found in Réim ríoghraidhe.

The lengthy account of Gaelic opposition to the Vikings, more precisely described here as Lochlannaigh, in the second book of *Foras feasa* was derived largely from *Cogadh Gael re Gallaibh*, an early twelfth-century tract. It had been written in the reign of Muirchertach Ó Briain (d.1119), great-grandson of Brian Bóroimhe (d.1014),[53] and told the story of Viking raids on Ireland. It described the oppression of Ireland by foreigners and then recounted the heroic exploits of Dál Cais heroes, Mathgamhain, his brother, Brian Bóroimhe, and their supporters, culminating in the Gaelic triumph at the battle of Clontarf. As an historical saga it was much prone to exaggeration. Its depiction of opposition to the Vikings as a national war was misleading, having been designed as a propagandist version of O'Brien exploits.[54] However, the text was very influential, becoming an accepted version of the story of the Lochlannaigh from a Gaelic, specifically O'Brien, perspective, and was still popular in the seventeenth century. Keating's summary of the text made the story even more widely available than before. It gave, moreover, a distinct Munster bias to his history which may explain later folklore tradition of Keating's bias against Ulster.[55] Keating supplemented the narrative with episodes from the *Caithréim Ceallacháin Caisil*, a Gaelic narrative on the Viking era which displayed a Mac Carthy rather than an O'Brien bias.[56] Slightly later in date than *Cogadh Gaedheal re Gallaibh*, being composed when Cormac Mac Carthaigh (d.1138) was king of Munster,[57] the *Caithréim Ceallacháin Caisil* described foreign oppression in Munster. Its focus was on the emergence of the heroic saviour in the person of Ceallachán.[58]

Foras feasa concluded with an account of the Normans that owed much to the *Expugnatio Hiberniae* of Giraldus Cambrensis. This twelfth-century source was then available in print in Latin and English,[59] but was also a familiar text in Irish translation and was in circulation in manuscript.[60] This account was supplemented

53 *Cogadh Gaedhel re Gallaibh: the war of the Gaedhil with the Gaill*, ed. J.H. Todd (London, 1867). **54** See Kathleen Hughes, *Early Christian Ireland: introduction to the sources* (London, 1972), pp. 288-300.   **55** Writing in the 1830s John O'Donovan recorded the tradition of the view of the O'Kelly's of Glenn Con Cadhain, County Tyrone, that Keating was biassed in favour of Munster and should therefore be denied access to historical records from northern parts of Ireland. Royal Irish Academy, Ordnance survey letters, Londonderry, pp. 180-1.   **56** Alexander Bugge, *Caithréim Cellacháin Caisil: the victorious career of Cellachán of Cashel* (Oslo, 1905). See *FFÉ*, iii, 224 for a story from *Caithréim Chellacháin Chaisil* not found in *Cogadh Gaedheal re Gallaibh* (Hughes, *Early Christian Ireland*, p. 299).   **57** AD 1127-1134, Donnchadh Ó Corráin, '*Caithréim Chellacháin Chaisil*: history or propaganda', *Ériu*, xxv (1974), p. 57.   **58** Hughes, *Early Christian Ireland*, pp. 299-300. *Caithréim Chellacháin Chaisil* appears alongside other Munster tales and annals, noteably *Cath Cnucha*, *Cath Maighe Léana*, *Cath Maighe Muccroimhe*, *Cath Crinna* and *Cath Cluana Tairbh*, in a melange of tales usually ending with the death of Cormac Mac Carthaigh as king of Munster [c.1134] in what Robin Flower described as 'a kind of Romantic history of Munster, AD 174-1138' (*BL Cat. Ir. MSS*, ii, 395-7, BL, Egerton MS 150). Flower suggests Eoghan Mac Carthaigh (1684) as originator of the collection in its modern form, but Ó Corráin suggests it may be earlier (Ó Corráin, '*Caithréim Chellacháin Chaisil*: history or propaganda', p. 3).   **59** The *Expugnatio*, in Latin was included in William Camden, *Anglia, Hibernica, Normannica, Cambrica a veteribus scripta ... ex bibliotheca Guillelmi Camden* (Frankfurt, 1602). An English translation by John Hooker was published in Raphael Holinshed, *The first and second volumes of chronicles ... now newly augmented and continued* (3 vols, London, 1587), ii.   **60** Whitley Stokes, 'The Irish abridgment of

by the narrative in Stanihurst's *De rebus in Hibernia gestis*, and by Stanihurst's contribution to Holinshed's chronicle.[61] It is clear therefore that the full framework of
Keating's narrative history was already available to his contemporaries in a range
of standard sources. His achievement lay in constructing an elegant prose narrative
that drew together the various strands of the historical record, both prose and
verse, into one accessible text. His reliance on established sources, a feature he
himself emphasised, enhanced the appeal of his history, and supported its claim to
be a true account of the past.

III

In addition to the major historical compilations which informed his narrative
framework, Keating also incorporated material from other standard sources of historical information. These included *Leabhar na gceart*, *Leabhar dinnsheanchuis*,
Leabhar bainseanchuis, *Cóir anmann*, *Amhra Choluimcille*, *Saltair na rann* and the
poem '*Fuaras i Saltair Chaisil*'.

In the form in which it is now extant, *Leabhar na gceart* (Book of rights) is a
compilation by a Munster poet, perhaps based at Cashel, and dates from a time
subsequent to Brian Bóroimhe becoming king of Ireland.[62] The text was regarded
as a record of the rights of the king of Ireland, the provincial kings and the tribal
kings within each province, itemising tributes and stipends due. The authorship of
the Book of Rights was attributed by Keating to a saint associated with Cashel,
'Beinén naomhtha mac Seisgnéin', an attribution supported by the text itself.[63] The
text as it now survives is in verse form, each passage of verse usually preceded by
a prose summary.[64]

An indication of Keating's working method in constructing his prose narrative
from earlier sources can be found in his use of materials from *Leabhar na gceart*.
One of the poems it preserved, '*Dligheadh gach rí ó rígh Caisil*' described the rights
and payments due from the kings of Cashel.[65] Keating presented this material as

the 'Expugnatio Hibernica', *English Historical Review*, xx (1905), pp. 77-115; Bodl., Rawl. MS B 475;
also some fragments in TCD, MS 1298.   **61** Raphael Holinshed, *The firste volume of the chronicles of
England, Scotlande, and Ireland* (London, 1577).   **62** *Lebor na Cert*, ed. Myles Dillon (Dublin, ITS,
1962). The text is now preserved in its most complete form in such manuscripts as the Book of Lecan,
the Book of Ballymote, The Book of Uí Maine, and also in the late fifteenth-century Book of Lismore
(*Lebor na Cert*, ed. Dillon, p. xii). The opening section of the text itself states that it is derived from
the Book of Glendalough. The present identity of the Book of Glendalough is a matter of ongoing
debate; see Pádraig Ó Riain, 'The book of Glendalough or Rawlinson B 502' *Éigse*, xviii (1981), pp. 161-
76; Caoimhín Breatnach, 'Rawlinson B 502, Lebar Glinne Dá Locha agus Saltair na Rann', *Éigse*, xxx
(1997), pp. 109-32; P.A. Breatnach, 'More on Ware's Psalter Narran', *Éigse*, xxxi (1999), pp. 133-4;
Pádraig Ó Riain, 'Rawlinson B 502 alias Lebar Glinne Dá Locha: a restatement of the case', *Zeitschrift
für Celtische Philologie*, li (1999), pp 130-47.   **63** *FFÉ*, i, 78; See *Lebor na Cert*, ed. Dillon, p. 18. The
other contender for authorship was Cormac mac Cuileannáin (Kenney, *Sources*, pp. 11-12), Either
author would have commended the text to Keating as a valuable source.   **64** *Lebor na Cert*, ed. Dillon,
p. ix.   **65** Ibid., ed. Dillon, pp. 6-12.

relating specifically to the reign of Feidhlimidh son of Criomhthann as king of Munster. Feidhlimidh was characterised as 'a wise and pious man' and Keating cited an extract in Latin from a set of annals he described as *Leabhar Irsi* that described the same king as *'optimus sapiens'*, an 'excellent wise man'.[66]

The various payments due – steeds, ships, slaves, goblets, rings, chess boards, swords, horses, coats of mail – were reasonably faithfully detailed in Keating's narrative. The poem ended the list of duties by asserting 'those are the stipends of the kings of Ireland from the king of Munster whom men praise; and it is certain to every one that he is entitled to his refection from all of them'.[67] Keating closed his list with the disclaimer 'Understand, O Reader, that I am not the author of these things, but St Beinén, as is plain from the Book of Rights'.[68] This suggests that Keating was aware of the implausible nature of some of the claims that the text contained, and of the fact that they did not remotely reflect contemporary realities. His presentation of this material as a description of an actual circuit of Leath Cuinn made by Feidhlimidh turned a technical record of indefinite date into a narrative exploit which the reader could associate with a particular king presented as a contemporary of the Lochlannaigh.[69]

Despite listing it among his authorities, and using it on a variety of occasions, Keating rarely cited the *Dinnsheanchas* directly.[70] However, he did cite this compilation of placelore in connection with the banqueting hall at Tara.[71] His description of the *teach miodhchuarta* at Tara was attributed to the *Dinnsheanchas* written by Aimhirgin son of Amhalghaidh. The poem *'Domun duthain a lainde'* appears to have been his source.[72] Keating's invocation of the *Dinnsheanchas* as an authoritative source was done to assert the authenticity of the record of the Irish past, but did not imply a total reliance on that source of information for his own discussion of places. *Foras feasa* included a great deal of placelore other than that contained in the *Dinnsheanchas*, and placelore was a subject on which he felt confident to contradict other authorities. His treatment of such material strengthens the theory that

---

66 *FFÉ*, iii, 166. For a detailed assessment of the evidence for the career of Feidhlimidh see Francis John Byrne, *Irish kings and high-kings* (London, 1973).   67 *Lebor na Cert*, ed. Dillon, p. 13.   68 *FFÉ*, iii, 168-9.   69 Ibid., 166.   70 *Leabhar Dinnsheanchuis*, a compilation of legends and stories associated with names of places, was assembled in the eleventh or twelfth century. It survives in a variety of forms. See Edward Gwynn (ed.), *The metrical Dindshenchas* (5 vols, Dublin, reprint 1991), v, 5-23. Versions are extant in a variety of manuscripts not least the Book of Ballymote (*c*.1400), the Book of Lecan (*c*.1400), and the Book of Uí Maine (*c*.1394). Closer to Keating's day are the sixteenth-century copies in RIA, MS D ii 2, transcribed by a Muiris Ó Clérigh, and in TCD, MS 1322 largely written by Seán Ó Cianáin, at Ard Choill, County Clare, a scribe associated with the Ó Maolchonaire school. It is evident from these that written texts of the *dinnsheanchas* were readily available to Keating's contemporaries and that its contents still had popular appeal.   71 *FFÉ*, ii, 250.   72 Cronin, Sources of Keating's *Foras feasa ar Éirinn*, p. 71; Gwynn (ed.), *Metrical Dindshenchas*, i, 28. The description of the fortress of Tara, built by Tuathal Teachtmhar, was taken from the same source as was the description of the Feis of Tara (*FFÉ*, ii, 132). The poem *'Feis Teamhrach gach treas bliadhna'* is taken from a long poem on Loch Garman beginning *'Rí na loch in loch-sa theas'* (Cronin, Sources of Keating's *Foras feasa ar Éirinn*, p. 71; poem printed in Gwynn (ed.), *Metrical Dindshenchas*, iii, 168-83).

5 Closing page of preface of *Foras feasa ar Éirinn* from a manuscript written in 1641–6. RIA, MS 24 P 23, p. 24

Keating had been trained in the bardic tradition where placelore was an inherent part of the body of knowledge preserved in the bardic schools.

Keating's two stories in connection with the placename Eamhain Mhacha[73] were drawn from the *Dinnsheanchas*.[74] The first tale related how Macha made prisioners of the sons of Dithorba and gave them the task of building a fort which she marked out with a bodkin.

> Whence men say 'Emain', that is eó-muin, that is 'the brooch at Macha's throat'... But see further the succession of kings, if thou desirest to learn the full story, which for brevity's sake I here omit.[75]

The second tale in the *Dinnsheanchas* related that Macha, though pregnant, was forced to run with the horses of Conchubhar, and at the end of the journey gave birth to a son and a daughter: 'From this Macha and from the twins (*emon*) she bore come the names of Mag Macha and Emain Macha'.[76] Keating told the story about a woman called Eamhain Mhacha the wife of Cronn son of Adhnaman. The version in the prose *Dinnsheanchas* is closer to Keating's version than is the metrical version, although the story told there explained the name 'Ard Macha' rather than 'Eamhain Macha'.[77]

Other material derived from the *Dinnsheanchas* found in *Foras feasa* included the description of Tailtiu[78] and the quatrain '*Gan teacht fear i bhfarradh ban*' taken from a poem beginning '*A chóemu críche Cuind chain*'.[79] Keating was probably working from memory for most of his placelore material, and any quest for one particular extant manuscript that was his source is likely to prove fruitless.

Similarly, although there are occasional references that may derive from the text known as the *Bansheanchas* (Lore of women) the means by which Keating accessed such material is unclear. This twelfth-century compilation of the lore of women provided a guide to the marriages contracted by Irish noble women from creation down to the twelfth century. It was divided into pre-Christian and early-Christian sections and concentrated on women connected to the reputed high kings of Ireland. Unlike the annals which were predominantly male-dominated and particularly the genealogies, which related exclusively to men, the *Bansheanchas* contained information on a large number of women, and in particular gave details of the multiple marriages of men and women in early Ireland.[80] Keating listed it among the major

---

73 *FFÉ*, ii, 152.   74 Gwynn (ed.), *Metrical Dindshenchas*, iv, 308.   75 Gwynn (ed.), *Metrical Dindshenchas*, iv, 308. It appears however that Keating consulted the fuller account in *Réim ríoghraidhe* using it in preference to the *Dinnsheanchas* version (Cronin, Sources of Keating's *Foras feasa ar Éirinn*, p. 72).   76 Gwynn (ed.), *Metrical Dindshenchas*, iv, 309-11. This episode is in a section of the *Dinnsheanchas* not found in the Book of Lecan version which ends at Gwynn (ed.), *Metrical Dindshenchas*, iv, 267.   77 Whitley Stokes, 'The prose tales in the Rennes Dindsenchas', *Revue Celtique*, xvi (1895), pp. 279-83.   78 *FFÉ*, ii, 248.   79 Cronin, Sources of Keating's *Foras feasa ar Éirinn*, p. 72; Gwynn (ed.), *Metrical Dindshenchas*, iv, 146.   80 The metrical version of the *Bansheanchas* now survives in four known manuscripts, the Book of Leinster, the Book of Lecan, the Book of Uí Maine, and NLI, MS G 3 (Muireann Ní Bhrolcháin, 'An Bansheanchas', *Léachtaí Cholm Cille*, xii (1982), 5-29;

sources for the history of Ireland, and although he did not specifically cite it as the source of any of his information, it may have been his source for information on Eochaidh Feidhlioch,[81] his wife Cloithfhionn and three of their children, Breas, Nár and Lothar.[82] The elopement of Conall Cearnach with Feidhlim Nuachrothach, daughter of Conchubhar, is also found in the *Bansheanchas*.[83]

Even where Keating cited a specific source, he did not feel bound to accept its evidence if it conflicted with other sources. Thus for instance he cited *Cóir anmann*[84] or 'Appropriateness of names' when discussing Lughaidh Laighdhe. Keating asserted that Lughaidh was son of Eochaidh, son of Oilill Fionn, but then noted that the *Cóir anmann* gave Lughaidh a different pedigree, and that that source contained stories of a prophecy associated with Dáire Doimhtheach and his five sons each called Lughaidh. However, Keating had doubts about this material and while not giving his reasons he noted that 'although the *Cóir anmann* states that Lughaidh Laighdhe was a son of Dáire Doimhtheach, I do not think that this is the Lughaidh Laighdhe the *Cóir anmann* refers to who was king of Ireland'.[85] This willingness to criticise written sources was characteristic of those who had read extensively and were aware of inconsistencies in the written record. Thus Tadhg mac Dáire Meic Bhruaideadha, writing in the 1620s, was similarly careful to point out that though in general the written record should not be challenged, there were cases where the historian had to exercise judgment in the face of conflicting evidence.

> *Aithcheodh na leabhar go léir,*
> *ní triallta do neach fan ngréin*
> *triallta do neach dá mbadh eol,*
> *gach ní badh ainbhfior d'aithcheodh.*
> ...
> *Is dearbh gur léigheas díobh sin,*
> *ní as mhó ná mar as mhaith libh,*
> *dearbhadh ar a léigheadh dhamh,*
> *toghaim cruithneacht is cogal.*
> *Dá ní as lia ar a mbí dearbhadh,*

Muireann Ní Bhrolcháin 'The Banshenchas revisited' in Mary O'Dowd and Sabine Wichert (eds), *Chattel, servant or citizen: women's status in church, state and society: historical studies xix* (Belfast, 1995), pp. 70–81). There are at least eight surviving manuscripts of the prose version, which though drawn from the metrical version is expanded by reference to the Bible and native Irish sources; Margaret Dobbs (ed.), 'The Ban-shenchus', *Revue Celtique*, xlvii (1930), pp. 283–339. 81 *FFÉ*, ii, 184. 82 *Bansheanchas* in Book of Lecan, p. 204; Book of Ballymote, f. 282a, although the information is also found elsewhere in Book of Lecan (p. 63) and Book of Ballymote (f. 68a); Cronin, Sources of Keating's *Foras feasa ar Éirinn*, p. 54. 83 *FFÉ*, ii, 214. 84 A tract consisting of discussion of the meanings of personal names, some historical, some fictional: Whitley Stokes (ed.), *Cóir anmann: 'Fitness of names'*, *Irische Texte mit Ubersetzunger und Worterbuch*, iii (Leipzig, 1897), pp. 285–444, 557, edited from TCD, MS 1337, pp. 565–96, with transl and notes. The section of this manuscript containing the *Cóir anmann* was purchased by Edward Lhuyd in Larne, County Antrim, in 1700. 85 *FFÉ*, ii, 148–51.

gach ní neimh-dhearbhtha neamh-ghlan
na leabhair na dteagmhaid so
eatorra do ním togha.

(No one on earth
should challenge all our books.
What one should do is
refute falsehood if one knew how.
...
I have indeed read those books
– more than suits you –.
A proof of my reading
is that I sift wheat from tares.
I choose between the books
where occur two opposite things
each backed by proofs,
or anything uncertain or hazy.)[86]

When discussing the four names of 'Mogh Nuadhat', Keating first cited a stanza detailing the four names, then added 'now if thou desirest to learn the reason of each of these names mentioned in this stanza, read the *Cóir anmann* and thou wilt find it there.'[87] This last recommendation implies that Keating believed that his readers were living in a world where such a manuscript would be accessible and they would have little difficulty in understanding such a text.[88] Alternatively, it may be that this is simply a rhetorical device and that Keating was simply reiterating the authority of his written source.

One of the oldest datable poems in Irish, *Amhra Choluim Chille*,[89] attributed to Dallan Forgaill (fl. *c.*AD 600), was used by Keating for the evidence it contained on the early Irish church. Its description of Colum Cille's journey from Iona to Ireland in the company of priests and bishops gave Keating cause for concern. The idea that bishops should be among the followers of an abbot, rather than being in a position of authority and leadership, required explanation and an assurance that such a scenario was exceptional.[90] Although Keating's knowledge of such early texts may in some instances have been derivative,[91] he would have valued their antiquity

---

86 McKenna (ed.), *Iomarbhágh*, poem 18, verses 15, 18, 19.   87 *FFÉ*, ii, 266-7.   88 Cronin, Sources of Keating's *Foras feasa ar Éirinn*, pp. 66-7. For one surviving example of a seventeenth-century version of this source see RIA, MS 24 P 13, pp. 257-92. The story of Eochaidh Muighmheadhóin given by Keating (*FFÉ*, ii, 360) is found in Stokes (ed.), *Cóir anmann*, p. 372 as well as in the Book of Lecan and Book of Ballymote. The poem '*Mac Eochaidh ard n-ordan*' (*FFÉ*, ii, 412) is found in Book of Lecan p. 86 and in Stokes (ed.), *Cóir anmann*, p. 338. The story of death of Daithí (*FFÉ*, ii, 412) is found in Book of Lecan, p. 72, and Book of Ballymote, ff. 107a, 248a, in a form that closely corresponds to Keating's text. Another account is found in Stokes (ed.), *Cóir anmann*, p. 352.   89 Thomas Owen Clancy and Gilbert Márcus, *Iona: the earliest poetry of a Celtic monastery* (Edinburgh, 1995), pp. 96-128.   90 *FFÉ*, iii, 84-86.   91 One version of the *Amhra Choluim Chille* to which Keating probably had access is BL, Egerton MS 1782 (*BL Cat. Ir. MSS*, ii, 263).

even if their meaning was not easily understood. Keating was involved in a dialogue with his sources, and moulded the material he knew from early sources into a seamless narrative that presented a version of the past consistent with his vision for the future.

IV

In addition to the major sources such as the *Dinnsheanchas*, Keating also enlivened his narrative with a range of prose tales and descriptions of battles which would already have been familiar to his earliest audiences. *Oidhidh na gcuradh* (Tragic fate of the champions) was recommended to readers of *Foras feasa* as a copious account of the adventures and history of warriors and champions.[92] The tale *Cath Mhuigh Léana* was mentioned by Keating as being available to readers who wished to have a more extensive account than was provided by *Foras feasa*.[93] Indeed a portion of the first book of *Foras feasa* could be described as a summary of this source.[94]

Part of the story of *Cath Muighe Muccraimhe* was likewise fitted into the *Foras feasa* narrative, in the episode on Art Aonfhear.[95] Several stanzas were cited, a very brief prose summary was outlined, and the reader was reminded that the material was being taken from the text of the narrative of the battle.[96] Keating appears to have combined his material from *Cath Muighe Muccraimhe* with a genealogical tract found in the Book of Lecan and a tract entitled *De Maccaib Conaire*.[97] His purpose seems to have been to fix these well known tales into his chronological framework so that readers would understand their message in the overall context of a history of the Kingdom of Ireland.

The story of *Cath Bealaigh Mughna* was cited by Keating in contradiction of Meredith Hanmer in relation to events that occurred in AD 905, Keating having narrated the story of this battle from the traditional source.[98] Keating's account told of the death of Cormac mac Cuileannáin (AD 908), in language that paralleled the biblical story of the death of Christ. Cormac, fortelling his death, told his followers that he would no longer be with them, but that someone would come after him to give them apples. As he died, Cormac uttered the words 'Into your hands, O Lord' a phrase that echoed the words of Christ on the cross at Calvary, and was

---

92 *FFÉ*, ii, 220. 93 Ibid., 260-8. 94 Cronin, Sources of Keating's *Foras feasa ar Éirinn*, pp. 56-7. With the exception of the poem beginning '*Eoghan Mór fa mór a rath*' which is from *Cath Magh Léana*, the remaining material on the battle can be found, in a form very close to that used by Keating, in Book of Lecan, p. 173. See Kuno Meyer, 'Mitteilunger aus Irischen Handschriften', *Zeitschrift für Celtische Philologie*, xii (1918), p. 292. In line with much other material that Keating appears to have taken from the Book of Lecan, he does not specifically mention his precise source for his account of the battle of Magh Léna. 95 *FFÉ*, ii, 268-72. 96 Ibid., 272. 97 Cronin, Sources of Keating's *Foras feasa ar Éirinn*, pp. 57-9. For this tract see Book of Leinster, f. 292, and Lucius Gwynn, 'De Maccaib Conaire', *Ériu*, vi (1911-12), pp. 144-53. 98 *FFÉ*, iii, 208-12. His account of the battle of Ballaghmoon corresponds closely with the text now published as J.N. Radner (ed.), *Fragmentary annals of Ireland* (Dublin, 1978).

cited in Latin in Keating's text. The story had obvious attractions for Keating, in its portrayal of the death of a Munster king (and bishop) using the biblical language of Christ at Calvary.[99] Stories such as this allowed Keating construct an image of early Ireland as a Christian kingdom and an appropriate homeland for the ancestry of his contemporary fellow Catholics.

Although Keating's treatment of these prose tales was very cursory, being just an outline summary, *Foras feasa* was important because it fixed these episodes firmly at particular points in the story of Ireland, each in the reign of a particular king. In doing so, Keating was not just presenting a summary history of Ireland, he was providing an interpretative framework within which the many historical tales then in circulation could be read and understood as history. The use of primary sources was not an end in itself, such sources were utilised in support of Keating's version of the myth of the Irish past. The re-use of known stories and poems in a new narrative form enhanced the credibility of Keating's history.

Keating's method of interpolating poetry into the prose narrative was part of a long tradition in medieval Gaelic saga. Thus, for example, the text *Caithréim Conghail Chláiringhnigh* (Martial career of Conghal Cláiringhneach)[100] the earliest extant version of which is dated to *c.*1650, although based on earlier material, has passages of verse interspersed through the prose in a style imitated by Keating's *Foras feasa*. The link between prose and verse, however, is rather more tenuous in some of Keating's text.

Keating had a clear view of the overall structure of his text – a history of the kingdom of Ireland through the lives and exploits of its kings, from earliest times to the arrival of the Anglo-Normans. His very selective and focussed use of the manuscript sources, inserting selected short extracts from a wide range of sources as fitted his narrative, indicates that this was far from being a struggle to salvage what could be preserved from sources threatened with destruction. It was a professionally constructed history, executed according to the normal standards of scholarship in his own day, telling the story of Ireland from the original manuscript sources, in a manner that would make the contents of those manuscripts meaningful to his contemporaries in the seventeenth century.[101]

V

The texts on which Keating relied for his history were those that had long been familiar to the keepers of the *seanchas*. Scholarly families such as Mac Craith, Ó Duibhgeannáin, Mac Eochagáin, and Ó Maolchonaire were the channels through which access to manuscripts containing such texts could be obtained. In most

---

99 *FFÉ*, iii, 202-8; Radner (ed.), *Fragmentary annals*, pp. 153ff.   100 *Caithréim Conghail Cláiringhnigh: martial career of Conghal Cláiringhneach*, ed. P.M. MacSweeney (London, ITS, 1904).   101 See also Breandán Ó Buachalla, '*Annála Ríoghachta Éireann* is *Foras feasa ar Éirinn*: an comhthéacs comhaimseartha', *Studia Hibernica*, nos. 22-3 (1982-3), pp. 59-105.

instances it has not proved possible to establish whether specific manuscripts still extant today were the exact copies used by Keating. This is largely because Keating's working method involved synthesis rather than transcription. The only extensive investigation of the manuscript sources used by Keating is the research of Anne Cronin.[102] Her analysis of Keating's use of the *Leabhar gabhála* and the *Réim ríoghraidhe* linked Keating's work with the Book of Lecan, but stopped short of concluding that Keating used the actual manuscript of the Book of Lecan now extant.[103] If Keating did indeed use the Book of Lecan this would most likely have been facilitated through Conall Mac Eochagáin who had the manuscript on loan from James Ussher in the 1630s.[104] While this particular connection cannot be conclusively demonstrated in the case of the Book of Lecan, Keating's likely use of another manuscript supports the idea of a scholarly association between him and Mac Eochagáin.

Although it had not featured on his list of chief books of the *seanchas*, Keating cited '*Leabhar ruadh Meic Aodhagáin*' (The Red book of Mac Aodhagáin), on the number of clergy in the household of Aonghus, son of Natfraoich king of Munster,[105] and he cited the same book, together with the *Naomhsheanchas*, on the number of saints of Ireland who had the same name.[106] No composite manuscript now extant is currently identified as the 'Red book of Mac Aodhagáin'. However, a vellum manuscript of the fifteenth and sixteenth centuries, now known as BL Add. MS 30,512, which was in the possession of Conall Mac Eochagáin from 1627 until after 1640 might possibly be the manuscript in question. One of the more prolific of late fifteenth-century scribes, Uilliam Mac an Lega, was the original scribe of Add. MS 30,512. Some later additions relative to the Fitzgeralds of Desmond were added by Torna mac Torna Uí Mhaoilchonaire (d.1532) while at Caher in 1561 Cosnamach Mac Flannchadha added material on Pierce son of Edmund Butler.[107] Its history thus associates it closely with Laud Misc. MS 610 in the sixteenth century, and its contents would have been known to Keating's scholarly contacts.

BL, Add. MS 30,512 contains the material cited by Keating from *Leabhar ruadh Meic Aodhagáin* on the 'rule' attributed to Comhghall of Bangor[108] and the text of a poem cited by Keating '*Anmann ceathrair ceart ro chinn*' to illustrate that Fionntain, Fearón, Fors and Andóid could not have survived the deluge.[109] The rubrics provided by the scribe to enhance the appearance of the manuscript would have been sufficient to earn it the title of 'red book'.

---

102 Cronin, 'Manuscript sources', pp. 122-35; Anne Cronin, 'Printed sources of Keating's Foras feasa', *Éigse*, iv (1943-4), pp. 235-79; Cronin, Sources of Keating's *Foras feasa ar Éirinn*.   103 Cronin, 'Manuscript sources', pp. 122-35; Cronin, Sources of Keating's *Foras feasa ar Éirinn*.   104 King's Inns, Gaelic MS 4, p. 54.   105 *FFÉ*, iii, 26.   106 Ibid., 109. See also Denis T. Brosnan (ed.), 'Comainmnigud Noem hErend so sis', *Archivium Hibernicum*, i (1912), pp. 314-65, edited from Book of Lecan, p. 366 col. 5 with variants noted from Book of Ballymote; BL, Add. MS 30,512, f. 48. *BL Cat. Ir. MSS*, ii, 496, item 91; Bodl., Rawl. MS, B 502, p. 92.   107 *BL Cat. Ir. MSS*, ii, pp. 470-73.   108 BL, Add. MS 30,512, f. 45b; *BL Cat. Ir. MSS*, ii, 495, item 88.   109 *FFÉ*, i, 148; *BL Cat. Ir. MSS*, ii, 500, item 103.

The material on St Comhghall cited from *Leabhar ruadh Mic Aodhagáin* provides an interesting example of Keating's working method, and his attitude to his
sources.

> St Comhghall of Beannchair, the holy abbot, a man who had forty thousand
> monks under his obedience or under his authority, as we read in the Red
> Book of Mac Aodhagáin; and this is the more to be believed because we
> read in an author of repute, namely St Bernard, in the life of Malachias,
> that there was a disciple of the abbot of Comhghall called Soanus, who built
> a hundred monasteries, and this Comhghall is of the race of Irial, son of
> Conall Cearnach, son of Aimhirgin, of Clanna Rudhruighe. In testimony of
> this, the poem on saint-history ('*duain naoimhsheanchais*') speaks thus:
>
>> Comhghall of Beannchair, son of Seadna,
>> Whom fear of death troubled not,
>> Was of Uladh's stock, who were not caught napping
>> Of the race of Irial, son of Conall.[110]

Evidently worried by the extravagant claims made in *Leabhar Ruadh Meic
Aodhagáin*, Keating sought to support its testimony by other sources he regarded
as more reliable, opting for a reputable clerical author – St Bernard. The fact that
the *Leabhar Ruadh* was not a particularly old source was perhaps sufficient for
Keating to have had reservations about relying solely on its evidence on matters of
greater antiquity. Here, as elsewhere, Keating strenghtened his argument by combining evidence from a native and a foreign source.

Some evidence of another dimension of Keating's scholarly network is provided
by an early sixteenth-century vellum manuscript, now BL, Egerton MS 1782. This
composite manuscript was also produced by Ó Maolchonaire scribes, and like Add.
MS 30,512 it contains a miscellany of material that corresponds very closely to a
range of sources used by Keating in *Foras feasa*. Egerton MS 1782 was evidently
written *c.*1516-18 for Art Mac Murchadha Kavanagh, who died while the work was
in progress.[111] It was in the hands of the O'Byrnes in the sixteenth century and
apparently remained with that family through the seventeenth century. As such, it
might have been possible for Keating to have had access to it, or to a copy made
from it.

Robin Flower's detailed description of Egerton MS 1782 draws attention to the
significant links between it and *Foras feasa*. The manuscript contains the *Amhra
Choluim Chille*, and the commentary on that text includes the story of Labhraidh
Loingseach, Moiriath and Craiftine the harper, in a version that corresponds to
that used in *Foras feasa*.[112] The tale of Labhraidh and his horse ears, betrayed by

---

110 *FFÉ*, iii, 48-9.   111 *BL Cat. Ir. MSS*, ii, 262; BL, Egerton MS 1,782 was primarily the work of
three sons of Sean mac Torna Uí Mhaolchonaire, who had become *ollamh* to the O'Conors in 1495.
The scribe of BL, Add. MS 30,512 was probably a member of the same family.   112 *FFÉ*, ii, 160. *BL
Cat. Ir. MSS*, ii, 266.

a harp made from the tree to which the secret had been revealed, also corresponds to the version found in this source.[113] Other close parallels between Keating's narrative and the texts found in Egerton MS 1782 include the tale of a priest in Tír Chonaill who made an altar of crystal with images of the sun and moon on it and was carried off by the devil. This episode formed part of the commentary on the *Amhra Choluim Chille*. Keating inserted this story in *Foras feasa* immediately after quoting a series of stanzas from the *Amhra* regarding Colum Cille himself.[114] The conditions attaching to service in the Fianna found in Egerton MS 1782 in the tract '*Airem muinntiri Finn innso*' was the source for Keating's descriptions in *Foras feasa* of requirements for entry into the Fianna.[115]

Two quatrains on national characters, in which the various provinces of Ireland were compared to foreign peoples, were attributed by Keating to Seán mac Torna Uí Mhaolchonaire, who was probably the father of the principal scribe of Egerton MS 1782.[116] Keating's version of the battle of Carn Conaill and his tales about Guaire closely resembled the versions of these stories found in Egerton MS 1782.[117] The tale of Deirdriu and the sons of Uisneach is found in a number of early manuscripts including the Book of Leinster and the Yellow book of Lecan, but in this instance also the version used by Keating corresponds most closely to that in Egerton MS 1782.[118]

The extent of this correlation provides important circumstantial evidence that this manuscript or a very similar collection of texts was one of Keating's direct sources. The evidence is not conclusive, but the close correspondence between *Foras feasa* and the versions of many of the episodes found in Egerton MS 1782 cannot have been purely coincidental.[119]

The *Black book of Molaga*, mentioned by Keating as one of the chief books of the *seanchas* of Ireland, was owned by Diarmuid MacCarthy in 1640, since in that year he gave it on loan to Domhnall mac Taidhg Óig Uí Shúilleabháin who made a copy.[120] The final section of the 1640 copy, now McClean MS 187 in the Fitzwilliam Museum, Cambridge, corresponds closely to a substantial section of *Foras feasa*.[121] The additions by Keating to the source text consist of little more

---

113 *FFÉ*, ii, 172; BL, Egerton MS 1782, f. 9b col. 2; *BL Cat. Ir. MSS*, ii, 266.   114 *FFÉ*, iii, 106; BL, Egerton MS 1782, f. 11b, col. 2.   115 *FFÉ*, ii, 332; *BL Cat. Ir. MSS*, ii, 270-1; the text has been edited from BL, Egerton MS 1782 in S.H. O'Grady (ed.), *Silva Gadelica* (2 vols, London, 1892), i, 92, with translation, ii, 99.   116 *FFÉ*, ii, 169. BL, Egerton MS 1782, f. 56. '*Fritha gach dá chosmuilius*'. A different version of the verses is found in BL, Harley MS 5280 and in Bodl., Laud Misc. 610, f. 10, col. 2. See also *BL Cat. Ir. Mss*, ii, 260-62.   117 BL, Egerton MS 1782, f. 59; *FFÉ*, iii, 58-66; *BL Cat. Ir. MSS*, ii, 284.   118 *FFÉ*, i, 190; BL, Egerton MS 1782, ff. 67-9; *BL Cat. Ir. MSS*, ii, 286.   119 Keating's account of the battle of Belach Mugna (*FFÉ*, iii, 200-214) for which he names the Annals of Cluain Eidnech as his source (*FFÉ*, iii, 212) is a paraphrase of the account in Radner (ed.), *Fragmentary annals*. BL, Egerton MS 1782 includes extracts from annals, in a version which closely follows the annals in Radner (ed.), *Fragmentary annals*. Flower has shown that the annals extracted in Egerton MS 1782 and those in Brussels, Burgundian Library MSS 5301-20, are both derived from the lost Annals of Cluain Eidnech, and that Keating also had access to these annals in some form (*BL Cat. Ir. MSS*, ii, 284-5).   120 Cambridge: Fitzwilliam Museum, McClean MS, 187; Pádraig de Brún and Máire Herbert (eds), *Catalogue of Irish Manuscripts in Cambridge Libraries* (Cambridge, 1986), pp. 104-5.   121 Fitzwilliam Museum, McClean MS. 187ff. 50-62v; *FFÉ*, ii,

than link sentences, introductory paragraphs and stanzas of poetry that support the
evidence of the prose narrative.[122] A story about Conchubhar mac Fachtna
Fáthaigh omitted from some early manuscripts of *Foras feasa*, is also an addition
not found in Keating's source text.[123] It seems, therefore, that Keating may well
have consulted the Black book of Molaga, and subsequently added material from
other sources to augment its evidence.

The material found in the latter part of McClean MS 187 and also in *Foras
feasa* provides evidence of Keating's method of adapting source texts. It is clear
that Keating had access to some version of the material found in McClean MS
187, but that he supplemented that material from a variety of other sources.
Sometimes such tampering with his original source upset the flow of his narrative.
Link sentences such as 'We shall come back again to Conchubhar and set down
here part of his story'[124] became necessary to knit the story together. Keating was
aware that he could get more seriously distracted from the central narrative, and
occasionally added paragraphs indicating that he was choosing not to pursue particular aspects of the story.

Thus, for example, having described briefly the death of Conlaoch, son of
Cúchulainn, in a narrative that corresponds to that found also in McClean MS 187,
Keating then intervened to address his readers directly.

> Know, O Reader, that if I were to relate here how Cúchulainn fell by the
> sons of Cailitin, and Fear Diadh son of Damhan by Cúchulainn, and the
> death of the seven Maines sons of Oilill Mór and of Meadhbh, and of many
> other stout heroes who are not mentioned here, a long narrative would be
> needed concerning them.

To avoid a lengthy digression and to allow himself to return to his source text, he
advised readers in this instance to read these other texts in which the history and
adventures of these heroes would be found.[125] Keating then returned to the story
of Cúraoi son of Dáire in a version that corresponds to that found also in McClean
MS 187. While the precise copy of these stories found in McClean MS 187 was
transcribed too late to have been Keating's source, it is evident that he must have
used a very similar text as a source.

The working method revealed here involved a sophisticated approach to a range
of primary sources such as could only be attempted by an historian thoroughly
familiar with the wide range of sources available to those who wished to read them.
In searching for the manuscripts actually consulted by Keating in *Foras feasa*, the
list of extant manuscripts named by him as important sources of *seanchas* is something of a distraction. The list of Ireland's most important manuscripts was indeed
a list of the oldest and most highly regarded manuscripts then believed to be still

ll. 3067-185; 3187-238; 3239-309; 3313-21, 3333-6, 3368-406; 3426-531; 3741-847; 3852-78; 3930-42, 3947-
56 and 3960-4.   **122** *FFÉ*, ii, ll. 3848-51; 3944-7.   **123** *FFÉ*, ii, ll. 3349-67, omitted, for instance, from
BL, Egerton MS 107.   **124** *FFÉ*, ii, 214-15.   **125** Ibid., 220-21.

extant, but was certainly not a list of the sources used in *Foras feasa*. In most instances, it appears, the compilations to which Keating actually had access were not themselves of great antiquity. Many had been compiled from older manuscripts, and in some instances this had been done within his own living memory. A plausible case can be made for Keating having had direct access to the manuscripts now known as BL, Add. MS 30,512 and Egerton MS 1782, to the Book of Lecan or a copy made from it, to Bodleian Laud Misc. 610 (or a copy of it), and to a manuscript of which Cambridge, McClean MS 187 is a copy. However, the evidence in each of these instances, though significant, is merely circumstantial. Keating's working method itself makes it largely futile to search for his precise source manuscripts. He was a synthetic historian, not a scribe, and he was interested in interpretation not transcription. Nevertheless, the investigation of possible source texts allows us to clarify a number of points. First, it is evident that contacts with the Mac Eochagáin, Ó Maolchonaire and Mac Craith families and their patrons must have been important. There were probably contacts with the O'Byrnes, the Kavanaghs, the MacCarthys and perhaps with influential clergy such as David Rothe. There may also have been indirect contacts with James Ussher and James Ware. While there is ample evidence of the influence of O'Brien patronage on many of Keating's source texts, for Keating himself the patronage of the Butlers of Cahir and Dunboyne may have been of pivotal importance. The evidence of the poetry, though problematic, certainly points in this direction. If the various laments for members of the Butler family included in the collection of Keating's poems edited by Éoin Mac Giolla Eáin (McErlean) can be accepted as his compositions, point to a special relationship with the Butlers. Two of these poems also provide the only extant evidence of Keating's activities after the completion of *Foras feasa*. '*A Bhanbha bhog-omh dhona dhuaibhseach*'[126] is a lament on the illness of Lord Dunboyne, Éamonn mac Piarais Butler, while '*Druididh suas, a chuaine an chaointe*'[127] is a lament following his death in March 1640. However, the authorship of these poems cannot be verified, the extant manuscript copies being early nineteenth-century texts. The attribution to Keating of another poem in these manuscripts, '*Múscail do mhisneach a Bhanbha*'[128] is almost certainly incorrect, and this fact casts doubt on the authorship of the other compositions also.[129] If the date '1646' is correct for '*Múscail do mhisneach*' then Keating cannot have composed it since it is clear that he had died no later than 1644.[130] The absence of any seventeenth-century copies of these poems and the confusion in the manuscript tradition whereby some of the poems attributed to Keating are also attributed to other poets, makes it unwise to place too much emphasis on the evidence of the poetry as a source of biographical information.

---

126 Mac Giolla Eáin (ed.), *Dánta*, poem 17.   **127** Ibid., *Dánta*, poem 12.   **128** Ibid., *Dánta*, poem 16. **129** RIA, MS 23 G 24, MS 23 N 15, Maynooth, Murphy MS 7, Murphy MS 2, are all the work of the Ó Longáin family of scribes.   **130** The date on the Tubbrid memorial clearly indicates that Keating was dead when the plaque was erected in 1644. He may have died some years prior to 1644. The attribution of this poem to Pádraigín Haicéad is much more likely to be correct. Ní Cheallacháin (ed.), *Filíocht Phádraigín Haicéad*, poem 36.

The internal evidence of the prose texts, therefore, is the most important guide to the intellectual and social world of Geoffrey Keating. The range of manuscripts available to him did not exist in a vacuum. In the process of consulting those manuscripts Keating had access not only to the historical literature and lore of Gaelic Ireland, but also to its contemporary patrons and custodians. Keating's knowledge of, and access to, this manuscript material, facilitated by patrons and fellow travellers in the pursuit of the truth about the past, equipped him for the daunting task of synthesising the complex Irish historical record for modern readers. While his efforts did not meet with universal approval, his ability to handle the manuscript sources and combine them with other historical writing and with the poetic record was an exceptional skill for which he won the respect and admiration of later generations.

5

Foreign writers and Irish readers:
the wider world of print in *Foras Feasa ar Éirinn*

Foras feasa ar Éirinn was rooted in the Gaelic manuscript tradition, but yet its author was also familiar with a range of printed histories in Latin and English that contained references to Ireland. It is evident that he was familiar with mainstream texts by English writers such as those used extensively by John Milton in his *History of Britain*, commenced about 1645.[1] The names Bede, Nennius, Geoffrey of Monmouth, John Speed, Raphael Holinshed, William Camden, George Buchanan and Hector Boece are to be found among Keating's sources as well as Milton's. These are unlikely reading materials indeed for a priest who was reputedly a fugitive in the glen of Aherlow, but yet citations from these authors form an intrinsic part of the methodology of *Foras feasa*. Indeed, the inclusion of extensive references to the writings of non-Irish historians is one of the significant differences between Keating's work and *Annála ríoghachta Éireann*. His methodology is much closer to that of Thomas Messingham, whose book on Ireland's saints, *Florilegium insulae sanctorum*, was published at Paris in 1624. Keating consciously demonstrated a keen interest in the wider world of historical scholarship, and absorbed both its style and its themes.

The extent of the printed material cited as evidence in his historical writing raises the question of how Keating had access to such books, and whether his wider historical interests were exceptional for a writer working in Ireland. The English, Scottish, and continental publications cited were mostly newly published in the early seventeenth century. While it is possible that he consulted some of these historical texts in France before his return to Ireland, in many instances the dates of publication makes this impossible. Furthermore, the bulk of his non-Irish source material was English and Scottish rather than continental. If he did not personally own the non-Irish texts he cited it is probable that the network of scholarly contacts which provided him with manuscript materials also supplied him with the printed histories cited in *Foras feasa*. It is noteworthy in this context that his con-

---

1 F. Fogle (ed.), *Yale complete prose works of John Milton*, v, pt. 1 (Yale, 1971); William Ferguson, *The identity of the Scottish nation: an historic quest* (Edinburgh, 1998), pp. 129-33.

temporary, Dubhaltach Mac Fhirbhisigh, also used the works of non-Irish authors such as Boece, Hanmer and Holinshed.[2] This chapter examines Keating's purpose in citing the works of foreign authors, and evaluates his historical method by assessing how he used those works.

I

Of three Scottish historians whose Latin writings had a noteable influence on *Foras feasa*, Hector Boece [Boetius] was probably the most influential. His *Scotorum historiae* was first published at Paris in 1526.[3] In general, Keating respected Boece's work and he was, in effect, seeking to produce a similar text for Ireland. This must surely have been one of the principal works Keating had in mind when he said that he wished Ireland to have a national history such as other nations have. Boece's history had as its central framework a list of Scottish kings, thereby underlining the value of the kingdom of Scotland. It had depicted the Scottish people as loyal Christians never veering from the true faith.[4] As was the case with other national histories Boece's narratives of war and defence were a mechanism through which national identity was delineated and defined. The king was depicted as a central symbol and focus of that identity.[5] This focus on the king ensured the Scottish character of the text was sustained even when foreign stories were told. In every instance the contextual framework was the reign of a Scottish king.[6] This aspect of Boece's work is very closely paralleled by Keating's choice of the succession of Kings of Ireland as the framework around which the *Foras feasa* was constructed. Nicola Royan's analysis of Boece's framework points out that the measurement of time by the passage of reigns of kings serves a highly political purpose. While there is a king of the people, the people cannot be deemed to be the subjects of another king. The king holds the throne from the people. The king does not choose his people, the people choose him.[7] This concept of kingship came to have a significant role in seventeenth-century Irish political thought and was developed by writers such as John Lynch, who relied on Keating for historical context.[8]

The kingship framework also permitted a conscious division into distinct eras, marking progress through time. In the Irish context, the framework of the succession of kings also allowed Keating establish the Norman kings as the legitimate successors of the Gaelic kings.[9] It allowed him make the case that the Irish people chose a Norman king, rather than a Norman king having chosen them.[10] The kingship framework had the great merit also of reflecting the expectations of Keating's

2 Ó Muraíle, *Celebrated antiquary*, pp. 236, 239, 242, 248, 350.   3 A second edition was printed at Lausanne and published in Paris in 1574.   4 Nicola Royan, The *Scotorum historiae* of Hector Boece: a study (D. Phil. thesis, Oxford University, 1996), p. 87.   5 Royan, Boece, pp. 106-8.   6 Ibid., pp. 239-41.   7 Ibid., see also Jenny Wormald, *Court, kirk and community: Scotland, 1470-1625* (London, 1981), p. 19.   8 See below, ch. 8, and see also Cunningham, 'Representations of king, parliament and the Irish people'.   9 Most clearly expressed in the synchronisms, *FFÉ*, iv, 123-49.   10 *FFÉ*, iii, 340-4.

contemporaries about how Irish history should be narrated. Keating's particular focus on Ireland as a kingdom, with a long history, gave him scope to establish, from the beginning, the idea of parity between Gaelic kings and their Briton and Saxon counterparts.[11] Such a case for the status of the kingdom of Ireland was a core objective of *Foras feasa* and one of the reasons for its lasting popularity.

Of the seven instances when Keating cited Boece's history, four were refutations of points of detail. Keating rejected Boece's evidence on the first king of the Scotic race in Scotland, and contradicted his arguments about the ancestors of the Gaeil, namely Gaedheal, Éibhear and Éireamhón, and also the Scot's assertion that Fionn Mac Cumhaill had been a giant. Boece was cited to more positive effect on evidence for the *Lia Fáil*, the stone of destiny, and on Gaedheal having been a contemporary of Moses in Egypt.[12] While these were all relatively minor points, the fact that three of the details in dispute related to the person of Gaedheal, his journeying and his descendants is significant. Keating was pointedly taking issue with a Scottish writer on the topical debate on the origins of the Gaeil.[13]

Boece's *Scotorum historiae* was in circulation in France and, given the evident similarity in authorial intent and chronological framework between his work and *Foras feasa*, it seems likely that Keating's encounter with this text, perhaps while still in France, convinced him that Ireland and the Irish people should have a similar narrative of their own kingdom. Boece, no less than Keating, was inclined to give a new lease of life to old fables, knitting them into the narrative in a manner that gave them respectability as quasi-history. In both works the stories, even if implausible, helped enliven the narrative, and must have contributed significantly to their sustained widespread popularity.

In contrast to Boece, Keating had little special regard for John Mair (Major) (1467-1550), a near contemporary of Boece, whose magnum opus had narrated the history of England and Scotland to the close of the fifteenth century. His *Historia Majoris Britanniae tam Angliae quam Scotiae*, with its pun on the word 'major', was first published in Paris in 1521. Deemed one of the first 'modern' historians of Scotland, he was wary of the mythological stories of Scotland's past.[14] While Keating described Mair as a 'reputable' Scottish author, he only quoted from the *Historia Majoris Britanniae* once, where he asserted that the Scots were descended from the Irish, and supported this by quoting Mair's view that the Irish and the Scots were originally of the same stock.[15] '*Dico ergo a quibuscunque Hivernici originem duxere ab iisdem Scoti exordium capiunt*.' (For this reason, I assert that whatever stock the Irish be from, the people of Alba are from the same stock.) In his Irish rendering of this citation, '*Éireannach*' (*Hivernici*) and '*Albanach*' (*Scoti*) were the terms chosen by Keating as the original names of '*Gaedhil Éireann*' and '*Gaedhil Alban*'.[16]

11 *FFÉ*, i, 14-16.   12 Cronin, 'Printed sources', p. 258.   13 Similar writing by other Irish clergy who had been educated in France includes the work of David Rothe and Thomas Messingham.   14 Roger A. Mason, 'Kingship, nobility and Anglo-Scottish union: John Mair's History of Greater Britain (1521)', *Innes Review*, xli, no. 2 (1990), pp. 182-222.   15 *FFÉ*, ii, 58-9.   16 Ibid., 59. Keating's one reference

Yet another Scottish history, George Buchanan's *De rerum Scoticarum historia* published in 1582,[17] was cited by Keating in connection with the idea that the sons of Míl had come to Ireland from France.[18] He outlined the three arguments Buchanan made on this point, refuting each of them in turn, and reaffirming the Spanish connection of Míl and his sons.[19] Buchanan's evidence was also cited in connection with the origin of the Scots.[20] It is significant that quotations from Buchanan on the Irish origins of the Scots were also contained in the introductory chapter of Thomas Messingham's *Florilegium insulae sanctorum*. Messingham was evidently the source for quite a number of Keating's references to non-Irish printed sources.[21] Keating also quoted from the work of another Scottish writer, John Barclay, whose *Icon animorum*, though published in London in 1614, was probably intended for circulation on the continent.[22] Its topic was the character of the principal European nations, and Keating quoted from the Latin version, on the matter of the dwelling houses of the Irish.[23] The debate over the true identity of the 'Scoti', the inhabitants of the original 'Scotia' had arisen on the continent among Counter-Reformation authors researching the lives of early Irish saints.[24] Thomas Dempster's publication claiming these saints for Scotland was greeted with dismay by the Irish scholars interested in hagiography and history.[25] Keating was doubtless aware of the controversy, which was reaching its height on the continent in the 1620s at the time when he was compiling the *Foras feasa* in Ireland.

Of more direct concern to Keating, among contemporary English-language publications, were histories of Ireland, notably those by Edmund Campion and Meredith Hanmer, and political tracts on the reform of Ireland, particularly the treatises of Edmund Spenser and Sir John Davies. These men, like Giraldus, were writing from the perspective of describing an alien people in a country in which they were themselves foreigners. Keating also noted histories of England that contained material on Ireland. James Ware's substantial composite edition, dated 1633, of narrative histories of Ireland by late Elizabethan and early Stuart authors may well have been the catalyst that led Keating to add an historiographical preface to his *Foras feasa*. However, references to this material are not confined to the preface.[26] Keating used the histories published by Ware in his core narrative also. Despite the tone of the preface to *Foras feasa*, Keating did not regard the evidence

to Mair's history may have been acquired indirectly.   **17** The work was prompted more by internal Scottish politics than by any desire to enhance Scotland's reputation abroad. His opposition to Mary Queen of Scots led him to take liberties with the historical record, and in general he displayed little concern to establish the truth of history.   **18** *FFÉ*, ii, 60.   **19** Ibid., 60-6.   **20** Ibid., 381, 389. In one case a page number was given (but inaccurately).   **21** Thomas Messingham *Florilegium insulae sanctorum* (Paris, 1624); Cronin, 'Printed sources', pp. 270-1.   **22** It was translated into English, by T.M. in 1631 as 'The Mirrour of mindes'.   **23** Cronin, 'Printed sources', p. 254.   **24** Among the first publications on this theme was Henry Fitzsimon, *Catalogus praecipuorum sanctorum Hiberniae recognitus sanctus* ([Liege], [1619]). See Paul Grosjean (ed.), 'Édition du *Catalogus praecipuorum Sanctorum Hiberniae* de Henri Fitzsimon', in John Ryan (ed.), *Féilsgríbhinn Eóin Mac Néill* (Dublin, 1940), pp. 335-93.   **25** Thomas Dempster, *Scotia illustrior, seu mendicabula repressa, modesta parecbasi Thomae Dempsteri* ([Lyons], 1620).   **26** Campion, cited in *FFÉ*, ii, 328.

of foreign authors as invariably hostile. Ware's compilation contained Edmund Campion's *A historie of Ireland*, a work completed in the 1580s but not widely available before 1633. Keating rejected Campion's evidence in two instances but accepted his work as a source for evidence of a tribute imposed on the Irish by King Arthur.[27]

Meredith Hanmer's *Chronicle of Ireland* written in 1571 was printed for the first time in Ware's 1633 edition.[28] It is clear that Keating did not like what he read about Ireland in Hanmer's work,[29] and he became a principal focus of Keating's attack on foreign authors. The polemical preface to *Foras feasa* contained eleven citations from Hanmer's *Chronicle*, refuting Hanmer's evidence in each instance. Likewise in the core of the history Hanmer's was twice criticised, once in relation to the death of Cormac mac Cuileannáin and Cearbhall mac Muireigéin, where Keating contradicted him by reference to the tract entitled *Cath Bealaigh Mughna*.[30] Earlier, Keating had argued that Hanmer had confused three different individuals called Roanus or Ronanus and Ruadhán, and concluded that 'we shall not follow any more of the lies of Hanmer, or of the authority he has'.[31]

Keating's account of the relationship between Ireland and Wales[32] also alluded to Hanmer's evidence, though Keating's version was not an accurate rendering of the material in Hanmer's *Chronicle*. Yet, while it seems clear that Hanmer was not highly regarded by Keating, nonetheless he sometimes relied on the chronicle for miscellaneous material. This included secondary references to the chronicles of Caradocus and Albion, and to a Spanish author Florianus del Campo.[33] As in the case of most other authors cited, Keating tended to use the materials published in Ware's edition primarily as a source book for miscellaneous information.

His approach to Edmund Spenser's *View of the present state of Ireland*, which had been written in 1596 based on Spenser's first-hand experience as a settler in Ireland, illustrates Keating's occasional reticence about confronting the ideology which underpinned his source texts. In many instances he was content simply to argue specific historic details so as to sustain the thrust of his own narrative.[34] Thus Keating accepted Spenser's assertion that the Saxons owed 'their letters, and learning and learned men' to the Irish,[35] while he had earlier rejected Spenser's notion that Egfrid, king of the Northumbrians, and Edgar, king of Britain, had authority over Ireland.[36] The point at issue here was the status of the kingdom of Ireland. Keating cited the appropriate page reference of the printed edition of Spenser's work,[37] thereby focussing the attention of the reader on specific short-

27 Cronin, 'Printed sources', pp. 255-6. 28 Hanmer's history was also in circulation in manuscript. See for instance Chetham's Library, Manchester MS A 677, pp. 1-22. 29 That Keating was working from the printed text is confirmed by his citing some accurate page references. 30 *FFÉ*, iii, 208. 31 *FFÉ*, i, 152-3. 32 *FFÉ*, ii, 70-2. 33 Cronin, 'Printed sources', p. 250. 34 Probably the most significant exception to this was his attitute to his fellow Catholic Old Englishman, Richard Stanihurst. See below, pp. 97-8, 115-6, and see also Brendan Bradshaw, 'Geoffrey Keating, apologist of Irish Ireland', in Andrew Hadfield and Willy Maley (eds), *Representing Ireland: literature and the origins of conflict, 1534-1660* (Cambridge, 1993), pp. 166-90. 35 *FFÉ*, i, 64-5. 36 Ibid., 24. 37 Edmund

comings of the printed text. However, it scarcely justifies one anonymous modern commentator's suggestion that Spenser was regarded by Keating as 'a leading calumniator of Irish culture and society, as he was indeed convinced of the need to eliminate the pre-conquest traditions of the Irish people'.[38] Keating's challenging of Spenser's notion that the Mac Mahons, Mac Sweeneys, Mac Sheehys, Mac Namaras, Kavanaghs, O'Tooles and O'Byrnes were of English origin[39] may have had greater resonance among contemporaries. The refutation of Spenser's account of the ancestry of these families was achieved by rejecting his etymological approach and citing instead the evidence of genealogical sources.[40] Dismissing Spenser's claim that the Mac Namaras were descended from a Norman family called Mortimer he asserted:

> however, that is not true, for it is from a person named Cumara they are called children of Cumara, the proper surname for them is the race of Aodh, and it is from Caisin, son of Cas, son of Conall of the swift steeds, of the race of Eibhear, they are derived, as may be read in the genealogical account of the Dál Cas.[41]

Keating similarly referred the reader to the genealogical account of Leinster families for the record of the true origins of the O'Byrnes, O'Tooles, and Kavanaghs.[42] The evidence of primary manuscript sources in Irish was Keating's principal yardstick in judging the shortcomings of Spenser as an historian. He concluded his dismissal of Spenser's evidence as grounded in ignorance by reference to his status as a poet who could indulge in poetic licence and fabrication.[43]

> I am surprised how Spenser ventured to meddle in these matters, of which he was ignorant, unless that, on the score of being a poet, he allowed himself license of invention, as it was usual with him, and others like him, to frame and arrange many poetic romances with sweet-sounding words to deceive the reader.[44]

Incidentally, this revealed a view of poetry quite at variance from the norm in *Foras feasa*, and suggests that his high regard for poetic sources in his own work was on the grounds of their antiquity.

In contrast to Hanmer and Spenser, John Stow was presented to Keating's readers as a reliable source. Stow's *Annales or a general chronicle of England ... to 1580* was first published in 1580.[45] The evidence Keating drew from Stow's *Chron-*

Spenser, *A view of the state of Ireland*, ed. W.L. Renwick (Oxford, 1970), p. 33; *FFÉ*, i, 24.   **38** Robert Welch (ed.), *Oxford companion to Irish literature* (Oxford, 1996), p. 532.   **39** *FFÉ*, i, 26.   **40** Ibid., 24-30.   **41** Ibid., 28-9.   **42** Ibid., 28-31.   **43** Ibid., 30-1.   **44** Ibid., 31.   **45** Stow's *Chronicle*, a substantial work, was in its fifth edition by 1631. Keating himself indicated that the version he consulted was the revised edition printed in London in 1614 (*recte* 1615) (*FFÉ*, ii, 396). This edition had been added to and altered by Edmund Howes.

icle ranged from the date of the reign of Gorguntius 342 years before Christ's birth, to an account of the pope having bestowed Ireland on Henry II in AD 1155. Although Stow, in turn, had derived some of his information on the papal bull of Pope Adrian from Giraldus Cambrensis' *Topographia Hiberniae*, Keating cited the material as though it had originated with Stow. While Keating took issue with the content of the bull as cited by Stow he did not challenge the detail, or suggest that Stow was guilty of misrepresentation.[46] Rather, Stow's *Chronicle* was probably another of those histories of other 'nations' that Keating wished to emulate in his own writing. He was not regarded by Keating as a hostile commentator on Ireland, and rightly so, since the intention of the compiler of Stow's *Chronicle* had little in common with the political purpose of Spenser's *View*.[47]

Keating derived his narrative of the Irish dealings of Magnus, king of Norway, from Richard Hakluyt's *Principal Navigations* (1589), perhaps using a secondary source. The events are placed in the reign of Muircheartach O'Brien as king of Ireland in the latter part of the eleventh century.[48] The episode illustrates that Keating's treatment of his sources took second place to the business of preserving Muircheartach O'Brien's reputation, and the material from *Cogadh Gaedhel re Gallaibh* was given priority over the external source.

> Maghnus, son of Amhlaoibh son of Aralt, who was king of Norway, sent envoys to Muircheartach Ó Briain, and sent his own shoes with them, to command Muircheartach to place the shoes on his shoulders; and when the nobles who were with him saw this, they became greatly enraged, and they reproached him for having done this deed. 'I prefer to do this', said Muircheartach, 'to Maghnus's plundering any province of Ireland'. After this Maghnus got ready a large fleet and came from Norway to Ireland to injure and ruin that country ...[49]

Keating was attracted by the anecdote of the shoes to be worn by Muircheartach on his shoulders, but he omitted to specify the meaning of the action as explained by Hakluyt, 'that thereby it might appear unto them that he was subject unto King Magnus'.[50] Keating also omitted to mention Hakluyt's claim that Magnus, king of Norway, was 'interred near unto the Church of St Patrick in Armagh'.[51] Instead

46 *FFÉ*, iii, 346-50.   47 Stow, a Londoner, devoted much of his life to collecting books, manuscripts and other material on English literature, archaeology and history. In 1565 he produced a *Summarie of Englyshe Chronicles conteyning the true accompt of yeres wherein every Kyng of this Realme ... began theyr reigne, howe long they reigned; and what notable thynges hath bene done durynge theyr reygne*, and there were at least nine editions of this work published in his own lifetime. His *Chronicles* likewise proved popular and ran to several editions, and his reputation was further enhanced by the publication of his *Survey of London* (1598). Howes, who reedited the *Chronicles* after Stow's death, judged him as one who 'always protested never to have written either for malice, fear, or favour ... and that his only pains and care was to write truth' (cited in *DNB*, s.n.). Keating himself would have aspired to similar assessment of his own historical writings.   48 *FFÉ*, iii, 308-10.   49 Ibid., 309.   50 Cronin, 'Printed sources', p. 272.   51 Ibid., p. 272.

Keating highlighted the fact that Muircheartach was buried in Munster at the cathedral of Killaloe.[52] In *Foras feasa* the roles of Magnus and Muircheartach were moulded into a version that prioritised the O'Brien king rather than the archdiocese of Armagh. It was instances such as this which helped give the history its strong Munster bias. Keating's account also added a description of burial rites appropriate to a Christian king.

The variety of other miscellaneous references to printed works confirms that Keating must have had fairly easy access to a substantial collection of books when compiling his history. His preface to *Foras feasa* incorporated four references to the first volume of Samuel Daniel's history of England.[53] Keating's use of this material was a means of supplementing the information contained in the native record. Two of the citations drawn by Keating from this source dealt with the Romans in Britain, their exclusion from Ireland, and the opposition they faced from the Picts and Scots. A third reference related to the name 'Britannia'.[54] In each instance Keating accorded Daniel the same credibility he allowed to native sources, while noting approvingly that Daniel himself was among those authors who admitted that some aspects of their histories were 'but a conjecture or an opinion'.[55]

Keating was able to cite a specific page reference of Edward Grimston's *Generall historie of Spain*, in the edition of 1612, for the story of Brigus, the first king to obtain sovereignty over all Spain. The discussion which followed gives a clue as to why Keating incorporated such miscellaneous references to printed books in the course of his narrative. Keating linked the story of Brigus as given in Grimston with the *Leabhar gabhála* personality called Breoghan, grandfather of Míl of Spain from whom the Brigantes took their name.[56] He then offered the reader two stanzas by the poet Giolla Caomháin (d.1072) on Breoghan and his descendants. There was a complication however. The second stanza listed Bile as the youngest of Breoghan's ten sons. This did not suit Keating's scenario where Bile was father of Míl himself. He therefore countered the evidence of the poem by the simple but unsubstantiated statement that 'the authors of *our* records assert that he was the eldest of Breoghan's sons'.[57] He was here appealing to the idea of primacy of authority being given to written sources, but not actually producing the reference to substantiate his claim.

A clear impression of Keating's approach to his sources emerges here. The specific reference to a source, the English historian Grimston in this case, added credibility and authenticity to Keating's account of the royal Spanish pedigree of Míl, ancestor of the Gaeil. The reader was expected to accept that Brigus and Breoghan were the same person without further explanation. The next evidence offered was extracted from an eleventh-century poem beginning '*Gaedheal Glas ó dtáid*

---

52 *FFÉ*, iii, 311.   53 *The first part of the historie of England* (London, 1613). first published 1612 and reissued 1613. A second volume, from the reign of Stephen to the reign of Edward III, published in 1617, was not cited by Keating.   54 *FFÉ*, i, 7, 9, 25, 47.   55 Ibid., 47.   56 *FFÉ*, ii, 38–9.   57 *FFÉ*, ii, 40–1 (my italics). Grimston was the author of a range of 'national' histories in English, including works on the French and the Turks.

Gaedhil. The fact that one of these stanzas conflicted with the evidence of *Leabhar gabhála*[58] troubled Keating and he expediently chose to treat all three sources as equally reliable.

As in the case of Hakluyt, John Speed's *History of Great Britaine ... from Julius Caesar ... to King James*, published in 1611, with further editions through the 1620s and 1630s was used by Keating as a source of information not readily available in native sources.[59] One reference to Nennius was probably derived from Speed.[60] The *History of Great Britaine* may also have been the source of Keating's computations from Hebrew, Latin and Greek authors on the length of time from Adam to the birth of Christ. Keating's dates, given without any indication of source, agree with the dates given by Speed.[61] His difficulty in reconciling various sources on this point prompted him to explain his method:

> And since these chief authorities agree not with each other in the computation of the time which is from Adam to the birth of Christ, it is no wonder that there should be discrepancy among some of the antiquaries of Ireland about the same calculation. However, I have not found among them a computation I rather think to be accurate than the numbering which some of them make of four thousand, fifty and two years, for the time from Adam to the birth of Christ; and what I desire is to follow the standard author who comes nearest to this reckoning in the synchronism of the sovereigns, of the epochs, of the popes, and of the general councils at the end of the book in their own proper places.[62]

It seems clear from this that one of Keating's objectives in citing foreign authors was to supplement his text with information that placed the Irish material in an appropriate context. His method also allowed him to reaffirm the credibility of native sources. For example, having quoted a passage from Stow, on one occasion, he added 'I imagine that the account we shall give of Niall from the *seanchas* of Ireland will appear the more credible if I set down these things from a foreign chronicle'.[63] In such instances what mattered most was the status of the source cited rather than merely its content. He valued the work of some authors more highly than others, accepting some as 'standard' works. This attitude to particular published works, whether in Latin or English, suggests that Keating wanted the history of Ireland to be judged by international rather than native Irish standards of historical scholarship. It confirms that he was writing for readers whose cultural interests transcended the merely local.[64]

---

58 *Lebor Gabála*, ed. Macalister, iv, p. 260.   59 Published in 1611, with further editions through the 1620s and 1630s.   60 *FFÉ*, ii, 394. Other references to Nennius are derived by Keating from alternative secondary sources.   61 Book 1, p. 19 of his *History of Great Britaine*. Cronin, 'Printed sources', pp. 274-5.   62 *FFÉ*, i, 90-1.   63 *FFÉ*, ii, 388-9.   64 The prompt translation of the work into English (RIA, MS 24 G 16) and the subsequent translation into Latin (RIA, MS 24 I 5) each accompanied by a translator's preface as though ready for publication, suggests that others shared the view that *Foras*

That this strategy of citing well known and authoritative sources was a deliberate attempt to enhance the status and credibility of his narrative is further confirmed by the manner in which Keating approached the writings of Thomas Messingham. In 1624 Messingham's *Florilegium insulae sanctorum* was published in Paris. Its focus was on Ireland's best-known saints, particularly Patrick, Brigid and Colum Cille, but also included saints renowned for their activities in Europe, notably Columbanus, Fursey, Gall and Kilian. The collection also included St Bernard's *Life of Malachy*. Messingham's stated purpose was to provide an example of devout living for Catholics and to convert heretics.[65] It is evident from his introduction, however, that it had the additional purpose of enhancing Ireland's image abroad. Although Keating owed a clear debt to this source, particularly in his discussion of the names of Ireland, he never mentioned Messingham's name.[66] Keating quoted a range of authors to support his contention that Scotia was a former name for Ireland. The sources he cited were Jonas, Bede, Orosius, Serarius, Capgrave, Marianus Scotus, Caesarius and Buchanan.[67] The arguments used to demonstrate that Scotia was the name of Ireland were those given in the introductory chapter of *Florilegium*, and there is a very close correlation between the references and quotations in both works.[68] The names of Ireland, recorded by ancient writers, which Keating gave at the beginning of *Foras feasa*, were also given in the introductory chapter of the *Florilegium*. These similarities clearly point to the likelihood that the *Florilegium* was Keating's source for these quotations. If so, Keating probably embarked on these sections of *Foras feasa* after the publication of the *Florilegium* in 1624. Indeed, Messingham's work on the saints of Ireland may well have been part of the inspiration that prompted Keating to present the story of the kings of Ireland to a wider audience.

Keating's failure to cite Messingham as a source is perhaps paralleled by his failure to mention his reliance on the work of sermon writer Pierre de Besse in his *Trí bior-ghaoithe an bháis*.[69] It would probably be unfair to accuse Keating of plagiarism in either instance. He was following the accepted practice of his day, and he normally only cited authors whose authority was well established. He would not have regarded the work of his own contemporaries as having the same authority to convince his audience as the *Leabhar gabhála* or the Venerable Bede.

---

feasa should be transmitted widely. See below, ch. 10.   **65** Messingham, *Florilegium*, sig a, iii(v).   **66** Cronin, 'Printed sources', pp. 263, 268.   **67** *FFÉ*, ii, 374-81. Jonas, *Life of Columcille* [recte Columbanus], ch. 2; Bede, *History of the English church and people*, translated by Leo Sherley-Price (rev. ed. London, 1968) book 1, ch. 1 and his writings on saints; Oriosus, book 1, ch. 2; Serarius on St Kilian and St Boniface; Capgrave on St Colum; Marianus Scotus on St Kilian, Caesarius, *Dialogorum*, book 12, ch. 38; Buchanan, *De rerum Scoticarum historia*, book 2.   **68** Messingham cited Jonas, *Life of Columbanus*, which Keating incorrectly interpreted as being a life of Columcille, *FFÉ*, ii, 374 (Bodl., Fairfax MS 29, f.91r). Messingham also cited book 1 of Bede's *history*, and his *Martyrology*; Oriosus, *Adversus Paganos*, book 1 ch 2; Serarius, Life of St Kilian, and Life of St Boniface; Capgrave, The beginning of his *Life of Colum*; Marianus Scotus on St Kilian; Caesarius; and Buchanan, *Historia*, ch. 2. Cronin, 'Printed sources'.   **69** See above ch. 3, and see also Cunningham, 'Sources of *Trí bior-ghaoithe an bháis*'.

Bede's *Historia ecclesiastica gentis Anglorum,* a history of the English church and people, was originally written in the eighth century. It retained the respect of later generations because of its careful attention to primary sources and its conscious effort to distinguish historical fact from fiction.[70] It was first printed in the late fifteenth century and was regularly reissued in western Europe during the sixteenth century. It seems likely that the edition of Bede's history used by Keating was either that printed at Basle in 1563 or the one printed at Cologne in 1601.[71] The work itself may have formed part of the inspiration for Keating having embarked on a history of Ireland that was, in part, a history of the Irish church.

Bede was not among those foreign writers whom Keating accused of making hostile comments about Ireland. Instead his work was used to support Keating's preferred theory on the origin of the Picts and Scots, as descendants of the Gael. Keating did not feel it necessary to explain to his readers who Bede was, assuming they would be familiar with the work of one of the western world's best known historians.[72] This was a justifiable approach, given that Bede's history had long been available in Irish translation. It was said to be one of the texts in the highly regarded 'Psalter of Cashel', and would probably have been accessible to scholars in Keating's neighbourhood in the sixteenth century in the manuscript now known as Bodleian Laud Misc. 610.[73]

While agreeing with Bede's contention that 'The Pictish race came from Scythia, as is stated, in a small fleet of long vessels',[74] Keating modified the story to give it a southern focus. He claimed that 'it was not in the north of Ireland they landed, but at the mouth of Innbhear Slainghe in the harbour of Loch Gormain'.[75] His source for this alternative geography of migration was given as the Psalter of Cashel.[76] Bede also featured in *Foras feasa* as an authoritative source in support of the idea that the Irish were initially called Scots, and that Ireland was the true homeland of the Scots. While Keating's array of other lesser known sources on this point of Scots origins was apparently derived from Thomas Messingham, he returned to Bede's evidence on other matters in a way which indicates that he particularly valued Bede as a reliable source. Keating did not rely on Messingham for most of his references to Bede. Keating reminded his readers that Bede lived *c.*AD 700 and was thus an eyewitness to some of the events he described.[77] Bede was the source of Keating's information that Pope Celestinus had sent Palladius to Ireland in AD 430 'as first bishop to the Scots who believed in Christ'.[78] Bede was also a

70 Bede, *History of the English church and people,* ed. Sherley-Pryce, preface. **71** His chapter references match these two editions. The edition of 1563 contains the *Life of Columbanus* by Jonas to which Keating also refers, citing Bede and Jonas in succession (Cronin, 'Printed sources', pp. 260-1). However, it has already been noted that the references to Jonas were probably derived second hand from Messingham, *Florilegium,* see *FFÉ,* ii, 374-6. **72** *FFÉ,* ii, 58. Although he did give book and chapter numbers, not all of Keating's citations from Bede are accurate, and one item he claimed to be derived from that source would appear to be cited in error (Cronin, 'Printed sources', p. 263). **73** Próinséas Ní Chatháin, 'Bede's ecclesiastical history in Irish', *Peritia,* iii (1984), pp. 115-30. **74** *FFÉ,* ii, 110-11. **75** Ibid., 110-11. **76** Ibid., 108-10. **77** Ibid., 376. **78** *FFÉ,* iii, 16-17.

source for the information relating to St Colum Cille having gone to Scotland in AD 565, and for the detail of the unusual ecclesiastical arrangments on Iona whereby priests and even bishops were subject to the abbot,[79] a feature Keating might have chosen to ignore if found in a less reputable source. Other ecclesiastical details derived from Bede relate to the Pelagian heresy together with a very brief allusion to the controversy over the date of Easter.

Bede was also cited on a secular matter in relation to incursions made by the British into Ireland under the leadership of Berthus, in AD 684, an episode which culminated in the battle of Ráth Mór in Magh Line, and the death of Cumascach, king of the Cruithin.[80] In this episode Bede's rather negative view of the Gael as plunderers was accepted by Keating and incorporated into *Foras feasa*.[81] Bede's work contained other details on Irish matters which Keating did not find room for in his history, such as an account of St Fursey[82] and most of the detail of the Easter controversy.[83] Keating's treatment of Adamnán and the Easter controversy was very brief. He fixed the date of Adamnán's coming to Ireland in his chronology, but did not explain the context. Having consulted Bede, he cannot have been ignorant of the episode, but chose to omit it. Likewise most of the detail on Irish saints contained in Bede's *Historia* was omitted by Keating.[84] It seems likely that such material was omitted because it concerned church history rather than the history of the Irish kingdom, and can be assumed to have been left out because irrelevant rather than because unpalatable.

Next to Bede, the English historian for whom Keating had greatest regard was probably William Camden. His *Britannia*, a history of Britain, was first published in Latin in 1586. It had reached its sixth, extended, edition by 1607.[85] Although the work was published in English translation in 1610, Keating's quotations from Camden are from the Latin version.[86] Camden was mentioned frequently in the preface to *Foras feasa*. Three instances where Camden was criticised feature material derived from Giraldus Cambrensis.[87] Most of the remaining references to Camden's *Britannia* show that Keating respected Camden's authority and reliability as an historian. It is evident that Keating had himself consulted this work, and his citations from it are accurate. Having mentioned Strabo, St Jerome, Solinus and Pomponius Mela and 'many other ancient foreign writers' who wrote rashly without evidence concerning Ireland, Keating drew on Camden to refute them. Supported by an extract from Camden's *Britannia* in Latin, he made the case that

79 Ibid., 86.   80 Ibid., 138-40.   81 Bede, *Historia*, book 1, ch. 14; *FFÉ*, ii, 394.   82 Bede, *History of the English church and people*, book 3, ch. 19.   83 Bede, *History of the English church and people*, book 5, ch. 15. The controversy over the difference between Rome and the Celtic churches in calculating the date of Easter was resolved by the synod of Whitby, AD 664.   84 The material in *Foras feasa* on St Colmán in Inishbofin (*FFÉ*, iii, 138) may have ultimately derived from Bede, *History of the English church and people*, book 4, ch. 4, but remains unattributed.   85 Anne Cronin established that the edition of 1607 was the first to contain all the material cited by Keating from this source, so that is probably the edition he used (Cronin, 'Printed sources'). Subsequent editions were published in Holland in 1617 and in 1639.   86 Cronin, 'Printed sources', pp. 250-1.   87 *FFÉ*, i, 58-60.

'we have not credible witness of these things'.[88] Quotations from Camden were also presented to support Keating's argument that Ireland had never been under the authority of the Roman Empire.[89]

In rejecting Meredith Hanmer's statement on Parthalón and the coming of the Gael, Keating cited the 'ancient record of Ireland' (though without actually mentioning any specific document). He then introduced Camden to validate the authority of the 'ancient record', specifically citing Camden's comments on the antiquity of the historical records of the Irish.[90] Similarly, following a defence of some of the customs of Gaelic society against the criticisms of Sir John Davies, Keating proceeded to cite Camden's *Britannia* as a source of evidence for the status and privileges of poets, brehons, antiquaries and physicians in Ireland.

> These princes (he says) have their own lawgivers, whom they call 'brehons', their historians for writing their actions, their physicians, their poets, whom they name 'bards', and their singing men, and land appointed to each one of these, and each of them dwelling on his own land, and, moreover, every one of them of a certain family apart; that is to say, the judges of one special tribe and surname, the antiquaries or historians of another tribe and surname, and so to each one from that out, they bring up their children and their kinsfolk, each one of them in his own art, and there are always successors of themselves in these arts.[91]

He concluded that Camden's evidence made clear that proper provision was made in Ireland for the arts. Citing an external source here served a function other than mere cumulation of information. A foreign writer's favourable comments on Gaelic society were deemed to be particularly worthy of mention. Keating's own elaboration on the reasons for the rules guarding the professions in Gaelic society was presented as an elucidation of Camden's statement of fact. Presenting material in this way ensured that the argument of *Foras feasa* was difficult for foreign commentators to undermine. Here, as elsewhere, Keating was unable to cite a written Gaelic document supporting his assertions and this made Camden's comments especially valuable in enhancing Keating's credibility as an historian. Keating concluded his discussion of this point by referring to the immunity of druids in France noted by Julius Caesar.[92] Although it was not so attributed by Keating, this detail too was taken from Camden's *Britannia*.[93] In such instances it emerges that Keating's reliance on Camden is greater than he admits.[94]

88 Ibid., 10-13.   89 Ibid., 16-18.   90 Ibid., 44-5; William Camden, *Britannia sive regnorum Angliae, Scotiae, Hiberniae ... descriptio* (6th ed. 1607), p. 728.   91 *FFÉ*, i, 70-71.   92 Caesar, *History*, book 6. 93 Cronin, 'Printed sources'. It is most likely therefore that all Keating's references to Caesar's *History* are second-hand. *FFÉ*, i, 72; *FFÉ*, ii, 63.   94 Other instances of references derived second hand from Camden have been detailed by Anne Cronin (Cronin, 'Printed sources', pp. 253-4) who suggests that Keating's occasional quotations from 'a certain author' may also have been derived from Camden, *Britannia*. Keating asserts that some Latin authors say that Gaedheal was the son of Argus or of

Although Keating had an obvious respect for Camden he still included him in his list of hostile foreign writers.[95] The discrepancy between this polemic and the reality of Keating's debt to Camden raises questions about Keating's purpose in prefacing his history with such a controversial *dionbhrollach*. While the criticism levelled at writers such as Giraldus Cambrensis and Richard Stanihurst may have been warranted on ideological grounds, overall the case against foreign authors was less clear cut than Keating implied.

The principal target for attack in the preface to *Foras feasa* was the Welsh author, Giraldus Cambrensis. His two works on Ireland, *Topographia Hiberniae* and his *Expugnatio Hiberniae*, had been written in the late twelfth century. They had circulated in manuscript form during the later middle ages, and an abridged version of the *Expugnatio* was available in Irish.[96] Giraldus's work became widely available to Keating's contemporaries when published at Frankfurt in 1602 in William Camden's composite work entitled *Anglica, Hibernica, Normannica, Cambrica, a veteribus scripta*. Keating evidently had access to this printed version since he used it for material other than Giraldus Cambrensis.[97] The *Topographia Hiberniae* had earlier been issued by the Catholic palesman Richard Stanihurst, with extensive annotations, as an appendix to his *De rebus in Hibernia gestis*.[98] While Keating was probably familiar with Stanihurst's version also, it was the edition of Giraldus as published in Camden's *Anglica* that he cited in his history.[99]

Although Keating was highly critical of Giraldus in the preface to *Foras feasa*, with seven negative references as against five instances where the evidence of Giraldus was accepted, he often accepted Giraldus' version of events when required to support the main narrative.[100] In one instance in the opening section of the narrative, having described the division of Ireland made by the Fir bolg, Keating added 'Cambrensis agrees with this division in the book he wrote of an account of Ireland where he says "*in quinque enim portiones (inquit) fere aequales antiquitus haec regio divisa fuit* (in five parts, indeed, almost equal (he says), this country was anciently divided)"'.[101] In the closing section of the history Keating drew extensively, if silently, on *Expugnatio Hiberniae* as a source for his account of the Normans. Thus, despite Keating's attack on Giraldus as a hostile writer, who had presented Ireland in an unfavourable light, Keating willingly used Giraldus's version of events when required for his own narrative. It is only in the preface that Keating began seriously to evaluate Giraldus's negative influence on the image of Ireland.

Cecrops. It is likely in this instance that Camden and Buchanan are the 'Latin authors' in question. Camden, *Britannia*, p. 85; George Buchanan, *De rerum Scoticarum historia* (1582), p. 13.   **95** *FFÉ*, i, 4.   **96** Stokes, 'The Irish abridgment of the '*Expugnatio Hibernica*', pp. 77-115. Bodl., Rawl. MS B 475; TCD, MS 1298.   **97** Cronin, 'Printed sources'.   **98** Antwerp, 1584. See introduction to *Holinshed's Irish Chronicle*, ed. Liam Miller and Eileen Power (Dublin, 1979), p. 9.   **99** Most of his page references correspond to the Frankfurt 1602 edition (Cronin, 'Printed sources', p. 237).   **100** Cronin, 'Printed sources', pp. 237-41.   **101** *FFÉ*, i, 107.

II

Keating's polemical introduction consciously sought to present *Foras feasa* in oppo-̇ sitional terms. The key focus for Keating's wrath in the preface, was not a for- eigner, however, but a fellow Catholic of Anglo-Norman descent, Richard Stanihurst, and a near contemporary of his own. Stanihurst was born in 1547, into the elite of Pale society, the son of a Speaker in the Irish Parliament. He spent his early life in Dublin and was educated at Peter White's school in Kilkenny. He went to the University of Oxford in 1563 where he came under the influence of Edmund Campion. He completed his formal education at the Inns of Court, and returned to Dublin.[102] His link with Campion resulted in him working on the Irish section of Holinshed's chronicles, which Keating refers to as 'Stanihurst's English chronicle'. After leaving Ireland for the continent, and having modified his views on Ireland and the Irish from the altered perspective of mainland Europe, Stanihurst's major historical work, *De rebus in Hibernia gestis* was published at Antwerp in 1584. Keating's references to the writings of Stanihurst are principally to *De rebus*.[103] Although this work was considerably less critical of Gaelic society than the writer's earlier contributions to Holinshed's chronicles it nevertheless offended Keating's sensibilities.

Though they were both Old English, their divergent views are better explained by contrasting cultural environments than by reference to shared ethnicity.[104] Ethnicity was evidently of little concern to Keating when he criticised some of Stanihurst's assertions about the Irish people. Keating linked Stanihurst directly with hostile writers on Ireland. He was specifically criticised for lack of knowledge of Irish affairs.[105] His ignorance of Irish geography and of the contents of the *Leabhar gabhála* and other records of Irish history were singled out for special mention.[106] His rejection of native Irish historical tradition was noted. From Keating's perspective, that a writer should attempt to write about Ireland in igno- rance of the *Leabhar gabhála* and the *Dinnsheanchas*, fundamental elements of his- torical Gaelic scholarship, was inconceivable. Stanihurst's criticism of lawgivers and physicians[107] was challenged by Keating's assertion that Stanihurst neither under- stood those professions nor the language in which Gaelic legal and medical knowl- edge were recorded. This was not so much an attack on Stanihurst *per se* as a spir- ited defence of the learned families of Gaelic Ireland with whom the written records of the Irish past, legal, medical and historical, were directly associated. The point was made that Stanihurst did not belong to that traditional cultural elite, and was therefore ignorant of the traditions of Gaelic learning. Stanihurst 'was not capable of reading either the law of the land, or the medicine in their own lan- guage, and if they had been read to him, he had no comprehension of them'.[108]

---

102 Lennon, *Stanihurst*, ch. 2.   103 *De rebus in Hibernia gestis*. Not reissued subsequently. See Lennon, *Stanihurst* for translation of book 1 only.   104 Bradshaw, 'Geoffrey Keating, apologist of Irish Ireland', pp. 166-90.   105 *FFÉ*, i, 32-3.   106 Ibid., 30, 32.   107 Lennon, *Stanihurst*, pp. 149, 153-6.   108 *FFÉ*, i, 39.

Keating was not merely accusing Stanihurst of not being able to read Irish – a rare enough skill, though more common by Stanihurst's day[109] – but rather of having no comprehension of the source texts of Irish antiquity.[110] 'He never understood the books in which they were written ... because Gaelic alone was their proper language, and he was out and out ignorant of it'.[111] This failure meant that Stanihurst fell short of contemporary standards of Renaissance historical scholarship.

In spite of this criticism of Stanihurst, there were also occasions, even in the preface to *Foras feasa*, when Keating used Stanihurst's positive statements about the Irish people in support of his own case. He quoted directly from Stanihurst on the hospitality shown by the Irish and again on their religiosity.[112] More significantly, in the main narrative of *Foras feasa* all of Keating's citations from Stanihurst presented his evidence as valid.[113] Keating relied on Stanihurst for some of the detail of the activities of the Normans, as well as for one version of the episode of the papal bull given by Pope Adrian IV to King Henry II.[114]

III

While some sources were included for polemical effect as much as for the significance of the historical material they recorded, the work of Polydor Virgil (*c*.1470-1535) entitled *De rerum inventoribus* was used by Keating specifically for its advice on the writing of history. It is probable that Keating had encountered *De rerum inventoribus* as part of his curriculum of study in France. First published in 1498, and with many editions through the sixteenth century, it is likely that the version Keating had encountered was the expurgated edition printed at Rome in 1576. The full work had been deemed to contain sections offensive to the clergy and was placed on the index of forbidden books. Keating's use of *De rerum inventoribus* was limited to two references on the proper method of the historian. Keating was keen to follow the advice of Polydor Virgil that the historian should not assert anything false and should not omit to set down every truth so that he could be trusted.[115] Although Polydor Virgil's later work, the *Historia Anglia* (1534) was the closest English equivalent of Hector Boece's 'national history' of the Scottish people, Keating did not mention or cite it. Nevertheless, it is evident that Keating had particular respect for Polydor Virgil's reputation as a historian, and his failure to men-

109 Katharine Simms, 'Literacy and the Irish bards', in Huw Pryce (ed.), *Literacy in medieval Celtic societies* (Cambridge, 1998), pp. 238-58.   110 *FFÉ*, i, 38-9.   111 Ibid.   112 Ibid., 20-1, 60-1.   113 *FFÉ*, iii, 332-3, 350-1, 358-9, 360-1, 362-3, 364-5.   114 Though Keating described the source as '*croinic Bhéarla Stanihurst*' ('Stanihurst's English chronicle') the detail he cites is found both in Stanihurst's *De rebus*, and in Holinshed's *Historie of Ireland*, ii. (It would probably not have been known to Keating that Stanihurst's contribution relied on Campion's history.) Since Keating specified the 'Engilsh ' chronicle of Stanihurst, it would appear that he used a version of Holinshed (probably the 1577 edition, or a manuscript version). It seems unlikely that he used the three-volume edition by Hooker published in 1587, since he does not cite Hooker at all (Cronin, 'Printed sources', p. 245).   115 *FFÉ*, i, 56; Vergil, *De Rerum* i, pt. xi, p. 56 (1561 ed.) (Cronin, 'Printed sources').

tion this second work is most probably because it lacked relevant Irish material on pre-Norman topics.

Occasionally, Keating's citations from particular publications were chosen for rather more subtle reasons, and none more so than Sir John Davies' *A discovery of the true causes why Ireland was never entirely subdued until the beginning of His Majesty's reign.* This book first published in 1612 was written by a prominent English member of the Irish administration.[116] The book criticised the Gaelicisation of early generations of settlers in Ireland. It strongly advocated anglicisation as the cure for Ireland's ills. Keating took issue with Davies on the matter of the Irish legal system. Refusing to adopt Davies' language of conquest, he astutely chose to quote the closing sentence from Davies' tract to support the case of the law-abiding inclinations of the Irish.

> There is no nation of people under the sun that doth love equal and indifferent justice better than the Irish, or will rest better satisfied with the execution thereof, although it be against themselves, soe as they may have the protection and benefit of the law when upon just occasion they do desire it.[117]

Keating cannot have been unaware that such a sentence, out of context, was not an accurate reflection of the tenor of Davies' argument. In the preface to *Foras feasa*, Keating ignored Davies' conceptual framework of a 'conquest', highlighting instead the nature of Gaelic 'civilisation'. He strove to use his explanation of the nature of Gaelic society in the past as the basis on which to present the Irish, especially the native Irish in this particular instance, in a more favourable light. He defended, in particular, three key elements of traditional Gaelic social organisation, tanistry, gavelkind and *éric*.[118] Keating explained why the circumstances of the past, where warfare was commonplace, made these three elements of the legal system necessary in Ireland. While he agreed with Sir John Davies that they were no longer suited to contemporary society, he insisted 'they were necessary at the time they were established'. Discussing the system of compensation known as *ér c* he concluded 'it is not honest in John Davies to find fault with the native jurisprudence because of it'. Similarly he insisted in relation to the other two customs 'there was no way of doing without them in Ireland when they were appointed'.[119]

Keating showed considerable understanding here not just of the way Gaelic society worked and of the reasons why particular legal structures had evolved in that society. He was also aware of the significance of the element of anachronism

116 Sir John Davies was born in Wiltshire and had ten years experience of Irish government when his work was published. Keating referred to *Discovery of the true causes* as Davies' first book on Ireland, indicating that he was aware of the existence of other writings by the same author. These presumably included the work published in 1615 under the title *Reports and cases* which contained much historical and antiquarian detail about Ireland in addition to the legal information that was its primary focus. 117 *FFÉ*, iii, 368-9. 118 *FFÉ*, i, 66-71. 119 Ibid., 70-1.

in Sir John Davies' analysis. He was conscious that in Ireland in the 1630s the system being described by Davies was no longer the norm. He did not concede that Davies was writing about the past rather than the present. And rightly so, since Davies' text had been using the past to justify current political strategies.[120]

Keating only rarely looked beyond the British Isles for printed works containing references to Ireland. Nevertheless occasional references to the works of European authors indicate that he was aware of the wider world of historical scholarship, and was keen to cite material from such external sources where appropriate. Caesarius Heisterbacensis (*c*.1180-1240) *Dialogus magnus visionum atque miraculorum*,[121] was quoted in connection with St Patrick's purgatory. Since the purgatory was more renowned in Europe than at home it is not surprising that Keating took this material from a continental source. Keating confused the author, however, with the much earlier Caesarius of Arles (*c*.470-543), a mistake which undermined his argument. As with other continental sources, Keating was probably working from extracts rather than a full version of this text.[122]

The chronology contained in Cardinal Robert Bellarmine's *De scriptoribus ecclesiasticis ... cum chronologia* (1612) was used as the basis for the synchronisms, given as an appendix to *Foras feasa*.[123] A direct Latin quotation from Bellarmine was cited in relation to the bestowal of the Island of Ireland on Henry II by Pope Adrian IV,[124] the quotation being taken from the *varia* attached to the *Chronologia*.[125] This incidental use of passing references to a range of foreign authors, interwoven with his synthesis of native sources, gave *Foras feasa* the semblance of being a truly innovative Irish history.

IV

John Roche, bishop of Ferns, reported to the Franciscan Luke Wadding in Rome in 1631 that 'One Doctor Keating laboureth much, as I hear say, in compiling Irish notes towards a history in Irish. ... I have no interest in the man, for I never saw him, for he dwelleth in Munster'.[126] While Roche's comments on the one hand highlight the restricted geographical sphere in which many individuals lived out their lives, it is simultaneously evidence that there was already an interest in Keating's writings, as far away as Rome, before he had put the final touches to his *Foras feasa ar Éirinn*.[127] The fact that he was writing in Irish not Latin, however, may have increased Roche's inclination to be dismissive of his efforts. Nevertheless, the kind of history he wrote reflected the values of the age, and was much more than just an attempt to give permanent form to the moral and historical tales that

120 On Davies see Hans Pawlisch, *Sir John Davies and the conquest of Ireland: a study in legal imperialism* (Cambridge, 1985).   121 First printed 1481 with a cluster of later editions in 1591, 1599, 1601 and 1604/5.   122 Cronin, 'Printed sources', pp. 271-2.   123 *FFÉ*, iv, 121-49; ii, 8-9.   124 *FFÉ*, iii, 348-9.   125 Cronin, 'Printed sources', p. 273.   126 Jennings (ed.), *Wadding papers*, p. 544.   127 See also Thomas Strange in HMC, *Franciscan Mss*, p. 6.

were his stock in trade. By communicating his ideas in writing he shaped the thinking of his own and later generations of Irish people about the world in which they lived, its past and the world that was to come. By combining native and foreign sources, he was creating an Irish history that had a new focus. He was writing for an Irish people whose horizons were wider than those of the compilers of the *Leabhar gabhála*. While building on the flexible narrative framework of an historical kingdom of Ireland that underlay the *Leabhar gabhála*, Keating was writing a history that would give recognition to that kingdom's status in the wider world.

He was embracing the literate world, addressing Irish audiences he believed to be immersed in a world of reading.[128] One of the technical ways in which *Foras feasa* differed fundamentally from the *Leabhar gabhála* tradition was in its author's assumption that he was addressing an audience living in a world of authoritative written texts in which assertions made could be compared and contrasted and thereby verified or refuted.[129]

It is evident that Keating himself was thoroughly immersed in the world of books, keeping abreast of the latest publications as well as absorbing the detail of ancient manuscripts. He was not writing narrative history as an exercise in preservation; he was providing the readers in the community in which he lived with a work of historical interpretation that would fill a gap in the reading materials available to his own contemporaries.[130]

Keating consciously limited the size of *Foras feasa* in the hope that he was thereby making its subsequent transmission more feasible.[131] His skilful summary of the available manuscript and printed sources attracted readers from a variety of backgrounds. He probably lived on for only a few years after the completion of his history, but in the hands of scribes, translators and readers the *Foras feasa* soon took on a life of its own. In subsequent decades Keating's history of Ireland reached audiences he could scarcely have imagined, his words had an impact that transcended his own initial objectives, and his work became known, posthumously, far beyond the Suir valley from whence he came.

128 He was aware for instance of the potential influence of one of Stanihurst's works then in print for circulation in Ireland *FFÉ*, i, 42; see also Katharine Simms, 'Literacy and the Irish bards'. 129 *FFÉ*, ii, 398-401. 130 Ó Buachalla, '*Annála ríoghachta Éireann* agus *Foras feasa ar Éirinn*'. 131 *FFÉ*, i, 94-5. See below, ch. 6.

6

Irishness and the recall of the past

Nations need myths and pasts if they are to have a future, and such pasts cannot be forged out of nothing, nor can myths that will have resonance be fabricated. (Smith, *The ethnic origins of nations*, p. 214)

The life and world of Geoffrey Keating as seen through his writings were considered in part one of this study. Part two adopts a thematic approach to the work of Geoffrey Keating, assessing the significance of his writing as a guide to beliefs and attitudes in Irish society in a period of transition from medieval to modern. Attitudes to history, the contemporary purpose of origin myths, and the motivations for attachments to language and place are among the themes examined through the medium of his writings in this and the following chapter. His texts also reflect political, social and moral values in seventeenth-century Irish society, and these themes are discussed in chapters eight and nine.

I

The theology of Trent was not the only inheritance of those from Ireland who studied in seminaries and universities on continental Europe in the early seventeenth century. Living abroad, they necessarily saw Ireland from a different perspective. Their sense of home was no longer focussed exclusively on a particular locality within Ireland; they developed a more abstract sense of the island of Ireland as their homeland. This changed perspective is reflected, for instance, in the *Annála ríoghachta Éireann* produced under the direction of Irish Franciscans working from Louvain. These annals were envisaged as relating to the whole island rather than a specific region such as had been the case with the earlier *Annals of Loch Cé* or the *Annals of Ulster*. This sense of the whole island of Ireland as homeland finds expression in Keating's writing also.

A student like Geoffrey Keating would have arrived in Europe with ideas about his own ethnic and national identity formed out of the experience of living in a predominantly Old English region of Munster where Butler influence was significant, where the Keating family network was, for him, the most important set of social relationships, and where Gaelic families like the Meic Craith were an established cultural group. Given the proximity of the Munster plantation he would probably also have been aware of English newcomers as outsiders in parts of Munster, but there would have been little reason for Keating to have developed any sense of a national rather than local identity while living in Munster.

Once in Europe, Keating was among strangers for the most part, people from more than one national group about whom he initially knew or understood little. Among the more readily available sources of information, or mis-information, about Ireland were the writings of Giraldus Cambrensis, written in the twelfth century, and Keating must have been among those Irish uncomfortable with the idea that unflattering stories of the Irish were being transmitted without challenge. Yet Keating's history of the Irish nation as presented in *Foras feasa* was no mere refutation of the adverse propaganda about the island of Ireland and its inhabitants found in Cambrensis' account. That was but one element of his broader purpose. Keating's was a complex text combining a justification of the altered perspective of Irishness formed on the continent with the provision of an origin myth for the Old English community from which he had emanated. It was written so as to be comparable to the histories other nations had available to them, drawing both on the example of other national histories and on the source material of Gaelic origin available at home. It filled the vacuum that had existed until then whereby the Gaelic community had an origin myth – in the form of the *Leabhar Gabhála* – but the descendants of the Anglo Normans did not. It was written as an inclusive history of the Irish Catholic people who saw themselves as '*Éireannaigh*'.

Keating's motives in compiling the *Foras feasa ar Éirinn* were formulated in the light of contemporary trends and fashions in historical writing. The text of *Foras feasa* is itself the best guide to his sources of inspiration. Apart from the example of other writings, he was also motivated by the political circumstances of the people among whom he lived in Tipperary, the people for whom the *Foras feasa* was written. If 'ideologies are fundamentally descriptions not of a present state, but of a past history',[1] then Keating's *Foras feasa* was designed to give his readers a meaningful interpretation of their world. In this way it can be regarded as a story that encapsulates the values Keating considered most important. In a pre-modern, semi-literate world, that a priest should be the one to tell the story of the community and be the arbiter of standards in terms of social and political order, morality and even language, was unexceptional.[2] Keating's historical writing, no less than his theological texts, grew out of his personal experience as priest and preacher in Ireland, combined with his personal experience of having once been an Irishman in exile.[3]

---

1 Anthony Kemp, *The estrangement of the past* (Oxford, 1991), p. 106.   2 H.J. Martin, *The history and power of writing* (Chicago, 1994), p. 377.   3 Anthony D. Smith, *Ethnic origins of nations* (Oxford, 1986), ch. 2.

Here followeth the Chief
Sirnames that are in Linster
of the Milesian race

O Conor faügie and all the branches
that spread from him

Kavanaghs
Kinsellaghs   Fitspatrick
Byrnes   Dunns
Tooles   Dempsyes
Ryans   Dwyers

And the branches that spread from
the above names the most part of the gentry
of Linster came from Charles the great King
of Ireland. and the Fitzpatricks came not
from him, for they parted at the man called
Breasall Breack, which was fourteen
degrees before Charles the great aforesaid

This Breasall Breack had two Sons
viz Lugh leigh fion and Conly, he being
King of Linster divided the Province betw—
ixt his said two Sons. from the River
Barrow

6 Late seventeenth-century copy of the Catholic 'A defence' translation of
Foras feasa ar Éirinn into English. NLI, MS G 288, p. 238

II

In sixteenth-century Europe the new trend in history writing was to emphasise the history of peoples, or individual nations. This was in contrast to the earlier preference for universal chronicles.[4] As European peoples began to perceive themselves as forming distinct nations and kingdoms, their intelligentsias turned to writing the kind of history that illustrated the descent and relationships of particular peoples and nations. In Ireland, the historians and scribes who compiled *Annála ríoghachta Éireann* were, like Keating, reformulating past history in line with current political perspectives. Others chose to write much more personal memoirs, such as Richard Bellings, secretary to the Catholic Confederation. His *History of the Irish Confederation and the war in Ireland* may have been partly a defence of his political activities in the Confederation in mid-century, but it was also a commentary on the 1670s.[5]

Keating's approach seems to have been based on a more fundamental understanding of the significance of history for the Irish Catholic nation. He himself stressed the importance of recording the history of Ireland and her inhabitants and clearly believed that Ireland's honourable reputation should be asserted in similar manner to that of other nations.[6] Hector Boece's *Scotorum historiae* certainly captured his imagination.[7] Kingship was a central concept in each text, with a list of kings forming the framework of the narrative. The king, whose sovereignty was derived from the people, was portrayed as a symbol of national unity[8] and the status of the clergy as advisors of the king was emphasised in each instance.[9] Where Boece's narrative history of Scotland drew on and was probably intended to replace the *Scotichronicon*,[10] Keating's similar narrative of Irish history was designed to rework the *Leabhar gabhála* into a narrative that took account of the concerns of Irish Catholics in the early seventeenth century. Keating may also have been following Boece in his decision to include fabulous stories in his history, and in his concern that the work might be widely disseminated.

The contemporary political agenda in early seventeenth-century Ireland created a need for new approaches to the past. The kind of history required by Catholics in Ireland, whatever their ethnic origin, in the reign of Charles I, was one which affirmed that theirs was the true faith, that Ireland was their homeland and they its rightful inhabitants, that Charles was their true king, and that God's providence would favour them in the future, as it evidently had done in the distant past.

Much of the history was probably written in the late 1620s, a time when negotiations were underway between the Old English and King Charles I concerning the Graces. Following the outbreak of war with Spain, the English king needed

---

4 Eric Cochrane, *Historians and historiography in the Italian renaissance* (Chicago, 1981), p. xv; May McKisack, *Medieval history in the Tudor age* (Oxford 1971), pp. 99-124.   5 *History of the Confederation and the war in Ireland*, ed. J.T. Gilbert (7 vols, Dublin, 1879); Raymond Gillespie, 'The social thought of Richard Bellings', in Micheál Ó Siochrú (ed.), *Kingdoms in crisis: Ireland in the 1640s: essays in honour of Donal Cregan* (Dublin, 2001), pp. 212-28.   6 *FFÉ*, i, 6, 76.   7 Royan, Boece, p. 87.   8 Ibid., pp. 107-8, 239-41.   9 Ibid., p. 79.   10 Ibid., p. 218.

financial support for his military activities. By May 1628 a series of Instructions and Graces had been agreed with the king in return for annual payments in support of the army. The Graces specified a range of detailed social and legal reforms designed to improve the ordinary conditions of life in Ireland. Among the more significant were changes in the functioning of the court of wards. Heirs taking possession of the estates were no longer to be required to take the oath of supremacy. Legal processes in relation to title to land were to be reviewed. New regulations were to be made regarding official, commercial, and ecclesiastical fees, a provision designed to deal with the issue of clandestine marriage and baptism. Other concessions related to new controls over the leasing of the crown's financial rights to private individuals, a system that had led to exploitation in the past. The core articles, however, were those relating to title to land. Most particularly, article 24 effectively removed the threat of land confiscation.[11]

In the context of *Foras feasa* as a reflection of Old English political sentiment, it was of particular significance that the Graces were negotiated directly with the king rather than through the Dublin government. The Old English in the 1620s believed that their declining political influence could only be reversed by direct appeal to the Stuart king. Their concern to assert their rights to property and influence in Ireland, revealed in the protracted negotiations over the Graces, could be enhanced by an appropriate historical underpinning of their political claims. While Keating did not overtly discuss the political dilemmas facing Old English Catholics in Ireland in the reign of Charles I, both the preface and the text of *Foras feasa* interpreted their world for them through the language of myth, religion and history.

For those Irish who regarded themselves as of Gaelic descent, and sought to interpret history in a way that legitimised current political allegiances, a retreat into Irish antiquity was an obvious and attractive option. It is rather less clear, at first glance, why the political circumstances of seventeenth-century Ireland would have prompted someone of Anglo-Norman descent, such as Geoffrey Keating, to embark on such an enterprise, concentrating almost exclusively on the history of Ireland before the arrival of his own Norman ancestors. Yet that is precisely what he did. His chronology began with Adam, and drew to a chose in the late twelfth century with the establishment of King Henry II as the holder of legitimate sovereign power in Ireland. In doing so he specifically rejected his fellow Old Englishman, Richard Stanihurst, who sought to disregard the significance of the Gaelic heritage in early modern Ireland.

If Keating's history was written with the aim of formulating an ideology, or creating 'a purposeful nation', 'a community of history and destiny in charge of its political fate', what was to be the nature of that 'nation'?[12] That nation, as perceived by Keating was a community of 'Éireannaigh': persons born in Ireland. It

11 Aidan Clarke, *The Old English in Ireland, 1625-42* (London, 1966), pp. 47-52.   12 Smith, *The ethnic origins of nations*, p. 219.

included all those of Gaelic or Anglo-Norman descent who were Irish-born and
Catholic. It excluded those who were not Irish-born, in particular the recently
arrived, usually Protestant, settlers. It disregarded the minority who were Old
English and Protestant. In this sense the history was designed to define a select
'nation' in opposition to others who were deemed to be outside of, and hostile to,
that nation.

In *Trí bior-ghaoithe an bháis* Keating warned his audience not to make an
enemy of God for the sake of transitory friendship on earth.[13] In particular, he
noted the human failing that made people want what was forbidden them. He suggested that those who had given in to heresy had given in to temptation, thereby
warning Catholics not to be tempted to abandon their faith for the sake of worldly
political or financial gain.[14]

The distinctive ideology being formulated by reference to a Christian antiquity,
and foreshadowed by a heroic pre-Christian era back to the beginning of time, was
designed to assert Catholic confidence in the validity of their religious allegiances.
That this was designed to persuade Catholics to keep their distance from the
authorities who sought to ensure their adherence to the state church is supported
by the political stance evident in *Trí bior-ghaoithe an bháis*.[15] The same ideology
underpinned *Foras feasa*. The use of an historical narrative rather than a political
tract for this purpose was significant. It meant that the reformulation and validation of Catholic identity was linked to a wider reconstruction of the historical context within which Irish identity was defined. It was addressed to audiences who
were expected to understand that their Irishness and their Catholicism were intrinsically intertwined through their heroic and Christian past. The narrative form and
its combination of myth and history helped integrate into a coherent unity the various elements of what it meant to be Irish and Catholic.

The story of the origins of a Christian people was one in which a sense of continuity with the past had a particular significance. Commitment to the Christian
tradition necessarily involved a commitment to history, because Christianity was a
religion in which history mattered.[16] Keating, like James Ussher,[17] believed it was
necessary for a Christian community to have a history that enriched their understanding of their religious allegiances, duties, and obligations. *Foras feasa* provided
just such a history for the people of Ireland, firmly linking the contemporary
reader, through history, back to their biblical origins.

Ancient biblical history linked people to a particular view of the early church
and early society. Those seventeenth-century historians who chose to write ancient
history were principally concerned with establishing continuities.[18] The sustained
narrative, progressing through time, conveyed a sense of a nation with a long past.

---

13 *TBB*, ll. 3550-6. 14 *TBB*, book 2, ch. 6. 15 *TBB*, l. 3549. 16 Owen Chadwick, *Catholicism and
history* (Cambridge, 1978), p. 2. 17 James Ussher, *A discourse of the religion anciently professed by the
Irish and British* (Dublin, 1631). 18 By analogy, historians such as Hugo Grotius and Pieter Hooft
(seventeenth-century Dutch) who wrote contemporary histories rather than antiquarian chronicles were
usually concerned to emphasise discontinuity and change.

The modern nation was underpinned by its ability to trace itself back to its origins at the beginning of time.[19] *Foras feasa* began with Adam, devoted the larger part of the text to the era of paganism, and continued a long narrative sweep through to the twelfth century. Keating did this to show that his people were the inheritors of an illustrious past, the proud possessors of a very ancient history. That long history defined his people, revealed to them who they were, and demonstrated to all the world that the Irish were an ancient and worthy nation.

Foras feasa focussed on a kingdom of Ireland and the two peoples whom Keating perceived to be rightfully part of that kingdom. It linked those two peoples together in one Christian history. Through skilful use of placelore it linked those peoples to the land of Ireland. By associating the people with the land, their implicit right to be permanently linked to that land was given an historical validity.[20] Through the genealogical framework, with its emphasis on affinity rather than difference, a sense of belonging was nurtured.[21] Through the precise naming of the specific ancestor from whom kin groups were descended, families were linked together in the community of the nation as constructed through its history.

The *Leabhar gabhála* already provided an Irish origin myth that was biblically based, and could easily be reused as the basis of an Irish Catholic origin myth. Versions of the text, in either its verse or prose forms, could be found in some of the most highly regarded medieval manuscript compilations available to Irish historians in the seventeenth century. Acceptance of this framework allowed Keating scope to retell well-known stories of heroes of old without diminishing the idea of a Christian kingdom, thus meeting the need of the people for an heroic past. Heroes, as the representatives of a more perfect past, embodied the ideals valued by people in the present.[22] The retelling of stories of such heroes in a narrative history helped re-imagine a golden age that allowed the Irish Catholic 'nation' root itself in a past it could claim as its own.[23] The emphasis on continuity through the ages had a religious purpose, establishing that the Catholic church was the true successor to the church of Patrick. The idea of an Irish Catholic nation was a new construction of the seventeenth century, a new kind of 'nation' in search of an appropriate past.

Since the framework of *Leabhar gabhála* facilitated the legitimisation of newcomers establishing themselves in Ireland as their homeland, it had a particular relevance for those of Anglo-Norman descent, whom Keating was able to present as the final wave of settlers who had long ago chosen to make Ireland their homeland and thereby establish their credentials as *Éireannaigh*.

At a secular level, an origin myth that portrayed the Old English as having long ago been legitimately absorbed into an ancient kingdom, where the rule of law was

---

19 See Royan, Boece, 1996, p. 173, and Roger Mason 'Chivalry and citizenship: aspects of national identity in Renaissance Scotland', in Roger Mason and Norman Macdougall (eds), *People and power in Scotland: essays in honour of T.C. Smout* (Edinburgh, 1992), pp. 50-73. 20 See Royan, Boece, 1996, p. 282. 21 Colin Kidd, *British identities before nationalism: ethnicity and nationhood in the Atlantic world, 1600-1800* (Cambridge, 1999), p. 10. 22 Smith, *Ethnic origins of nations*, p. 213. 23 Ibid., p. 209.

determined by a contract between king and people, had obvious political implications in the early seventeenth century. Their traditional power was under threat
from more recent 'upstarts', and they relied increasingly on the king as their main
hope of securing political favour. An historical myth that linked them, however
tenuously, to an 'ancient constitution' had very significant advantages over conquest theory as an historical underpinning for Old English political aspirations.

III

The theories of history expounded by most historians of the Reformation era were
essentially biblical.[24] The invocation of a symbol such as the Bible was a powerful
means of establishing credibility, or justifying a position.[25] The Old Testament story
of a chosen people was a particularly attractive theme, and was already an established idea in Irish literature, as well as in European Reformation discourse. It
required little innovation on Keating's part to construct a narrative of the Irish past
that was biblically based. One of the attractions of the structure lay in the parallel
between the pre-Christian and Christian epochs of Irish history with the biblical
division into Old and New Testaments. This allowed scope to admit the prehistoric myths and legends as a valid element in the Irish story, without undermining the values being emphasised in the second part of the narrative. Before ever
embarking on his studies in Europe, Keating would have been familiar with the
version of the past recorded in *Leabhar gabhála*. That knowledge would, therefore,
have been part of the foundation on which was overlaid an awareness and understanding both of universal church history, and of the histories of other individual
nations and peoples. That both the Four Masters and Keating instinctively turned
to the *Leabhar gabhála* text as one of their principal sources indicates that its message was relevant to both native Irish and Old English historians.[26] Its revival in
the early seventeenth century coincided with a renewed search for origins by those
who had experienced exile.

When Keating set about providing an '*Hibernorum historia*' to rival Hector
Boece's *Scotorum historiae*, he already knew that a ready-made framework for that
history existed in the *Leabhar gabhála* tradition, and the continuation of the story
of the kings of Ireland found in the *Réim ríoghraidhe*.[27] As has been seen, much of
the material for the later sections of the narrative, taking account of the encounters
between Gaeil and Lochlannaigh, was available to Keating in *Cogadh Gaedheal re
Gallaibh*, while his account of the coming of the Normans was mainly indebted to
the writings of Giraldus Cambrensis.[28] The inclusion of a large number of genealo-

---

24 Joshua Mitchell, *Not by reason alone* (Chicago, 1993).   25 Raymond Firth, *Symbols, public and private* (London, 1973), p. 84.   26 RIA, MS 23 K 32; *Leabhar gabhála: the book of the conquests of Ireland:
the recension of Micheál Ó Cléirigh*, eds R.A.S. Macalister and John Mac Neill, part 1 (Dublin, 1916).
27 *Lebor Gabála Érenn: the book of the taking of Ireland*, ed. R.A.S. Macalister (5 vols, Dublin, ITS,
1938-56).   28 *Cogadh Gaedhel re Gallaibh, The war of the Gaedhil with the Gaill*, ed. James H. Todd

gies at the end of his narrative history was an indication of his awareness of the continuing importance of the kin group as a building block of society. The incorporation of these genealogies gave families their own key to the text, presenting them with a means of establishing precisely how they fitted into the narrative. It allowed them to trace their individual family histories back to Adam. It affirmed the ongoing value of the genealogical record while asserting, in the case of each person whose ancestry was recorded, that the story of the Irish past recorded in *Foras feasa ar Éirinn* was indeed *their* family history.

In Ireland by the seventeenth century, the genealogical record was no longer exclusively a record of Gaelic families. Genealogies of Anglo-Norman families are found in the latter half of the sixteenth century in texts such as *Seanchas Búrcach* and *Seanchas Buitlérach* and most comprehensively in Dubhaltach Mac Fhirbhisigh's *Leabhar na nGinealach*, compiled in 1649-50.[29] The increased interest in heraldry displayed by both Old English and Gaelic families in the 1620s and 1630s, not least in Tipperary, was another means to the same end.[30] All of these genealogical compilations reflected the ideology found also in *Foras feasa* and *Annála ríoghachta Éireann* that the Old English were to be regarded as an integral part of the Irish population.[31] Above all, they were used as a mechanism for asserting status within contemporary society. *Foras feasa's* inclusion of genealogies for families of Anglo-Norman descent was an affirmation of Keating's concern with affinity rather than ethnic difference. The ultimate purpose of the history was not to make distinctions on grounds of ethnicity but rather to integrate peoples into a shared model of a Christian kingdom and people.[32]

In addition to the genealogies, there was a further addendum to *Foras feasa* comprising synchronisms of church patriarchs, secular emperors and monarchs, and kings of Ireland. The synchronisms were a means of placing Irish history in a world setting, fitting it into the history of the universal church and of the historical record of emperors and kings, while recording the succession of sovereigns of Ireland from earliest settlement down to the seventeenth century. The sequence of Irish kings emphasised a continuity from pagan antiquity through to the Christian era and then presented the Norman kings as the successors to the Gaelic high-kingship in an unbroken sequence of legitimate sovereigns of Ireland. The acces-

(London, Rolls Series, 1867); Giraldus Cambrensis [Gerald of Wales], *The history and topography of Ireland*, trans. John J. O'Meara (London, 1982); *Expugnatio Hibernica, the conquest of Ireland*, ed. & trans. A.B. Scott and F.X. Martin (Dublin, 1978). **29** See also from the seventeenth century the O'Clery Book of Genealogies (Seamus Pender (ed.), 'The O'Clery book of genealogies', *Analecta Hibernica*, no. 18 (1951), pp. 1-194). Ó Muraíle, *Celebrated antiquary*; Nollaig Ó Muraíle, '"Aimsir an chogaidh chreidmhigh": An Dubhaltach Mac Fhirbhisigh, a lucht aitheantais agus polaitíocht an seachtú haois déag' in Máirín Ní Dhonnchadha (ed.), *Nua-léamha: gnéithe de chultúr, stair agus polaitíocht na nÉireann, c.1600-c.1900* (Baile Átha Cliath, 1996), pp. 89-117. **30** Terence Francis McCarthy, Ulster office, 1552-1800 (M.A. thesis, QUB, 1983), pp. 165-74. See especially NLI, GO MS 69, pp. 172-3, for the funeral certificate of Mortagh Magawly (1638) which could only have been compiled by a specialist in the Gaelic genealogical tradition. **31** Ó Muraíle, *Celebrated antiquary*, p. 180; Ó Buachalla, 'Introduction' *FFÉ* (new ed., London, 1987). **32** Kidd, *British identities before nationalism*, chs 1-2.

sion of the Stuart king, James I, in 1603 was usually recorded in the seventeenth-century manuscripts of *Foras feasa* that contain synchronisms.[33]

IV

Keating's lengthy preface to *Foras feasa*, written after the main narrative had been completed, was deliberately controversial. It left the reader in no doubt but that the unflattering stories about Ireland promulgated by Giraldus Cambrensis and other hostile historians could and must be refuted. It conveyed to the reader that there were basically two types of history, one was biassed, unfair, inaccurate history, which portrayed people in an unfavourable light, and the other was the truthful history of an honourable people who were therein presented in a fair and favourable light. This confrontational approach, denigrating other writers, echoed the attack on the views of Luther and Calvin found in the preface to Keating's tract on the Mass. It probably also reflects a hardening of attitudes towards a government perceived as hostile.[34] In each instance the preface was intended to galvanise readers into taking the text seriously and to make it clear to them why its message was important. The oppositional tone alerted the reader to the reality that the history of both Gaeil and Old English was being misrepresented by other authors. Keating portrayed both groups together as an honourable people whose history was distorted by unreliable, usually foreign, writers. Defining Gaelic Irish and Old English together against 'others' conveyed the idea that they shared a common fate. It formed an image of the Irish as one people with a shared past (and hence a shared future).[35]

> Having undertaken to investigate the groundwork of Irish historical knowledge, I have thought at the outset of deploring some part of her affliction and of her unequal contest; especially the unfairness which continues to be practised on her inhabitants, alike the Sean Ghaill who are in possession more than four hundred years from the Norman invasion down, as well as the Gaeil who have had possession during almost three thousand years. For there is no historian of all those who have written on Ireland from the epoch that has not continuously sought to cast reproach and blame both on the Sean Ghaill and on the Gaeil.[36]

Keating named those who had given hostile testimony: Giraldus Cambrensis, Edmund Spenser, Richard Stanihurst, Meredith Hanmer, William Camden, John

---

33 Seventeenth-century copies of *FFÉ* containing synchronisms include FLK, MS A 15; TCD, MS 1394; King's Inns, Gaelic MS 2; FLK, MS A 14; BL, Add. MS 4,779; NLI, MS G 117, NLI, MS G 17. The synchronisms in TCD, MS 1332 end with Ruaidhrí Ó Conchobhair in the twelfth century; TCD, MS 1397 ends with accession of Henry VIII in 1509. Some later manuscripts extend the synchronisms further, and Tadhg Ó Neachtain's copy commenced in 1704 (NLI, MS G 192) continues the list of popes to 1723.   34 This was certainly how it was read by Michael Kearney. See below, ch. 10.   35 cf. Leerssen, *Mere Irish and fíor-Ghael*, 2nd ed, pp. 276-7.   36 *FFÉ*, i, 2-3.

Barclay, Fynes Moryson, Sir John Davies and Edmund Campion had conducted themselves in the manner of a beetle, he asserted. 'for it is the fashion of the beetle, when it lifts its head in the summertime, to go about fluttering, and not to stoop towards any delicate flower that may be in the field, or any blossom in the garden, thougth they be all roses or lilies, but it keeps bustling about until it meets with dung of horse or cow, and proceeds to roll itself therein'.[37] The introduction continued in this vein, accusing various writers of 'malicious unwarranted lies'.[38]

It was argued that the hospitality and generosity, the valour and piety, the respect for learning and the church, the care for the poor, and the other good qualities of the nobility of both the Sean Ghaill and the Gaeil had been disregarded, while the ways of inferiors and wretched little hags were highlighted so as to present the Irish in an unfavourable light.[39] Having set the confrontational tone, Keating then systematically refuted points made by a succession of authors about the Irish past. Some of the refutations were short on hard evidence. The criticism of one point made by Edmund Spenser was more rhetorical than factual.

> Spenser, in his narrative, says that Egfrid, king of the Northumbrians, and Edgar, king of Britain, had authority over Ireland, as may be read in the thirty-third page of his history: yet this is not true for him, because the old records of Ireland are opposed to that, and moreover British authors themselves confess that the Saxons did not leave them any ancient texts or 'monumenta', by which they might know the condition of the time which preceded the Saxons.[40]

Fully aware of Spenser's high reputation as a poet, he added 'I am surprised how Spenser ventured to meddle in these matters, of which he was ignorant, unless that, on the score of being a poet, he allowed himself license of invention, as it was usual with him, and others like him, to frame and arrange many poetic romances with sweet-sounding words to deceive the reader.'[41]

It was frequently Keating's practice to base his refutations of particular authors by citing contrasting views expressed by other historians. His criticism of Spenser relied on Gildas and Samuel Daniel.[42] Earlier he refuted Giraldus Cambrensis' assertion that the Irish were an inhospitable people by reference to no more authoritative a source than Richard Stanihurst's statement to the contrary. Whereas he might have cited poetry in praise of the hospitality of any number of individuals, he chose merely to cite Stanihurst, concluding that 'hence it may be inferred, without leave of Cambrensis, that they are hospitable people, and truly generous in

---

37 Ibid., 4-5; see also note by Tadhg Ó Dúshláine, 'More about Keating's use of the simile of the dung beetle', *Zeitschrift für Celtische Philologie*, xl (1984), pp. 282-5. 38 *FFÉ*, i, 24. 39 Ibid., 4-7. 40 Ibid., 24-5. 41 Ibid., 30-1. 42 For Gildas [*c.*516-70], see '*De Excidio Britanniae*, or "The ruin of Britain"', in *Gildas: the ruin of Britain and other documents*, ed. M. Winterbottom (Chichester 1978), pp. 87-142; N.J. Higham, *The English conquest: Gildas and Britain in the fifth century* (Manchester, 1994); Samuel Daniel, *The first part of the historie of England* (London, 1613).

regard to food'.[43] Given Keating's subsequent onslaught on Stanihurst's shortcomings as an historian, his case for hospitality was rather poorly constructed.[44]

On other points Keating was on surer ground. He took issue with Giraldus's
statement that the rivers Suir, Nore and Barrow rise in Slieve Bloom. This being
Keating's home territory he could confidently assert 'that it is from the brow of
Slieve Bloom on the east side the Barrow springs, and that it is from the brow of
Slieve Aldun, which is called the mountain of the Gap in Ikerrin, the Suir and the
Nore rise'.[45] In Keating's view the evidence of the landscape spoke for itself; no
reference to a written source was deemed necessary in this case. It was, in any case,
a landscape that he could assume would have been familiar to many of his readers.

Despite his criticism of foreign writers, it is evident that Keating held some
authors in high regard. His obvious respect for the opinions of those same authors
whom he initially castigated as 'beetles in a dung heap' indicates that the controversial tone of the introduction was deliberately constructed. It was designed to help
create a self-image of the Irish as a people who needed to have their history told
from their own point of view, and whose need was answered in *Foras feasa ar Éirinn*.

Keating stated that he wrote the history of the Irish people because those
people had been denigrated by New English historians and by those of Old English
origin such as Stanihurst, even while the land of Ireland was being praised.
Highlighting some of the more serious accusations, he systematically rejected the
idea that the Irish were barbarous. He refuted accusations of cannibalism,[46] of soldiers bathing in the blood of their victims,[47] of contracts being sealed by mutual
drinking of blood.[48] In particular instances he categorised the hostile comments as
deliberately vindictive and false.[49] He asserted that he had decided to write so as
to defend the Irish people from such unwarranted attack. This defensive stance
allowed him to counter hostile comment by boasting that the Irish people were
comparable with 'any nation in Europe in three things, namely, in valour, in learning, and in being steadfast in the Catholic faith'.[50] He emphasised the high regard
for learning as documented in the lives of Irish saints, the regard for law and for
the preservation of the historical record.[51] His picture of early Irish society was one
of moral order as exemplified by the saints, of social order as revealed in respect
for the law, and of political order underpinned by the proper recording of history.

V

Keating's historical method derived from his stated belief that three elements of
the record of the past were required to prove the truth of history: the oral tradition of the ancients (*béaloideas na sean*), old written documents (*seinscríbhne*), and
surviving antiquities (*seanchomharthaidhe dá ngoirtear i Laidin monumenta*).[52] The

---

43 *FFÉ*, i, 20-1. 44 Ibid., 40-3. 45 Ibid., 20-1. 46 Ibid., 8-9. 47 Ibid., 10. 48 Ibid., 18. 49
Ibid., 34; i, 74. 50 Ibid., 78-9. 51 Ibid., 78. 52 *FFÉ*, ii, 324.

compilation of historical material that Keating presented to his readers as a 'basis of wisdom' about Ireland drew on all three of these kinds of sources.[53] As seen above the written documents he used consisted of both published and unpublished works in a number of languages. Despite, or perhaps because of, his facility for languages he took delight in the fact that he could read manuscript sources in the Irish language, whereas foreign writers could not. This was no mere academic triumphalism. He was drawing attention to the necessity of using primary sources in the search for the 'truth' about the past. He was also affirming the significance of the Irish language and the bardic heritage in the search for the origins of the people of Ireland.

In general, Keating demonstrated great respect for the written word, and only rarely questioned the reliability of any statement he found in the manuscript record. In keeping with his contemporaries, while he appreciated the historical value of primary sources, he tended to be rather uncritical in his use of those source materials, being reluctant to doubt the written word. He gave preference to Irish manuscripts over foreign printed materials. When he used the two in conjunction he cited the foreign printed source to reaffirm his conclusions drawn from a manuscript source, or if they disagreed he pointed out the error of the foreign source on the grounds of it being contradicted by the native record. Where there were discrepancies between different accounts, he strove to reconcile them, or to give reasons for choosing one rather than the other.[54] Anne Cronin drew attention to the fact that where faced with a choice, Keating consistently chose the evidence of the poetry in preference to a prose account of a particular episode.[55] He specifically asserted the authoritative nature of poetry as historical evidence, even though many of the poetical sources he cited were anonymous.[56] Such a view was a valid judgment of the nature of the historical record in a pre-literate society. The poet in such a society was not merely a creative artist. Rather he used the rhythm of the language itself 'to preserve whatever needs preserving, regardless of whether it constitutes poetry in the modern sense'. The Irish bardic poet, in the words of M.T. Clanchy, was a 'mnemotechnician', 'expert in making language memorable', and poetic diction has long been a valued mechanism for remembering the past.[57]

While Keating treasured the literature that had emanated from this largely pre-literate society, he was himself working in an intellectual milieu where written documents were becoming increasingly significant. His writings were the product of a literate culture, and were addressed to literate audiences. Part of the challenge facing Keating in compiling *Foras feasa* was to communicate to his literate contemporaries the essence of the traditional learning and lore about Ireland that had

---

53 The reader was reminded, by reference to the evidence of Polydorus, that it was the duty of a good historian to explain 'the customs and way of life, the counsels, causes, resolves, acts, and development, whether good or bad, of every people who dwell in the country about which he has undertaken to write'. (*FFÉ*, i, 56-7). 54 Cronin, 'Manuscript sources' p. 124. 55 Ibid., p. 124. 56 *FFÉ*, i, 90. 57 M.T. Clanchy, 'Remembering the past and the good old law', *History*, lv, no. 184 (1970), pp. 165-76, esp. p. 169.

emanated from a cultural environment where the written word did not have pivotal significance. Thus, while Keating's method of using sources was grounded in
the values of a literate society, he was careful to recognise the particular value of
the poetic record of earlier times. He was happiest when he could refer readers to
manuscripts containing the texts of poems he cited. Thus, for instance, the lengthy
poem '*Aithne dhamh gach meirge mór*', on the emblems of the Children of Israel,
was one which could be found, according to Keating, in 'the old Book of Leacaoin,
in Urmhumha, and in many other old books'.[58] The comment implies that Keating
believed his readers would regard the poem as more authoritative if he made reference to a written version in a manuscript of some antiquity.[59]

The second category of material on which Keating relied was oral tradition.
That he gave credit to oral tradition should not be considered as undermining the
value of his historical scholarship; the secular world in which he lived was only
beginning to regard the written word as somehow more reliable than the memory
of the people. However, in practice Keating did not draw extensively on purely
oral material when compiling *Foras feasa*.[60]

Keating viewed surviving antiquities as further tangible evidence in support of
stories about the past. In discussing whether Fionn and the Fianna really existed,
he argued that not only was there oral and documentary testimony, there were also
places in the landscape that were known to have been intimately associated with
the Fianna. 'Suidhe Finn on Sliabh na nBan, called from Fionn descendant of
Baoiscne, and Gleann Gharaidh in Uí Faithche, called from Garaidh son of Morna,
and Leabaidh Dhiarmada Uí Dhuibhne agus Ghráinne at Poll Tighe Liabhain in
Ui Fiachrach Eidhne'.[61] Such placelore evidence was regarded by Keating as reliable, and while he admitted that imaginative romances had been written about the
Fianna, he insisted that some of the stories that existed about them were true and
credible.[62] Such use of placelore to assert the truth of stories of saints rather than
secular heroes was also used by contemporaries of Keating, especially the Irish
Franciscans. Thus rocks or wells associated with particular saints were taken as
verification of the truth of stories told of those saints.[63] In practice, Keating mentioned relatively few antiquarian artifacts and the vast bulk of the sources he used
for his history were manuscript materials in the Irish language. He was conscious
that there was far more material available to him in the manuscript sources than he
could possibly hope to incorporate in his history, a synthetic narrative derived from

---

58 '*Seanleabhar Leacain i nUrmhumhain is i mórán do leabhraidh oile*', *FFÉ*, iii, 126-7.   59 The manuscript cited by Keating here is not the Book of Lecan (RIA, MS 23 P 2), but rather a manuscript from
Ormond. (Paul Walsh, 'The Book of Lecan in Ormond', *Irish Book Lover*, xxvi (1938), p. 62.) The
poem referred to is found in *Leabhar Breac* (RIA MS 23 P 16), a manuscript complied by Murchadh
Ó Cuindlis, one of the scribes of the Book of Lecan at Loch Riach, Clonmacnoise in 1408-11. It was
also known as the great Book of Duniry and was consulted by Micheál Ó Cléirigh in County Galway
in 1629. Dinneen (*FFÉ*, iii, 374) described the poem as 'rare and interesting' and printed the *Leabhar
Breac* text.   60 Cronin, 'Manuscript sources', pp. 122-35.   61 *FFÉ*, ii, 324-5.   62 Ibid., 326. See
ibid., 348, 390, 396, 406 for further examples.   63 Mac Aingil, *Scáthán*, ll 4137-41.

a selection of the available source material. The introductory paragraph most often found as a title page in most seventeenth-century manuscripts of *Foras feasa* accurately summarises the author's approach.

> Here is a vindication or defensive introduction to the groundwork of knowledge on Ireland, in which is a compendium of the history of Ireland briefly: which has been gathered and collected from the chief books of the history of Ireland, and from a good many trustworthy foreign authors by Geoffrey Keating, priest and doctor of divinity, in which is a brief summary of the principal transactions of Ireland from Parthalón to the Norman Invasion: and whoever shall desire to write fully and comprehensively on Ireland hereafter, he will find, in the same ancient books, many things desirable to write of her which have been purposely omitted here, lest putting these all in one work, thereby this compilation should less likely come to light from the greatness of the labour of putting them in one writing.[64]

In consciously limiting the size of his text, so as to make it more feasible to have it circulated, he was most probably thinking in terms of scribal publication.[65] He did not consider that his text had to be all-inclusive. He reminded his readers that saints' lives, tales of battles and historical romances were in circulation, and he invited them to read such works to supplement the coverage of his own outline narrative.

VI

Although the motivation for writing history in the seventeenth century frequently owed much to the desire to authenticate a confessional standpoint, there is little evidence that Keating's *Foras feasa* was written for such straightforward religious reasons. The contrast in attitude between the preface to *Eochair-sgiath an Aifrinn* and that of *Foras feasa* may be explained by the changed circumstances of the author. The first work was written while the author was probably still living in France, teaching theology and immersed in the polemical literature of Suarez and Bellarmine. *Foras feasa*, on the other hand, was the product of an Irish political environment where the political threat to the status of the Old English may have been of more immediate concern than the challenge to their Catholicism. Whereas the preface to *Eochair-sgiath an Aifrinn* took issue with the views expressed by Luther and Calvin, *Foras feasa* did not, for instance, take issue with the views expressed by the Church of Ireland archbishop James Ussher (incidentally, a

---

64 *FFÉ*, i, 92-5. 65 The Louvain Franciscans may have intended to publish the Irish text in the 1630s, and certainly the Latin translation by John Lynch was intended for publication on the continent. That one of the extant manuscript copies of Lynch's translation (MS 7, Woodstock Theological Centre Library) has attached to it a letter by Thomas O'Sheeran [Sirinus], who saw several works by Irish authors through the continental presses certainly supports this idea.

nephew of Richard Stanihurst), whose *Veterum epistolarum Hybernicarum sylloge* had been published in 1632. Keating was aware of this work, and even cited it on minor points of detail.[66] He did not, however, explicitly challenge the overall argument of the book though it made the case for the claim of the established church to be the true successor of the church of Patrick in Ireland. It appears that Keating did not feel it necessary to elaborate on the opposing case for the benefit of the Catholic readers he wished to address. This stance contrasts with the concern indicated by Ussher in the note to the reader prefixed to the 1631 English language work entitled *Discourse of the Religion anciently professed by the Irish and British*. Ussher, like Sir Robert Cotton, in England, was conscious of a need to explicitly counter the arguments of Catholic writers.

Other Irish Catholic writers, however, did take issue with Ussher on matters of historical interpretation. There was a lengthy correspondence betweeen Ussher and David Rothe over the true successors of St Patrick as archbishops of Armagh.[67] Philip O'Sullivan Beare's *Patriciana decas* (1629) contained a life of St Patrick, and argued strongly for the loyalty of the Catholic Irish to the faith of their patron saint. The book also included a tract which refuted the claims made by James Ussher on the history of the early Irish church.[68] Ussher's polemical writings did not prevent his being respected as a scholar by his Catholic contemporaries. David Rothe, bishop of Ossory, with whom he corresponded regularly, was but one of the network of contacts maintained by Ussher with Irish scholars and historians.[69] Keating did not consider that the scholarly researches of Protestants like Ussher concerning the early ecclesiastical history of Ireland aroused feelings of antagonism among those to whom *Foras feasa* was addressed. The perceived threat to Irish Catholics was a political rather than a religious one, and Keating was more concerned with defining Irishness than defining Catholicism. This reading of the core message of *Foras feasa* is borne out by the evidence of how the text was read by Michael Kearney in the 1630s.[70]

Though not presented as a response to Protestant historical polemic, *Foras feasa* nonetheless put forward a clear and confident case for the Catholic religion as the

---

66 *FFÉ*, iii, 4-6; 300.   67 O'Sullivan, 'Correspondence of David Rothe and James Ussher, pp. 7-49; Sir Christopher Sibthorpe, *A friendly advertisment to the pretended Catholics of Ireland .. in the end whereof is added an epistle written to the author of the Religion anciently professed by the Irish and Scottish by James Ussher* (Dublin 1622, 2nd ed. 1623).   68 Philip O'Sullivan Beare, *Patritiana decas, sive libri decem, quibus de diva Patritii vita, purgatorio, miraculis rebusque gestis* (Madrid, 1629); Matthew Byrne (ed.), *Ireland under Elizabeth ... being a portion of the history of Catholic Ireland by Don Philip O'Sullivan Bear* (Dublin, 1903).   69 O'Sullivan, 'Correspondence of David Rothe and James Ussher'; Rothe encouraged Ussher's endeavours in historical research into 'remarkable matters for illustrating your country which had much need to be remembered by some exact pen before all memory be abolished wherein your studious industry may make the posterity beholding to you'; on the impetus to write down material that had previously been remembered, see M.T. Clanchy, *From memory to written record* (London, 1979), esp. pp. 11-28. It was not so much the loss of the written record that was feared by Ussher, Rothe and Keating in the 1620s and 1630s, rather it was the loss of the oral record.   70 See below pp. 182-7 for discussion of the work of Michael Kearney, the first translator of *Foras feasa*.

religion of Patrick. The placing of a discussion of the twelfth-century Church in Ireland at the end of a long discourse on the origins of the Gaelic Irish and the Old English gave them a common Catholic version of their history. An Irish Catholic mythology had been forged out of an atmosphere of conflicting interests. New definitions of native and foreigner, self and other, had been formulated.

This was a self-assured history for a people who had confidence in the future of the kingdom of Ireland. The Irish Catholic people of that kingdom were given a clear message concerning their responsibilities in living up to the standards of their illustrious ancestors. They were reminded of the need to avoid suffering the fate of those in earlier ages who had transgressed the moral order. The polemical account of the coming of the Normans in the concluding section of *Foras feasa* offered a parable for the 1630s that operated at several levels. First, it reminded those of Anglo-Norman descent that those of their ancestors who had behaved dishonourably had not prospered. It served as a warning that those who collaborated with unacceptable New English activities were contravening the moral order. Secondly, it made clear that those who were newcomers had a moral responsibility to treat the indigenous population with respect. Thirdly, it reaffirmed the respect for the law that was a characteristic of the indigenous population when subject to a just ruler. When new accommodations were being made, and the Old English in particular found their access to political power diminishing, it restated a belief in just rule as the means of maintaining an ordered society. It provided a multi-faceted political manifesto for the future of the Catholic people in the kingdom of Ireland.

7

Origin myths: people, language, place

It is rarely the case that stories told in Keating's writings had originated with him. His creative impulse lay in the selection and adaptation of material for re-telling, the style of language he employed, and the interlinking of diverse materials into a readable form. The fact that many of his themes are unoriginal does not make them any less central to Keating's imagined world. His inclusion of a particular story should be sufficient for us to take that element seriously as having been considered significant in his world.

I

A reader of Keating's prose works would have encountered a wide range of themes which narrated aspects of the story of Ireland and her people. Much of the content would have appeared very familiar. The geographical setting immediately appealed to readers' sense of identity with the land of their birth. Not only his history of Ireland but also his theological tract, *Trí bior-ghaoithe an bháis*, located the ideology and values of these works within a specifically Irish context. Of the three major prose works only *Eochair-sgiath an Aifrinn* lacked an Irish setting, but it too dealt with a topic that had an air of the familiar. Many of the stories told, whether mythical accounts of Irish origins or moral tales drawn from standard preachers' handbooks, were stories that had often been told before. The language in which the stories were told made the text readily accessible and even attractive.

Against this backdrop, the more universal topics of the nature of human existence and the moral order were treated in some detail. The political world of earthly kings and heroes, and the corresponding leaders in the realm of religion, such as Moses and Christ, were all interpreted in an interrelated way. It was a world where monarchy was the focal point around which society was conceptualised, a world in which human loyalties were necessarily hierarchical.[1] The church, past and present, and the kingdom of Ireland, past and present, were social constructs which formed

---

1 Benedict Anderson, *Imagined communities: reflections on the origin and spread of nationalism* (London, rev. ed, 1991), p. 40.

core elements of Keating's understanding of the Irish people as a distinct Christian nation of great antiquity whose origins could be traced, through biblical genealogies, to Adam. The idea of the kingdom of Ireland as delineated through the medium of Keating's historical imagination was closely intertwined with his concept of the kingdom of God. These themes underlie all of Keating's narrative writings, whether on the history of the origins of the Irish people, or the more universal theme of the road to salvation in the kingdom of God.

The Irish language, which he chose as his medium of communication, itself conveyed a message to the reader on the nature of Irish identity. The Irish language as used by Geoffrey Keating was not a neutral vehicle with which to convey his ideas to the reading public. Linguistics, too, had its origins in sacred history.[2] His view of the origins of the language was part of his overall interpretation of the origins of the Irish people and his use of the written language in modern prose form was integral to his reordering of a valued heritage for the modern age. The availability of Keating's Catholic theological tracts in the Irish language would have had the effect of promoting an understanding of the Counter-Reformation Catholic doctrines which they contained as something intrinsically Irish. The writings of Geoffrey Keating worked at several levels to create for his readers a sense of Irishness intertwined with Catholicism, and an understanding of Catholicism that was presented as being peculiarly Irish.

II

The main text of *Foras feasa ar Éirinn* was divided into two books, the first narrating the history of Ireland from the beginning of time to the coming of Christianity. The second book continued the narrative from the great watershed of the fifth-century Christianisation of Ireland down to the coming of the Normans in the twelfth century. Appended to the prose narrative was a collection of genealogies, and tables of synchronisms spanning the generations from the Flood to the opening years of the seventeenth century. The genealogies purported to record the succession of major Gaelic families over more than a hundred generations, back to the beginning of time. The narrative history of pagan Ireland, from the time of Adam down to the coming of St Patrick to Ireland, occupied the largest portion of the history compiled by Keating.[3] The emphasis given to pre-Christian Ireland was not merely a reflection of the available sources but also a measure of the importance the author attached to documenting the origins of the Irish people. Those origins began, for him, with the creation of Adam, 'the first father from whom we have sprung'. The story of the Irish people (Keating's people, for he uses the first person plural in his preamble)[4] began in earnest with Noah, 930 years after Adam.

---

2 Kidd, *British identities before nationalism*, p. 11. 3 The first book, comprising the pre-Christian narrative, contained 92,000 words. The second book, covering the period after the coming of Christianity contained 64,000 words. 4 *FFÉ*, i, 132.

The three sons of Noah were identified, Sem, Cham and Japheth, and the peoples of Asia, Africa, and Europe were then distinguished from each other as having descended from these three distinct individuals. The main focus thereafter was on the descendants of Japheth who was ancestor of all the people of Europe. The focus was then narrowed further to Magog, one of the fifteen sons of Japheth, and the one from whom the people of Scythia were descended. The Scythians were presented as the ancestors of the tribes who occupied Ireland after the deluge, before the arrival of the sons of Míl.[5]

In due course, according to Keating's account, Galamh, who was called Míl of Spain, travelled to Scythia,[6] and married Seang, daughter of Reaflóir the king of Scythia, who bore him two sons. Míl subsequently travelled to Egypt and there married Scota, daughter of Pharaoh, who bore him six sons, so that in the person of Míl the contact with the near East was renewed, and the biblical origins of the inhabitants of Ireland thereby reaffirmed.

The genealogical framework of the opening section of *Foras feasa*, with its obvious biblical overtones, was used to convey an understanding of the honourable origins of the Irish people. The idea that some people had honourable origins, while others did not was repeatedly emphasised. The fate of the rootless Fomorians, for instance, contrasted sharply with their challengers from Clann Neimhidh.[7] That only the honourable prospered and had progeny was a recurring theme.[8]

The people that featured in *Foras feasa*, whether or not they were of royal blood, were perceived not as individuals but as members of kin groups with origins ultimately extending to Noah and thus back to Adam. When Keating named contemporary kin groups they were presented as the descendants of particular named persons in the past, the credentials of their forbears usually being described in some detail.

With few exceptions the Gaelic families in Ireland in Keating's own day whose ancestry was alluded to in *Foras feasa* were portrayed as members of Clann Mhíleadh, being descendants of Éibhear or of Éireamhón, the sons of Míl. Thus, for example, the ancestry of 'true Leinstermen' was traced back to Labhraidh Loingseach and thence to Éibhear son of Míl. Naming the contemporary families involved gave them a personal genealogical connection to their ancient ancestors, and drew attention to the bond of shared origins.

> Know, O reader, that all true Leinstermen that survive of the race of Éireamhón are descended from this Labhraidh Loingseach, except Ó Nuallain who sprang from Cobhthach Caol mBreagh. The following are the principal families that sprang from the Leinstermen, namely, Ó Conchubhar Failghe with his family branches, Ó Caomhánaigh, Ó Tuathalaigh, Ó Branaigh, Mac Giolla Phádraig, Ó Duinn, Ó Diomsaigh, Ó Duibhidhir, muinntear Riain, and every branch that sprang from these families. It was from Cathaoir Mór that most of the Leinster families sprang. But it was not from him that Mac Giolla Phádraig sprang, since Mac Giolla Phádraig and

5 Ibid., 138.   6 *FFÉ*, ii, 40-2.   7 *FFÉ*, i, 162-88.   8 *TBB*, ll. 5444-76; *FFÉ*, iii, 369.

himself separated in pedigree from one another at Breasal Breac son of Fiachaidh Foibhric, the fourteenth ancestor from Cathaoir upwards. Now this Breasal had two sons, namely, Lughaidh Loithfhionn and Connla: and the province of Leinster was divided between these two: thus Lughaidh and his descendants obtained from Bearbha eastward, and Connla and his descendants from the Bearbha westwards.[9]

It was perhaps unfortunate, considering his renown as the king with horses ears, that the Leinstermen had Labhraidh Loingseach as their ancestor, but it seems that it was not Keating's intention to insult them by telling unsavory stories, but rather to fix the Leinster families firmly within the genealogical framework of Clann Mhíleadh. However, it was this sort of incidental story that left the author of *Foras feasa* open to accusations of credulity and the text being dismissed as being full of 'ridiculous stories'.[10]

Elsewhere in *Foras feasa* a number of midland and Connacht families were grouped together as the descendants of Cian son of Oilill Ólom of the race of Éibhear[11] and later their associated territories were also identified.[12]

> For Tadhg son of Cian, son of Oilill Ólom had two sons, namely, Connla and Cormac Gaileang. From Iomchaidh son of Connla comes Ó Cearbhaill, and from Fionnachta son of Connla comes Ó Meachair. From Cormac Gaileang son of Tadhg, son of Cian, comes Ó Eadhra and Ó Gadhra and Ó Conchubhair Ciannachta. The following are the territories they acquired, namely, Gaileanga, east and west; Ciannachta, south and north; Luighne, east and west. Moreover, another company of the race of Éibhear took possession of other territories in Leath Cuinn, these are the descendants of Cochlan son of Lorcan.[13]

To modern tastes, Oilill Ólom was a considerably more unsavory individual than Labhraidh Loingseach, but again it was kinship rather than political correctness that was at the core of the political values Keating sought to portray. Other kin groups associated with Connacht (part of Leath Cuinn) were portrayed as being descended from Clann Mhíleadh.[14]

In Keating's day, the '*Clann Mhíleadh*' was a term still used to denote virtually all of the indigenous population of Ireland. While outsiders could write of 'the meere Irisch, called Clan na Milegh', for the Irish-speaking population whose origin myth was drawn from the *Leabhar gabhála*, the term '*Clann Mhíleadh*' conveyed to them a sense of their honourable origins.[15] Its value was strengthened for

9 *FFÉ*, ii, 168-9.　10 Cox, *Hibernia Anglicana*, 'An apparatus', sig. [e 2v]; For a commentator who took offence at the story of Labhraidh Loingseach see Brian Ó Cuív (ed.), 'A seventeenth-century criticism of Keating's *Foras feasa ar Éirinn*', *Éigse*, xi (1965), pp. 119-40.　11 *FFÉ*, ii, 276.　12 Ibid., 294.　13 Ibid., 294-7.　14 Ibid., 294-6.　15 Another compilation which built on this concept, 'Foras feasa Chloinne Mhíleadh Espaine', dating from *c.*1648, did so from a MacCarthy perspective. See RIA, MS 23 K 37; BL, Egerton 106; BL, Egerton 150. *RIA Cat. Ir. MSS*, pp. 433-8; *BL Cat. Ir. MSS*, ii, 396-7.

them by the continued understanding that the ultimate honourable genealogical connection was biblical.[16]

While Keating derived much of his genealogical material from earlier sources, he adapted it as suited his own purpose. Thus, in addition to noting the genealogies of leading Irish families in the text and appendices of *Foras feasa*, he was careful to allocate an appropriate pedigree to the monarchs of his own day by asserting that the Stuart king, Charles I, and his father James I, were themselves descendants of the race of Éibhear.[17] They thus shared a pedigree with one of the heroes of *Foras feasa*, Brian Bóroimhe, of Dál Cais, the king hero who fell in the battle of Clontarf, 1014.[18] This was an affirmation of sentiments expressed by some Gaelic poets following the accession of James I in 1603. Fearghal Óg Mac an Bhaird in '*Trí coróna i gcairt Shéamais*' affirmed that James Stuart, by his ancestry, was rightful king of Ireland.[19] Soon afterwards, in the contest known as the 'Contention of the bards', rival poets put forward variant claims as to whether the Stuart king was of Ulster or Munster origin.[20] By the early eighteenth century variant Irish paternal and maternal pedigrees for the Stuart kings could be found as a preliminary to the Fermanagh genealogies compiled by the Ó Luinín family.[21]

The major grouping of people living in Ireland who were not part of the Clann Mhíleadh were, of course, those of Norman descent. In contrast to his treatment of the Stuart kings, and the practice of some early seventeenth-century Gaelic poets,[22] Keating did not attempt to knit the Old English into the Gaelic genealogical framework. Instead, recognising their different origins, he simply stated in the closing section of the history that these families were the descendants of lesser known leaders who came to Ireland at the time of the Norman invasion. He emphasised that they were not descended from those who had behaved treacherously, but rather were descended from others who

> did much good in Ireland by building churches and abbeys and giving church lands to clerics for their support, together with many other good deeds besides, and God gave them as a return for this that there are many descendants after them at this day in Ireland.[23]

A list of family names followed. This naming of Old English family groups established their credentials as long established inhabitants of Ireland whose pedigrees, though different from those of the Gaeil, could not be faulted.[24] They were simply

---

16 Brian Mac Cuarta (ed.), 'Mathew de Renzy's letters on Irish affairs, 1613-1620', *Analecta Hibernica*, no. 34 (1987), pp. 107-82, esp p. 20; Brian Mac Cuarta, 'A planter's interaction with Gaelic culture: Sir Matthew de Renzy, 1577-1634', *Irish Economic and Social History*, xx (1993), 1-17.   17 *FFÉ*, ii, 44, 46.   18 *FFÉ*, iii, 256.   19 Breandán Ó Buachalla, 'James our true king', p. 10; Lambert McKenna (ed.), *Aithdioghluim dána* (2 vols, London, ITS, 1935-40), poem 44.   20 Lambert McKenna (ed.), *Iomarbhágh na bhfileadh* (2 vols, London, ITS, 1918), poem 15, verses 26-28; poem 18, verse 55.   21 Cormac Ua Cadhla, 'Geinealaighe Fearmanach', *Analecta Hibernica*, no. 3 (1931), pp. 68-70. Cf. poem in praise of Theobald Dillon, '*Maith an seanadhsa ag Síol Néill*', claiming descent for the Dillons from Niall Naoighiallach. RIA, MS A v 2, f. 27.   23 *FFÉ*, iii, 368-9.   24 Ibid., 368.

the latest wave of settlers to arrive on the island. The story of their origin was such that it could be accepted as parallel to that of the arrival of the Clann Mhíleadh many centuries before. In a story of Irish origins structured around the idea of a series of invasions, with kin groups descended from sons of invaders, those of Anglo-Norman descent could find their origins also.

Any reader, whether Gaelic or Old English, who encountered the text of *Foras feasa*, finding his family name there, would probably have identified strongly with that kin group. Kinship represented the strongest social bond in Keating's Ireland. During his own life in Munster, as seen in chapter two, the extended network of Keatings would have constituted his most significant set of social relationships. Both Keating and his readers would have been aware of the strength of these ties of kinship, which had scarcely diminished over time. Their sense of belonging to a particular family, with a particular pedigree, was something that still mattered. That sense of belonging also conjured up a sense of place, and increasingly, in the changing world of the seventeenth century, a sense that language was one of the identifiers that marked out those who belonged.

III

The choice of Irish as the language of both his theological tracts and his history of Ireland was determined by Keating's perception of his intended audience, and by the nature of his message for those people. They were his own kinsmen and neighbours in a predominantly Irish speaking region of Munster. He chose not to write in Latin, still the language of scholarship, because his writings were no mere academic exercises. He chose not to adhere to the archaic form of the Irish language still being preserved by a tiny cultural elite in Ireland. Rather he opted to write in modern, accessible Irish, something close to that which he would have used orally when delivering a sermon.

Foras feasa was written to define the Irish people in terms of who they were and where they had come from. The use of the Irish language was an integral part of that process of defining the Irish people. Language was a potent and vibrant tool in defining identity, and here it was deliberately chosen, and skilfully used so that the linguistic medium was a significant part of the message.[25]

Keating was a master of the Irish language, and his writings were carefully crafted pieces, drawing on the full riches of the linguistic heritage that he valued. Keating's choice of a modern vernacular prose narrative as the medium through which to express his ideas to a wider audience probably originated in his continental experience. Temporarily exiled from the cultural environment of his youth, but encountering scholars of diverse nationalities writing in their vernacular languages for their own people, he was exposed to a view of language that contrasted

---

25 For the trend towards vernacular histories elsewhere in Europe see Kelley, *Foundations of modern historical scholarship*.

with that of the bardic schools. Keating's use of the Irish language reflected the ideology expressed by his fellow Old English secular cleric, Theobald Stapleton, who claimed that every nation should be proud of its language. 'There is no nation on earth that does not respect, read and write its own language as a matter of honour', Stapleton wrote in the prologue to a Latin-Irish dual language catechism he compiled in 1639.[26]

The poem '*Milis an teanga*' encapsulates an understanding of Irish as an ancient language which provides a voice free from foreign elements.

> *Milis an teanga an Ghaedhealg,*
> *Guth gan chabhair choigcríche*
> *Glór géar-chaoin glé glinn gasta*
> *Suairc séimhidhe sult-bhlasta.*
>
> *Gidh Eabhra teanga is seanda,*
> *Gidh Laidean is léigheanta,*
> *Uatha uirthi níor fríth linn*
> *Fuaim nó focal do chomaoinn.*
>
> (Irish is a sweet language,
> a voice without foreign aid,
> A refined, distinct, clear, clever voice
> agreeable, gentle and pleasant sounding.
>
> Though Hebrew is the oldest tongue,
> Though Latin is the most learned
> We did not find in them
> A sound or word to enhance it.)

While it is unlikely that the attribution of these verses to Keating is accurate, the fact that such a poem was attributed to him by later generations emphasises Keating's reputation as one who valued and thereby enhanced the status of the Irish language.[27] The detail of the poem, particularly on the status of the Irish language, as compared with Hebrew and Latin, however, does not concur with the portrayal of the origins of the Irish language outlined in *Foras feasa*. It seems improbable that the author of *Foras feasa* would have conceded that Hebrew was an older language or Latin a more scholarly one.[28]

There were other Catholic clergy among Keating's contemporaries who were compiling religious texts in Irish prose and verse. Of particular significance was the work of some Irish Franciscans associated with the Irish college of St Anthony at Louvain.

---

26 Theobald Stapleton, *Catechismus, seu doctrina Christiana Latino-Hibernica* (Brussels, 1639; fascimile reprint Dublin, 1945) prologue, sig. b.v.   27 The earliest extant manuscript version of this poem appears to be TCD, MS 1365, pp. 350, 380, written by Tadhg Mac Namara in 1757.   28 E.G. Quin, 'Irish studies' in T. Ó Raifeartaigh (ed.), *The Royal Irish Academy, a bicentennial history, 1785-1985* (Dublin, 1985), p. 169.

In the early decades of the seventeenth century they published a range of devotional and catechetical texts in Irish intended for use in teaching religious doctrine and devotion to Irish-speakers on the continent and at home. These poets turned priests, most notably Bonaventure Ó hEodhasa and Aodh Mac Aingil, were less than comfortable with the way they themselves were using the Irish language as a mere functional tool to communicate the basic tenets of the faith to the less well educated. Aodh Mac Aingil apologised for his lack of style, as though writing the living language for pedagogical purposes was a betrayal of the scholarly values of a bardic training.

> If it is said that we should not write in Irish something that is not crafted, our reply to that is that we are not writing to teach Irish but to teach repentance, and we are satisfied if we are understood even if we do not have correct Irish.[29]

Their work ensured that books available in print encapsulated the essence of Counter-Reformation Catholic doctrines adapted for Irish audiences and written in a modern, accessible form of the Irish language.

Closer to home in the 1620s there were the beginnings of a consciousness among the learned classes of the need to value the Irish language. In tandem with this was the gradually growing awareness of the threat being posed by the growth of English as the language of government and law. In 1627, for example, Conall Mac Eochagáin translated an Irish text known as the Annals of Clonmacnoise into English. Such translation of Irish texts into English was an innovation, and it concerned him that there were people anxious to read the record of the Irish past whose lack of knowledge of Irish prevented them doing so. He criticised those parents who 'neglect their books and choose rather to put their children to learn Eng[lish] than their own native language'.[30] His contemporaries understood the link between language and power in their increasingly bilingual society. The perception that the increased use of English was associated with a degree of social mobility was reflected in other literary texts, notably *Pairlement Chloinne Tomáis*, from the early seventeenth century. There was an awareness that English was becoming 'now the more respected language' as Michael Kearney, first translator of *Foras feasa*,[31] asserted, but a concern also, among those who were bilingual, that Irish was not to be regarded as in any way inferior.

Geoffrey Keating had moved in similar European circles to Theobald Stapleton and the Francisan catechists, and on his return to Ireland must have had contact with Conall Mac Eochagáin and his associates. Keating's work in Irish epitomised the values these men had variously expressed in relation to the language. He wrote con-

---

29 '*Dá n-abarthaoi gur dána dhúinn ní dho sgríobhadh a nGaoidhilg 's nár shaothruigheamar innti, as i ar bfhreagra ar sin, nach do mhúnadh Gaoidhilgi sgríobhmaoid acht do mhunadh na haithridhe, 7 is lór linn go ttuigfidhear sin gé nach biadh ceart na Gaoidhilgi aguinn.*' Mac Aingil, *Scáthán*, p. 5; cf. Nicholas Canny, 'The formation of the Irish mind: religion, politics and Gaelic Irish literature, 1580-1750', *Past & Present*, no. 95 (1982), pp. 91-116. **30** *Annals of Clonmacnoise*, ed. Murphy, p. 8. **31** RIA, MS 24 G 16, f. 36v.

fidently in stylish modern prose. The language of Keating's *Trí bior-ghaoithe an bháis* was characterised by Osborn Bergin in the 1930s as the work of a writer who had 'the idiomatic grasp of the language possessed by one who wrote it while the literary tradition was still unbroken'.[32] The language of this tract has been valued through the centuries as exhibiting 'the real structure of the language' by an author thoroughly familiar with Gaelic modes of expression. 'It is veritably Irish uncontaminated by English phrases, and written by a master of the language while it was yet a power'.[33]

Keating's concern with origins included the story of the origins of the Irish language, and he was particularly concerned to explain the name '*Gaedheal*'. Drawing on materials from the *Leabhar gabhála* and ultimately from *Auraicept na nÉces*, he traced the language back to the story of the tower of Babel, and Féinius Farsaidh, king of Scythia, who decided to study all the languages of the three inhabited continents, that had evolved from the collapse of the tower.[34] In Keating's version of the story, the Gaelic language was named after Gaedhael, son of Eathór, who had been appointed by Féinius Farsaidh to oversee the schools in Scythia where the languages were studied.[35] From among various etymologies of the name Gaedheal, Keating favoured '*Gaoith dhil*' or 'lover of wisdom', which he equated with the Greek term '*philosophos*'.[36] He stressed that this individual named Gaedheal associated with the origins of the Gaelic language was distinct from Gaedheal Glas, son of Niúl and Scota, who was the ancestor of the Gaelic peoples.[37] This distinction, which deviates from the *Leabhar gabhála* tradition, permitted Keating to present the Gaelic language as having a separate origin from that of the Gaelic people and to be the language of Irish people other than the race of Gaedheal. Though Keating did not labour the point, he was keen to show that the Gaelic language was not solely to be equated with the Gaelic race. In his discussion of these matters Keating weighed up the evidence of the *Leabhar gabhála* with other evidence, noting that much of the *seanchas* was derived from the *Leabhar gabhála* tradition. Among the evidence he assessed was that provided by Richard Creagh, primate of Ireland who had written a book on the origin of Gaelic and the race of Gaedheal.[38] This supported the view that Gaelic was a very ancient language and had been in use in Ireland 'from the coming of Neimhidh, 630 years after the Deluge, to this day'. He considered that Gaelic, or '*Scoitbhéarla*', was the mother tongue of the Clann Neimhidh and the Fir bolg and that it was the language used by the Tuatha Dé Danann in conversation with those they encountered in Ireland.[39]

Keating emphasised that the language of Scotland shared its origin with the language of Ireland, rejecting Hector Boece's views in favour of the majority opin-

---

32 *TBB*, p. xiii. 33 Geoffrey Keating, *Trí bior-ghaoithe an bháis*, ed. Robert Atkinson (Dublin, 1890), preface. For a traditional discussion of Keating's prose style see Gerald O'Nolan, *Studies in modern Irish, part iv, being a critical analysis of Keating's prose* (Dublin, 1922). 34 *Leabhar gabhála*, ed. Macalister, ii, especially pp. 52-5. See also *Auraicept na nÉces*, ed. Anders Ahlqvist (Helsinki, 1983); R. Thurneysen, 'Auraicept na n-Eges', *Zeitschrift für Celtische Philologie*, xvii (1928), pp. 277-303; Anders Ahlqvist, *The early Irish linguist* (Commentationes Humanarum Litterarum, 73, 1982). 35 *FFÉ*, ii, 10. 36 Ibid., 10-11. 37 *FFÉ*, i, 232-4; ii, 16-20. 38 *FFÉ*, ii, 52-4. 39 *FFÉ*, i, 174-5; ii, 52-3.

ion as expressed by John Mair, Bede and even Giraldus Cambrensis.[40] Keating cited a Welsh author, Humphredus, in support of the view that 'The Scots themselves, and all besides, know well that they are the descendants of the Irish; and our countrymen (i.e. the Welsh) call them by the same name, that is, Gaels'.[41]

The Irish language was important to Keating because he wished to use it to help define an Irish identity. He presented the language as one of the elements that distinguished clearly between those of his contemporaries who were Irish and those who were not. Stressing that the New English could not understand Irish-language sources allowed Keating to imply that they had no claim to the history recorded in that language. The Irish language was the medium through which the story of the Irish people had been preserved until Keating's own time. The Old Englishman Richard Stanihurst's ignorance of the language placed him culturally among the New English to whom access to the true history of Ireland would be forever denied. Keating extended the politicisation of the language by asserting that people like Stanihurst who sought to banish the Irish language were also seeking to banish those whose language it was.[42]

Keating encouraged the idea that the status of the Irish language, though no longer the language of the political elite by the 1620s, was the language of the indigenous people of Ireland. The Norman conquest, he asserted, had been a Christian conquest, because it had not sought to destroy the indigenous people or their language:

> he who makes a Christian conquest thinks it sufficient to obtain submission
> and fidelity from the people who have been subdued by him, and to send
> from himself other new people to inhabit the land over which his power has
> prevailed, together with the people of that country ... he who makes a
> Christian conquest extinguishes not the language which was before him in
> any country which he brings under control.[43]

The argument allowed Keating to present the Norman conquest in a favourable light while re-emphasising that Gaelic was the language not just of the Gaeil but of those of Anglo-Norman descent also. These views on the status of the language, underpinned by a revised interpretation of the origins of the language that involved adaptation of the *Leabhar gabhála*, allowed him claim the language as an identifier not just of the '*Gaeil*', but of the broader category of '*Éireannaigh*', that included those Irish born of Anglo-Norman stock.

In a seventeenth-century world of dissension between native and newcomer, Keating was presenting the Irish language as a marker of Irish identity. Those who read his history in its original Irish form would have absorbed his message about the significance of the language for Irish identity in a rather more personal way than those who read his work in English translation. The linguistic medium of the original text itself constituted the most potent representation of the message Keating sought to convey.

40 *FFÉ*, ii, 58-60. 41 Ibid., 58-9. 42 *FFÉ*, i, 36. 43 Ibid., 34-7.

IV

While the people and the language were central elements of Keating's interpretative framework, the island of Ireland provided a geographical setting that was integral to his story. In the poem '*Mo bheannacht leat a scríbhinn*', Keating, the exiled poet, remembered fondly not just the people he had left behind in Ireland but the very hills, lakes, woodland, bogs and plains.[44] The island of Ireland itself as a physical entity was important to him. Throughout *Foras feasa* both the internal physical features of the island and its location in the wider world were regularly alluded to. His descriptions echoed the world view of the *Leabhar gabhála* so that his perspective was one that was deeply rooted in Irish culture for many generations.

The people and the landscape were seen as having lived through time in a closely integrated manner. The names people gave to the island, the specific features and places on the island, and the names of kin groups were all valued as evidence of that symbiotic relationship between the place and the people. Both the peopling of the island and the physical creation of the landscape were depicted as processes rooted in the distant past. There was a consciousness of the landscape as an artifact that recorded the peopling of Ireland. Thus the evolution of particular mountains, rivers and lakes was narrated in a manner that associated those physical features of the landscape with particular events significant for the peopling of the island. Placenames were no mere curiosities, they were an integral part of the historical record. Drawing from the *Leabhar gabhála* tradition Keating augmented the authority of his placelore by citing manuscript authorities for his descriptions, particularly the *Dinnsheanchas*.

The names for the island were brought to life with stories of the people behind the names. Thus the reader was told that when the descendants of Míl arrived in Loch Garman, 'the Tuatha Dé Danann assembled and congregated round them, and spread a magic mist above them, so that they imagined that the island in front of them was a hog's back, and hence Ireland is called Muicinis'.[45] The story then described the wandering of the sons of Míl in Munster and Meath and successive encounters with each of the triad Banbha, Fódla and Éire, as various personifications of the name of Ireland.[46] Drawing on the tradition of the *Dinnsheanchas*, Keating viewed the Irish language itself as a repository of historical evidence about the island of Ireland, its people and its customs. Names of peoples, placelore and etymology were all important analytical tools.

The story of the origins of the kingdom of Ireland was narrated as the story of successive kings interspersed with mention of the emergence of lakes and rivers.

> The fourteenth year after the death of Éibhear, Éireamhón died in Airgeadros at Ráith Beitheach, beside the Feoir, and there he was buried. The same year the river called the Eithne burst over land in Uí Néill; and the river called Freaghobhal burst over land between Dál nAruidhe and Dál Riada.[47]

---

44 Mac Giolla Eáin (ed.), *Dánta*, poem 2, see above, ch. 2.   45 *FFÉ*, ii, 82-3.   46 Ibid., 82-4.   47 Ibid.,

The recounting of such episodes linked these early kings with specific locations, Éireamhón's death and burial were made more significant, more relevant to the contemporary reader, by the fact that the precise place the event took place could be named and located. The integral link between these early kings and the island of Ireland was affirmed in a way that strengthened the sense of the symbiotic relationship between the institution of kingship and the land of Ireland.

Many placenames were exhalted by association with early personages associated with the kingship of Ireland. Thus, for instance, the name of the river known as Innbhear Colpa was linked to Colpa of the Sword, son of Míl who was drowned as he was coming ashore with Éireamhón son of Míl.[48] In another episode the emergence of a lake and a well were described in a manner that gave the holy well at Tobar Finn an authenticity deriving from antiquity.

> After that was fought the battle of Bealach Cró by Criomhthann, son of Éanna, where fell Fionn, son of Arb, at Tiobraid Fhinn, and the Dealbhna were slaughtered around him; and it is from this event that the lake in that place is called Loch an Bhealaigh Chró, and the well that is in the same place is called Tobar Finn.[49]

Examples of such snippets integrated into the grand narrative could be multiplied. One more case, that of Irial Fáidh, son of Éireamhón, will suffice here. The reader was first told that Irial Fáidh held the sovereignty of Ireland for ten years, and that he slew the four sons of Éibhear. The focus then moved to changes in the landscape during his reign. 'Sixteen plains were freed from wood in Ireland in the reign of Irial,'[50] The place and location of each of these plains was given. Then it was recorded that:

> Irial Fáidh son of Éireamhón built seven royal forts in Ireland in his time, namely Ráith Ciombaoith in Eamhain, Ráith Croichne in Magh Inis, Ráith Bachaill in Lotharna, Ráith Coincheadha in Seimhne, Ráith Mothaigh in Deaghcharbad, Ráith Búireach in Sleachta, Ráith Lochaid in Glascharn. The year after that the three rivers called the three Fionns burst over land in Ulster. The following year Irial won four battles'.[51]

In intertwining places with persons in a manner that enhanced the significance of both for the reader, Keating was not usually inventing connections. Rather he was retelling established stories from traditional placelore in his own style.

The narrative continued in this vein alternating between stories of the exploits of successive kings and stories of the evolving landscape, in a way that integrated the origin legend of the people, focused on the person of the king, with an origin legend for the landscape. The cumulative effect of repeated stories of this kind created the sense of the kingdom and people and land of Ireland having a shared heritage by which Irishness itself was defined.

114-17. **48** Ibid., 88. **49** *FFÉ*, iii, 150-1. **50** *FFÉ*, ii, 116-17. **51** Ibid., 116-19.

The various divisions of Ireland were explained in terms of the people who had introduced those divisions. Thus the reader was told of the division of Ireland into 25 parts for the 25 children of Ughaine Mór. It was according to these divisions, Keating explained, that rents and duties were paid to kings of Ireland for 300 years until a new division was made by Eochaidh Feidhlioch, who came to the throne in the year of the world 3940.[52] This next division was based on provinces, a topic Keating dealt with at length, because provincial divisions were very much a reality for his seventeenth-century readers.

> And this Eochaidh Feidhlioch it was who first divided Ireland into provinces and instituted provincials. For he divided the province of Conn-acht into three parts, between three, namely, Fidheac son of Feig, Eochaidh Allad, Tinne son of Connraidh. He gave to Fidheac Fir na Craoibhe, from Fidheac to Luimneach; he gave to Eochaidh Allad Iorrus Domhnann, from Gaillimh to Dubh, and to Drobhaois; he gave to Tinne son of Connraidh, Magh Sainbh and Sean-tuatha Taidhean, from Fidheac to Teamhair Bhrogha Niadh; he gave, moreover, the province of Ulster to Fearghus son of Léide, he gave the province of Leinster to Rossa son of Fearghus Fairrge, he gave the two provinces of Munster to Tighearnach Tead-bhannach and to Deaghaidh; so that he brought all Ireland under his own sway and rule during his reign.[53]

The successive divisions of Ireland were portrayed as the personal allocation of territory by a sovereign. The divisions were thus presented as an integral part of the political evolution of kingship in Ireland. The formation of Meath as the terri-tory of the high kings of Ireland was closely associated with the sovereignty of the king, a sovereignty pledged to him by the nobles of Ireland. Tuathal, a king who had won many battles, was proclaimed king of Ireland at Tara, having rescued the free races of Ireland from the tyranny of the Athachthuaith, a lower order of people with an ignoble pedigree. Having convened a gathering at Tara, 'a great general assembly to regulate the laws and customs of the country',[54] the nobles of Ireland pledged their support. In a section of narrative which was apparently not derived from his documentary sources Keating described how

> It was then, too, that he [the king] was given four portions of the provinces, out of which he made the present Meath, as the peculiar territory of the successive high kings of Ireland. For although Meath was the name of the territory which is beside Uisneach from the time of the children of Neimhidh to the time of Tuathal, still Meath was not the name of the por-tions that were taken from the provinces until the time of Tuathal, and he made it into a territory distinct from the provinces.[55]

---

52 *FFÉ*, iv, 130-1.   53 *FFÉ*, ii, 184-5.   54 Ibid., 244-5.   55 Ibid., 246-7.

He then described the four chief fortresses built by Tuathal in the four parts of the royal province of Meath: Tlachtgha, Uisneach, Tailtiu, and Tara.[56] The reader was thus presented with the setting for four institutions which Keating associated with the high-kingship: the fire of Tlachtgha, where the druids of Ireland offered sacrifice to the Gods on the eve of *Samhain*, and the men of Ireland were forbidden to kindle fires except from that fire; the Convention of Uisneach (*Mórdháil Uisnigh*) a fair that took place at *Bealtaine*, at which time sacrifices were offered to the God Beil, to secure protection of cattle from disease. Thirdly, there was the fair of Tailtiu which Keating associated with the formation of alliances of marriage and friendship among the men of Ireland. The fourth fortress at Tara was described as the venue for the *Feis* of Tara, presented as a royal assembly where the men of Ireland met to review and revise the laws and customs, annals and records of Ireland.[57]

D.A. Binchy has shown that the stories presented by Keating here were the product of the fabrication of 'national institutions' by synthetic historians of the tenth, eleventh and twelfth centuries and further adapted by Keating.[58] The idea of a high kingship had been created retrospectively, and validated by reference to these institutions which were portrayed as drawing the power of the four provinces towards a central focus of sovereignty. According to Binchy, the Fair of Tailtiu was a 'genuine historical institution', and the origin of the idea of a gathering of people there may well be pre-Christian. Tailtiu had been a place of religious significance, associated with a fire cult, and stories of a sacred fire at the site were preserved in the *Dinnsheanchas*.[59] Uisneach is more problematic and the description of commercial activities at Uisneach may have been invented by Keating himself, in an ongoing adaptation of the story of Uisneach as 'centre' of Ireland. Apart from Keating's one reference in *Foras feasa*[60] the only other mention of an assembly at Uisneach is in an entry that confuses the event with Tara, in a passage interpolated in a list of royal auspices and tabus.[61] Keating's entry regarding Uisneach contradicts the idea of a meeting of provincial kings under the king of Tara convened every seven years when each king paid 'rent' for his place at Tara to the 'king of Meath'. No other evidence of an assembly at Uisneach can be found in sources that predate *Foras feasa*.[62]

The claim that Tlachtgha originally belonged to Munster is dismissed by Binchy as a 'ludicrous fable', and the story of a tradition of fire-worship at that site is not found in earlier sources.[63] We must conclude therefore that Keating's story of the way the province of Meath evolved as the portion of the high king was simply a myth reformulated in line with the need to present an historical underpinning for a high-kingship of Ireland. The process of historical revision was an ongoing one in Keating's day and his version was at least partly his own fabrication. Indeed Keating was aware of the risk of contradicting some earlier documen-

---

56 Ibid., 246-52. 57 Ibid., 250. 58 D.A. Binchy, 'The fair of Tailtiu and the feast of Tara', *Ériu*, xviii (1958), pp. 113-38. 59 Gwynn (ed.), *Metrical Dindshenchas*, ii, 42-5; Binchy, 'Fair of Tailtiu', p. 114. 60 *FFÉ*, ii, 246-7. 61 See Myles Dillon, 'The taboos of the kings of Ireland', *PRIA*, liv, C (1951-2), pp. 1-36, at p. 28; Binchy, 'Fair at Tailtiu', p. 113. 62 Binchy, 'Fair of Tailtiu', p. 113. 63 Ibid., pp. 129-30.

tary evidence and he had to check himself and say that there was an earlier Meath, with a different origin to that associated with the high king's portion of each of the four other provinces.[64]

The name Meath, along with the names of places such as Tara and festivals such as *Bealtaine*, *Samhain* and *Lughnasa*, had resonance for those already familiar with stories of the Irish past and they were appropriated in this narrative.[65] They were used to create a plausible synthetic story of the highkingship, all the more credible because the use of these names allowed Keating to tell a story that appeared familiar.

Readers of Keating's narrative were not expected to, and for the most part did not, judge the 'reliability' of Keating's version of the past by reference to older 'definitive' versions of the stories he narrated. That is not how the stories of early Ireland were used, and that is not how the *Foras feasa* was meant to be read. He reassured his readers that if there was anything in his history that they had not heard before, he had the evidence of song or story to support it. 'If I make statements here concerning Niall Naoighiallach which the reader has not heard hitherto, let him know that I have song or story to prove every statement I advance here.'[66] Where different strands of the early evidence did not entirely agree, he exercised his judgment in choosing between them. But it is evident that he always bore in mind that much of the material he included in his history was already familiar to his readers.

V

For most people, Keating's history of Ireland was made more credible by its careful blending of the known with the unknown, the visible with the invisible, the familiar and named with the forgotten. Placelore was the crucial element which constantly linked the narrative back to territories and the peoples that inhabited them. The geographical entity that was Ireland was further defined in relation to its place within the known world. The interaction between the various peoples of the known world and various groups of the inhabitants of Ireland was all integrated into Keating's story of the shaping of the Christian kingdom of Ireland.

There were two main foci for the external world in *Foras feasa* as contextualised as part of the history of the Irish people. The first focus was the Near East, the lands of the Bible, a region which formed part of the necessary geographical backdrop to the way the story of Christian Ireland had evolved through the early medieval period. Since the corpus of Irish genealogical material traced the origins of Irish families back through Noah to Adam, there had to be a narrative explanation of how people with biblical origins came to be the indigenous population of Ireland. Keating did not neglect to describe the geographical setting appropriate to the *Leabhar gabhála* account of the origins of the Gaeil. The reader was given sufficient information to locate Ireland at the opposite extremity of Europe from

---

64 *FFÉ*, i, 32.   65 On Meath see RIA, MS D iv 2, Bodl., Rawl. B 512, Paul Walsh, 'A fragment used by Keating', *Archivium Hibernicum*, i (1912), pp. 1–9.   66 *FFÉ*, ii, 398–9.

Scythia, the place of origin of the early inhabitants of Ireland.[67] Four successive waves of invasion of Ireland, by the Parthalonians, Clann Neimheadh, Fir bolg and Tuatha Dé Danann, were described. Drawing on the evidence of the *Polychronicon* also, the etymology of the word *Scotia* and its link with the word *Scythia* was explained.

> And I think that is why Scot is more especially called to the posterity of Gaedheal, son of Niúl, son of Féinius Farsaidh ... Niúl (not having inherited any patrimony) enjoined on his posterity to denominate themselves from Scythia, and forever to call themselves Scots.[68]

Keating presented all of the invasions of Ireland after the Flood as being interconnected.

> Every invasion which occupied Ireland after the deluge is of the children of Magog. At Srú, son of Easrú, Parthalón and the children of Neimhidh separate from each other: and at Searea the Fir bolg, the Tuatha Dé Danann, and the sons of Míl separate. And it is the Scotic language every tribe of these had.[69]

Parthalón was described, by Keating, on the authority of a poem beginning '*Adhamh athair sruith ar slógh*', as having set out from, 'Migdonia', or Middle Greece, and travelling through the 'Torrian' sea to Sicily, and with the right hand towards Spain till he reached Ireland.[70]

Later, the journey of Neimhidh from Scythia, in the vicinity of the Black Sea, to Ireland was described in *Foras feasa* as a journey through a narrow sea with the mountains of Riffe, or the Urals, on the right, until he reached the northern ocean, and then travelled with Europe on his left until he reached Ireland. The feasibility of such a journey for a fleet of thirty-four ships may be doubted, but the specific naming of geographical reference points helped fix the idea of the invasion as a reality, and supported the idea that such a journey was entirely plausible.[71]

This geography of Asia on the right and Europe on the left, which Keating found in the *Leabhar gabhála*, was very simplistic, but he did not attempt to modernise it. The narrow sea leading north from Scythia to the ocean remains unnameable, yet to readers whose knowledge of the geography of foreign lands was unavoidably vague, the idea of a journey from beyond the extremity of Europe was effectively conveyed. Neimhidh was portrayed here in a manner that invited the reader to see him as a fore-runner of Míl, just as the biblical Moses was a fore-runner of Christ. The route of Neimhidh's journey from beyond Europe was repeated by Míl himself, with the difference that on reaching Alba Míl proceeded towards the Rhine and France to Biscay.[72] Two conflicting accounts of the journey

---

67 On medieval geographical perceptions of Ireland see Kenney, *Sources*, pp. 141-2. 68 *FFÉ*, i, 228-31. 69 Ibid., 174-5. 70 Ibid., 158, For further detail see Cronin, Sources of Keating's *Foras feasa ar Éirinn*. 71 *FFÉ*, i, 172-4. 72 *FFÉ*, ii, 44.

of Srú, son of Easrú, son of Gaedheal[73] from Egypt to Scythia were offered, with Keating opting for the version which described travelling 'from the mouth of the Nile through the Torrian Sea to Crete, which is now called Candia' and thence to Scythia. Evidently there was some controversy on this point and Keating added:

> and whoever should state that it was not possible to go from Egypt to Scythia by ship or vessel, considering how Scythia was bounded at that time, would not be stating a fact, since it is plain from every writer who has treated of geography that the river called Tanais flows into the Mediterranean Sea, and that that sea extends to Egypt, where the river Nile is; and according to the limits of Scythia at that time the river Tanais is reckoned among the rivers of Scythia according to Herodotus, an ancient author of weight.[74]

The second focus for the external world, against which the island of Ireland was to be defined, was an Atlantic-European one. Ireland's geographical location was placed by Keating in a firmly west-European context.

> Spain to the south-west side of it, France to the south-east side of it, great Britain to the east side of it, Scotland to the north-east side, and the ocean to the north-west side and to the west side of it. And in the form of an egg it is shaped, and its foot to Scotland north-eastwards, its head to Spain south westwards.[75]

Having located the island in relation to neighbouring countries, Keating then defined its extremities in Irish terms: 'The length of Ireland is from Carn Uí Néid to Cloch an Stocáin, and its breadth from Innbhear Mór to Iorrus Domhnann'.[76] While few people would have seen more than one of these extremities, the description was valuable in defining a sense of the island's geographical limits in its own terms as well as defining its location in the wider world. This approach, drawing on the author's own awareness of contemporary links with French and Spanish territories, and of the various links with England and Scotland and Wales, together with the documentary evidence, was used as a backdrop for the presentation of Ireland as a kingdom of considerable antiquity. It was 'a little world in itself', but one which was and continued to be capable of influencing neighbouring peoples in a variety of ways. Citing the English historian Camden as evidence, Keating asserted that in the era of Roman dominance, many people from Spain, France and Britain sought refuge in Ireland, it being the only place strong enough to have escaped Roman plundering.[77] Again the geographical perspective was an Atlantic one.

In a later episode, it seems that it was a reversal of the idea of invasion and conquest of Ireland that Keating had in mind in his description of Irish plunderers in Britain.[78] In the context of the life of St Patrick, the reader was told that in the reign of Niall Naoighiallach, the Scots of Ireland were plundering the three

---

73 Ibid., 30. 74 Ibid., 30-1. 75 *FFÉ*, i, 130-1. 76 Ibid. 77 Ibid., 16. 78 *FFÉ*, ii, 394-402.

kingdoms of Scotia, Anglia and Britannia[79] in opposition to Roman sovereignty. The twenty-seven years of Niall's sovereignty were portrayed as a period when the Irish king exercised his sovereignty strenuously ('*go nearthmhar*'), and Keating deduced from the authoritative evidence of 'an old vellum book' that 'from the above words we may believe that Niall Naoighiallach entered Great Britain and that he made conquests there'.[80] There was nothing unusual in this. The Irish, he asserted, had often gone on expeditions to plunder Britain.[81]

This perspective was then broadened to France and particularly Brittany, and Keating allowed himself further speculation as to where St Patrick might have been taken captive, bearing in mind that the saint's mother was said to have been a sister of the French saint Martin of Tours.[82]

> I am also of opinion that it was while Niall was making conquests in Great Britain that he sent a fleet to pillage the borders of France, to the country which is called Armorica, which is now called Little Britain, and that it was thence Patrick and his two sisters were brought as captives. I am the more convinced of the truth of this from the fact that Patrick's mother was sister to Martin, who was bishop of Tours in France, and because I read in an old book, in which is the life of Patrick in Irish, that it was from Armorica Patrick and his two sisters were brought into captivity.[83]

Some of the early contacts with France were portrayed as aggressive acts or invasions, as in the case of Ughaine Mór who went to conquer France[84] or Niall Naoighiallach and others who did likewise. On even slimmer evidence it was asserted that the Gaeil regularly plundered Africa.[85] The point being made was that the Gaeil were powerful not just in Ireland, but also exercised power and influence beyond Irish shores. In narrating the story of Ireland as the story of an independent kingdom of great antiquity, Ireland's assertions of status in relation to other powers were given special emphasis. It was also important to balance the stories of invasions of Ireland with some stories of exploits of the Gaeil overseas. Drawing on the evidence of saints lives, Keating reminded his readers of scholarly contacts in early Christian Ireland with France, Italy, Germany, Flanders, England and Scotland.[86] Long-established contacts between Ireland and Spain were traced to the last king of the Fir Bolg,[87] and the Roman historian Cornelius Tacitus was cited as evidence for the commercial links between France and Ireland.[88] In a passage which began by explaining why Labhraidh Loingseach went to France, but which ended by reflecting 1630s Ireland as much as any earlier era, Keating described

> a special friendly understanding between the Leinstermen and the French. Indeed every province in Ireland had formed a special friendly alliance beyond the sea, as the alliance between Clann Néill and the Albanaigh,

---

79 Ibid., 400.   80 Ibid., 402-3.   81 Ibid., 394.   82 Ibid., 402.   83 Ibid., 402-3.   84 Ibid., 64.   85 Ibid., 396.   86 *FFÉ*, i, 78.   87 *FFÉ*, ii, 50.   88 Ibid., 64-7.

between the Munstermen and the Sacsain, between the Ultonians and the
Spanish, between the people of Connacht and the Welsh.[89]

A Roscommon historian, Sean mac Torna Uí Mhaolchonaire, whose school of history was renowned in the late sixteenth century, was cited as his source for these
assertions.[90] These claims, coming in the context of a story with strong folklore
characteristics[91] about Labhraidh Loingseach going to France, were building on an
idea in contemporary circulation involving links between an Irish king and France.
They were also drawing on an awareness of the strong trading links between
France and Keating's own homeland in Decies, which had been reinforced by a
generation of contacts among students, particularly clerical students from East
Munster and South Leinster, including Keating himself, who had travelled to
France for their education. There were also resonances here, perhaps, of the
Norman invasion and the links between France and eastern Ireland established in
the twelfth century. Keating's reference to historical links between Munster and
England should probably be read in the context of the reality of the Munster plantation which had gone a considerable way to shaping Munster society into a world
that resembled southern England. Similarly, Keating's allusion to the links between
the Ulster family of O'Neill and the Scots, and between the Ulstermen and Spain
reflected recent rather than ancient history. The late sixteenth-century associations
of the O'Neills with Scots mercenaries, the subsequent departure of the earls of
Tyrone and Tyrconnell to Spanish lands in 1607, and the strong links established
by Ulster clerical students with the university towns of Spain and the Spanish
Netherlands, were all part of the contemporary context that confirmed the connection that Keating noted. Each instance was a clear example of an historical
veneer being given to a contemporary reality.

While Keating did not make any qualitative distinction between Irish links with
England as compared with any other region within the Atlantic world, he did have
a clear eye to the significance of French and Spanish links with the Ireland of his
own day. Although there is ample evidence that Keating viewed Ireland and the
Irish through the eyes of a returned migrant who had been stimulated by the
opportunity of seeing his homeland from an altered perspective, his account of the
origins of the Irish people was informed primarily by the written sources available
to him and on uncontroversial matters like geography he confined himself primarily to the perspective of his twelfth-century sources.

89 Ibid., 166-9.   90 Ibid., 166-8; *ARÉ*, i, p. lxviii.   91 I owe this interpretation to Tadhg Ó Dúshláine.

8

Political and social hierarchies

The 'invasions' framework of the early part of Keating's narrative history, with its strong biblical overtones, was followed by a lengthy section structured around a chronology of kings. This material, drawn from the *Réim ríoghraidhe*[1] found in manuscript compilations as a continuation of the *Leabhar gabhála*, allowed Keating full scope to develop his idea of a kingdom of Ireland. Using the succession of kings as the structure on which to build his narrative, he could narrate the history of an island kingdom so ancient that its origins could be traced to the beginning of time. As seen in the previous two chapters, that kingdom was depicted as having been peopled by a race of the highest pedigree, bound together by bonds of kinship, language and geography, that had their origins in scripture. Contemporary political and social hierarchies, however, exercised a considerable influence on the way Keating portrayed the past. The nature of the Irish kingdom in Keating's own day and the significance of the contemporary relationship between king and parliament were reflected in his construction of the past. His description of the role of law in early Ireland, his portrayal of heroes, his distinctions between differing social hierarchies, between the noble and the ignoble, his depiction of foreigners and his account of the arrival of the Normans, all had resonances for seventeenth-century readers.[2]

I

The idea that Ireland was a separate kingdom unto itself 'like a little world' was at the core of Keating's view of the history of his native country.[3] There were two key political dimensions to this perception. The first involved the immediate world of Ireland's kings, the sovereigns who had ruled that distinct kingdom. The second necessitated definitions of the kingdom and people of Ireland against others. Those others might be named individual opponents, or other specific groups of attackers. They could form elements of a legendary unfree tribe, the Athachthuaith, hostile

---

1 Anne Cronin, Sources of Keating's *Foras feasa ar Éirinn*. 2 For discussion of how later writers drew on Keating's ideas see Cunningham, 'Representations of king, parliament and the Irish people'. 3 *FFÉ*, i, 38-41.

to the interests of the free tribes of Ireland.[4] Alternatively they could be ill-defined *gaill* (foreigners), whose origins were sometimes made clear from the context,[5] but at other times were kept suitably vague.[6] Yet again, they could be contemporary heretics hostile to the values of a Catholic people, such as were alluded to in the preface to *Eochair-sgiath an Aifrinn*.[7]

In Keating's view of the past there were three distinct epochs of kingship in Ireland. Ireland before the coming of Christianity was the first era, firmly brought to a close with the coming of Patrick. The second great era was that of the kingdom of Ireland in the early Christian period down to the coming of the Normans. The final period of kingship began when Henry II of England aquired the sovereignty of Ireland. Keating devoted particular attention to establishing the legitimacy of the claims of the Norman kings to the sovereignty of Ireland, but only after he had characterised the nature of Irish kingship in considerable detail through the stories of the individual exploits of successive kings of Ireland. The narrative focussed on each of the kings of Ireland in succession, in a progression from pagan to pre-Christian to Christian to Anglo-Norman.

The political theory of kingship espoused by Keating was outlined in the section of *Foras feasa* that described the inauguration of kings.[8] Keating began this description by explaining

> Now, the reason why one person is made king over tribes and over districts is in order that each one in his own principality should be obedient to him, and that none of them should have power to resist or oppose him during his sovereignty, and to have it understood that it was by God who is Lord and ruler over all that he has been appointed king over the peoples to govern them, and hence that they are bound to obey him and to bear in mind that it is the same only God who is lord of heaven and of earth and of hell that gave him that authority and that it was from Him he obtained sovereignty.[9]

At first glance this seems like an assertion of the idea of the 'divine right' of kings, but on closer examination this is not so. The king's sovereignty, in the Irish context, did not come immediately from God, because the kingship was elective not hereditary. Before the coming of Patrick, Keating recorded, 'it was the learned and those who were most zealous for the aggrandisement of the public weal that the men of Ireland elected' as king.[10] In relation to the early Christian period, Keating was more specific on the identity of the electors. 'Since the coming of Patrick, it was the bishops and the nobles and the chroniclers who elected the kings and lords until the Norman invasion'.[11] Keating was here affirming the role of the Christian church in early Irish society, and simultaneously enhancing his portrayal of Irish kingship by associating it directly with Christianity.

---

4 *FFÉ*, ii, 238-44.   5 *FFÉ*, i, 60, 68, 72, 84, 120, 230.   6 *FFÉ*, ii, 310, 318.   7 *ESA*, pp. 1, 10.   8 *FFÉ*, iii, 8-14.   9 Ibid., 8-9.   10 Ibid., 10-11.   11 Ibid.

The inauguration of kings was presented as having particular significance, and Keating felt it necessary to outline its purpose. In the ceremony of inauguration, a

> chronicler came forward bearing the book called the Instruction for Kings, in which there was a brief summary of the customs and laws of the country, and where it was explained how God and the people would reward the doing of good, and the punishment that awaited the king and his descendants if he did not carry out the principles of justice and equity which the Book of Kings and the Instruction for Kings direct to put in practice.[12]

The white wand used in the inauguration ceremony signified equity and justice, truth, and freedom from bias.[13] The description of these various aspects of the inauguration procedure conveyed Keating's sense of the honour attaching to kingship in an Irish context. His interpretation of this old symbol of just kingship was intended to be read by contemporary readers in the light of their own experiences of kingship in seventeenth-century Ireland.

In addition to describing the inauguration of kings in some detail, Keating emphasised the significance of kingship in many other ways. It was a truism in his narrative, as in much early Irish literature, that during the reign of a good king, the whole kingdom prospered. During the reign of Eochaidh, last of the Fir bolg to be king of Ireland, for example, 'there was no rain nor bad weather ... nor yet a year without fruit and increase'.[14] Conversely, when the sovereignty of the rightful king was usurped, famine and crop failure followed. Thus when the story was told of the serfs and rustic tribes who plotted against Cairbre, king of Ireland, and killed the free tribes of Ireland with the exception of three unborn sons of king Cairbre, the usual prosperity of Ireland did not return until these three had come back and accepted their father's inheritance as kings. Even in this instance, however, it should be noted that the sovereignty of Ireland was not acquired by heredity alone. The sons of Cairbre were asked by the men of Ireland to assume sovereignty.[15] Sovereignty was in the gift of the people.

This same point, which had a contemporary relevance for the relationship between the Old English and their Stuart king, was implicit in the description of the inauguration of the O'Donnell chiefs also. When an O'Donnell was installed as king, he was surrounded by his nobles, epitomising civility within Gaelic society. The king's status was enhanced by the support he enjoyed from the nobility in his territory. They were both the source and sustenance of his sovereign authority.

Keating did not analyse the nature of sovereignty in any detail. Rather he focussed on the idea of a rightful king, under whom the country would prosper, and on the disaster that would befall if that rightful king was usurped. A Munster king of the Christian era, Cormac mac Cuilennáin, was portrayed as one under whom the province enjoyed great prosperity and constant peace. Such was the tranquility, he

12 Ibid. 13 *FFÉ*, ii, 12. 14 *FFÉ*, i, 198-9. 15 *FFÉ*, ii, 240-1.

asserted, that cattle did not need herdsmen, nor sheep shepherds; Ireland was then a land of scholarship, just laws, piety, almsgiving and hospitality.[16] That the well-being of Ireland and its people was intrinsically linked to the rule of a just king was made abundantly clear. Early Irish kings regularly asserted their sovereignty over Ireland on the battlefield, often claiming the crown following the death of the previous incumbent in battle. Few early kings died in their beds. Thus an early pagan king, Slanóll son of Ollamh Fódla died of unknown causes, but the fourteen kings who succeeded him all died violently, with the exception of one who was killed by lightning.[17] Ollamh Fódla himself, who 'died in his house', was another exception to the rule. His reputation was that of a law maker, and originator of the *feis* of Tara, which Keating described as 'a great general assembly like a parliament, in which the nobles and ollamhs of Ireland used to meet'.[18]

The sometimes unpalatable exploits of the pagan inhabitants of Ireland seem not to have posed a difficulty for Keating who was quite happy to record one regicide after another. Kim McCone has argued that these stories of Ireland before the coming of Christianity were acceptable to Irish Christian audiences because they were perceived as being the indigenous equivalent of the Old Testament period in the Bible, which was not without its violent episodes.[19] It is no mere coincidence that Keating's history is in two books, and that the dividing point between the first and the second parts is the coming of Christianity to the Kingdom of Ireland. The structure deliberately mirrors the division of the Bible into Old and New Testaments.

In relation to the early Christian period, the personal attributes of the individual king were a major focus of concern in the Irish literary tradition, and the text containing the advice of King Cormac to his son, known as *Tecosca Cormaic*,[20] was used by Keating as a guide to kingship worthy of the kingdom of Ireland.[21] His physical appearance, military prowess, and the wisdom of his judgements were measures of the quality of a king, and these were the values intrinsic to the *Tecosca Cormaic* text.[22] The best kings were portrayed as having successfully combined military prowess with wise judgements. Essentially, Cormac was portrayed as a king whose heroism was asserted by intellectual rather than martial activities.[23]

Though there may be doubt as to whether a real personage existed on the basis of whom the heroic tales associated with Cormac mac Airt evolved, the story of this king, whom Keating claimed was sovereign of Ireland for forty years, encapsulates the model of an ideal king.[24] The value of the heroic tales of Cormac, some of which date perhaps to the ninth century, is that they adapt the model of heroic biography to the native ideology of kingship.[25] Keating popularised this old tradition for a new generation of readers in the seventeenth century. His portrayal of

---

16 *FFÉ*, iii, 194.   17 *FFÉ*, ii, 132-42.   18 Ibid., 132-3.   19 Kim McCone, *Pagan past and Christian present in early Irish literature* (Maynooth, 1990), p. 77.   20 Kuno Meyer (ed.), *The instructions of King Cormac Mac Airt* (RIA, Todd lecture series, xv) (Dublin, 1909).   21 McCone, *Pagan past*, pp. 121-2.   22 *FFÉ*, ii, 304; iii, 10.   23 Tomás Ó Cathasaigh, *The heroic biography of Cormac Mac Airt* (Dublin, 1977), pp. 9-10.   24 *FFÉ*, ii, 298.   25 Ó Cathasaigh, *Heroic biography*, pp. 25-6.

Irish kingship was not done in a vacuum but drew its inspiration from the traditional intermingling of the story of Christianity and Irish kingship.

Keating's description of the ascent of Brian Bóroimhe to the position of king of Ireland illustrated central aspects of kingship in an Irish context. Brian Bóroimhe obtained the kingdom of Ireland 'by the strength and bravery of his feats of valour and championship, driving the foreigners and the Danair out of the country, and not by treachery as others assert'.[26] He was not a usurper, Keating assured his readers, 'for it was not the custom in Ireland that the son should succeed the father in the sovereignty of Ireland, as is plain from the history up to this point, but the sovereignty of Ireland was given to him who was the most powerful in action and exploit'.[27] In Brian Bóroimhe's case then, his predecessor, Maoilseachlainn, had forfeited his claim on sovereignty, because he had given in to 'luxury and comfort and ease' when he should have been devoting his energy to expelling foreigners.[28] Because of this the majority of the nobles of Ireland chose Brian Bóroimhe to be sovereign in his place. Those who did not choose Brian, we are told, were forced to submit against their will.[29] Military prowess, therefore, was the key to winning the support of the people and the award of sovereignty. When a rightful king was installed, the whole country prospered and bore fruit. The three elements of kingship as analysed by modern scholars, of sovereignty, military prowess and fecundity, thus permeated the narrative history of the kingdom of Ireland.[30]

The idea that the king was chosen by the people, and not by right of heredity was emphasised in *Foras feasa*.

> We do not read in the seanchus that there was ever any king of Ireland from the time of Sláinghe to the Norman invasion but a king who obtained the sovereignty of Ireland by the choice of the people, by the excellence of his exploits, and by the strength of his hand.[31]

The implication was that there was a contract between king and people, an idea found in texts associated with the idea of kingship in Ireland from at least the eighth century.[32] A reader of *Foras feasa* could be in no doubt that kingship was still central to the Irish polity. In a narrative ranging over many hundreds of years, the reigns of kings were the episodes around which much of the story of Ireland was structured. That the structure was borrowed from the *Leabhar gabhála* and the *Réim ríoghraidhe* does not diminish the significance of Keating's choice of the succession of kings as the framework of his narrative.

---

26 *FFÉ*, iii, 256-7. 27 Ibid. 28 Ibid., 248-9. In the work entitled *Cogadh Gaedheal re Gallaibh*. See above, ch. 4. 29 *FFÉ*, iii, 256-7. 30 Ó Cathasaigh, *Heroic biography*; Breandán Ó Buachalla, 'Aodh Eangach and the Irish king-hero', in Donnchadh Ó Corráin, Liam Breatnach and Kim McCone (eds), *Sages, saints and storytellers: Celtic studies in honour of Professor James Carney* (Maynooth, 1989), pp. 200-32. 31 *FFÉ*, iii, 182-3. 32 Thomas Charles Edwards, 'A contract between king and people in early medieval Ireland: *Crith Gablach*', *Peritia*, viii (1993), pp. 107-19.

II

The Ireland of Keating's historical imagination was a kingdom that absorbed waves of outsiders. The story of Ireland in *Foras feasa* did not portray the indigenous population as resisting newcomers. Rather was it that the newcomers successfully established an entitlement to the sovereignty of Ireland. Ireland was portrayed as being and remaining an independent kingdom in its own right, a kingdom where the king had never been subject to any higher authority before the eleventh century. Quoting directly from the Latin of Giraldus Cambrensis himself, Keating asserted that 'from the first, Ireland has remained free from the invasion of any foreign nation',[33] a quotation he valued so much that he repeated it later in the volume, translating '*incursu*' alternately as '*iomruagadh*' and '*ruathar*'.[34] The reader was supplied with the context in which to interpret this statement:

> From these words it is evident that neither Arthur, nor any other foreign monarch, ever had supremacy over Ireland from the beginning till the Norman invasion: and moreover, it is not conceivable that the Britons had any control over Ireland, since even the Romans did not venture to meddle with it, and it is not alone that the Romans, or other foreigners, had no control over Ireland, but it is Ireland that was a refuge to the other territories to protect them from the violence of the Romans and other foreigners.[35]

There was a clear distinction in Keating's mind between the idea of tribes arriving in Ireland and establishing themselves there, and the notion of a foreign power gaining control over Ireland. In his account, successive tribes had arrived to inhabit Ireland who were the precursors of the modern peoples of Ireland. These peoples were the link between the island of Ireland and the peoples of Old Testament times. Particular emphasis was placed on the story of Míl, father of the Gaeil. Sovereignty was linked with destiny in the case of Míl, who 'bethought him that Caicher the druid had foretold, long before, to his ancestor Lámhfhionn, that it was in Ireland his descendants would obtain permanent sovereignty'.[36] The scene was thus set for the arrival of the sons of Míl from whom the Gaeil traced their descent. They were clearly not to be seen as invaders:

> Were we to assert that no foreign nation ever acquired full supremacy over Ireland except the tribes that successively occupied it, namely, Parthalón, the Clann Neimhidh, the Fir bolg, and the Tuatha Dé Danann, and the sons of Míl, perhaps we should not be believed unless the reader had seen what Gulielmus Nubrigensis has written, treating of Ireland, in the twenty-

---

33 *Hibernia, ab initio ab omni alienarum gentium incursu libera permansit.*   34 *FFÉ*, i, 16–17, 82–3. He gives the reference alternately as ch. 26 and ch. 46 (perhaps scribal error?).   35 *FFÉ*, i, 16–17.   36 *FFÉ*, ii, 44–5.

sixth chapter of the second book of his history, in which he says 'Ireland never submitted to a foreign power'.[37]

Irish origins were traced through Míl to the Scythians. They were older than the Egyptians, who in turn were older than the Greeks, and they had never been subordinate to any other earthly power. Citing Becanus, and ultimately Epiphanius, as his authority, Keating asserted that the people of Scythia obtained sovereignty (*ardfhlaitheas*) shortly after the deluge, and that their sovereignty continued until the predominance of Babylon.[38] The worthiness of these Scythian origins was made abundantly clear: 'great was the bravery and the valour which was among the people of Scythia'. They were 'never subdued by any dominion'. They were doers of very great deeds, their gallantry, bravery and valour was such that they were 'always without foreign power affecting them or seizing their spoils'. 'They had heard of the power of the Romans, and [yet] had never felt it'. Moreover, it was from Scythia that 'other countries used to receive institutes and laws and ordinances' emphasising that these Scythian origins were a source of civility.[39] Not only were the people of Ireland never conquered by the Romans, they were descended from a civilisation older, and thus worthier, than the Roman Empire. The kingdom of Ireland had not adopted Roman law, but had inherited its own laws from a civilisation older than Rome. He thus presented his readers with an idea of Ireland as a truly ancient, independent, kingdom, exceptional in Europe in not having succumbed to Roman influence, and to be more higly prized than any territory that had fallen under the influence of that more recent civilisation that was Rome. It was in giving substance to such arguments that the antiquity of the origin legend was important.

Keating added context to the Arthurian legends then in circulation among Irish readers by emphasising that King Arthur and Muircheartach, king of Ireland, were equals. He denied that Muircheartach owed tribute to Arthur, likening their relationship to that between the king of Spain and the Holy Roman emperor.[40] In this as in other instances throughout the text, Keating's historical evidence was drawn from Irish and European traditions, but the political context of his interpretation was the relationship between the kingdom of Ireland and the kingdom of England. The political institution of the kingship was the element that gave a sense of continuity and coherence to Keating's story of Ireland through the upheavals associated with successive waves of settlement in pre-Christian Ireland.

In a rare reference to the contemporary era, Keating reminded his readers that the present king of Ireland, Charles I (1625-49) and his father James (1603-25)

---

37 *FFÉ*, ii, 398-9. 38 *FFÉ*, i, 228-9. 39 Ibid. 40 *FFÉ*, i, 14-17; For examples of Arthurian romances in circulation in early seventeenth-century Ireland see Máire Mhac an tSaoi (ed.), *Dhá sgéal Artúraíochta: mar atá Eachtra Mhelóra agus Orlando agus Céilidhe Losgaide Léithe* (Dublin, 1946). See also Joseph Falaky Nagy, 'A new introduction' to R.A.S. Macalister (ed.), *Two Irish Arthurian romances* (London, ITS, 1908, 1998 reprint), esp. p. [10]; William Gillies, 'Arthur in Gaelic tradition: part 1, folktales and ballads', *Cambridge Medieval Celtic Studies*, no. 2 (1981), 47-72; 'part 2, romances and learned lore', *Cambridge Medieval Celtic Studies*, no. 3 (1982), pp. 41-75.

'came from the Scotic race (that is to say, from the posterity of Máine son of Corc son of Lughaidh, who came from Éibhear son of Míl of Spain)'.[41] The reference was made in the context of explaining stories relating to the *Lia Fáil*, a coronation stone. Citing Hector Boece's *Scotorum Historiae*, Keating recounted the prophecy associated with the *Lia Fáil*. Wherever the stone was located, a descendant of Míl of Spain would have sovereignty there.[42] Keating considered the accession of the Stuart king James VI of Scotland to the crown of England as James I of England in 1603, and his being succeeded in turn by Charles I, as a fulfilment of the prophecy. He further asserted that the stone was used in the inauguration ceremonies of the Stuarts as kings of England. This idea conflates two inauguration stones, the so-called Stone of Scone, which would have been used at the inauguration of James I, and the pillar stone at Tara known as the *Lia Fáil*. Such conflation epitomised Keating's model of the kingdom of Ireland.[43] Keating referred to Charles I as 'the king we have now' (*an rígh so againn anois*) in a manner which made plain that he was entirely comfortable with the idea of one king for the three separate kingdoms of Scotland, England and Ireland. The validation of Charles as rightful sovereign was achieved by reference to Milesian genealogy and a long-established mode of inauguration. Such thinking reflected early seventeenth-century values as expressed by a variety of Gaelic poets, including Eochaidh Ó hEodhasa and Fearghal Óg Mac an Bhaird.[44] The Stuarts, however, were not Keating's central contemporary concern. Though Keating regarded himself as 'Irish', his own Norman ancestors could not be portrayed as Milesian, and therefore could not be easily be depicted as a branch of the Irish genealogical tree. Secondly, if the kingdom of Ireland were to be portrayed as having a continuous existence from earliest times to the present, the legitimacy of monarchs since Henry II as sovereigns in Ireland had to be established. Given the particular emphasis placed by Keating on the idea of Ireland as an independent kingdom that had never been subject to any higher secular authority in the pagan or early Christian era, his treatment of the coming of the Normans requires particular consideration.

The arrival of Henry II in 1172 marked the beginning of the third great epoch in the history of the kingdom of Ireland. The first epoch had been the era of pagan kings, the second that of the kings of Ireland since the coming of Christianity. Keating had previously argued that the transition from pagan to Christian kingship had been a period 'without change'[45] with the exception of the druids being replaced by Christian clerical counsellors in the king's retinue. The transition from the highkingship of Ireland under Ruaidhrí Ó Conchobhair to the sovereignty of Henry II was more complex and had political resonances in Keating's day.

---

41 *FFÉ*, i, 208-9. 42 Ibid., 206-8. 43 T. Ó Broin, 'Lia Fáil: fact and fiction in the tradition' *Celtica*, xxi (1990), pp. 393-401; P.J. O'Reilly, 'Notes on the coronation stone at Westminster and the Lia Fáil at Tara', *JRSAI*, xxxii (1902), pp. 77-92; J. O'Rourke, 'The Lia Fáil, or stone of destiny', *IER*, 3rd ser., i (1880) pp. 441-53; L.S. Gogan, 'Dála Lia Fáil', *Feasta*, iii, no. 2 (1951), pp. 10-12. 44 Ó Buachalla, 'Na Stíobhartaigh agus an t-aos léinn: Cing Séamas', pp. 81-134; Carney, *Irish bardic poet*. 45 *FFÉ*, ii, 342-3.

Henry II's position was given an appropriate constitutional legitimacy which underpinned the idea of the continuity of the kingdom of Ireland. Keating focussed on the notion of an assignment of sovereignty through the papacy. Keating's history contained a story that Donnchadh mac Briain son of Brian Bóroimhe, and king of Ireland, had visited Rome on pilgrimage. There, together with the nobles of Ireland, he had 'consented to the bishop of Rome's having authority over them'.[46] Keating placed this event 'about 77 years before the Normans came to Ireland'. Although his chronology here was incorrect, Donnchadh mac Briain having died in Rome in 1064, he reused the same story later. This was done to re-emphasise the idea that the papacy had possession of and sovereignty over Ireland until the time of Pope Adrian IV.[47]

Keating's portrayal of the status of this Munster king contrasts with the accounts in the northern Annals of Ulster and in *Annála ríoghachta Éireann*, where Donnchadh is described as a deposed king at the time of his pilgrimage to Rome.[48] Keating's story is corroborated, however, by the Munster Annals of Clonmacnoise and his version provided a context for the 1155 papal bull, *Laudabiliter*, issued by Adrian IV, that had a particular appeal to the Old English.[49] This bull conferred conditional power on Henry II to govern Ireland, specifically requiring him 'to maintain and protect every privilege and every termon land that was in the country' of Ireland.[50] In this version of events Henry II was not portrayed as a conqueror of Ireland. Rather he had come to Ireland on legitimate business and had gained recognition from the nobility and clergy of Ireland as their legitimate overlord.[51] That foreigners had arrived in Ireland, at the invitation of Diarmait Mac Murchadha, was not denied, nor did Keating claim that there had been no violent clashes. Drawing on the local history of his own home territory of Decies, he first noted that a military expedition of foreigners had landed at Dún Domhnaill, four miles south of Waterford, 'and when they had landed they built a strong embankment of stones and clay in that place'.[52] Such claims were verifable for Keating's contemporaries: the fortifications were still there almost five centuries later. Probably equally credible for Keating's readers was the story of a battle in the Waterford region between the Normans and the people of Decies, a story that may well have been still alive in local memory. Keating recorded that

> when news reached Port Lairge and Maoilseachlainn Ó Faoláin, king of the Deise, that these foreigners had arrived in their neighbourhood, they were all seized with hatred and fear of them, and they came to one place to take

---

46 *FFÉ*, iii, 6-7. **47** *FFÉ*, iii, 346-7. For further description of Donnchadh in Rome see *FFÉ*, iii, 290-7. **48** *The annals of Ulster to AD 1131, text and translation*, eds Seán Mac Airt and Gearóid Mac Niocaill (Dublin, 1983), s.a. 1064; *ARÉ*, s.a. 1064. **49** *Annals of Clonmacnoise*, ed. Murphy, s.a. 1063. **50** *FFÉ*, iii, 348-9. **51** Bradshaw, 'Geoffrey Keating: apologist of Irish Ireland', pp. 176-78; *FFÉ*, iii, 342-50. The idea, if not the precise detail, of Keating's account of this episode was accepted in the 1650s by the author of *A contemporary history of affairs in Ireland*, ed, J.T. Gilbert (3 vols in 6 parts, Dublin, 1879), i, 2. **52** *FFÉ*, iii, 332-3.

counsel in reference to this matter, and the decision they came to was to attack the strangers in the stronghold in which they were, and to slaughter and destroy them.

After this they came to one place, and their number was three thousand men when going to oppose these foreigners. When Raymond [de la gros] saw them approach him he went out quickly and unwisely with his small party to meet that large host with a view to engaging them in battle and conflict. But when he saw that he was not strong enough to fight them, he retreated to the fortress he had himself raised. When the Gaeil saw the foreigners retreating, they followed them vehemently and boldly into the fortress. But when Raymond de la gros observed that his enemy were boldly in pursuit of him he turned on them and made indescribable slaughter upon that great host of Gaeil, so that apart from all he slew of them he maimed and wounded five hundred of them on the spot.[53]

An attack on Waterford and the capture of Dublin followed, and Mac Murchadha accompanied by the 'earl of Stranguell' (Strongbow) and his foreigners had achieved such fame and renown 'that the men of Ireland conceived a horror and dread of them'.[54] In Keating's version it was at this point that Henry II, the king of England, came to the rescue, arriving in Waterford to restrain the unruly and disruptive foreigners from their unwelcome activities in Ireland. By degrees all the kings and lords of Ireland came to him and pledged obedience to him, even a somewhat reluctant Ruaidhrí Ó Conchubhair.

> Now when Ruaidhrí Ó Conchubhair, king of Connacht and of Ireland, heard that his provincial kings and those who paid him rent and tribute, and those to whom he himself gave wages and stipends, had put themselves under the protection of the king of England, he judged in his own mind that it would be less an indignity for him to submit to the king of England voluntarily than to do so against his will.[55]

Eventually, 'there was no king or leader or lord in Ireland who did not at that time make submission to the king of England and acknowledge him as their lord'.[56] Keating reiterated that Mac Murchadha looked for assistance from the king of England rather than the king of France or any other king 'because of the grant the pope had previously made of Ireland to the king of England', which authority over Ireland made it 'his duty to demand amends or satisfaction for the injury done to Mac Murchadha'.[57] In this way Henry II was portrayed as having proved himself worthy of the trust the nobility and clergy of Ireland placed in him. The unworthy leaders of the foreigners who had invaded Ireland were named and were accused of committing 'more evil deeds than all the Gaeil that lived from the time of Brian to the Norman invasion as regards the plundering of churches and cler-

---

53 Ibid., 332-5.   54 Ibid., 334-9.   55 Ibid., 342-3.   56 Ibid., 344-5.   57 Ibid., 350-1.

ics, bloody deeds of treachery and violent tyrrany'. In an assertion of his belief in the triumph of good over evil, Keating reassured his readers that such misdeeds did not go unpunished, noting that 'the majority of these persons on account of their own misdeeds left behind them no son to take up his father's inheritance'.[58] The consequence of the arrival of the Normans, in Keating's view, was a victory for the moral order.

In Keating's scenario Ireland had not been conquered by the Normans. Rather Henry II had been welcomed by clergy and nobility as a monarch whose obligation it was to protect those over whom he had been legitimately assigned sovereignty by the pope. Ruaidhrí Ó Conchubhair, king of Ireland, had agreed to Henry's role as lord and protector, and the legitimacy of the Anglo-Norman kings was thereby established. The reality of conflict was explained away as constituting the atrocities of a small minority, who had ultimately been punished by God for their misdeeds. Being himself of Anglo-Norman descent, Keating felt it necessary to emphasise that the unruly invaders had no descendants among the Anglo-Normans of Ireland. The Gaeil who had resisted them were exonerated from blame on the grounds that they had not been justly treated and that, given good government, they were a peace-loving, law-abiding, civilised people. It was important that in this climax to his narrative, both Gaeil and Gaill were shown in a favourable light. It remained only to establish the credentials of those Anglo-Norman families who did establish themselves in Ireland under the protection of Henry II and his successors. This was achieved by the simple device of introducing 'other leaders' who 'came to Ireland in the beginning of the Norman invasion, besides the five we have named above, who did not commit the deeds of treachery that the said five committed, and who did much good in Ireland by building churches and abbeys and giving church lands to clerics for their support, together with many other good deeds besides, and God gave them as a return for this that there are many descendants after them at this day in Ireland, to wit, the Fitzgeralds, Burkes, Butlers', and many others.[59] Later scribes added names to the list as they felt appropriate. Not least, they added the name Keating, thus revealing that they understood the point of the narrative in purifying the pedigree of the Irish families of Anglo-Norman descent. The very survival of those of Anglo-Norman descent was, in Keating's view, evidence of their worthy origins. While those origins were different from those of the Gaeil, their merits were delineated in a manner that echoed the qualities shared by the Sean-Ghaill and Gaeil mentioned at the beginning of *Foras feasa*. He was drawing to a close a history that had told

> of the virtues or good qualities of the nobles among the old foreigners and the native Irish who then dwelt in Ireland, such as to write on their valour and on their piety, on the number of abbeys they had founded, and what land and endowments for worship they had bestowed on them ... insomuch that it cannot truthfully be said that there ever existed in Europe folk who

---

58 Ibid., 358-9. See below, ch. 9. 59 Ibid., 368-9.

surpassed them, in their own time, in generosity or in hospitality according to their ability.[60]

In choosing these particular attributes of the Normans, Keating was bringing together the values of good kingship and respect for the church as his twin ideals for a Catholic kingdom of Ireland.

III

The structure of society as depicted by Keating was hierarchical. In repeatedly making the point in his theological writings that death comes to all, '*idir uachtarán agus iochtarán*' (both upper and lower orders),[61] Keating was drawing attention to the hierarchical nature of society. The biblical description in Daniel 2 of a vision of a golden statue – 'the head of this statue was of fine gold, its chest and arms were of silver, its belly and thighs of bronze, its legs of iron, its feet part iron, part earthenware'[62] – was used to describe the components of society in hierarchical terms. Keating's analysis equated the fine gold head with kings and princes, the silver chest and arms with the noble advisors of princes. The bronze belly and thighs were the nobility and the gentry who supported them with rents and taxes, the legs of iron the servants and volunteer defenders of the territory, the feet part iron part earthenware were the common people.[63] While Keating's didactic point here was about the universality of death, the passage also explained the structure of contemporary society as he understood it.

It was made clear at the beginning of *Foras feasa* that writing about the lower orders of society was inappropriate in the context of the history of a nation.

> Whoever should determine to make a minute search for ill customs, or an investigation into the faults of inferior people, it would be easy to fill a book with them; for there is no country in the world without a rabble. Let us consider the rough folk of Scotland, the rabble-rout of Great Britain, the plebeians of Flanders, the insignificant fellows of France, the poor wretches of Spain, the ignoble caste of Italy, and the unfree tribe of every country besides, and a multitude of ill-conditioned evil ways will be found in them; howbeit, the entire country is not to be disparaged on their account. In like manner, if there are evil customs among part of the unfree clans of Ireland (*daor-chlannaibh Éireann*), all Irishmen are not be reviled because of them.[64]

The people of Ireland whose history Keating sought to present consisted of the nobility whose lives and deeds were closely bound up with the activities of their kings. Thus John Barclay's description of the Irish living in cabins in which people shared their habitations with cattle was criticised because

60 *FFÉ*, i, 4-5.   61 *TBB*, line 82.   62 Daniel 2:32.   63 *TBB*, ll. 69-75.   64 *FFÉ*, i, 4-7, 56-9.

> this man stoops to afford information on the characteristics and on the habitations of peasants and wretched petty underlings ... he does not endeavour to make mention or narration concerning the palatial princely mansions of the earls and of the other nobles who are in Ireland.[65]

Keating did not deny that the hovels of the poor existed, but insisted that their description had no place in his narrative of the kingdom of Ireland.

The language used to describe the lower orders, or the rabble, was the language of 'otherness'. Thus the story of a peasant revolt against the kings and nobles of pre-Christian Ireland was the story of the negative consequences for the whole country that resulted from the actions of the lower orders in attempting to usurp the proper social hierarchy. The slaying of three kings was followed by famine, and adversity continued until the sons of the three slain kings were old enough to bear arms and regain their rightful inheritance.[66]

Irish society, as perceived by Keating, was one in which kinship was crucial. It was a world where fathers needed heirs, where children needed their parents.[67] It was a world where the sins of earlier generations had serious consequences for posterity. In *Trí bior-ghaoithe an bháis*, having cited Exodus 20:5, 'For I, the Lord, your God, am a jealous God punishing the children for the sins of the parents to the third and fourth generation of those who reject me.'[68] Keating related this to named persons in contemporary society in a manner which contrasts with his depiction of the Irish nobility in *Foras feasa* where the tone was designed rather to enhance the status of these families. Many of the same families of nobles were mentioned in a refutation of the claims made by Stanihurst about the status of the Gaelic nobility. Taking offence at Stanihurst's claim that the people of Fingal would not condescend to marry any of the Irish nobility, Keating retaliated by asking

> which were the more honourable, the more noble, or the more loyal to the crown of England, or which were better as securities for preserving Ireland to the crown of England, the colonists of Fingal, or the noble earls of the foreigners who are in Ireland, such as the earl of Kildare, who contracted alliance with Mac Carthy Riabhach, with O'Neill and with others of the nobles of the Gael; the earl of Ormond with O'Brien, with Mac Gil Patrick, and with O'Carroll; the earl of Desmond with Mac Carthy mór, and the earl of Clanricard with Ó Ruairc. I do not include the viscounts nor the barons, who were as noble as any settler who was ever in Fingal, and by whom frequently their daughters were given in marriage to the nobles of the Gael.[69]

It is evident that the status of the provincial nobility, both native Irish and Old English, was a matter of particular concern, and Keating was anxious that they be presented in a favourable light as honourable noblemen.

65 Ibid., 54-5; John Barclay, *Icon animorum* (London, 1614), p. 93; Cronin, 'Printed sources', p. 254.
66 *FFÉ*, ii, 236-41.   67 *TBB*, ll. 1160-7.   68 *TBB*, ll. 5340-50.   69 *FFÉ*, i, 32-5.

There was a close relationship between the nobility and the church in Keating's account of the early Christian period. Patronage of abbeys and churches was regularly mentioned as a virtue characteristic of the Irish nobility. After the coming of Christianity, it was the nobility of Ireland who decreed that the clergy should be the keepers of the *seanchas*.[70] Later, nobility and clergy together were credited with laying down laws for laity and clergy at a series of ecclesiastical councils in the twelfth century, culminating in the synod of Kells in 1152.[71]

Keating depicted the nobles (*fíor-uaisle*) of pre-Norman Ireland as pious Catholics. Penance and pilgrimage was second nature to them:

> It is plain, from the number of genuine nobles who, towards the close of their lives, betook themselves to the principal churches of Ireland to end their days in penance, from the time of Brian to the Norman Invasion, that the faith was then alive in Ireland. Here follow some of these, to wit, Flaithbheartach Ó Néill, who was called Flaithbheartach of the Pilgrim's Staff, he first began to do penance in Ireland, and after that he went to Rome on a pilgrimage in the year of the Lord 1073; and Donnchadh, son of Brian Bóroimhe, who went on a pilgrimage to Rome and who ended his days in penance in the monastery of St Stephen; and Tadhg, son of Lorcán, king of Uí Cinnsealaigh, who ended his days in penance in the church of Caomhghín in Gleann da Loch ... and so it was with many others of the true nobles of Ireland who closed their days in piety and as Catholics from the time of Brian to the Norman invasion.[72]

The description Keating provided of the assemblies that took place at Tara cast further light on his understanding of the role of the nobility in early Irish society. The nobility were the kingmakers: they chose the person who would be their king.[73] In conjunction with the *ollamhs*, they renewed the customs and laws of Ireland at the assembly convened at Tara by the high king. Thus, they were the decision-makers, and the law-makers for Ireland.[74] They met in assembly arranged hierarchically.

> Now the *Feis* of Tara was a great general assembly like a parliament, in which the nobles and the ollamhs of Ireland used to meet at Tara every third year at Samhain, where they were wont to lay down and to renew rules and laws, and to approve the annals and records of Ireland. There, too, it was arranged that each of the nobles of Ireland should have a seat according to his rank and title. There, also, a seat was arranged for every leader that commanded the soldiery who were in the service of the kings and the lords of Ireland.[75]

70 *FFÉ*, iii, 32.   71 Ibid., 356.   72 Ibid., 352-3.   73 *FFÉ*, i, 100.   74 *FFÉ*, iii, 36-8.   75 *FFÉ*, ii, 132-3.

This description of the *feis* of Tara, with its echoes of a contemporary parliament, stressed the value of the close symbiotic relationship between the monarch and the nobility in establishing the laws of the country. Taken in conjunction with Keating's earlier assertion that the Norman kings had ruled the country by relying on the assistance of provincial earls, naming Ormond, Desmond and Clanricard, the description indicates that Keating considered it appropriate that the day-to-day government of the kingdom of Ireland should be entrusted by the monarch to the responsible care of the Old English nobility.[76] His description of the Synod of Dromceat, associated with St Colum Cille, also had echoes of a modern parliament. Citing the *Book of Glendalough*, Keating described the synod of Dromceat as having 'sat for a year and a month instituting laws and regulating tributes and forming friendly alliances between the men of Ireland'.[77]

Keating's concern with the status of the contemporary nobility was reflected in his depiction of the *fior-uaisle* of early Ireland. The nobles in *Foras feasa* are depicted as being in close alliance with their kings, advising and assisting them.[78] The story of the opposition to Turgesius, leader of the Lochlannaigh, drew attention to the virtues of the indigenous nobility.

> When the nobles of Ireland saw that Turgesius was upsetting the country, and that he had it is his power, and that he was enslaving and tyrannising over it, these nobles assumed a magnanimous courage and a valorous steadfast spirit, and they underwent great hardship and distress in their conflict with these tyrants.[79]

The defeat and subjection of the Gaelic nobility at the hands of the Lochlannaigh were portrayed as having had very serious consequences for the church, for learning, music, feasting and hospitality, even for luxurious clothing, in other words for all the cultural activities and luxuries that were considered to have been characteristic of society under the patronage of the indigenous nobility. Contemporary readers would have drawn their own comparisons about the status of the nobility within their own society.

In a status-conscious society, there were mechanisms in place to give expression to hierarchical differences. One way in which this could be done was through customs of dress. Thus Keating recorded for the pre-Christian period that:

> it was in the time of Tighearnmhas that clothes were first dyed purple, blue and green in Ireland. It was also in his time that embroidery, fringes, and filigree were first put on mantles in Ireland. It was he in the same way that introduced into Ireland the custom of having but one colour in the dress of a slave, two colours in the dress of a peasant, three in the dress of a soldier or young lord, four in the dress of a brughaidh, five in the dress of a district chief, six in the dress of an ollamh, and seven in the dress of a king or queen.[80]

---

76 *FFÉ*, i, 32-4.   77 *FFÉ*, iii, 96-7.   78 *FFÉ*, i, 38-40; iii, 36-8.   79 *FFÉ*, iii, 172-5.   80 *FFÉ*, ii,

Keating's hierarchical sense of the structure of early Irish society was expressed here by reference to colour of dress.[81] His description of Irish hierarchies in his own day, found in *Trí bior-ghaoithe an bháis*, would have been more readily recognisable to an Old English elite. Citing the vision of 'a hugh red dragon which had seven heads and ten horns, and each of the seven heads crowned with a coronet' in Apocalypse 12:3, Keating compared the seven heads with the seven levels of honour in a commonwealth. Here the degrees of status defined by Keating were pope, emperor, king, prince, duke, marquis and earl,[82] reflecting in its latter elements English rather than Gaelic hierarchical criteria. Keating was at home in both worlds, and he had little difficulty in equating the status of the nobility in Gaelic society with that of the largely Old English world of his readers and his patrons.

This hierarchical kingdom, where honour and social status were attributes to be valued, was one in which social upheaval was unwelcome. There is some slight evidence that Keating was conscious of threats to the status of the nobility being posed by the lower orders. The poem '*Om sceol ar ardmhagh Fháil*', sometimes attributed to Keating, laments the decline in status of the nobility, and the rise to prosperity of base peoples at the expense of the rightful nobility.[83]

> *Atáid foirne ag fás san gclár so Logha liofa*
> *dár chóir bheith táir gé hard a rolla scaoile*
> *síol Eoghain tláith 's an Tálfhuil bodhar claoite*
> *'s na hóig on mBántsrath scáinte i gcoigcríochaibh.*

> (A new tribe is growing in this plain of fluent Lugh
> who should be lowly however highly they reveal their genealogies;
> Eoghan's seed ignored and the race of Tál dumbstruck
> and the young (O'Briens) of Bántsrath scattered in foreign lands.)

The families perceived to be under threat were the major Munster families including the O'Briens, Fitzgeralds, Butlers and MacCarthys. The disruption to the traditional hierarchical social order concerned the poet. The precise identity of the upstarts who were the source of the disruption was not specified, but the implication was that they were unacceptable for primarily social rather than ethnic reasons.

The sentiments expressed in this poem were paralleled in other contemporary texts, not least the satirical prose text *Pairlement Chloinne Tomáis*. This satire, set in an imaginary parliament of churls, comprised two parts the first of which was apparently composed in Munster sometime after the 1613-15 parliament. Nicholas Williams has argued that the first part is 'based on the assumption that the Gaelic nobility have a divinely ordained right to rule the churls throughout Ireland'.[84] However, an alternative reading of the text, taking the 'Clan Thomas' as representing the Old English whose fortunes had declined, is also possible.

122-3. 81 Cf. reference to Daniel 2 above. 82 *TBB*, ll. 7858-9. 83 Pádraig de Brún, B. Ó Buachalla, T. Ó Concheanainn (eds), *Nua-dhuanaire, i* (Baile Átha Cliath, 1975), poem 15. 84 *Pairlement Chloinne Tomáis*, ed. N.J.A. Williams (Dublin, 1981), p. xxvi.

> It happened then, that as a result of the extensive war, there came diminution upon the men and inhabitants of much of Ireland, so that many of their noble men and base ones became extinct, and Clan Thomas began to dye their clothes blue and red, having previously spent a period of their existence in theft, oppression and violence; and then with the scarcity of population, they began to take holdings and to seek marriage alliances that were unseemly for them to seek or get, and gradually they became village headmen, and they began to make land expensive for the nobility, and set to dyeing their clothes stylish colours and to cutting them stylishly. ...
>
> When King James ascended the throne, as a result of his goodness and graciousness under him Ireland was filled with peace and prosperity for a long time, and Clan Thomas set about sending their children to school and to study for the priesthood; and none of them was satisfied unless he sent them to be taught rhetoric and natural philosophy, and their daughters to learn silk-work and sampler-making, so that land became more and more expensive, and the wealth of Clan Thomas began to diminish.[85]

It is very clear from this text that the upstarts who were perceived as disrupting the traditional social order were not the recently arrived New English, but rather came from within Irish society. While Keating's approach to the issue is less cynical, he shared the sentiment of regret over the social change that had impacted on Irish society in the first quarter of the seventeenth century. He was aware that a landholder could forfeit his land if accused of treason.[86] More pertinently he criticised the greed of those who sought to acquire land at the expense of its traditional owners. Keating insisted that those who amassed wealth and land for their families in an illegal manner were guilty of the sin of greed and were offending against the will of God.[87] The behaviour of individuals acquiring land not rightfully theirs, explicitly criticised in *Trí bior-ghaoithe an bháis*, was a reflection of the same social phenomenon of change to the traditional social order.

In similar vein, in the poem '*Och mo chreach-sa faisean chláir Éibhir*', the poet Brian Mac Giolla Phádraig (*c.*1580-1652) complained that beggarwomen's sons were parading about dressed like lords, speaking English and lacking in respect for the traditional values which the poet represented.[88] There are two issues here. The status of poets themselves was being undermined in the early decades of the seventeenth century because of the changing status of their elite patrons. But there was also a broader phenomenon of social mobility which challenged hierarchies and the traditional social order.

The status of poets mattered to Keating because he regarded respect for learning and the arts as an indicator of civility. He recorded that proper measures had been traditionally taken in Ireland to support the brehons, bards and historians, and to ensure the preservation of these scholarly families.

---

85 *PCT*, p. 23, transl., p. 83.   86 *TBB*, ll. 3320-5.   87 *TBB*, ll. 3542-7.   88 Seán Ó Tuama (ed.), *An duanaire, 1600–1900: poems of the dispossessed* (Dublin, 1981), pp. 90-1.

They assigned professional lands to each tribe of them, in order that they might have sustenance for themselves for the cultivation of the arts, that poverty should not turn them away; and moreover, it is the most proficient individual of one tribe or the other who would obtain the professorship of the prince of the land which he held.[89]

The status of the poets depended on the status of the nobility who were their patrons, and it is clear that Keating, like Brian Mac Giolla Phádraig and the anonymous author of *Pairlement Chloinne Tomáis*, placed a particular value on the traditional status of the nobility, both Old English and Gaelic. Their well-being was integral to the right ordering of society. At the next hierarchical level an appropriate reciprocal relationship between the nobility and the king was considered crucial. Each element of the social hierarchy was important for the prosperity of the kingdom of Ireland.

89 *FFÉ*, i, 72-3.

9

The moral order

I

Although the story of Ireland told in *Foras feasa ar Éirinn* was not ostensibly a moral tale of the triumph of good over evil, Christian religious and moral values permeated the narrative. Despite the warring exploits of kings it was made clear that the world of the Irish past was a world in which moral order had existed. That order was rooted in kingship and in law. It was overseen by a judgmental, sometimes vengeful, God who was actively at work in the world. Thus Keating recounted that God gave the Scoti victory over the Britons in the time of Vortigern 'on account of the evil passions and the pride and the sins of the Britons at that time'.[1] When German soldiers were brought in to assist, 'God used these Germans as a scourge to deprive the Britons of the sovereignty of all Britain ever since'.[2]

The Norman William Fitz Aldelmel after having committed many atrocities, as recorded in *Leabhar Breac Mhic Aodhagáin*, was punished by God for his misdeeds 'in a miraculous manner'. It was noted that God 'inflicted a foul deformity and an incurable disease on him through which he died a loathsome death, and that he received neither extreme unction nor penance, and that he was not buried in any churchyard but in a deserted grange.'[3]

The long episode recounting the dispute between the free and unfree tribes of Ireland following the revolt of Cairbre Chinn Chait concerned the triumph of good over evil. The Athachthuaith, the unfree tribe, when they consulted their druids on the cause of Ireland's current misfortunes, were told that the slaying of the kings who were the rightful sovereigns was the cause. The prosperity of the land could only be restored when a descendant of the rightful sovereign was restored to the kingship. This was ultimately achieved when Tuathal Teachtmhar gained the sovereignty of Ireland. To emphasise that order had now been restored to the country the reader was told that Tuathal held a *feis* at Tara 'to regulate the laws and customs of the country'.[4] Thus *Foras feasa* was a history of the kingdom of

---

1 *FFÉ*, ii, 396-7.　2 Ibid., 396-7.　3 *FFÉ*, iii, 362-3.　4 *FFÉ*, ii, 236-45.

Ireland in which the approved moral order was continually asserted through stories of the fate of kings, good and evil.

Keating's world was one in which the due punishment of sin could be directly
experienced by the living when God avenged evil-doing by allowing wrong to be
committed against a person or a community.[5] Thus, for instance, the sin of pride
among the Gaeil was offered as an explanation for the oppression suffered at the
hands of the Lochlannaigh. 'The saints of Ireland foretold that evil would befall
Ireland through the pride of their rulers, and through their tyranny, hence the
oppression of the Lochlannaigh came on them'.[6] The Lochlannaigh too, had only
themselves to blame when they were eventually defeated at the hands of
Maolseachlainn. Their sexual immorality left them open to being tricked by the
promise of women being sent to their bedrooms.

> Now at this time Maoilseachlainn with a body of soldiers was with his
> daughter, and he directed a number of those youths who were with her dis-
> guised as women, the moment Turgesius should lay hands on his daughter
> for the purpose of detaining her with him, to seize him by force and take
> him captive ... and that he would rush into the house at the first cry to
> help them to slay the Lochlannaigh.[7]

The story implied that the immorality of the Lochlannaigh rather than any supe-
riority of the Gaeil brought about their defeat. It was a story of the triumph of
Maolseachlainn and his virtuous youths over Turgesius and his immoral men.

Even the coming of the Normans was portrayed in these terms. Keating argued
that the loss of Irish sovereignty through conquest by the Gaill, was the result of
the sinfulness of Ruaidhrí Ó Conchobhair and Diarmait Mac Murchadha. The
adulterous behaviour of the king of Connacht and the king of Leinster prompted
God to allow the Gaeil to lose their sovereignty.

> Thus, I believe it was in revenge for the adultery of Ruaidhrí mac
> Toirdhealbhaigh Uí Chonchubhair, king of Connacht and the adultery of
> Diarmait Mac Murchadha, king of Leinster, that God allowed the Gaeil to
> lose the high kingship of Ireland and the Gaill to conquer them.[8]

This perception of the moral order pervaded Keating's historical writing (although
he modified his ideas on the conquest). He affirmed that the deeds of the evil
minority among the Normans in Ireland, who plundered churches and committed
deeds of treachery and violent tyranny, did not go unpunished by God. 'The
majority of these persons on account of their own misdeeds left behind them no
son to take up his father's inheritance'.[9] The virtuous, in contrast, were rewarded
with many descendants.[10]   .

5 *FFÉ*, iii, 6, 18, 166. 6 Ibid., 158-9. 7 Ibid., 180-3. 8 *TBB*, ll. 5461-6. 9 *FFÉ*, iii, 358-9. 10
Ibid., 368.

The idea that God would punish peoples whose sins offended him was treated in *Trí bior-ghaoithe an bháis* also. God would even allow Catholic Christians to be defeated by pagans, if the Christians had committed sin. Drawing on stories such as that of Attila the Hun, the triumph of the Goths in Italy, the Moors in Spain, the Vandals in France, and the Lochlannaigh in England, Scotland and Ireland, and offering Old Testament parallels, Keating hoped to persuade his readers of the calamitous consequences of sin, particularly the sin of pride, for the whole community.[11] Three crimes in particular were noted by Keating as drawing divine wrath on a community: criminal violence, adultery and bias against the church.[12] That there was a direct link between suffering and sin was implicit in *Trí bior-ghaoithe an bháis*. The idea of the sins of the nation having been responsible for the misfortunes of the nine years war was expressed in the writings of Aodh Mac Aingil, Philip O'Sullivan Beare, Fear Flatha Ó Gnímh and Aonghus Fionn Ó Dálaigh.[13] The same idea permeated the latter sections of *Annála ríoghachta Éireann* in the section partly derived from Lughaidh Ó Cléirigh's 'Life of Aodh Ruadh Ó Domhnaill'.[14]

II

The religious and moral values which Keating usually took for granted in *Foras feasa* were more coherently and comprehensively stated in his theological writings. Using the evidence of *Trí bior-ghaoithe an bháis* in particular, a clear impression can be formed of Keating's understanding of the moral order. In his series of sermon-like meditations on the theme of how to live a life that will be rewarded by eternal glory, the possibility of eternal damnation was portrayed as a very real alternative to salvation. The preacher's mission of reminding sinners of their ultimate fate if they did not repent was apparent throughout. Heaven, hell and purgatory were all realities to be contended with both now and in the future, and the reader was repeatedly reminded of the transitory nature of life on earth.

Keating's theology of sin was grounded on the medieval teaching on the seven deadly sins:[15] pride, covetousness, lust, envy, gluttony, anger and sloth. The classification had originated among monks in the Egyptian desert, but had been adapted in the medieval west for laymen by Gregory the Great and his follower Alcuin. For Gregory, the seven deadly sins represented successive stages of a decline into evil. Pride was deemed the root of all evil, leading to vainglory and on to envy, anger and avarice. Thomas Aquinas too had discoursed at length on the seven deadly sins, in the context of the seven cardinal virtues.[16] The theology faculties of early seventeenth-century French universities operating under Jesuit influence drew heavily on the teachings of Aquinas. It is not necessary to argue for such

---

11 *TBB*, ll. 9750-95. 12 *TBB*, ll. 5356-67. 13 Ó Buachalla, *Aisling ghéar*, p. 36; Bernadette Cunningham and Raymond Gillespie, 'The east Ulster bardic family of Ó Gnímh', *Éigse*, xx (1984), pp. 106-14. 14 *ARÉ*, vi, pp. 2288, 2294. 15 See especially *TBB*, ll. 7893-8266; 9249-385; 9796-10003; 10362-663; 10800-6. 16 Thomas Aquinas, *Summa theologica*, i, 2, q. 61; ii, 1, q.84.

a neat chain of influence on Keating's writings, however. The seven deadly sins had such a prominent place in moral teaching, and indeed in literature,[17] at home and abroad that it was unthinkable that the concept would not have surfaced in Keating's writings about sin and death.[18]

The institutional church, and particularly the preacher, were portrayed as offering advice and guidance to the sinner that would steer him towards repentance and thus save him from spiritual death. Despite this general assumption that the church knew the way to salvation, there was very little discussion of any sacraments or rituals of the church throughout *Trí bior-ghaoithe an bháis*. Some occasional concession was made to church doctrine on the two sacraments that were deemed to counteract sin: baptism and penance. The circumstances of the human race in the aftermath of original sin and before baptism was equivalent to an absence of the most fundamental goodness a person was expected to have. Even after baptism, the human condition was likened to the circumstances of a family whose father was guilty of treason. The discussion focussed on the implications of original sin rather than the efficacy of baptism.[19] Confession was likened to a shepherd of the soul, necessary because the devil treated the sinner as the wolf treats the sheep.[20] A story borrowed from *Leabhar na Seacht dTiodhlaictheadh* (*Liber de Septum donis*)[21] had an incidental story on confession,[22] but Keating did not use the opportunity to expand on the function of the sacrament. The sinner envisaged by Keating in these meditations seems to have lived in a world where the role of the priest was a rather peripheral one.[23]

There was a strong sense of a community context in Keating's discussion of sin. Examples were given of sins against one's neighbour. Theft of gold or silver, land or cattle from a neighbour was a rejection of God. Fornication and excessive drinking were also unacceptable behaviour.[24] The moral code being promulgated was expressed in terms of avoiding such sins against one's neighbour. The social world constructed by Keating presented the individual living in community with others. The cultivation of neighbourliness extended to the idea of helping the souls in purgatory by interceding for them. Readers were advised that they should pray for those in purgatory out of friendship and love and in thanks for favours received while the person was alive. God would reward the living for their care of the souls in purgatory, and there was also the promise that when the soul of the person who prayed for others finally reached heaven, the favour could be returned.[25]

The theological premise on which the community of the living and dead was based was the doctrine of purgatory. Although the living could not know for certain whether the person who had died had gone to heaven, hell, or purgatory, the likelihood that very many souls were destined to spend some time in purgatory was sug-

17 In the writings of Geoffrey Chaucer, Dante Alighieri and William Shakespeare, for example.   18 *Superbia, avaritia, luxuria, invidia, gula, ira acedia.* See A.B.D. Alexander 'Seven deadly sins' in James Hastings (ed.), *Encyclopedia of religion and ethics* (13 vols, Edinburgh, 1908-26), s.n.   19 *TBB*, ll. 3316-58.   20 *TBB*, ll. 2323-31.   21 A work by Nicolas of Dinkelsbühl (*c*.1360-1443), that would have circulated in manuscript form.   22 Tubach, *Index exemplorum*, no. 4777; *TBB*, ll. 9143-71.   23 *TBB*, ll. 10664-75.   24 *TBB*, ll. 2000-22.   25 *TBB*, ll. 4870-960.

gested as the guiding rule. A soul going straight to heaven was an exception. A story of a vision of St Colum Cille seeing the soul of a good king going straight to heaven was used to demonstrate the exceptional worthiness of the king, in a universe where the more usual journey of the soul followed the path through purgatory.

The doctrine of purgatory taught that those who died having committed venial sin, having unconfessed sins, or having neglected to make reparation for confessed sin, though confirmed in grace and certain of salvation, were temporarily denied the presence of God.[26] Keating's description added much physical detail to this abstract idea and insisted that the fire of purgatory was as real as the water of baptism.[27] The souls in purgatory were powerless to help themselves, and could only be freed from the pains of purgatory through the intercession of the community of the living. All the faithful were members of the 'communion of saints'. They comprised the community of all Christians who were joined in the faith of Christ in heaven, on earth or in purgatory. Though they suffered pain for sin committed during their lives, Keating emphasised that the souls in purgatory were not in despair of seeing God or of achieving salvation. The doctrine stated that the souls in purgatory could be helped by the prayers of their family and friends who were still alive, and by alms giving, fasting and other sacrifices.[28] The idea of a communion of saints was presented in a similar manner in the Irish Franciscan catechism by Bonaventure Ó hEodhasa, published in 1611.[29] A theological discussion of purgatory was also given prominence in the Franciscan Aodh Mac Aingil's treatise on penance, *Scáthán Shacramuinte na hAithridhe*.[30]

The doctrine of purgatory had been reaffirmed at the Council of Trent as an intrinsic part of Catholic teaching, in opposition to the Protestant reformers who denied that the concept had any biblical foundation.[31] Keating's discussion of purgatory included a series of scriptural references, chosen to demonstrate that he considered the doctrine to be scripturally based.[32] He avoided any reference to indulgences to be gained for souls in purgatory – a point of controversy which divided the Christian churches. Such a treatment would not have been necessary since the *Trí bior-ghaoithe an bháis* was not primarily a work of controversial theology; its readers were assumed to be committed members of the Catholic church.

Keating considered it his duty to draw attention to faults and abuses within the Catholic community where the responsibility of the living towards the dead had not been heeded. He emphasised the responsibility of the living in ensuring that the wills and testaments of the deceased were executed as stipulated.[33] It appears likely that Keating may have encountered cases of reluctance to hand over money or other bequests left by the deceased to clergy for masses for the benefit of the soul of the dead. A second abuse of which Keating was aware was that of clergy accepting money for such masses and subsequently neglecting to say the masses

---

26 *TBB*, ll. 4863-9.   27 *TBB*, ll. 5025-59.   28 *TBB*, ll. 3940-4279.   29 Ó hEodhasa, *An Teagasg Críosdaidhe*, p. 19.   30 Mac Aingil, *Scáthán*, pp. 121-2.   31 *The canons and decrees of the … Council of Trent*, transl. J. Waterworth (London, 1848), pp. 232-3.   32 John 5, Deuteronomy 22, Jeremiah 1; *TBB*, ll. 4724-75.   33 *TBB*, ll. 5158-92.

promised. A section of *Trí bior-ghaoithe an bháis* intensely critical of negligent clergy suggests that the quality of clergy was sometimes less than that required by the standards laid down by the Council of Trent.[34]

III

The typical individual addressed in *Trí bior-ghaoithe an bháis* was male, lay and literate. A knowledge of the fundamentals of Catholic doctrine was assumed. The reader was addressed as an individual who had an understanding of the purpose of prayer, who valued the teachings of scripture and was persuaded by its authority, who was familiar with the nature and purpose of the sacraments. Keating could take for granted that his readers accepted the doctrine on purgatory.[35] He assumed that his readers would be likely to have Masses said for the dead. He assumed that his readers knew something of or could be expected to have particular respect for the teachings of the church Fathers.[36] Keating reminded his readers that ignorance of the law of God was no excuse and asserted that 'the law of God is being widely broadcast and announced to Christians in general'.[37] While he was clearly confident that the Catholic message was being widely promulgated, there was an awareness that the Catholic church was not the only institutional church that would be encountered by the reader. Keating believed that his readers were in some danger of making inappropriate choices of pastors and needed to be advised to choose their spiritual mentors with care.[38] He specifically warned against timidly acquiescing in false doctrine for the sake of a quiet life on earth. Among those not in a state of grace he counted 'another group of them renouncing and hiding their faith for fear of disobeying their worldly superiors'.[39] In what should be taken as an exhortation against nominal conformity to the state church in order to avoid persecution, quoting Ecclesiasticus 6:1, Keating advised his readers that they must bravely take risks for their faith.[40] Later, he indicated that loyalty to the will of God in the face of persecution meant that Irishmen should be prepared to suffer and die for their faith.[41]

Perhaps the most colourful descriptive passage in *Trí bior-ghaoithe an bháis* is the description of the torments of hell. Such descriptions were commonplace in medieval literature, and Keating could not resist following in this tradition, conjuring up memorable images of the fires of eternal damnation. Hell was depicted as a place from which there was no return. There the souls of the dammed were eternally in company with Lucifer and a rabble of devils. It was full of ghosts and phantoms, monsters and demons, deformed and injured bodies. Using analogies his readers might identify with, Keating explained that the occupants resembled broken bands of soldiers without protection, or a wretched class of people without a shepherd; the horror and chaos were like a battlefield.[42] Such disorder reflected

34 *TBB*, ll. 4557-75.   35 *TBB*, ll. 3940-4030.   36 *TBB*, ll. 3470-4.   37 *TBB*, ll. 3388-9.   38 *TBB*, ll. 10664-75.   39 *TBB*, ll. 3547-9.   40 *TBB*, ll. 3552-6.   41 *TBB*, ll. 6056-74; 6097-118.   42 *TBB*, ll.

Keating's concept of the earthly chaos that would ensue in the absence of a king who offered protection and guidance. In the reign of a good king, evil was repressed, crime was absent and peace ensued, the crops grew, the weather was favourable, piety and learning prevailed.[43] A subverted world without order and hierarchy was the consequence of the absence of a benevolent king. A kind of hell on earth, would persist until the rightful king was restored to sovereignty.[44]

Keating used exceptionally long sentences in his description of the pains of hell, to reinforce the idea of the unending nature and the extensive range of the torments there. It was a physical place where every imaginable earthly pain and horror was multiplied. The emphasis was on physical pain, where the fires of hell really burned the soul, rather than mental torture suffered by the absence of the love of God.[45]

The alternative scenario was that in which the soul gained entry to heaven, the palace of paradise. Since the repentant needed a foretaste of what was in store in the kingdom of heaven (Isaiah 32), Keating provided a brief description of the joys of heaven.[46] Heaven was depicted as the place where the righteous, God's true friends, would receive countless divine gifts.[47] Peace and perfect tranquility prevailed, there was no evil and no sorrow or crime to be suffered. The delight of eternal glory was promised to the righteous as a life in the company of Christ sharing the inheritance of the friends of God as co-heirs with Christ.[48] It would be life without death, freedom without slavery, joy without sorrow, for all eternity.[49] Drawing on Matthew 13, Keating affirmed that the righteous in heaven would be so beautiful and bright that even the sun would not be brighter.[50] Heaven was the mountain of virtue and good deeds provided by God as a reward at the end of a journey through the desert of repentence.[51]

I V

The idea of a contract between God and the individual was paralleled by the idea of a contract between a king and his followers in the secular world. The religious aspects of the idea of a kingdom were interpreted in the light of contemporary political and hierarchical understandings of the structure of society. Secular perceptions of a contract between king and people were echoed in the idea of a contract between God and people. However, while in *Trí bior-ghaoithe an bháis* the need for a personal faith and repentance was emphasised, the religious imagery and values depicted in *Foras feasa* focused more consistently on the institutional church than on individual piety.[52]

The transition from paganism to Christianity, as it impacted on the kingship of Ireland, was presented in terms of Christian ecclesiastical advisers to the king taking the place of the druids. Having described the ten advisers of the high-king

6149-743. **43** *FFÉ*, i, 198; iii, 10; iii, 194. **44** *FFÉ*, ii, 238. **45** *TBB*, ll. 6149-743. **46** *TBB*, ll. 10883-8. **47** *TBB*, ll. 10962-7. **48** *TBB*, ll. 10975-8. **49** *TBB*, ll. 10990-5. **50** *TBB*, ll. 10978-83. **51** *TBB*, ll. 9000-12. **52** *FFÉ*, i, 4-5.

in the time of Cormac mac Airt as a prince, brehon, druid, physician, bard, sean-chaí, musician and three stewards, Keating added that:

> this custom was kept from the time of Cormac to the death of Brian son of Cinnéide without change, except that, since the kings of Ireland received the faith of Christ, an ecclesiastical chaplain took the place of the druid, to declare and explain the precepts and the laws of God to the king, and to his household.[53]

The transition to Christianity was presented here in legalistic, externalised fashion, where the trappings of church officialdom rather than a personal faith were emphasised.

Keating was careful to show that the days of druids and magic were over, and that pagan beliefs and customs were no longer current. Thus the reader was told that the *Lia Fáil*, the stone of destiny that the Tuatha Dé Danann brought to Ireland and which was subject to taboos, roared under the person who had the best right to the sovereignty of Ireland. However, the stone was silent now, 'for the false images [*bréig-dhealbha*] of the world were silenced when Christ was born'.[54]

Similar editing of the traditional story occurred elsewhere in *Foras feasa* also. The description of the death of Cormac mac Cuileannáin, king of Munster and bishop of Cashel, was apparently adapted by Keating from a version of the text now published as the *Fragmentary annals of Ireland*. The story is very similar in both texts.

> A party came to Flann Sionna, king of Ireland, bringing with them the head of Cormac, son of Cuileannáin, and they said to Flann: 'Life and health be thine, O slaughtering powerful king; behold we have the head of Cormac, king of Munster, for thee, and according to the custom of the other kings lift thy thigh and put the head under it and press it beneath thy thigh. For it was the custom of the kings that preceded thee, when they had slain a king in battle to cut off his head and to press it beneath their thighs'. But instead of thanking this party he reproached them severely for this deed, and said that it was a pity to behead the holy bishop and added that he would not press it; and Flann took the head in his hand and kissed it, and thrice turned round in full circle with the blessed head of the holy bishop. And then the head was reverently carried from him to the body, at which was Maonach, son of Siadhal, comharba of Comhghall, and he took the body of Cormac to Dísirt Diarmada, and it was there buried with honour.[55]

In this account Keating apparently adapted the concluding phrase, substituting 'and it was there buried with honour' in place of 'where it produces omens and miracles' of the presumed source.[56] Although Keating's editorial hand was not

---

53 *FFÉ*, ii, 342-3.   54 *FFÉ*, i, 100-1.   55 *FFÉ*, iii, 210-11.   56 Radner (ed.), *Fragmentary annals*, p.

always so clearly in evidence, the compilation of *Foras feasa* involved an ongoing process of selection, adaptation and omission from his source material.

Even pre-Christian kings were assigned attributes that accorded with Christian values. Cormac mac Airt was presented as personally resisting the influence of the druids.

> On a certain day, when Cormac was in the house of Cleiteach, the druids were worshipping the golden calf in his presence, and the general body of the people were worshipping it after the manner of the druids. Maoilgheann the druid asked Cormac why he was not adoring the golden calf and the gods like the rest. 'I will not', said Cormac, 'worship a stock made by my own artificer; and it were better to worship the person who made it, for he is nobler than the stock'. Maoilgheann the druid excited the golden calf so that he made a bound before them all. 'Dost thou see that, O Cormac?', said Maoilgheann. 'Although I see' said Cormac, 'I will worship only the God of heaven, of earth, and of hell'.[57]

Keating's christianisation of Cormac mac Airt, the ideal king hero,[58] was a significant modification of the heroic king genre.

> On account of the excellence of Cormac's deeds, and judgements and laws, God gave him the light of the Faith seven years before his death. And accordingly, he refused to adore gods made with hands; and he set himself to reverence and honour the true God; so that he was the third man in Ireland who believed before the coming of Patrick.[59]

These attributes of Christian kingship were, in truth, difficult to reconcile with the heroic king genre, but when faced with a choice, Keating's Christian values usually prevailed. The story of Conchubhar mac Neasa involved a case of incest with his own mother, who bore him a son named Cormac Conluingeas.

> Now Cormac is the same as Corbmac, an incestuous son; for it was through *corbadh* or incest that Cormac was the offspring of Conchubhar by his own mother, whose name was Neasa. And in punishment of this misdeed all his sons died without issue except three ... But there is no one to-day in Ireland descended from these.[60]

It is evident that Keating's sensibilities were offended by some aspects of the lore of pre-Christian Irish kings, and he sought to minimise the implications of the stories for contemporary readers.

---

159. These edited annals are from a seventeenth-century copy of a text penned by Dubhaltach Mac Fhirbhisigh in 1643 from a source presumed to be the now lost Book of Clonenagh: Ó Muraíle, *Celebrated antiquary*, pp. 89-90. Keating evidently had access to the Book of Clonenagh (*FFÉ*, iii, 212, 314, 316). **57** *FFÉ*, ii, 346-7. **58** Ibid., 344. **59** Ibid., 344-5. **60** Ibid., 214-17. See *FFÉ*, ii, 232 for a case of incest where the child succeeded to the sovereignty of Ireland.

V

Saints were significant figures in the Irish past as depicted by Keating. In a world where God was constantly at work, saints were the intermediaries between man and God, acting as God's agents on earth, implementers of the will of God. They usually featured in *Foras feasa* in the capacity of supporters or validators of the actions of kings. Thus in the case of the conflict between Guaire and King Diarmait it was made clear that battles were not won by large armies but by the will of God. The battle was lost by Guaire because a holy man, Caimín of Inis Cealltrach, had fasted against him. Guaire went to Caimín and paid him respect, and came to see that God's law was greater than any other. King Diarmait likewise recognised this and Guaire's submission to God was then accepted by King Diarmait in lieu of submission to himself.[61] This story was told as one of a series showing the power of the saints implemented through prayer and fasting, and emphasising the due respect that should be shown them, to win their protection.[62] In the battle of Cúil Dreimhne 'many of the people of Corcach fell through the prayer of Midhe, that is, a noble female saint of the race of Fiachaidh Suighdhe, son of Feidhlimidh Reachtmhar, to whom these people showed disrespect.'[63] In a similar episode,

> Fearghus and Domhnall, two sons of Muircheartach Mac Earc, won the battle of Cúil Dreimhne over Diarmait, son of Fearghus, and he was routed and most of his people were slain, through the prayer of Colum Cille. For he had slain, in violation of Colum's protection, Cuarnan, son of Aodh, son of Eochaidh Tiormcharna, and God avenged that deed on him in this battle.[64]

The selection of these stories presented these holy men and women to be models worthy of emulation. Very occasionally the contemporary parallel was made explicit as in the story of Mochua and Colum Cille. Mochua was a hermit in the desert whose only livestock were a cock and a mouse and a fly. The cock kept the matin time of midnight; the mouse ensured he slept no more than five hours in the day-and-night, while the fly marked his place in the Psalter that he read. When these companions died Mochua wrote a letter to Colum Cille and complained of the death of his flock. 'Colum Cille wrote to him, and said thus: "O brother", said he, "thou must not be surprised at the death of the flock that thou has lost, for misfortune exists only where there is wealth"'. Keating concluded the episode by drawing out the moral. 'From this banter of these real saints I gather that they set not store on worldly possessions, *unlike many persons of the present time*'.[65]

Such a viewpoint was made more explicit in *Trí bior-ghaoithe an bháis* where saints were depicted as following a penitential lifestyle appropriate for all to follow. Patrick, Colum Cille and other saints are mentioned in connection with fasting, alms-giving, and prayer, as well as preaching and administering the sacraments.[66]

---

61 *FFÉ*, iii, 60-3. 62 See also *FFÉ*, iii, 56. 63 *FFÉ*, iii, 56-7. 64 Ibid. 65 *FFÉ*, iii, 70-3 (my italics).
66 *TBB*, ll. 2255-73; See Cunningham and Gillespie, '"The most adaptable of saints"'.

In *Foras feasa* the exemplary status of the saints was taken for granted, and was used to enhance the reputation of those with whom they came into contact. Thus a story was told of St Mochuda arriving in Decies,

> and when he arrived there the king of the Déise went to meet him, and reverenced and honoured him, and commended his body and soul to his protection; and they both proceeded to Dún Scinne, which is now called Lis Mór. There Mochuda and his community dwelt, and there they built a church, so that the place has been honoured and celebrated for piety and learning ever since.[67]

Such stories integrated the lives of saints and kings in a way which helped depict the kingdom of Ireland as a virtuous entity permeated with Christian values.

The imprimatur of the national apostle, St Patrick, was given to the pre-Christian history of Ireland through the collection of middle-Irish tales known as 'Agallamh na senórach'. This work is based on the pretence that the 300-year-old Caoilte mac Rónáin had survived until the time of Patrick and had recounted to him stories of Irish antiquity relating to the reign of Cormac mac Airt.[68] By using this material Keating was reaffirming the validation of the history of early Irish kingship by association with the national apostle. Keating also included Patrick's supposed encounters with Aonghus, king of Munster,[69] and his (equally supposed) attendance at the inauguration of Duach Galach as king of Connacht.[70]

Stories about Colum Cille were also treated in a rather unsophisticated way. In contrast to the Louvain Franciscans who had a more European audience in mind, Keating displayed little concern for the significance of Irish hagiography either for the image and status of the contemporary Irish church or as a didactic tool. Keating was not particularly concerned to depict Colum Cille as an unblemished holy man. Where the Franciscans had described Colum Cille's sojourn on Iona as a pilgrimage for Christ, Keating, using unrevised sources, retold the story of Colum Cille having been banished from Ireland for having caused three battles, the battle of Cúil Dreimhne, the battle of Cúil Rathan, and the battle of Cúil Feadha.[71] Keating's account of the life and times of Colum Cille concluded with stories that showed he had been a special child destined for a life of sanctity. These were added almost as an afterthought following stories of the saint cursing his opponents, and using his staff to provide protection enforced through fear.[72] The core of Keating's discussion of St Colum Cille centred on the saint's return to Ireland to participate in the convention of Druim Ceat. His role was portrayed as political, influencing the decisions of the king. Having presented his picture of Colum Cille

---

67 *FFÉ*, iii, 122-3. 68 *FFÉ*, i, 150-4. 69 *FFÉ*, iii, 24, 26. 70 *FFÉ*, iii, 28; Cunningham and Gillespie, '"The most adaptable of saints",' pp. 82-104. 71 *FFÉ*, iii, 88. Keating was probably using Maghnus Ó Domhnaill's early sixteenth-century life of Colum Cille. (The Battles of Cúil Fheadha and Cúil Rathain are not mentioned by Adamnán, but they are found in Maghnus Ó Domhnaill's text.) I am grateful to Nollaig Ó Muraíle for this observation. 72 *FFÉ*, iii, 86-106.

as an influential abbot, not above cursing and swearing to achieve his objectives, a shrewd political operator who could act as intermediary between man and God, to achieve the right political result, Keating concluded by echoing other Irish writers in reasserting Colum Cille's Irish pedigree. 'Know, O reader, that Colum Cille was a genuine Irishman on his father's and mother's side, and not a Scot as some Scots say.'[73] He cited the *naomhsheanchas* to clarify Colum Cille's Irish paternal and maternal ancestry and then, almost as an afterthought, recited some evidence of the holy life which the saint lived. In Keating's version of the past it would appear that the priority was to prove Colum Cille's Irishness rather than his holiness.

As an advocate of a diocesan parochial structure rather than the monastic structure of the religious orders, Keating had difficulty in accommodating stories of monastic saints within his vision of the most appropriate structures for the contemporary church. Nevertheless, by allowing the stories of the moral worth of kings to be validated by their association with saints, Keating succeeded in conveying a sense of moral virtue at the core of early Irish kingship.

It was not necessary to use stories of saints to achieve this end. The story of Donnchadh Mór mac Ceallaigh, king of Ossory, fitted Keating's conceptual model rather better, in that it highlighted the significance of the Mass in association with this particular king's battle against the forces of evil:

> a doubt arose in the minds of clergy and laity, for they were surprised that demons should be openly attending the body of that most virtuous king. Indeed among the pious practices of the king were frequent confession and the receiving of the Body of Christ and fervent prayers; and among his exercises of holy zeal was to send food and provisions to be given to God's poor in each principal church in Osruighe on each of the apostles' feasts.[74]

An angel of God appeared and explained to the clergy that since the demons could not find opportunity to attend the king during life they were causing a disturbance over his body after his death. The angel instructed them to have Mass said and water blessed and sprinkled on the grave and the churchyard and all the demons would go away.[75] Such stories survived and were retold by Keating because they affirmed the sanctity of Irish kings.

Keating's understanding of the moral order was not compartmentalised into his theological writings alone. It permeated all his thinking, and his view of the supernatural world paralleled many dimensions of his perception of the nature of good and evil in secular society. His prose writings treated at length of many aspects of his understanding of the moral order, retelling well-known stories, reusing well-tried topics and themes, in the manner he deemed most appropriate to the needs of readers in the contemporary world.

---

73 *FFÉ*, iii, 102-3. This was a point of contention that had concerned other Old English secular clergy, particularly David Rothe and Thomas Messingham.   74 *FFÉ*, iii, 218-21.   75 Ibid.

PART 3
SCRIBES, TRANSLATORS AND OTHER READERS

Catholic readers and translators of
Foras feasa ar Éirinn in the seventeenth century

I

The Irish text of *Foras feasa ar Éirinn* was completed by 1634/5. Although not printed in full, in Irish, until the early years of the twentieth century it did not remain 'unpublished' in the intervening period. The text was already being made available to the reading public during the 1630s, by Irish scribes operating within several largely distinct scribal networks.

Not even a fragment of a manuscript known to be in Keating's own hand is now known to survive.[1] It was claimed in the early eighteenth century that Keating's autograph copy of *Foras feasa* was in the possession of the barons of Cahir, being descendants of Keating's patron. If true, this autograph manuscript and its whereabouts are now unknown.[2] No scribe claims to have worked from Keating's own text, though one mid-eighteenth-century Tipperary manuscript does claim to be based on a copy derived in direct line from that source.[3] Keating's works are known to us, therefore, only through the intermediary work of scribes. We can only assume that the earliest copies, made while the author was probably still living, resemble the author's text fairly closely. There are, however, many minor variations between copies of the *Foras feasa*, even those transcribed before 1644. It may well be that the pursuit of Keating's 'original' text is not a valid exercise, since more than one version of the author's work may have gone into circulation, with the consent of the author.

The existence of so many seventeenth-century copies of *Foras feasa*, in all their variety, is testimony to the vibrant scribal tradition through which the text was transmitted. Approximately thirty extant seventeenth-century manuscripts contain

1 The manuscript formerly supposed to have been in Keating's own hand (Hayes, *MSS sources*), once owned by the Revd P. Power and now UCC, Power MS 92, contains no internal evidence to support this supposition; see Dinneen's comments in *FFÉ*, ii, pp. xiii, xvii, xxxii, manuscript 'P'. 2 O'Sullevane, 1722, in Ó Cuív (ed.), 'An eighteenth-century account', p. 264. 3 BL, Add. MS 31,872 (1763). Edmond Purtil of Cahir, County Tipperary, writing in 1865, stated that this MS was a transcript of one that had been written by John Cody who had copied from Michael White's transcript of Keating's autograph text (*BL Cat. Ir. MSS*, i, 33); for one Michael White see above p. 20.

the text of *Foras feasa*; one third of these pre-date 1650. Copies of the work, in Irish, continued to be made throughout the eighteenth and nineteenth centuries.

The earliest scribes to copy *Foras feasa* were mostly from well-known families of scribes. Prominent among them were members of the Ó Duibhgeannáin and Ó Maolchonaire families. The earliest extant dated copy, was the work of Flaithrí Ó Duibhgeannáin.[4] In BL, Egerton MS 107, the scribal colophon at the end of the first book indicates that Flaithrí Ó Duibhgeannáin had finished copying it on 17 October 1638 in 'Baile Coille Foghair'. This was Castlefore, county Leitrim, one of the centres of learning traditionally supported by the Ó Duibhgeannain family of historians.[5] A second member of the family, Fearfeasa Ó Duibhgeannáin made a copy of *Foras feasa* in 1646, this time at Tombrick in Wexford.[6] A scribe of the same name, Fearfeasa mac Conchobhair Riabhaigh Uí Dhuibhgeannáin, working at Cill Tochomharc (Kiltoghert) in county Leitrim, made a further copy of *Foras feasa* in 1666.[7]

Keating's links with another scribal family may have been more significant for the dissemination of his works. Iollan mac Torna mic Muiris Uí Mhaolchonaire who transcribed *Foras feasa* in 1643[8] and Séamus Ó Maolchonaire of Ballymacooda, in the parish of Kilmaley, County Clare[9] were both members of the Thomond branch of this family of hereditary historians. Also from the County Clare branch of the family was the most prolific of seventeenth-century copyists of Keating's work. Seán mac Torna Uí Mhaolchonaire, of Ardchoill, County Clare,[10] became more closely involved with the full range of Keating's writings than perhaps any of his contemporaries. He is probably not, however, the person of that name of whom Flann Mac Aodhagáin wrote in 1636

> numerous the uncertain number of ancient and modern books which I saw written and being transcribed in the school of Seán mac Torna Uí Mhaolchonaire, the tutor of the men of Ireland in general in history and chronology, and who had all that were in Ireland learning that science under his tuition.[11]

Foras feasa and Keating's theological works all fell within the scope of Seán mac Torna's interests. In 1657 he was commissioned by Domhnall Ó Cearbhaill to provide a transcript of *Foras feasa*[12] and he was also responsible for several other copies of the work prepared on behalf of other, unidentified, patrons.[13] The same scribe also copied the earliest extant manuscripts of both *Eochair-sgiath an Aifrinn* and *Trí bior-ghaoithe an bháis*.[14] An Ó Maolchonaire link has also been suggested

4 BL, Egerton MS 107. Though undated, FLK, MS A 14 is almost certainly earlier than Egerton MS 107. These two texts, along with Paris, Bib. Nat. Fondes Celtique MS 66, do not contain certain passages normally included (apparently as later interpolations by the author) in later copies of *Foras Feasa*.   5 *BL Cat. Ir. MSS*, i, 28. They were also associated with Cill Rónáin in the north of County Roscommon, and with Seanchuaidh (Shancoe), County Sligo, and acted as hereditary historians to the Uí Fhearghail of Longford. 6 TCD, MS 1394.   7 RIA, MS 24 N 3.   8 RIA, MS 23 O 19.   9 Hayes, *MSS sources*: Copy in possession of Miss G. Hess, Howth, 1966. Current location of this MS not traced.   10 See Comyn's comments in *FFÉ*, i, p. vii.   11 *ARÉ*, i, p. lxviii, cited in Brendan Jennings, *Michael O Cleirigh, chief of the four masters, and his associates* (Dublin, 1936), pp. 153-4.   12 King's Inns, Gaelic MS 2.   13 TCD, MS 1397, MS 1439; TCD, MS 1403 is partly in his hand.   14 TCD, MS 1403. The complex question of Seán mac

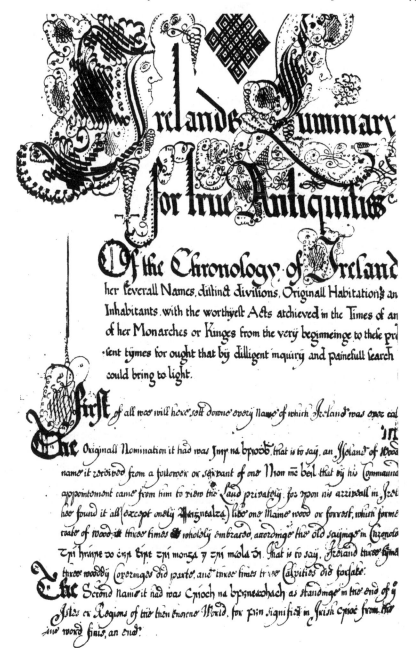

7 Opening page of book 1 of Michael Kearney's 1635 translation of *Foras feasa ar Éirinn*.
RIA, MS 24 G 16, f. 37

for the copy of *Foras feasa* preserved in Maynooth MS C 2.[15] Several copies remained in the Ó Maolchonaire family. TCD MS 1397 was subsequently owned by Muiris Óg mac Muiris mic Briain Óig Uí Mhaolchonaire, while RIA MS C iv 1, probably the work of Seán Ó Maolchonaire,[16] was in the possession of 'John Conry' of Rathmore in the 1690s.[17]

It is clear from the surviving manuscripts that the work of Ó Maolchonaire scribes made an important contribution to the early transmission of *Foras feasa*. Keating probably lacked the secular patronage that might have facilitated publication in print. In the circumstances, the best facilities available were provided by the Ó Maolchonaire scribes who shaped the text according to contemporary standards of scribal publication.

Given the prominence of Dál Cais and of the O'Briens in Keating's version of the history of Ireland, not least in the narrative of the exploits of Brian Bóroimhe and his depiction as epitomising the best of Irish kingship, it should come as no surprise that Thomond scribes, in particular, would have found a steady demand for their work. When *Foras feasa* was written the traditional mechanism for transmission of texts was still flourishing in Thomond and the history had an obvious appeal for readers with O'Brien connections. Seán mac Torna did not just concentrate on *Foras feasa*, however, and one of his manuscripts, now TCD, MS 1403, contains in addition to *Foras feasa* copies of *Eochair-sgiath an Aifrinn* and *Trí bior-ghaoithe an bháis*. Although now incomplete, this impressive manuscript was used by Bergin as a source for his edition of *Trí bior-ghaoithe an bháis*[18] and by Dinneen for his text of *Foras feasa* prepared for the Irish Texts Society.[19] A large folio manuscript, it was described by Dinneen as 'an excellent and accurate copy of the work', and was clearly the work of a practiced scribe.[20]

It is evident from the surviving work of members of these families that *Foras feasa* went into circulation in the traditional manner of Irish historical texts as soon as it had been completed by its author. The extant manuscripts suggest that Thomond and north Connacht, rather than the author's home territory of south Tipperary, was a principal centre of activity in the transmission of the *Foras feasa* text in the mid-seventeenth century. However, Bodl., Fairfax MS 29, copied in 1643, appears to have had Tipperary connections, and RIA, MS 23 Q 14, was transcribed in 1662 by Tomas Ua Faoláin of Tullamoylin, County Tipperary. It is also significant that the first translator of *Foras feasa* into English, in 1635, was Michael Kearney, of Ballylusky in County Tipperary.[21] He enjoyed the patronage of the

---

Torna Uí Mhaolchonaire's precise role in relation to these theological texts will be discussed below. **15** Original MS too fragile to consult in 1998. P. Ó Fiannachta (ed.), *Lámhscríbhinní Gaeilge Choláiste Phádraig Má Nuad* (Ma Nuad, 1968), v, pp. 1-2. **16** *RIA Cat. Ir. MSS*, p. 1672. **17** Dinneen's assertion that this copy was the work of Seán mac Torna Uí Mhaolchonaire is incorrect (*FFÉ*, ii, p. xxix), but it was probably the work of a scribe associated with the Ó Maolchonaire school. **18** Dublin, 1931. Manuscript 'H' in Dinneen's analysis, *FFÉ*, ii, introduction. **19** *FFÉ*, ii, pp. xxviii-xxix. Manuscript 'M1' in Dinneen's discussion. **20** It has been suggested by Dinneen that the second hand featured in this manuscript was that of Mícheál Ó Cléirigh. *FFÉ*, ii, pp. xxviii-xxix. **21** RIA, MS 24 G 16.

Butlers of Dunboyne,[22] and may have been encouraged by them to undertake the work of translation.[23]

In addition to circulating in the milieu of Gaelic historians, the text also went into circulation in another closely related community: Irish Franciscan scholars at home and abroad. In the early seventeenth century the Franciscans had a particular interest in the study of Irish history, their best known work being the renowned *Annála ríoghachta Éireann*. There is a direct link between one of the scholars who worked on *Annála ríoghachta Éireann* and the manuscript that is probably the earliest extant copy of *Foras feasa*. Although unsigned, it is believed that Micheál Ó Cléirigh, the principal compiler of the annals, was the copyist of most of the text of *Foras feasa* now preserved in Killiney, Gaelic MS A 14. This manuscript was written in the month of September (in an unspecified year in the 1630s, very probably no later than 1636) in the Franciscan convent at Kildare, apparently by Micheál Ó Cléirigh. While the year is not stated, the last occasion Ó Cléirigh might have had the opportunity to be in Kildare in September was 1636.[24] Since *Foras feasa* was not used by the Four Masters in their annals, completed in August 1636, it may be that the transcription of *Foras feasa* was undertaken after their own *magnum opus* was completed. Ó Cléirigh evidently did not have time to complete the copy himself, and another scribe was assigned to the task.[25] At any rate, it seems that the copy was complete in time for Ó Cléirigh to take it to Louvain on his return there early in 1637. It was used and annotated extensively by John Colgan at Louvain and was cited in the first volume of his *Acta sanctorum Hiberniae* published in 1645.[26] A slightly later Franciscan copy of *Foras feasa* that found its way to the continent[27] was prepared by Pól Ó Colla in county Leitrim in 1644. A further copy with a Franciscan pedigree, now preserved as Killiney, Gaelic MS A 15, dates from 1641. In 1652 it was owned by '*Jacobus Dulaeus, Limericinus Sorbonicus*', probably the Limerick man, James Dooley, connected with the Sorbonne in Paris. It appears that this manuscript remained on the continent and was associated with the Irish Franciscan college of St Isidore in Rome by 1739. By 1663, another copy of *Foras feasa* was being transcribed as far away as the Irish college in Prague, by Éinrigh Mac Ardghuil for the use of Micheál Ó Raghailliogh.[28]

In attempting to reconstruct the pattern of transmission of the text of *Foras feasa* it would not be prudent to read too much into the pattern of survival of the extant manuscripts in modern repositories. The proportion of extant early copies of *Foras feasa* that were associated with the Franciscans may simply be evidence of

22 NLI, GO MS 71. **23** The transcript made in 1668 of this translation (RIA, MS 24 G 16) may have been at the instigation of the earl of Orrery (*Clanricarde*, p. cxxv). **24** Jennings, *Michael O Cleirigh and his associates*, pp. 141, 147-8, 167-73. **25** The *díonbhrollach* was not in Ó Cléirigh's hand, suggesting that his interest was in the basic narrative rather than the polemical introduction. His other activities in 1636 are documented in Jennings, *Michael O Cleirigh and his associates*, and it is possible that Sept 1635 saw Ó Cléirigh commencing the work on copying *Foras feasa*. **26** FLK, MS A 14; John Colgan, *Acta Sanctorum veteris et Maioris Scotiae, seu Hiberniae sanctorum insulae* (Louvain, 1645), pp. 583, 654. **27** Paris, Bib. Nat. Fonds Celtique, MS 66. **28** Maynooth, Renehan MS 68.

a given manuscript's greater chances of survival in the long term if in the possession of a religious order rather than in private hands. There is no doubt, however, that the Irish Franciscans in the early seventeenth century, particularly those associated with St Anthony's College, Louvain, were active participants in the transmission of *Foras feasa* and were among its first and keenest readers.

II

Unlike in the case of publication in printed form, standardisation was never likely to be a feature of a text disseminated by scribes. One important variant in the Irish language versions of Keating's works in circulation in the seventeenth century was noted by Dinneen. A small number of manuscripts of *Foras feasa* contain more archaic language than that found in the earliest texts. There are four extant manuscripts of portions of *Foras feasa* which adopt more archaic language and syntax and more precise terminology. The archaic copies, for instance, use the word 'flaith' rather than 'rí' to denote petty princes. The archaic copies also transcribe the verse passages more carefully.[29] Curiously, Seán mac Torna Uí Mhaolchonaire made copies of *Foras feasa* in both the archaic[30] and the modern styles, which suggests that the explanation for the existence of two versions was not merely scribal preference.[31] Dinneen asserted, rightly, that the earliest form of *Foras feasa* was the 'modern' version, and made the plausible suggestion that the 'archaic' version which brought the text into line with the traditional style of the chroniclers may have been the work of a scribe expressly employed by the author for this purpose.[32] It is certain, at any rate, that the text circulated in both forms at an early date.[33] All eighteenth-century copies are in the modern style, which suggests that this was the form that most appealed to patrons.

It may have been the author's intention to seek an approbation from the hereditary historians for a version of his text presented in the more formal archaic style. However, there is no evidence that Keating's work received the sort of approbations sought in the mid-1630s by the compilers of *Annála ríoghachta Éireann*. The extent of the author's probable contacts with learned scholars such as Conall Mac Eochagáin and Seán mac Torna Uí Mhaolchonaire when seeking source materials for his history, and the respect subsequently shown for *Foras feasa* by the traditional learned families, suggests that such approbations would have been forthcoming if sought.

Indeed, the author seems to have encountered only a favourable response from the scribes.[34] They usually referred to him as 'Doctor' Keating, not a traditional

29 *FFÉ*, ii, p. xiv.   **30** TCD, MS 1397.   **31** King's Inns, Gaelic MS 2; first portion of TCD, MS 1403.   **32** *FFÉ*, ii, p. xvii.   **33** TCD, MS 1397; RIA, MS C iv 1; UCC, MS G 92 (previously owned by P. Power), and the latter portion of TCD, MS 1403 which is not in the hand of Seán mac Torna Uí Mhaolchonaire.   **34** But see Brian Ó Cuív (ed.), 'A seventeenth-century criticism of Keating's *Foras feasa ar Éirinn*', *Éigse*, xi (1965), pp. 119-40.

8 *Foras Feasa ar Éirinn*. Interpolated (?) text of on the theme of inauguration. RIA, MS 24 P 23, p. 295

Irish title, and his reputation evidently rested on the quality of his work rather than on his status as an hereditary historian.

It may well be that Keating never regarded his text as being quite finished. This might also explain the manner in which variant versions of the history went into circulation. These variants may represent drafts rather than a final version as approved for 'publication' by the author.[35]

In his preface to the printed text, Dinneen explains that there are two strands of the 'modern' version, one represented by the very earliest manuscripts and another, based on the work of the Ó Maolchonaire scribes, with more precise orthography. He has suggested that the versions of *Foras feasa* now preserved in Killiney MS A 15 (1638-41) and RIA MS 24 P 23 (1641-46) probably reflected Keating's orthography most closely before the text was modified in the copies made by the Ó Maolchonaire scribes.[36]

It seems reasonable to conclude that these early copies, along with the slightly shorter texts in BL Egerton MS 107 and Killiney MS A 14 and Paris Bib. Nat. Fonds Celtique MS 66 are the closest we can now get to the lost original text from the hand of Geoffrey Keating. But these five texts are far from being identical, and are a reminder that scribal publication did not impose the kind of standardisation inherent in the mechanical process of print.

While BL Egerton MS 107 was described by S.H. O'Grady as a 'condensed' version of *Foras feasa*[37] it would probably be more accurate to consider it an incomplete preliminary version of the text, to which a number of paragraphs were subsequently added by the author when supplementary information became available. In the full text as published by the Irish Texts Society, several passages read like interpolations, and some of these are missing in the early manuscripts of the Egerton MS 107 type. In the world of scribal publication it was not unusual for different drafts, representing stages towards a final text, to go into limited circulation.

One important instance of variant versions of *Foras feasa* in the extant seventeenth-century manuscripts is the passage describing the inauguration of kings. This passage is found in later manuscripts (from which the Irish Texts Society edition are drawn) at the beginning of the narrative of the kings of Ireland from the coming of Christianity.[38] This section was edited by Dinneen principally from TCD, MS 1403, but few seventeenth-century versions of *Foras feasa* place the inauguration passage at this point in the text. The description of inauguration reads like an interpolation in the manuscripts that insert it at the beginning of the narrative of Christian kings.[39] The more usual location for this passage in the seventeenth-century manuscripts is much later in the narrative, immediately preceding the description of the rights and dues of Brian Bóroimhe.[40] In the early manu-

---

35 Cf. Peter Lucas, *From author to audience* (Dublin, 1997), p. 2.   36 *FFÉ*, ii, p. xviii. RIA, MS 24 P 23 is manuscript 'R' in Dinneen's discussion.   37 *BL Cat. Ir. Mss*, i, 28.   38 *FFÉ*, iii, 9-15 (ll. 89-194).   39 Ibid., beginning at line 89.   40 RIA, MS 23 O 19 inserts it after *FFÉ*, iii, line 4162; RIA, MS 24 P 23 inserts it after *FFÉ*, iii, line 4192; TCD, MS 1394 also links this passage with the narrative of Brian Bóroimhe.

scripts where it occurs in the section on Brian Bóroimhe it is usually incorporated more smoothly into the narrative.[41] Some very early copies of *Foras feasa* do not contain this passage at all[42] and, curiously, in the important early manuscript of *Foras feasa* preserved in RIA MS 24 P 23 it is clearly marked off as separate from the surrounding text.[43] It appears that some scribe amended the text of *Foras feasa* because he wished to highlight this passage so as to associate the ideas of kingship it contained with all Christian kings of Ireland and not just Brian Bóroimhe.

Apart from providing an important commentary on the nature of kingship, this passage had a second significant function. It named the learned families who were associated with particular rites of inauguration. Thus, it affirmed, for instance, the traditional role of the families of Mac Craith, Mac Eochagáin and Mac Bruaideadha in relation to the kings of Munster. These were the same families through whom Keating achieved and maintained links with the traditional world of Irish historical scholarship.

III

The role of the Ó Maolchonaire scribes was not confined to the technical matter of producing copies of *Foras feasa*. They probably acted as cultural patrons, promoting Keating's history. Thus when an Ó Maolchonaire criticised an aspect of Micheál Ó Cléirigh's work, *Foras feasa* was put forward as evidence that Ó Cléirigh was mistaken.[44] This suggests that Keating's history was immediately accepted as authoritative by Ireland's professional scribes. Others, however, adopted a more critical approach.

A copy of *Foras feasa*, in Irish, was found among the books and manuscripts in John Colgan's room in the Irish Franciscan college of St Anthony at Louvain after his death in 1658. This manuscript, now Killiney MS A 14, partly in the hand of Micheál Ó Cléirigh, contains preliminary notes and annotations in the hand of John Colgan himself. These annotations reveal something of Colgan's reasons for consulting *Foras feasa* and the way he approached the text. His interest was in identifying the precise sources used by Keating, rather than in the story of Ireland that Keating told. His annotations include a list of authorities, '*Authores qui in prologo citantur*' (authors cited in the preface) and '*Authores qui citantur in corpore historiae*' (authors cited in the body of the history), and '*Chronica hiberniae aliaeque historiae*' (chronicles of Ireland and other histories). Colgan noted the folio numbers on which the various authorities are cited, but his list only reached folio 21v.

---

41 King's Inn's, Gaelic MS 2 (1657), and Marsh's Library, MS Z3.1.7 (76) (1651). Michael Kearney's translation, RIA, MS 24 G 16 is another example of an early text that associates the inauguration passage with Brian Bóroimhe. 42 FLK, MS A 14 (1636?), BL, Egerton MS 107 (1638) and Bodl., Fairfax MS 29 (1643) are among the early manuscripts that do not contain the passage on inauguration. These texts share other omissions also. 43 RIA, MS 24 P 23. See also the treatment of this passage in NLI, G 192. 44 *Geneal. Reg. Sanct. Hib.*, ed. Walsh, pp. 148-9.

He may have been discouraged from proceeding when he realised the high proportion of sources that he had to list as '*anonymus*', despite the impressive list of
chronicles drawn from the list provided in *Foras feasa* itself.[45]

The section of *Foras feasa* which began with the creation of Adam '*Ar dtús do
cruthuigheadh Adhamh*'[46] in which Keating cited numerous extracts from poetry as
supporting evidence was repeatedly annotated '*anonymus*' in the margin of Killiney
MS A 14. Keating's disclaimer in his account of Ceasair, daughter of Bioth, and
the invasions of Ireland before the deluge, 'Know, O reader that it is not as genuine history I set down this occupation, nor any occupation of which we have
treated up to this; but because I have found them written in old books' attracted
the annotation '*Apocrypha*' from Colgan.[47] Keating's discussion of the dubious
nature of the evidence that one Fionntain survived the deluge was marked '*Fiontain
fabulosus*' by Colgan.[48] On one occasion when Keating cited the poem '*Fuaras i
Psaltair Caisil*' as a source (as he frequently did) the item was underlined and
annotated '*anonymus fabulator*' by Colgan.[49]

While Colgan proceeded to make some notes on the Irish connection with
Scythia[50] it would appear that he soon realised that the sources used by Keating to
support his narrative of early Irish history were of doubtful historical accuracy. In
particular there was relatively little in *Foras feasa* that provided reliable information
for Colgan's *magnum opus* on the lives of Irish saints. *Acta Sanctorum Hiberniae*, the
first volume of a projected multi-volume work, published in 1645, cited *Foras feasa*
as a source,[51] but Colgan's use of Keating's history was not extensive and he has not
left a record of any special interest in the polemical dimension to *Foras feasa*.

A second reader of Killiney MS A 14 also left his annotations on the manuscript. In contrast to Colgan's notes, this unidentified second annotator was interested in the story being told rather than in the sources cited. Significant points in
the narrative are marked 'NB' in the margin, with the addition of a very occasional
note in Latin.[52] While little else can be deduced from this second annotator's
marks, it is evident that while Colgan was only too well aware of the tenuous
nature of the sources used, other readers of the text were far less concerned with
such technical details and read *Foras feasa* as a straightforward narrative history of
Ireland which documented historical events that were significant for contemporary
readers of Irish history in the seventeenth century.

IV

The ink was scarcely dry on the Irish language version of *Foras feasa* when an
English translation was begun. Keating's text cannot have been completed before

45 *FFÉ*, i, 78-80; FLK, MS A 14, f. xvi.   **46** *FFÉ*, i, 132ff; FLK, MS A 14, ff. 4-4v.   **47** *FFÉ*, i, 146-
7; FLK, MS A 14, f. 5.   **48** *FFÉ*, i, 148-50; FLK, MS A 14, f. 5.   **49** *FFÉ*, i, 154; FLK, MS A 14,
f. 5v.   **50** FLK, MS A 14, f.11v.   **51** Colgan, *Acta Sanctorum Hiberniae*, pp. 583, 654.   **52** FLK, MS
A 14, ff. 37v, 67, 72v.

1633, and by 1635 Michael Kearney of Ballylusky was working on a translation. Only one copy of his translation is known to survive,[53] transcribed by Domhnall mac Thomáis Uí Shuilleabháin[54] in 1668. This latter date, inserted by the copyist in a colophon at the end of the manuscript, has been erroneously interpreted as the date of the translation itself. The manuscript was correctly described by S.H. O'Grady and he also identified the scribe.[55]

The translator, Michael Kearney, was well-connected in Tipperary society. He was second son of Patrick Kearney and Ellen Carrane. His grandmother was a Butler from Ballyvadlea, a cadet branch of the Dunboyne Butlers. Michael Kearney's older brother, Brian, was born in 1585 and Michael was born a few years later.[56] As a younger son, Michael was apparently not a landowner. However, he was mentioned in the Civil Survey for County Tipperary as holding a share, together with Conor Meagher, in a lease of the tithes of two parishes, his own parish of Magowry and the adjoining parish of Drangan both before and after the rebellion of 1641.[57] The lease in the parish of Drangan was held from Patrick, son of Viscount Netterville, 'for term of years yet unexpired' and was valued at £20 per annum, while that in Magowry was valued at £10.[58] The population of Ballylusky, in the barony of Middlethird, was almost exclusively classified as 'Irish' in the '1659 census', with very few 'English' residents.[59] At the time of the Civil Survey, Ballylusky was a village containing a castle which was 'ready to fall'. The proprietor of the lands of Magowry parish in 1640 was Thomas Butler of Kilconnell, described as an 'Irish papist', and it was recorded that he held the lands of the parish 'by descent from his ancestors'.[60]

Ballylusky townland contained 357 profitable acres and it was noted that 'the said land hath on it an old broken castle which is cloaven in three quarters, and some few thatched cottages, and a corn mill which hath water only in winter'.[61] If the castle, known as Kearney's castle, was uninhabitable, it may be that Kearney lived elsewhere. Since he was described in a mid-1630s funeral entry as servant to the dowager baroness Dunboyne, it may be that he lived comfortably.[62]

In his manuscript translation of *Foras feasa*, Kearney gave no direct information about himself, and gave no indication that he knew Keating personally, or that he had encountered him except through his writings. Nevertheless some of the preoccupations in Kearney's preface hint at his circumstances. He considered that the

53 RIA, MS 24 G 16. **54** For identification see *BL Cat. Ir. Mss*, i, 17, 51. **55** The date information given in Hayes, *MSS sources*, drawing on *RIA Cat. Ir. MSS*, is incorrect. For O'Grady's comments see *BL Cat. Ir. MSS*, i, 51. The manuscript was bought by John O'Daly at the auction at Sharpe's, Anglesea St, Dublin, of Colonel Howard's library and in 1847 it was, according to O'Daly 'in the hands of a gentleman in this city' (John O'Daly, *The kings of the race of Éibhear* (Dublin, 1847), p. 5). It was among the collection of O'Daly manuscripts purchased by the Academy in 1869. **56** Three younger brothers survived to adulthood. Michael was married to Joan Fitzgibbon, and they had seven sons and one daughter born between 1614 and 1626. NLI, GO MS 71. McCarthy, Ulster office, p. 275; Jackson, 'Michael Kearney of Ballylosky', pp. 84-5. **57** *Civil survey*, i, pp. 163-5; 159. **58** Ibid., 163. **59** *Census Ire., 1659*. **60** *Civil survey*, i, 163-4. **61** Ibid., 164. **62** Jackson, 'Michael Kearney of Ballylosky', pp. 84-5.

possession of Irish soil, in a land comparable with the land of Canaan, a land of wheat and barley and a land of honey, would be enjoyed by the Irish 'if the envy of wicked intruders did not ... as it doth, hinder our happiness'. Tension over landownership seems to have been an issue of concern to this non-landowning inhabitant of Ballylusky. Although he stated that he was not a clergyman he was concerned over the status of the church and clergy and the restrictions on Catholic education which forced students to travel overseas for their higher education.

> To hinder them from learning, their schooling at home being prohibited if it were not under Protestant teachers, it is there further directed that their scholars studying overseas, and gentlemen and others leaving this nation, their native country for their religion sake, should be learned fugitives ... the project was to keep them blindfold, that their desired alteration of religion meeting with blunt capacities may be the sooner embraced.[63]

Kearney's link with the Butlers of Dunboyne would explain this concern since members of that immediate family had been contemporaries of Keating at the Irish college at Bordeaux.[64]

Kearney echoed Keating's sentiments in asserting that 'there is no nation in the world (making their case equal) that better maintain their ancient Catholic Roman religion, learning, good literature and civility in their dealings and carriages, than the Irish generally do'. Kearney's views indicate a world of elite scholarship and literary culture challenged, but not suppressed, by hostile legislation. The translator was at pains to demonstrate his own classical education, using Latin quotations, citing Ovid and also discussing Machiavelli.

The lengthy address from 'the Translator to the courteous and Friendly Reader' was a more pointedly political text than *Foras feasa* itself, making explicit many of the themes touched on in Keating's narrative. The address took the form of a summary history of Ireland. It presents first-hand evidence of how the message of *Foras feasa* was interpreted by one of its earliest readers.

Kearney depicted *Foras feasa* as being a readily accessible digest of information on the true antiquities of the nation. He saw the kingdom of Ireland as having existed from time immemorial and viewed all newcomers from the Fir bolg forward as 'colonists' trying to gain a foothold in the kingdom. He attributed the troubles of the kingdom throughout history to internal dissensions, with war and strife being perennial problems. The coming of Christianity he equated with the coming of civility to the kingdom.

Although Kearney criticised the anti-Catholicism of Elizabethan legislation and complained of the exclusion of Catholics from office, loyalty to the Stuart monarchy was stressed, because the concept of the kingdom of Ireland was of paramount importance. He reiterated several times the loyalty of the Irish to the imperial king

---

63 RIA, MS 24 G 16, f. 34v.   64 *Calendar of state papers Ireland, 1615-25*, pp. 318-22.

of England – 'Charles son and heir of the late illustrious king James'. James I who came to the throne in 1603 was, he asserted, the first 'absolute king of all Ireland' since Maolseachlainn in the eleventh century, being 'the first monarch of the nation itself that since reigned over Ireland of whose ancestors may have been before him kings of all Ireland.'[65] The Irish people were

> inflamed with a fervent desire to continue the ancient lustre and credit of this their native country and ancestors, whom no rewards in their times did or could invite, nor no perfection enforce them either to forsake their anciently professed Catholic Roman Religion nor their true allegiance to the Imperial Crown of England.[66] ...
>
> As they are men and born subjects, they owe loyalty to their king, and as they are Christian and mystical members of God's church they owe (above and before all things in this world) truth and sincerity to God and his church, their Christianity no way impeaching their humanity, nor their Catholic and spiritual obeisance to their undoubted pastor of Christ's flock on earth, any way hindering or infringing their earthly and due obedience and homage to their sovereign lords the kings of England unto whom they did and ever will keep the depositum of their natural subjection.[67]

The common law was also respected by Kearney, provided it was correctly administered. He believed that 'the common laws of England are in themselves very just and agreeable to the government and nature of the people of Ireland, and that the statutes and Acts of Parliament anciently of force in this kingdom were specially made and provided for the great benefit of this nation'. The problem arose from the exclusion of many from the benefits thereof.[68] The difficulty was not with the king of England, but with those who administered the law in Ireland.

> If any grants were made by the king of England to the Irish, a way pro-pounded for to avoid and overthrow them and a secret resolution for the effecting as well thereof as of their other projects for overthrowing of the Irish devised and seriously prescribed.[69]

The problem for the Irish 'and this their oppressed country' was one of upstarts, 'blood-suckers and moths that among them daily breed', who were denying the Irish the status and esteem due to them. They were

> wasting and rooting out not only her ancient Irish from their lives and estates, but also in as much obscuring and blemishing with mis-reports and approby the good fame and assured credit and approved honour of the Nation and its inhabitants in general.

65 RIA, MS 24 G 16, f.31.   66 Ibid., f. 33v.   67 Ibid., f. 33v.   68 Ibid., f. 33.   69 Ibid., f. 34v-35.

Her 'new adopted English children', having 'received advancement in honour and riches beyond their merits or deserts', were such that even the Secretary of State, Sir Robert Cecil, described them as 'wanton lechers'.[70] Echoing the attitude towards upstarts found in *Pairlement Chloinne Tomáis* as well as in Keating's history and poetry, Kearney argued that the justice, grace and clemency of their King Charles, son and heir of 'their late sacred sovereign King James', was denied the Irish 'underhand by men of mean condition and quality'. These undesirable upstarts,

> who to raise for themselves a fortune founded upon the destruction and ruins of the Catholic natives of this nation with their false and malicious informations, always endeavoured to possess their majesties of an evil opinion of their faithful and true subjects here'.[71]

In the light of this, it seems clear that Kearney valued *Foras feasa* as an important weapon in a propaganda war, a valuable tool with which to help restore the honour of the Catholic Irish. He noted, like Keating, that the Old English were now being tarred with the same brush as the native Irish. He objected that

> the old descendants English which by birth and natural inclinations in time grow to like and affect this country, should be termed degenerated and counted more malicious towards the English than the very Irish themselves, a comparison most odious for to be inferred against a nation most tractable and ameasurable to civil government and common laws of England.[72]

Clearly, Keating's history prompted this commentator to reflect on the contemporary status of the Old English community in Ireland.

Kearney's attitude to language was slightly ambivalent, as befitted a translator. He presented the translation of *Foras feasa* for the benefit of those who could not read Irish, noting that English was 'now the more respected language among us'. Despite this admission of current attitudes towards the language, he was at pains to assert that the Irish language was not inferior to English, and that knowledge of English was not a mark of higher status or scholarly achievement. English perceptions of the Irish language as barbarous arose, he argued, because 'they understand not our language'. He suggested that the converse argument could 'as justly repute them barbarous that they learn not our language'.[73] The Irish language, 'for antiquity, propriety of character (being the archetype of their letters) and copiosity of phrase, without little or no beholdingness to any other tongue, is unto their language nothing inferior'.[74]

Kearney's preface indicated that he shared Keating's sympathies on many issues including the Catholic religion, the Irish language, the status of the Old English,

---

70 Ibid., f. 36r.   71 Ibid., ff. 32v-33.   72 Ibid., f. 34-34v.   73 Ibid., f. 34.   74 Ibid., f. 34.

and that elusive concept of the honour and reputation of the kingdom of Ireland. His work reveals, however, a more explicit awareness of the tensions of Anglo-Irish relations than that offered in *Foras feasa* itself. There seems little doubt but that Kearney's reading of the text of *Foras feasa* was one which took full account of the nuances of the contemporary political message inherent in Keating's narrative of early Irish history. Kearney read *Foras feasa* in the way Keating would have hoped it would be read.

V

While it is evident that Michael Kearney engaged with the message of *Foras feasa* on an immediate and highly political level, others who came in contact with the work took a more academic approach. Among the most influential was John Lynch, a near-contemporary of Keating, whose best-known publication, *Cambrensis eversus*,[75] was inspired in large part by Keating's polemical preface to *Foras feasa*. Lynch, who was closely involved in interpreting and disseminating *Foras feasa*, was a secular priest who lived much of his life in Galway, but spent his last years in exile in France.[76] Lengthy extracts from *Foras feasa* were cited in Latin in *Cambrensis eversus*. It seems likely that Lynch decided on the desirability of a full Latin translation of *Foras feasa* while at work on his own defence of Ireland's reputation. Lynch also translated part of the *Annála ríoghachta Éireann* into Latin. This suggests that he believed there was a demand, among seventeenth-century readers who could not read Irish, for histories of Ireland from a Catholic perspective.

When John Lynch translated *Foras feasa* into Latin, probably in the late 1650s, he added a lengthy preface of the kind one might expect in a text intended for publication. The autograph copy of Lynch's translation is not known to survive, but three manuscript copies of it are extant, and each has a story to tell. The Woodstock Theological Center Library copy of Lynch's Latin translation of *Foras feasa*[77] is a hurried late-seventeenth-century copy made by at least six scribes. It contains some annotations and corrections indicating that it was checked against another copy and that errors and omissions were corrected. Titles of sources given only in Latin in the text were annotated in Irish in the margin, thus '*Libro Migrationum*' was annotated '*Leabhar gabhála*' and '*Iurem liber*' annotated '*Leabhar na gCeart*'.[78]

A more complex manuscript containing Lynch's Latin version of *Foras feasa* is in Aube, Bibliothèque de Troyes MS 919.[79] A two-page preface, dated 1703,

75 [St Malo], 1662.   **76** Nollaig Ó Muráile, 'Aspects of intellectual life in seventeenth-century Galway', in Gerard Moran (ed.), *Galway: history and society* (Dublin, 1996), pp. 155-65.   **77** Now Woodstock Theological Center Library, MS 7, located within Georgetown University Library, Washington DC. The manuscript is not dated but in is in a range of seventeenth-century hands, and affixed to it (p. 109) is a letter from Fr Th. Sirinus in Louvain dated 15 Sept 1672, thanking the recipient for having sent him lives of saints and commenting on the Irish language.   **78** Woodstock MS 7, ff. 23, 51.   **79** A copy is

asserted that the first part of the work was originally completed on 6 March 1657; that it was an abridgement made by a holy man and that it was later revised. The text of the history itself was hurriedly written in this manuscript, book two being in a different hand from book one. The manuscript was later reworked with the insertion of section headings in a script imitating print.[80] A supplementary section between books one and two of this manuscript comprised notes and corrections to the text, in various hands including that of the main scribe, most of the notes being critical of Keating's credulity.[81]

The section dealing with kingship and inauguration was tagged in the margin as '*additio translationis*'.[82] It would appear that Lynch's Latin translation was originally made from a manuscript that did not have the section on inauguration, but was subsequently compared with one that did. The section on inauguration was of particular relevance to Lynch, given his particular concern with the issue of kingship that pervaded his own writing in *Cambrensis eversus*.[83]

The detail of the translation of *Foras feasa* itself also reveals Lynch's particular approach to *Foras feasa*. It is significant, for instance, that Keating's distinction between the Old English and the Gaeil, '*Sean Ghaill is Gaedhilibh Éireann*' was not retained in John Lynch's Latin translation.[84] At first glance this suggests that by the 1660s, in Lynch's judgement, the idea of an ethnic distinction within the Irish Catholic community no longer had significance for readers. This was, however, at odds with Lynch's later publications which attached much more importance to ethnic difference.[85] It may be that Lynch considered it necessary to minimise the ethnic distinctions within Irish Catholicism for those readers for whom his Latin translation was intended. In contrast to Lynch, the later seventeenth-century English translation of *Foras feasa* – discussed below as the 'A defence' text – retained the distinction between 'the Old English and Irish gentry',[86] and 'as well the Old English as the inhabitants of Ireland'[87] 'as for the Old Irish before the English conquest'.[88]

Of the three extant copies of Lynch's translation of *Foras feasa*, that transcribed by the Dominican priest John Donnelly in 1712 is now the most significant.[89] It is particularly valuable because it contains the only extant copy of Lynch's own '*Interpres ad lectorem*' in which he placed the *Foras feasa* in the historiographical context in which he wished it to be understood. Lynch's preface, probably add-

---

available in NLI, microfilm P 804. A preliminary note in French in a later hand recorded that this copy had been in the possession of the Revd Richard Farrell *c.*1660 (author of *Commentarius Rinuccinianus*). 80 It has not been ascertained whether any of the hands in this MS is that of John Lynch himself. There are very extensive marginal notes in Irish and Latin. Some of these, probably in the hand of the main scribe, give the Irish forms of names given in Latin in the text, in other cases another hand has written the Irish sections in a more practised Gaelic script. See Troyes, MS 919, p. 47. 81 Troyes, MS 919, pp. 159-64. 82 Ibid., pp. 231-2. 83 See Cunningham, 'Representations of king, parliament and the Irish people'. 84 *FFÉ*, i, 4; RIA, MS 25 I 5, ff. 13-14. 85 John Lynch, *Alithinologia sive veridica responsio ad invectam mendaciis* ([St Malo], 1664); *Supplementum alithinologiae* ([St Malo], 1667); Ó Muraile, *Celebrated antiquary*, p. 227. 86 NLI, MS G 293, p. 4. 87 Ibid., p. 2. 88 Ibid., p. 5, etc. 89 RIA, MS 24 I 5. It gives '1669' on the spine as the date of original translation into Latin.

ressed to a primarily French readership,[90] placed Keating firmly in the context of the classical historians of Greece and Rome. He likened him to Herodotus, the father of history who, like Keating, included many *'fabulae'* in his work.[91] On Keating's use of poetry as evidence, Lynch began by citing Cato, *'Admiranda canunt, sed non credenda poetae'*, recommending that poetry be admired but not believed. However, he then proceeded to explain and defend the use of poetry as an historical source in the Irish context. Irish poetry, he noted, recounted the reigns of the kings of Ireland and of its provincial kings and the histories of famous Irish families, so that they were not collections of ill-digested facts, but were indeed a source of erudition on Irish politics. Appealing to the classical learning of his intended audience, Lynch likened Keating's poetical sources to the work of Livy and Sallust who had written history in the form of poetry.[92] In an attempt to focus attention on Ireland's rightful place in world culture Lynch made special mention of the synchronisms attached to *Foras feasa* which fitted Irish kings into the wider chronology of Persian and Greek kings and Roman emperors.[93] In exhorting his readers to approach Keating's text as they would the narrative of Herodotus, or the work of Livy or Sallust, perhaps Lynch protests a little too much. There is a sense that Lynch, while welcoming Keating's trenchant refutation of the negative aspects of Giraldus's description of Ireland and the Irish, was somewhat less than comfortable with the kind of history Keating had written. Lynch was aware that Keating's work was very highly regarded among the Catholic Irish at home, but he probably would have preferred rather fewer *'fabulae'* in the work that had established itself as the Catholic history of the kingdom of Ireland.

Keating was, he asserted, the most renowned of over 200 historians who had written of things Irish.[94] Lynch presented *Foras feasa* as a text that fulfilled the role of a standard history of the Irish nation, and he informed his readers that he had prepared this Latin version because the histories of other nations were in Latin.[95] Lynch considered the Latin language to be the most appropriate medium in which to present to the wider world the history of the Irish nation. British writers, being ignorant of Irish, he asserted, could only read Latin writings on Ireland, which meant that they could read Giraldus Cambrensis but not the authentic native texts such as the Psalter of Cashel containing the fragments of the Latin history of Cormac mac Cuileannáin, king, archbishop and martyr.[96] Evidently he hoped that the availability of a Latin version of *Foras feasa* would undermine the traditional place enjoyed by Giraldus as chief commentator on the Irish past for foreign audiences.

Lynch's magnum opus, *Cambrensis eversus*, written in the light of the experience of having read *Foras feasa*, also provides evidence of the way in which Keating's history was read and interpreted in the seventeenth century. He developed and adapted some of the key political ideas inherent in Keating's history, while rejecting others. An examination of Lynch's work casts light on the post-

---

90 RIA, MS 24 I 5, p. 10. 91 Ibid., p. 3. 92 Ibid., p. 11. 93 Ibid., p. 9. 94 Ibid., p. 1. 95 Ibid., p. 2. 96 Ibid., pp. 5-6.

1641 legacy of Keating, and also illuminates the evolution of concepts such as sovereignty, kingship, parliament, law and liberty among seventeenth-century Irish
historians.[97] By the later part of the century, the ancient world of the kingdom of
Ireland was seen as something of a golden age when there existed a harmonious
relationship between king and people. *Foras feasa* was read in the later seventeenth
century as evidence that in early Ireland king and parliament acted in unison as
guarantors of justice and impartial government for the prosperity of the whole
kingdom on behalf of the people of Ireland.

VI

An English translation of *Foras feasa*, prepared independently from that of Michael
Kearney, was completed by the 1680s. The name of this second translator is not
known, and with one exception the surviving transcripts do not name a scribe. To
judge by the detail of the occasional scribal errors and corrections a reasonable case
can be made that NLI MS G 293 may be the translator's autograph copy. Some
deletions and interlineations in this manuscript are amendments of the translation
rather than corrections of transcription errors.[98] The untidy columns in the
genealogical tables also suggest that perhaps this was the translator's autograph
copy.[99] However, the evidence is not conclusive, and the deletion of two lines of
text inserted in the wrong place on page 342 hints that NLI MS G 293 might not
be the translator's autograph copy. However, it may well be the first 'fair copy'
made by the translator or his employee, based on a preliminary draft. Other copies
of the same translation, referred to here on the basis of its opening words as the 'A
defence' text, are located in a range of archives. These include Marsh's Library,[100]
Armagh Public Library,[101] Bodleian Library,[102] British Library[103] and National
Library of Ireland.[104] One of few clues to the dating of this series of closely related
manuscripts is the note in NLI, MS G 293 indicating that it was on loan to Mr
[Richard] Cox in 1689-90. A slightly different copy of the same text is found in
TCD, MS 1443. This adaption re-inserted the verse quotations in Irish, generally
omitted from the 'A defence' translation. The revision was competently done by
scribes of the Moynihan family, evidently working from both an Irish and an

---

97 See chapter 8. For Keating's influence on these political concepts as understood later in the seventeenth century see Cunningham, 'Representations of king, parliament and the Irish people'.   **98** NLI,
MS G 293, examples include: '... to seat and place the nobility, gentry and commanders at meals, in
the feeding rooms, according to their degrees and qualities, in that <kings rolls> meeting ...' (p. 346).
'I shall not be delivered of him <until the morrow> during that time.' (p. 367) '...for there were
four<teen> score and eight years from the death of Cahir before Cormac ...' (p. 392); The words in
angle brackets are deleted by the scribe and replaced by the word underlined.   **99** NLI, MS G 293,
pp. 287-311.   **100** Marsh's library, MS Z3.1.17.   **101** Armagh Public Library, MS H.3.1.   **102** Bodl.,
MS Ir. d. 1.   **103** BL, Add. MS 4,818.   **104** NLI MS G 288. The suggestion in *NLI Cat. Ir. MSS*,
Fasc vii, p. 8 that NLI, MS G 288 might be the autograph copy is incorrect. It is in fact the latest
known copy (dated 1718).

English exemplar of *Foras feasa*. This copy was purchased by Edward Lhuyd in 1700 from Thomas Moynihan, near Killarney.

Although undated, it is probable that most copies of the 'A defence' translation of *Foras feasa* date from the 1670s onwards.[105] The latest in date is NLI, MS G 288 (1718), and no copy of the 'A defence' translation prepared subsequent to the publication in 1723 of O'Connor's alternative translation has been located. The availability of a printed text of Keating's history, albeit in a translation with entirely different emphases, undermined demand for scribal publication of that text in English. However, during the forty years prior to O'Connor's publication, the 'A defence' translation of Keating's *Foras feasa* was clearly in demand.

In contrast to the Irish language copies in circulation, most manuscripts containing this English version are uniformly impersonal, with no colophon, no name of scribe, and they are simplified for English readers by the omission of the Irish verse. The Latin quotations, however, are retained as in the original. It may be that the translator was not competent to translate the Irish verse accurately. More probably it may be that the intended audience of this version would have been expected to be able to read Latin, but not Irish, and would not have been expected to place any particular value on the quotations in Irish verse.

This 'A defence' translation was clearly written from a Catholic standpoint. It was faithful to Keating's text in noting, for instance, the Irish people's 'valour, stoutness and constancy in the Catholic religion'.[106] Such references in O'Connor's quite different printed translation, first published in 1723, substitute the word 'Christian' for the word 'Catholic'. This is just one indication of how particular textual communities adapted and experienced *Foras feasa* in quite different ways.

Whereas the synchronisms appended to some Irish language copies of *Foras feasa* were omitted from the 'A defence' translation, the genealogical tables were included in most copies of 'A defence'.[107] The Bodleian copy[108] includes further genealogical material on the O'Kellys added at a later date, perhaps indicating that this section of the history was regarded by the owner of the manuscript as particularly significant. The Moynihan copy[109] includes only summary extracts from the pedigrees, possibly suggesting a different set of priorities in the mind of the patron who commissioned this copy. The 1718 copy[110] contains neither genealogies nor synchronisms. However, in this manuscript family names are given particular prominence throughout through the use of very large lettering.[111] Despite omitting the genealogical tables, therefore, the scribe nevertheless gave prominence to family origins. The interest in family history prevalent in Ireland in the closing decades

---

105 The translation of *Foras Feasa* available to the earl of Anglesea in the 1670s was probably the 'A defence' version. See below p. 204, n. 12.   106 NLI, MS G 293, p. 55.   107 NLI, MS G 293 contains what might be the translator's autograph copy of the genealogies. Marsh's Library copy closely resembles NLI, MS G 293 and contains the genealogies also. Armagh Public Library, MS H.3.1 has extensive genealogies.   108 Bodl., MS Ir d 1.   109 TCD, MS 1443.   110 NLI, MS G 288.   111 NLI, MS G 288, p. 238 for instance, which contains 'the chief surnames that are in Leinster of the Milesian race', and p. 400 'surnames of those that went with William, king of Scotland from England'.

of the seventeenth century may explain much of the demand for this particular English translation of *Foras feasa*.

VII

Access to the full text of *Foras feasa* in manuscript either in Irish, English, or Latin, was a luxury only available to those who could afford it, or at least moved in circles where a copy could be borrowed. However, lack of money did not imply a lack of interest in the story of the past. Ideas close to those contained in *Foras feasa* were in circulation in other ways also.

The lengthy poem entitled '*Tuireamh na hÉireann*', written by Seán Ó Conaill, probably between 1655 and 1659, has been viewed as the poor person's *Foras feasa*.[112] Cecile O'Rahilly noted that 'judging by the frequency with which it occurs in eighteenth and nineteenth-century manuscripts, the poem '*Tuireamh na hÉireann*' must have enjoyed an extraordinary popularity'.[113] There are copies of the poem in no less than seventy-four different manuscripts in the Royal Irish Academy alone, and there are several nineteenth-century translations of the poem into English. Not surprisingly, in view of its wide availability, there are echoes of the poem and, through it, *Foras feasa* in the poetic compositions of many later poets including Aodhagán Ó Rathaille, Seán Ó Gadhra, and Raifteirí.[114]

'*Tuireamh na hÉireann*' was a virtual summary of *Foras feasa* in verse, but with an added contemporary messsage since the early history was presented in the political context of Cromwellian Ireland. The poem opened with an account of the Flood, and recorded Noah's descendants through his sons Shem, Cham and Japheth, inheritors of Asia, Africa and Europe respectively. Although the poem included the story of the Tower of Babel and the wanderings of the race of Gaedheal Glas, the emphasis was on the history of Ireland from the coming of Patrick. Brian Bóroimhe was depicted as a king who was also saviour of Ireland who, like Christ, gave his life for his people on Good Friday so that they could be free.

> *Do shaor Brian Bóraimhe Banba ó dhaorbhruid*
> *i gcath Chluana Tairbh, Aoine an Chéasta.*[115]
> (Brian Bóroimhe freed Banba from bondage
> at the battle of Clontarf, on Good Friday.)

After a brief mention of the coming of the Normans the poem then departed from the *Foras feasa* tradition by discussing in some detail the history of the sixteenth and early seventeenth centuries. The poem referred in hostile terms to some of the English laws being applied in Ireland, and then told the story of the war in Ireland

---

112 Pádraig Ó Fiannachta, 'Stair, finnscéal agus annála', *Léachtaí Cholm Cille*, ii, (1971), pp. 5-13. 113 Cecile O'Rahilly (ed.), *Five seventeenth-century political poems* (Dublin, 1952), p. 50. 114 O'Rahilly (ed.), *Five seventeenth-century political poems*, pp. 53-8. 115 Ll. 245-6.

in the 1640s culminiating in the arrival of Oliver Cromwell and his son Henry who completed the 'conquest' of Ireland.

> *'S iad so do chríochnaigh conquest Éireann,*
> *do ghabh a ndaingin 's a mbailte le chéile*
> *ó Inis Bó Finne go Binn Eadair*
> *'s ó Chloich an Stacain go Baoí Béarra.*[116]

(It was these who finished the *conquest* of Ireland
who captured her forts and towns
from Inishbofin to Howth
and from Cloghastucan to Beare.)[117]

The poet recorded the Old English and the Gaelic families who had lost out as a result of the Cromwellians, mentioning with particular regret the banishment of Mac Carthy mór from Munster. The poem concluded with a prayer to God and the saints to restore their faith and their rights to the Irish people.

Drawing on the tradition of *Foras feasa*, the poem explained to the Irish Catholic people, both native Irish and Old English, where they had come from and who their ancestors were. It had the effect of engendering a sense of pride in the origins of a people that could be very intense.[118] It affirmed their sense of identity as combining Irishness and Catholicism. The sense of oppression and suffering that gave the poem its direction, however, did not derive primarily from the *Foras feasa* tradition, but from the more immediate political realities of 1650s Ireland. It could be argued that these political poems are not a direct 'legacy' of *Foras feasa*, and that such poems would have been composed even if Keating had not written his history. Given the essentially derivative nature of the story of Ireland recorded in *Foras feasa*, articulating popular stories and traditions, it is difficult to prove 'influences' on later tradition. Poems such as '*Tuireamh na hÉireann*' represent, in parallel to *Foras feasa*, another dimension of the use of history for present purposes. The poet's motive in drawing on the extended history of the Irish people helped shape perceptions of the Irish past that would draw contemporaries and later generations back again and again to that story of Ireland, a story which was narrated in attractive, accessible prose in Keating's *Foras feasa ar Éirinn*.

VIII

Probably the best-known Munster poet writing in the second half of the seventeenth century, Dáibhí Ó Bruadair, was particularly conscious of the legacy of Geoffrey Keating and the achievement that was *Foras feasa*. Ó Bruadair's histori-

---

116 Ll. 377-80.   117 See O'Rahilly (ed.), *Five seventeenth-century political poems*, p. 150, for discussion of these placenames.   118 Ó Fiannachta, 'Stair, finnscéal agus annála', pp. 5-13.

cal poems are one measure of the nature of the legacy of *Foras feasa* among the Gaelic literati, and Ó Bruadair, in particular, valued Keating's work highly. In his poem '*Searc na suadh an chrobhaing chumhra*', Ó Bruadair recalled the historian's work in a poem prompted by the activities of his later namesake John Keating. Geoffrey's work was interpreted as having brought the truth to light, restoring reputations by revealing the honour of princes and providing genealogical information. While the immediate subject of the poem was Lord Chief Justice John Keating, who was involved in the trial and acquittal of a group of Munster Catholics in 1682, the poet was reminded of Geoffrey Keating, and chose to draw analogies between the two men.

> *Searc na suadh an chrobhaing chumhra*
> *do chraoibh ghealghall Innse Fáil,*
> *nach tug cúl re béim a bhíodhbhadh*
> *géill a nglún gur díoladh dáibh.*
>
> *Séathrún Céitinn cnú don mhogal*
> *maoidhfidh mise ar chách a chóid*
> *tug a foras dleacht a diamhraibh*
> *solas ceart a riaghail róid.*
>
> *D'fhoillsigh onóir ardfhlath Éireann*
> *iul a bpréamh sa ngéaga gaoil*
> *tug anall dá mbladh ar bhradadh*
> *ar nach gann re cabghall claoin.*

> (Love of sages in the fragrant cluster
> Of this branch of Inis Fail's fair Galls,
> who never turned their backs on strokes of foemen,
> But forced them to pay homage on their knees.
>
> One nut of that bunch is Geoffrey Keating,
> Whose code above all others I extol,
> That brought her real story forth from darkness
> Rule to show the road with correct light.
>
> The honour he revealed of Erin's princes,
> The knowledge of their stems and families
> Restoring to their fame what has been pilfered
> No trifling task 'gainst mouther's vaunts.)[119]

---

119 J.C. Mac Erlean (ed.), *Duanaire Dhaibhidh Uí Bhruadair: the poems of David Ó Bruadair* (3 vols, London, 1910-17), ii, poem 36, pp. 264-81, stanza 1-3. Among the numerous manuscript copies of this poem is one (RIA, MS 23 M 28) by Eoghan Ó Caoimh, a scribe who was closely associated with Keating's prose works. The manuscripts containing this poem were read by a wide range of readers and

Ó Bruadair was particularly taken with the idea of Keating's role in defending the reputation of the Irish.

> *D'fhág Séathra fál scéithe ar cháil clé gach úghdair*
> *dár éilnigh clár Fhéidhlim d'áirc bréag i bprionnta*
> *ó táid méirligh fá éitheach lán d'fhéile cúighte*
> *is fearrde Éire Seán Céitinn d'fhás gléasta i ngúna.*

> (Geoffrey hath left us a wall of defence against author's base tales,
> That polluted the fair plain of Feidhlim with infamous falsehoods in print,
> And now that the lies of these rogues have been nobly exposed
>   and avenged,
> Increased hath been Erin's delight by John Keating arrayed in his gown.)[120]

The spring assizes in Limerick in 1682, when men charged in connection with the 'Popish Plot' were being tried for high treason, provided the setting for the poem. The poet argued that the men were loyal to Charles II and that the verdict of acquittal was in reality a verdict for the king. The point was made that both Keatings had undermined detractors and liars through their work. In a letter to Justice Keating (1682) enclosing the poem, Ó Bruadair mentioned having read *Foras feasa*:

> A famous work formerly undertaken and firmly finished by a venerable and most revd person of the name, to wit, Doctor Jerome Keating in defence and vindication of his native soil against the partial writers that offered to calumniate and vilify both the soil and the seed, and with their envious aspersions to obfuscate their grandeur.[121]

The implication of the poem was that the elite of Gaelic society, despite their impeccable genealogies, were being usurped by deceitful inferiors, who were deliberately behaving like informers. The Gaeil, in consequence, were in need of defence and vindication. The idea earlier expressed in prose by the author of *Pairlement Chloinne Thomáis*, as well as by Keating, of upstarts undermining the values of society, was echoed in the poetic compositions of Ó Bruadair. It appears that the upstarts being complained about were most frequently 'newcomer' upstarts. In one of his earlier poems '*Créacht do dháil mé*', Ó Bruadair focused on the Cromwellian era and contrasted honourable kings of old against contemporary upstarts. He asked why the descendants of Gaedheal Glas have become degraded and unheeded.[122] The poem again stressed the issues of honour and status, linking them with religion. Ó Bruadair's poem called on the Gaeil not to surrender to 'hireling monsters' but to 'drive to jeopardy all these new-come aliens'.[123]

some surviving transcripts contain annotations in Latin, Irish and English. 120 Ó Bruadair, *Poems*, ii, poem 36, pp. 264-81, stanza 43. 121 Ibid., p. 286. 122 Ibid., i, poem 5, pp. 27-51. 123 Ibid., p. 49.

IX

The tradition of narrative historical poems represented in the mid-seventeenth century by compositions like '*Tuireamh na hÉireann*'[124] continued in the eighteenth century, by which time Keating's work was firmly established as part of the heritage that was being recorded. A Connacht poem entitled '*Tuireamh na Gaeilge agus teastas na hÉireann*'[125] specifically mentioned a range of seventeenth-century historical works. The poem is preserved in a manuscript dating from 1758 but internal evidence shows it was written before 1720 while the Connacht poet Sean Ó Gadhra (c.1648-1720) was still alive.[126]

This historiographical poem began by recalling Keating's *Foras feasa*, particularly the preface. Next, John Lynch's *Cambrensis eversus* was presented as a faithful rendering of Keating's argument. James Ware's *Antiquities of Ireland* was also mentioned together with John Colgan's *Trias thaumaturgae* and the work of Micheál Ó Cléirigh in collecting saints' lives and history. The poet noted that Peter Walsh's elegant history in English also followed in the style of *Foras feasa*. Finally the Connacht scholars, Roderick O'Flaherty, Tadhg Ó Rodaigh and Sean Ó Gadhra were grouped together by the poet who regreted that only Ó Gadhra was still alive like '*Oisín in ndiadh na Féinne*'.[127] The poem elevated the status of these Connacht historians and poets by reference to the seventeenth-century tradition of which Keating was the instigator.

It was not only in overtly political poems that the legacy of Geoffrey Keating was revealed in Irish poetry in the century after the composition of *Foras feasa*. A lament for Murtagh Cruise (d.1702) composed by Séamas Dall Mac Cuarta (fl. 1647-1717), gave voice to Keating's core idea of the shared destiny of the Old English and native Irish. The idea that Gaelic descent from Milesius, or the alternative of Strongbow ancestry as one of '*Gaill Fhódhla*', were equally to be valued, confirms the ideology which underlay *Foras feasa*.[128] The same poem depicted death as a thief with no regard for an individual's worldly wealth, in a manner which echoed the sentiments of *Trí bior-ghaoithe an bháis*.[129] Though Keating was not specifically named in the poem, it is evident that both the political and theological ideas he represented were reflected in this lament by a Gaelic poet for a fellow Catholic of Old English ancestry.

Although *Foras feasa* was the most prominent of Keating's works alluded to in the later work of other writers, clearly *Trí bior-ghaoithe an bháis* also had an impact. The poem '*Mallacht ort, a bháis bhronaigh*' sometimes incorrectly ascribed to Muiris mac Dáibhí Dhuibh Mhic Gearailt, and sometimes ascribed to Dáibhí Mac

---

124 O'Rahilly (ed.), *Five seventeenth-century political poems*, poem 4.   **125** [S]. Mac Domhnaill (ed.), *Dánta is amhráin Sheáin Uí Ghadhra* (Baile Átha Cliath, 1955), poem 1.   **126** Mac Domhnaill (ed.), *Dánta is amhráin Sheáin Uí Ghadhra*, notes to poem 1.   **127** Ibid., p. 18, ll. 187-9.   **128** Seán Ó Gallchóir, (ed.), *Séamas Dall Mac Cuarta: Dánta* (Baile Átha Cliath, 1971), poem 6, '*Tuireamh Mhurcha Crúis*', lines 157-8. '*De ghaill Fódhla nó dá nGaelaidh, Mhuintir Strongbow nó Mhilesius*'.   **129** Ll. 100-10.

Gearailt, is an example of a seventeenth-century poem on death that appears to have been drawn from the ideas in *Trí bior-ghaoithe an bháis*.[130] Stanzas 10-11 contain the 'Make reckoning' story from *Trí bior-ghaoithe an bháis*:

> *Cosmhail tú le fear ósta*
> *agá mbí deóra fá chaithis;*
> *ar n-imtheacht adeir dá lámhughadh:*
> *'Tabhair sásughadh 'nar chaithis!'*
> ...
> *'come here', adeir gan faitchios,*
> *'make raicin ina bhfuarais!'*

> (You are like an innkeeper
> where drink is consumed
> on leaving he says to his guests
> pay for what you drank.
> ...
> *come here*, he says without fear
> *make raicin* for what you got.)[131]

When this poem was edited by O'Rahilly, in *Measgra dánta*, he omitted the 'make reckoning' section considering it a later interpolation, even though he noted that most of the poet's illustrations were drawn from Keating's text.[132] More recently, Nicholas Williams has detailed the correspondence between other stanzas and particular sections of the prose text of *Trí bior-ghaoithe an bháis*, to emphasise the poet's familiarity with Keating's work.[133]

It appears from the poetry of Séamas Dall Mac Cuarta noted above, and also from the poetry of Pádraig Mac a Liondain, that Keating's reputation lived on among the people not just as an historian but as an historian who was also a preacher and a priest. Keating's appeal for these poets may partly have been the way in which he came to personify an intertwining of Irish history and the Catholic faith. This appreciation of the full range of values which Keating's writings represented, and which the poetry in Irish reveals, is generally missing from the prose texts in English derived from Keating, where the writers focused more particularly on the political implications of the story of the kingdom of Ireland, and less on the story of the Catholic people both Gaeil and Gaill.

Pádraig Mac a Liondain (1665-1733) assumed that his audience were familiar with Keating's work. In a poem he composed about 1730 in praise of a priest named Feidhlim Ó hAnluain of County Armagh, he praised his learning, teaching

130 Nicholas Williams (ed.), *Dánta Mhuiris mhic Dháibhí Dhuibh Mhic Gearailt* (Baile Atha Cliath, 1979), poem 12, and note on p. 20. 131 Williams (ed.), *Dánta Mhuiris*, poem 12. 132 O'Rahilly (ed.), *Measgra dánta* (2 vols, Cork, 1927) ii, poem 66. 133 Williams (ed.), *Dánta Mhuiris*, pp. 94-6; stanza 5 and *TBB*, ll. 1158-62; stanza 6 and *TBB*, ll. 2644-9, and stanzas 7-9 and *TBB*, ll. 16-28, etc.

and especially his preaching and noted, without feeling the need to explain the link, that the man's nickname was '*Foras feasa*'. The poem '*Tabhair a lao loinn lachta*' depicted a priest following in the footsteps of Melchizedek, an example to the community because of the excellence of his bearing. The poem also inferred that through his good scholarship, and his correction of the errors of others, the priest was also following in the footsteps of Keating.

> *Ainm dó 'Foras feasa',*
> *deismireacht sua n-ainbheasa,*
> *scáthán grianloinnreach sráide*
> *ar dhealbhdhreach 's ar chaoinráite.*[134]

> (His name is *Foras feasa*
> he corrects their errors
> he gives example bright as the sun
> in his manner and his elegant words.)

'*Tuireamh Phádraig Mhic a Liondain*', a lament on the death of Pádraig Mac a Liondain composed by Fearghas Mac Bheatha in 1733, praised the man as a poet and historian well versed in writings in English, Irish and Latin, whether in print, in prose or in verse.[135] The poem asserted that Mac a Liondain was without equal in Europe in his knowledge of the origins of the Gaeil and their journeying from Scythia to Spain and Banba through the ages and down to the time of Henry II and Strongbow. It was specified that this knowledge, which his wife shared, was drawn from Geoffrey Keating '*Bhí seo gan dearmad de réir scansail Séathrúin*'.[136]

X

While Keating's ideas were being transmitted to new audiences through the compositions of later poets, in some instances those poets participated directly in the scribal transmission of the full prose versions of Keating's works also. In the 1690s, Eoghan Ó Caoimh, a Cork poet and scribe, took a special interest in the works of Geoffrey Keating and was a prolific copyist of his works. Among the copies of *Foras feasa* made by this scribe, one was commissioned in 1693-4 by a priest named Séamus de Nógla, probably a close relative of the scribe's wife, Eleanor de Nógla.[137] The manuscript also includes religious poetry and the text of the poem '*Fuaras i Psaltair Chaisil*', frequently cited by Keating as a source of historical evidence. In the summer of 1696 the same scribe transcribed *Foras feasa* for Donnchadh Óg Mac Donnchadha, a copy which soon afterwards came into the hands of

---

134 Seosamh Mag Uidhir (ed.), *Pádraig Mac a Liondain: dánta* ([Baile Átha Cliath], 1977) poem 6. See also Mhag Craith (ed.), *Dán na mBráthar Mionúr*, poem 77.   135 Mag Uidhir (ed.), *Pádraig Mac a Liondain: dánta*, poem 1, ll. 24-40.   136 Mag Uidhir (ed.), *Mac a Liondain, dánta*, poem 1, ll. 131-48. 137 NLI, MS G 117.

Edward Lhuyd and was later owned by Charles Vallancey.[138] That the antiquarian Lluyd bought contemporary copies of *Foras feasa* both in Irish and in English[139] indicates that Keating's reputation by the end of the seventeenth century made the *Foras feasa* a desirable item for antiquarians to acquire.

Two further copies of *Foras feasa* were prepared by Eoghan Ó Caoimh in 1702-3.[140] One of these, RIA MS 23 E 23, had been commissioned by Diarmuid Ó Suilleabháin and was later owned by his wife Caitlín O'Brien.[141] The same scribe also made copies of *Eochair-sgiath an Aifrinn* and *Trí bior-ghaoithe an bháis* in 1703,[142] and a further four copies of *Trí bior-ghaoithe an bháis* in his hand survive from the years 1704-10.[143] Indeed, the work of Ó Caoimh accounts for a significant proportion of the extant early eighteenth-century manuscript copies of Keating's theological works. Apart from Seán mac Torna Uí Mhaolchonaire, he was probably the first to focus on the entire corpus of Keating's writings rather than primarily on the history. For Ó Caoimh, it would appear that his own religious concerns, combined with his interest in the Irish past, found expression in Keating's writings and he worked to make those ideas more accessible to others.

Ó Caoimh had been born at Glenville, County Cork, in 1656, and had married Eleanor de Nógla. His wife had died in 1707 and two years later his son, a clerical student, died at Rochelle in France. Ó Caoimh himself subsequently became a priest and served as parish priest of Doneraile before his death on 5 April 1726. He was buried at Old Court (Sean-Chúirt), where the later tombstone inscription indicates the scribe had been particularly highly regarded in the Cork community in which he lived. He was considered to be an exceptional individual involved in a highly skilled learned activity and his death was regarded as a blow to the cultural life of the community.[144] John O'Brien, later bishop of Cloyne, also added an epitaph in verse on the same stone.[145]

The work of Eoghan Ó Caoimh alone is probably sufficient to account for the proliferation of copies of *Foras feasa* that suggest 1629 as the date of composition, since his exemplar evidently bore this date.[146] Together with David Mohir, who was apparently based in Limerick in the 1720s, he made a significant contribution to the dissemination of Keating's theological tracts.[147] His work ensured that

---

138 NLI, MS G 17, Vallancey noted inside the front cover, 'This is the original Keating by which I detected many interpolations in O'Connor's translation'.   139 In 1700 he also acquired the translated copy of *Foras feasa* (now TCD, MS 1443) which had been written in 1697-9 by Humphry and T. Moynihan.   140 UCD, Gaelic MS 62; RIA, MS 23 E 23.   141 *RIA Cat. Ir. MSS*, pp. 1683-84.   142 Stonyhurst College Library, composite MSS (NLI, microfilm P471).   143 UCC, Gaelic MS 168; RIA, 23 E 17; RIA, 23 G 2; and NLI, G 312.   144 'Ag so ionad iodhlaicthe Eóghain Uí Chaoimh, thug tréimhsi dá aimsir pósda, agus tar éis éaga a mhná do ghlac Grádh Coisreagtha; iur ba dhuine gaosmhar, geanamnaidhe, greannmhar; agus do ba fhile fóghlamtha, fír-eólach, agus cléireach cliste, caoin, a bpríomhtheangach a dhúithche agus a shinnsear é. Gur ab uime sin do cuireadh an sgríbhinn neamhchoitcheann so ós a chionn. Do éag an cúigmhadh lá de'n Abrán AD 1726, agus ar doilg d'ógaibh na Múmhan é, agus fós dá chléir; óir as iomdha leabhar lan-fhoghlamtha, léirsgríobhtha, dá shaothar re na fhaicsin a nÉire aniugh' (John O'Daly, *The poets and poetry of Munster*, (Dublin, 1849), p. 38).   145 O'Daly, *Poets and poetry of Munster*, p. 38.   146 As seen above, p. 59, this date is incorrect.   147 Mohir's work includes FLK,

Keating's work was transmitted not just to those who commissioned the manuscripts but to many Catholic congregations who then and later heard sermons based
on those texts as transcribed for clergy.

This overview of the legacy of Geoffrey Keating within the Catholic community in the seventeenth century makes clear that the impact of his writings was
wide-ranging. The most striking feature, perhaps, is the immediacy with which
Foras feasa was accepted by his contemporaries as a work of special significance.
While the Franciscans were busy transcribing the Irish text to take it to Louvain,
Michael Kearney was at work on an English translation and the Ó Maolchonaire
scribes were disseminating it within traditional Gaelic scholarly circles. Within the
limitations of the medium of scribal publication, *Foras feasa* was clearly an instant
'best-seller'. John Lynch's production of a Latin version, and the late seventeenth-
century Catholic 'A defence' translation are evidence of its wider appeal. Its popularity among later poets is evidence of the crucial function served by *Foras feasa*
in maintaining a link with the past among those who no longer had the training or
the patronage to cope with the challenges of the older manuscript tradition. While
the success of *Foras feasa* is self-evident, the extent of that success was starkly
highlighted by the eclipse of the older scholarly tradition on which it was built.

Gaelic MS A 26, NLI, MSS G 55, G 83, G 196 and RIA, MS 23 I 13. Mohir was also responsible for
FLK, MS A 35, which ascribes the text known as *Saltair Mhuire* to Keating. Riseárd Ó Foghludha
(ed.), 'Saltair Mhuire', *Irish Rosary*, xii-xiii (1908-1909). The *Saltair Mhuire* is an Irish language version of a work by Thomas Worthington. There is no evidence of it having been ascribed to Keating in
his own time. See RIA, MS 23 I 9, ff. 101-24, for another text of *Saltair Mhuire*, transcribed by Tadhg
Ó Neachtain, Feb. 1740 (f. 107), but not ascribed to Keating. Tadhg Ó Dushláine has suggested that a
case could be made on linguistic grounds for Keating having translated the *Saltair Mhuire* (Ó
Dushláine, *An Eoraip agus litríocht na Gaeilge*, p. 217, n. 8).

11

Catholic history; Protestant history:
Foras feasa ar Éirinn in circulation, 1680-1740

Many prose histories of Ireland written in English in the late seventeenth and early eighteenth centuries drew extensively on *Foras feasa ar Éirinn* as a source of reference for the early history of Ireland. Of particular note, among Catholic writers, was work by Peter Walsh, Roderick O'Flaherty and Hugh MacCurtin. These, together with Protestant writers such as Thomas Harte and Richard Cox, were participants in an ongoing dialogue with and about the Irish past, the vocabulary for which was drawn largely from *Foras feasa*. That this trend was so pronounced before *Foras feasa* was available in print is a measure of the importance of the scribal tradition in making the text available even outside its traditional milieu. It serves as a reminder that publication did not necessarily require print and that early eighteenth-century readers did not distinguish between manuscript and print in the way that is usual today.

While language, in late seventeenth-century Ireland, could be an indicator of political and cultural allegiances, it was not the only characteristic distinguishing the various readers who had an interest in Geoffrey Keating's story of the origins of the Irish people. Each reader would have known that Geoffrey Keating was a Catholic priest, a Doctor of Divinity, educated in Europe. Individual reader's responses to the text would have been coloured by their own perceptions of Catholicism, their prior assumptions about the Irish past, and about the nature and purpose of history, about what it was appropriate to remember about the past, how the past could, and should, be recalled and recorded. Readers of the text also had their own views on contemporary society, its political, social and cultural dimensions, and these too affected the way in which they approached any author's interpretation of the past. Each reader brought to the text his own preconceptions about the author, about Ireland, and about history. History was read, not just to illuminate the past, but also to help explain the present.

Keating's manuscript history also had an appeal outside Ireland. In 1696, for instance, Patrick Logan, a Quaker schoolmaster from Lurgan, sent a newly transcribed copy of the *Foras feasa*, in Irish, to Edinburgh, to be placed in the Advocates' Library there. He judged that the recipient might find Keating's history advantageous 'in writing matters of controversy pertaining to history'.[1] Logan had heard that an English translation was in existence, but was not able to verify this. At any rate he was confident that the Irish language text would suffice in Edinburgh since 'these that have the Irish language will explain it'.[2] It is evident from these comments that Keating's history had an established reputation by the late seventeenth century among people who could not read Irish. That reputation was very considerably enhanced between about 1680 and 1740 because of the uses made of Keating's history by a variety of authors, Catholic and Protestant.

I

Among the most influential users of Keating's history was Peter Walsh, OFM (*c*.1614-1688), who in 1682 published a substantial history entitled *A prospect of the state of Ireland from the year of the world 1756 to the year of Christ 1652*. The book was published in London, where the author had been living since 1669 under the patronage of the duke of Ormond. Walsh himself was described by a contemporary, the Reverend William Burgat, who had met him in Dublin in 1662, as 'a well-educated man, of keen intellect, on which he presumes much; a fluent and prompt speaker given to loquacity'.[3] A Franciscan who was no stranger to political controversy, Walsh had been involved in the Remonstrance controversy in the 1660s, and although a very able man has been judged vain and egotistical.[4]

In his history, Peter Walsh in fact made no secret of his reliance on two works, John Lynch's large treatise, *Cambrensis eversus*, published in 1662 under the pseudonym Gratianus Lucius, and a translation of Keating's *Foras feasa* shown to him by the earl of Anglesea in the mid 1670s.[5] Walsh dedicated his book 'To the king' and reminded Charles II that being a history of Ireland 'tis an account of part of your people, and contains an account of part of your pedigree ... for it is the glory of the Irish nation to have contributed to your sacred blood, as well as the rest under your happy government'.[6] Walsh's text presented an Old English perspective on the state of Ireland and he made clear at the outset the nature of his source materials:

> although I have read whatever Cambrensis, or Campion, or Hanmer, or Spenser wrote of Ireland: yet in the whole former part of this Prospect, I have not borrow'd from any one or more of them above one paragraph of a

---

1 NLS, Advocates MS 33.4.11, f. vi.   2 Ibid., f. vii.   3 Cited from P.F. Moran (ed.), *Spicilegium Ossoriense, being a collection of original letters and papers illustrative of the history of the Irish church from the Reformation to the year 1800* (3 vols, Dublin, 1874-84) i, p. 445 in Benignus Millett, *The Irish Franciscans, 1651-1665* (Rome, 1964), p. 462.   4 Millett, *Irish Franciscans*, pp. 462-3.   5 This was probably the 'A defence' translation rather than Kearney's earlier text. See also note 12 below.   6 Peter Walsh, *A prospect of the state of Ireland from the year of the world 1576 to the year of Christ 1652* ([London], 1682), sig. a2v.

few lines: unless peradventure you account those other to be such (i.e. borrowed from them) which animadvert upon some few of their many errors.
Nor certainly would I have ventur'd on writing so much as one line of the
state of that kingdom before the English conquest if I had not been acquainted with another kind of authors, yea authors not only more knowing, but
incomparably better qualified to know the ancient monuments of that kingdom, than they or any other foreigners that hitherto have gather'd, written,
printed some here-say scraps of that nation, could possibly be. In short, when
I was a young man I had read Geoffrey Keting's manuscript History of
Ireland. And now when my Lord of Castle-haven would needs engage me to
write something, as you have seen before: I remembered how about four or
five years since, the R.H. Earl of Anglesey, Lord Privy Seal, had been pleas'd
to shew me another manuscript, being an English translation of that Irish history of Keting's. Besides I remember'd to have seen and read Gratianus
Lucius,[7] when he came out in print some twenty years ago. And because I
was sure to meet in the former, materials enough for such discourses upon
the more ancient Irish or state of their country before the Engish conquest,
as were to my purpose: and that the later too might be very useful in some
particulars: having borrow'd Keting first, (i.e. that English manuscript translation of him, such as it is, from my Lord Privy Seal) I ventur'd to begin
somewhat, in the method you have here, on so noble and illustrious a subject.
Though I must confess, I am still the more unsatisfied, that while I was
drawing these papers you have now before you, I could by no means procure
the reading either of Primate Ussher's *Primordia Ecclesiarum Britannicarum*,
or Sir James Ware's *Antiquities of Ireland*.[8]

Walsh's description of *Foras feasa* was designed to present Keating in a very
favourable light. He expressed none of the reservations that the more scholarly
Lynch had noted in the preface to his Latin translation. From Walsh's perspective
Keating was 'the chiefest of all the historians of later days'.[9] A small reminder that
some 'unlikely stories'[10] were to be found therein was all Walsh felt was necessary
'to prevent your prejudice against Keating's history'. How and why did Keating
relate these stories? he asked. 'It is manifest he does it, of set purpose to explode
'em every one as incredible, and mere poetical fictions. For so himself expressly
says. Adding withal that such only and no other was the repute they had in the
very days of yore among the best Irish Antiquaries.'[11] Walsh offered the reader
some background information on Keating and on the sources of *Foras feasa* as he
understood them.

Geoffrey Keating was a native of Ireland in the province of Munster, as
were his ancestors before him for many generations, though not of Irish but

---

7 John Lynch, *Cambrensis eversus* (1662).   8 Walsh, *Prospect*, sig. a1v-a2.   9 Ibid., p. [506].   10 Ibid.,
sig. a[7]v.   11 Ibid., sig. [a8].

English blood originally. He was by education, study, commencement abroad in France, a Doctor of Divinity, in his religion a Romanist, by ordination and calling, a secular priest. He had by his former study at home in his younger days, under the best masters of the Irish tongue and the most skillful in their Antiquities, arriv'd to a high degree of knowledge in both. In his riper years, when return'd back from his other studies and travails in foreign parts, his curiosity and genius led him to examine all foreign authors both ancient and modern who had written of that kingdom either purposely or occasionally whether in Latin or in English. And this diligent search made him observe two things chiefly. 1. That every one, even the very best and most knowing of those writers, were either extremely out in many, if not most of their relations concerning the state of that country before the English conquest, or rather indeed wholly ignorant of it ... [relating] monstrous fables derived from such romantic stories as were certainly written at first for mere diversion and pastime only. 2. That the generality of those British authors, who have written of that country since the English conquest, are against all justice and truth and laws of history, in the highest degree injurious to the ancient natives. These considerations improving by a fervant zeal for truth, and generous love to his country, made Father Keating undergo the laborious task of writing the history of Ireland ... And this history (besides which there is no other full, complete or methodical one extant of all the ages, invasions, conquests, changes, monarchs, wars and other considerable matters of that truly ancient kingdom) he lived to finish in his old age, that is, a little after Charles I, of glorious memory had been proclaimed king.[12] Nor did he only finish it, but prefix unto it a very judicious, large and learned preface to the reader.[13]

Marginal textual references to Keating's work abound in the pages of Walsh's *A prospect*, and it is likely that the publicity given to *Foras feasa* among readers of English by Walsh's book would have generated demand for copies of *Foras feasa* itself in English translation. The surviving series of manuscript copies of the 'A defence' translation prepared in the final two decades of the seventeenth century may be linked to this demand.

Roderick O'Flaherty's *Ogygia, seu rerum Hibernicarum chronologia*, published in London in 1685 to some acclaim, would have generated further interest in the sources for the early history of Ireland as conveniently summarised in Keating's *Foras feasa*. O'Flaherty, like fellow Galwegian Lynch, was interested in the pre-history of the kingdom of Ireland. He was particularly attracted by the issue of the Irish origins of the Stuart kings and the idea of the antiquity of the kingdom of

---

12 If, as is possible, Walsh was using a copy of 'A defence', he would have accepted 1629 as the date of completion of the text given in the copies of that translation. This supposition moves the date of that translation back to the 1670s, an idea reinforced by the fact that the earl of Anglesea also had access to a translation of *Foras feasa* (probably the 'A defence' text) in the 1670s. **13** Walsh, *Prospect*, sig. a2-a3.

Ireland relative to neighbouring kingdoms. The focus of O'Flaherty's work was on the period up to 1022, with a final chapter covering the period 1022-1684 in a mere nine pages.[14]

The publication also included a chronological poem in three parts. The first part began with creation and continued to the coming of Christianity to Ireland AD 432. The middle section of the poem recorded the forty-eight Christian kings of Ireland from Laoghaire to Malachy, AD 432–1022. The final section purported to cover the period AD 1022 to 1684 but in reality it treated the period from 1022 to 1198. After the death of Ruaidhrí Ó Conchubhair, last indigenous king of Ireland in 1198, O'Flaherty skipped several centuries and resumed his narrative in 1603 when 'After a lapse of 405 years Ireland is again governed by a Scottish king'.[15]

> James, the descendant of Conary by origin an Irishman, during his reign united the three empires, whom seven nations acknowledge as their ruler, each contending he was sprung from them. England gives him three nations, the Norman, the Welsh and the Saxon, and Scotland two, the Pict and the Scot. To him likewise, Ireland affords two races – the Milesians and those whom England sent forth, the ornament of their country. Not force but love inbred of their origin, by close connexion united them, though of discordant minds one from another.[16]

Throughout the text O'Flaherty's debt to Keating was considerable; *Foras feasa* was the only source from which verbatim quotations were given at length. Keating's material was usually discussed in favourable terms, being used as supporting evidence. Only rarely did O'Flaherty take issue with Keating on a point of detail. In addition to his use of *Foras feasa* in developing the debate about the nature of the kingdom of Ireland, on a personal level also O'Flaherty, who died in 1718, was one of those who provided a link between Keating's contemporaries, such as Mac Fhirbhisigh and John Lynch, and the antiquarian collectors of the early eighteenth century, including Edward Lhuyd.[17]

II

Books in circulation were read, perhaps with different emphases, by persons from all political allegiances. Thus, for instance, there is evidence that it was Peter

---

14 i.e. nine pages of Hely's English translation. The original Latin edition is similarly brief. Roderick O'Flaherty, *Ogygia, seu rerum Hibernicarum chromologia*, trans. James Hely (2 vols, Dublin, 1793), ii, ch. 94.   15 O'Flaherty, *Ogygia*, ii, p. 414.   16 O'Flaherty, *Ogygia*, ii, p. 414. The notes to the English translation, pp. 416-18 give genealogical details of King James' claim to be Irish, English, Welsh and Scots.   17 T.W. Moody and W.E. Vaughan (eds), *A new history of Ireland, iv, eighteenth-century Ireland, 1691-1800* (Oxford, 1986), p. 398.

Walsh's use of Keating that prompted Thomas Harte, a Sligo Protestant, to undertake his own work on *Foras feasa*. A few years after *A Prospect* was published
Thomas Harte noted in a letter to his son that:

> now of late I have seen a book of Father Peter Welsh dedicated to his late
> majesty the which in substance is nothing else but Keting in another dress
> with his own animadeversions [*sic*] and therefore I thought it would not be
> amiss to bring Keting himself to light that it may be known how far those
> who have written since do agree or disagree from that often quoted
> author.[18]

Harte, in these comments, was dismissive of Walsh's effort. It is evident that while
Walsh's version of Irish history was unpalatable to Harte, Keating's *Foras feasa* was
regarded more favourably. Its value as a source book that made accessible the early
history of Ireland meant that it was highly regarded by readers who would otherwise not have been sympathetic to the views of a Counter-Reformation Catholic
priest.[19]

Two copies of a seventeenth-century history of Ireland by Thomas Harte survive.[20] These are adaptations of *Foras feasa* with the addition of a third section bringing the narrative forward to the reign of James I. The text in NLI, MS G 292
(incomplete) is now prefixed by a letter from the scribe (Thomas Harte) to his son,
Mr Morgan Harte, at Tuam, county Galway.[21] The letter explained that the translation was done by Henry O'Hart and the scribe then 'digested it into the best order
I could without altering the sense of the author'. The preface to the other manuscript copy of Harte's work, (RIA, MS 24 G 15) made a different claim. There it
was asserted that 'T.H.' made the translation himself 'by the assistance of my very
good friend and tutor ... master Henry O'Harte ... a native of county Sligo'.[22]

Harte did not simply treat the *Foras feasa* as a text to be faithfully translated.
He was significantly less sympathetic to the text than Michael Kearney had been
in his translation. Harte approached the text as a 'source book' rather than a
polemical history. He selected and adapted Keating's work as he felt appropriate.
His description of the author as 'one Doctor Keating, an Englishman by descent
but of the Romish religion' who being 'very expert in the Irish tongue hath framed
a collection from their best authors now extant' suggests that Harte did not identify himself culturally with the milieu in which Keating operated.

---

18 NLI, MS G 292, inserted page. Transcribed in *NLI Cat. Ir. MSS*, Fasc vii, pp. 13-14. 19 Internal
evidence suggests that Harte's translation was undertaken after the death of Charles II, because he
described Peter Walsh's address to Charles II as an address to 'our late monarch' when mentioning that
it was Walsh's use of Keating that prompted him to make the *Foras feasa* available in English.
Curiously, he would have known, from the same source, that the *Foras feasa* had already been translated into English, yet he went to the trouble of proceeding with a new translation presumably believ-
ing it impossible to obtain a copy of the earlier translation in the possession of the earl of Anglesea,
which in any case was a 'Catholic' version of *Foras feasa*. 20 RIA, MS 24 G 15 and NLI, MS G 292.
21 Text of letter printed in *NLI Cat. Ir. MSS*, Fasc. vii, pp. 13-14. 22 RIA, MS 24 G 15, p. 3.

Harte was clear that his purpose could only be served by an English language text. Thus

> being penned in the Irish language ... I have translated into English and shall by God's assistance transmit unto the public view as much thereof as I shall find necessary for my purpose, together with what I conceive authentic and not contradicting the Irish history as I have read out of English authors.[23]

Harte, therefore, judged the *Foras feasa* and adapted it according to the standard of those very histories Keating has been at pains to refute. Not surprisingly, Keating's long controversial *Díonbhrollach* was omitted in the manuscripts which originated with Harte. Harte also made clear to the readers of his English version that he had omitted

> those many genealogies, fictions and miracles of saints which are inserted by Keating and others which I conceive fitter for a legend than an history which should contain nothing but certainty.[24]

While book one of *Foras feasa*, down to the coming of Patrick, was relatively uncontroversial, Harte found book two rather more problematic. The period from the coming of Christianity to the Norman conquest was necessarily viewed rather differently from a New English Protestant political perspective. Thomas Harte was unhappy with the way St Patrick and the pre-Patrician era was portrayed by Keating and he used Colgan's *Acta sanctorum*, Ussher's *Indice chronologicae* and Hanmer's history to revise the interpretation of Patrick as the individual who brought Christianity to Ireland.[25] Harte concluded 'that the gospel was preached in Ireland at least 75 years before St Patrick arrived with a commission from Rome for that purpose.'[26] This interpretation allowed Harte to argue that Christianity did not come to Ireland from Rome and that the true church in Ireland was not the Church of Rome. Harte explained that it was because Patrick converted the Gaelic kings and princes and baptised the vulgar sort who formerly did not believe that he had the honour of being accounted 'apostle of Ireland'.

Harte was here constructing a different version of the Irish Christian past from that found in *Foras feasa*. He considered that an unspecified elite, who were neither the Gaelic elite nor the lowly, had adopted Christianity in Ireland independently of Patrick and of Rome. Harte was content not to elucidate the matter at length because it had been asserted by 'so reverend and learned a judge as our late primate Ussher ... whose writings will be famous both among us and foreign nations to the world's end'.[27]

Thomas Harte also provided his own slant on the nature of the Norman conquest of Ireland. He was evidently in no doubt but that Ireland had been genuinely

23 NLI, MS G 292, p. 2. 24 Ibid., p. 2. 25 RIA, MS 24 G 15, p. 131. 26 Ibid., p. 134. 27 Ibid., p. 134.

conquered by Henry II in the seventeenth year of his reign.[28] In his account of the Norman invasion, the Irish were described as 'the enemy'[29] and in contrast to *Foras feasa*, Strongbow was presented as the hero of the hour. Harte's text was entitled 'The history of the kingdom of Ireland in three books' and the idea of kingdom was central to his interpretation. While omitting much of the detail of the earliest kings of Ireland recorded by Keating, he was in no doubt but that King James was the heir to the title of king of Ireland. It seems that it was this interest in the kingdom of Ireland, coupled with an interest in family history, that attracted post-Restoration readers and writers, whether Catholic or Protestant, to *Foras feasa* as an historical source.

Thomas Harte's translation of Keating's first book on pre-Christian Ireland, to which he appended a revised second volume with a different version of the Norman conquest, indicates that Keating was regarded as the best available, or most accessible, source on the origins of the kingdom of Ireland. It also indicates that the nature of the Norman conquest was debatable territory about which Harte felt at liberty to alter Keating's account. The addition of a third volume bringing the narrative forward to the Stuart period is a measure of Harte's New English Protestant sympathies. Having narrated the story of the Nine Years' War and the defeat of the earl of Tyrone, with Lord Deputy Mountjoy as the hero of the hour, he concluded

> Ireland being thus broken and ploughed, that glorious queen [Elizabeth] who died a victor over all her enemies, having made a final and full conquest of all that nation, she left the sowing of it to her diligent successor King James who brought another crown to aggrandise and add to the imperial and triumphant glory of England ... being descended from the ancient monarchs and provincial kings of Ireland.[30]

Harte regarded the story as complete when he had brought the narrative of the kingdom of Ireland as far as the end of the reign of 'King James, the first monarch of Great Britain and Ireland'.[31]

Thomas Harte's history, which he intended to have printed, concluded with the genealogy of James, monarch of Great Britain and Ireland, as recorded in Lynch's *Cambrensis eversus*, and perhaps derived from that source. He traced the line back through Earchan 'under whose conduct the Irish or Scots first began to inhabit Alba back to Éireamhón, son of Míl'.[32] That Harte chose to adapt *Foras feasa* rather than begin afresh is a measure of the extent to which Keating's history met the needs of readers from all backgrounds in the late seventeenth century. It is clear that when Harte encountered *Foras feasa* he saw it as a history of the Irish kingdom that had significance for his own circumstances and his own Protestant political perspective in Restoration Ireland.

---

28 Ibid., pp. 293-5.   29 Ibid., p. 263.   30 Ibid., p. 463.   31 Ibid., p. 462.   32 Ibid., p. 464.

III

In the debates about Ireland's past and on the nature of the Irish kingdom, which were a strong undercurrent to late seventeenth-century Irish political debate, one hostile reader of *Foras feasa* was Sir Richard Cox (1650-1733). He served as lord chancellor of Ireland and was author of *Hibernia Anglicana: or the history of Ireland from the conquest thereof by the English to this present time*.[33] Though born in Cork, Cox was culturally and politically 'New English' and his book was an exposition of the view 'that the Irish did continue in their barbarity, poverty and ignorance until the English conquest, and that all the improvements themselves and their country received ... is to be ascribed to English government'.[34] The book was written in the years 1685-9 when Cox, a strong exponent of the Protestant interest in Ireland, moved from Kinsale to England following the accession of James II. At the time of writing Cox believed the religio-political situation was such that:

> at this day we know no difference of nation but what is expressed by papist and Protestant, if the most ancient natural Irishman be a Protestant, no man takes him for other than an Englishman, and if a Cockney be a papist, he is reckoned in Ireland, as much an Irishman as if he were born on Sleve-logher; the earls of Inchiquin and Castlehaven are examples hereof.[35]

This identification of Irishness with Catholicism was at the core of Keating's *Foras feasa* as originally conceived[36] and it is not surprising that Cox was antagonistic to Keating's version of the past. The version Cox read was the Catholic 'A defence' translation as found in NLI, MS G 293. This manuscript was on loan to him in 1689-90.[37] The concern shown by Cox regarding the current status of the Old English was clearly at odds with that which was inherent in the *Foras feasa* narrative. Cox was careful to point out the 'degeneracy' of the Old English: 'whereas the Old English were heretofore on the British side in all national quarrels, they are now so infatuated and degenerated that they do not only take part with the Irish but call themselves *Natives* in distinction from the New English'.[38] He warned that, since Protestants now had three-quarters of the kingdom, the Irish 'interest to regain it is larger and more pressing than it was in former times'.[39] He believed the Old English and Old Irish to be 'more firmly united by the common tie of religion'. He argued that 'they are united in a common Interest, to recover their forfeited estates, if they can; and when that is done, the Irish have their particular interest apart, to recover their old estates from the first conquerors or intruders'.[40]

---

33 First published London, 1689-90, 2nd ed. 1692.   34 Cited in *New Hist. Ire.*, iii, pp. lix-lx.   35 Cox, *Hibernia Anglicana*, sig. c2.   36 Cunningham, 'Seventeenth-century interpretations of the past'.   37 'This booke was lent by Sir John Percivale to Mr Cox. And returned to Sir R. Southwell in London March 1689/90' (NLI, MS G 293, memorandum by Sir Robert Southwell on 2nd flyleaf).   38 Cox, *Hibernia Anglicana*, sig. c2.   39 Ibid., sig. d1.   40 Ibid., sig. c2.

Rejecting the idea that the Irish were a 'pure and ancient nation' descended from 'Hiber and Herimon', he regarded them as a 'mixt people' and contrasted the Irish and Scots with the British whom he defined as those who associated with the English in language, manners, customs, religion and interest.[41] Although John Lynch's and Roderick O'Flaherty's Latin publications expressing views on the history of the Irish kingdom would have been more immediately accessible to Cox's readers, Keating's work was still regarded, even by Cox himself, as influential. He rejected Keating's story of Irish Scythian and Milesian origins and concluded that 'it is rational to believe England peopled Ireland, being the nearest country to it'. He cited the etymological evidence of Welsh words in the Irish language in support of his case. He rejected the *Leabhar gabhála* version of Irish origins, dismissing 'those ridiculous stories which they have published of the *Fir Bolgs* and *Tuah-de-danans*'.[42]

'As for the government of Ireland', he argued, 'it is not to be doubted but it was governed by kings, but they were such as the Indian kings in Virginia or the lords of manors in England', and the boundaries of their territory were 'every day altered by force'.[43] 'These kings or monarchs were neither anointed nor crowned nor inaugurated by any ceremony, they did not succeed either by descent or election, but by pure force, so that the title of most of them is founded on the murder of his predecessor'.[44] While these comments might seem disingenuous, it should be noted that the version of *Foras feasa* read by Cox (the 'A defence' translation) did not contain the material on inauguration found in most Irish language copies of the text.[45] Perhaps the central reason Cox objected to Keating's account was because it presented Ireland as an independent kingdom.

Ireland was, in Cox's view, 'a subordinate kingdom to the crown of England' and 'the Irish are (as Campion says) beholding to God for being conquered'. As far as Cox was concerned the history of Ireland that really mattered began with Henry II, 'conqueror and lord of Ireland', and in his dedication to William and Mary he pointed out that, with one exception, kings of England since the twelfth century had retained 'Ireland inseparably united to the crown of England'. The exception was Henry II who gave the kingdom to his son John and that example 'was thought so dangerous, that Ireland was never given away since that time'.[46] The unionist sentiments of Cox emerge in the implied threat of disaster that would befall if any separate political status of the Irish kingdom were to be recognised in the 1690s. Cox looked forward to the day when Protestants would be preserved from ruin and there would be 'such a degree of reformation and religion as will restore that *Kingdom* to its ancient appelation, and *Ireland* will again be called *Insula Sacra*'.

It is clear, given his political views, that Cox could not have responded favourably to Keating's version of the Irish past. There was, he asserted, no 'complete or coherent history of that kingdom'.[47]

---

41 Ibid., 'To the reader'.   42 Ibid., sig. e2v.   43 Ibid., sig. f1v.   44 Ibid., sig. f1v.   45 As printed in *FFÉ*, iii, 8–14.   46 Cox, *Hibernia Anglicana*, 'Dedication'.   47 Ibid., 'To the reader', sig. b[1]v.

As for those histories that treat of the times before the English conquest, Doctor Keating's is the best, and is exceedingly applauded by some that did and others that did not know better; Peter Walsh thinks 'tis the only compleat history that we have of all the invasions, conquests, changes, monarchs, wars and other considerable matters of that truly ancient kingdom, but after all it is no more than an ill-digested heap of very silly fictions. And P.W.'s *Prospect* which is in effect the epitomy of Keating in English, with all the art he could use to polish it, will never pass for more than an Utopian achievement.[48]

Cox believed that 'An entire and coherent history of Ireland must be very acceptable to the world, and very useful to the people of England, and the refugees of Ireland, as least especially at this juncture, when that kingdom is to be reconquered, and perhaps time may produce such a one'.[49] This statement can be read as an awareness by Cox that a distinct 'textual community' existed that sought to have their own narrative history of Ireland written from a very different perspective to the Irish Catholic perspective of *Foras feasa*. The Protestant New English in late seventeenth-century Ireland and the 'people of England' mentioned by Cox, were busy compiling their own family histories that would legitimise their current political status.[50] Cox clearly believed that the Protestant New English as a political community also needed a 'national' history of their own, to match that available to Catholics in *Foras feasa*.[51]

Despite Cox's extreme reservations in the 1690s, it would appear that by the second decade of the eighteenth century Irish Protestant readers were rather more prepared to accept the narrative of the Irish past contained in *Foras feasa* as their history too.[52]

IV

In considering the legacy of Geoffrey Keating, and the textual communities that may have formed around his texts, it is not possible to draw a clear distinction between those who read and wrote in Irish and those who read and wrote in English, not least because certain individuals did both. There were many people in late seventeenth-century and early eighteenth-century Ireland, scribes and poets

48 Ibid. 49 Ibid., sig. b[1]*v* – b[2]. 50 Raymond Gillespie, 'The making of the Montgomery manuscripts', *Familia*, ii, no. 2 (1986), pp. 23-9; George Hill, *The Montgomery manuscripts: 1603-1706* (Belfast, 1869); G.F. Savage-Armstrong, *A genealogical history of the Savage family in Ulster* (1906); T.K. Lowry, *The Hamilton manuscripts* (1867). 51 Cox's sectarian views on the state of Ireland were reiterated in his brief *Aphorisms relating to the kingdom of Ireland* (London, 1689) published separately in 1689. 52 Jacqueline Hill, 'Popery and Protestantism, civil and religious liberty: the disputed lessons of Irish history, 1690-1812', *Past and Present*, no. 118 (1988), pp. 96-129, and Vincent Morley, *An crann os coill: Aodh Buidhe Mac Cruitín, c.1680-1755* (Baile Átha Cliath, 1995).

among them, who were part of two different cultural worlds defined in part by language, but to a greater extent by religious allegiance. While one politico-religious community moulded its identity, through its writing, around its continued association with the Irish language, and the other was characterised in part by its association with the English language, many people straddled these cultural boundaries. Hugh MacCurtin, (Aodh Buidhe Mac Cruitín, *c*.1680-1755), typified the dual world of scholarship in which an interest in the origins of particular cultural communities brought different groups of scholars into contact with each other.

Hugh MacCurtin (along with Aindrias Mac Cruitín, scribe of several copies of *Foras feasa*) enjoyed the patronage of a range of county Clare gentry in the early eighteenth century. Their traditional family role as hereditary poets to the O'Briens was carried on through the patronage of Sir Donnchadh O'Brien of Lemenagh.[53] Hugh was equally at home in Dublin, where he was a member of the Tadhg Ó Neachtain circle of scribes. While it is true, as Cullen argues, that individuals like MacCurtin continued to be a part of the cultural world of their rural origins, those origins did not define the limits of their cultural contacts.[54] Cullen draws attention to the gradual distancing between the cultural and social worlds of patron and scribe in the course of the eighteenth century, as scribal activity became increasingly urbanised. Over time, it was not just the patrons, but the scribes too, who were distanced from the cultural milieu from which the texts they copied had emanated.[55]

Hugh MacCurtin, came to the notice of the English-speaking cultural elite of Dublin in 1717 when his *Brief discourse in vindication of the antiquity of Ireland* was published. This book, which relied heavily on Keating's *Foras feasa*, was written as a refutation of Sir Richard Cox's *Hibernia Anglicana*. It also drew on the work of John Lynch, Peter Walsh and Roderick O'Flaherty. MacCurtin used the evidence of *Foras feasa* to make the case that Cox had misrepresented the laws and customs of Ireland prior to the Norman conquest. MacCurtin's account of early Irish history followed *Foras feasa* closely, just as an historical poem, beginning '*A Bhanba is feasach dom do scéala*', which he had written earlier had followed the Seán Ó Conaill's poem, '*Tuireamh na hÉireann*', on the same theme.[56] MacCurtin's effort was a poetic narrative of Irish history that linked the coming of the Normans and the Elizabethan Reformation in a way that presented a version of Irish history at odds with the legacy of Geoffrey Keating.[57] Alan Harrison and Vincent Morley concur in the view that the level of scholarship displayed by MacCurtin and his contemporary Irish scholars in the early eighteenth-century was low, and that their approach to history consisted of little more than rewriting *Foras feasa*.[58]

Nevertheless, the account of the Irish past provided in *A Brief discourse* was more even-handed than the work by Cox it was designed to refute, displaying none

53 L.M. Cullen, 'Patrons, teachers and literacy in Irish: 1700-1850' in Mary Daly and David Dickson (eds), *The origins of popular literacy in Ireland* (Dublin, 1990) p. 20.   54 Cullen, 'Patrons, teachers and literacy in Irish' p. 21.   55 Ibid., pp. 20-4.   56 Morley, *An crann os coill*, pp. 38, 43-5.   57 Ibid., p. 45.   58 Ibid., p. 145; Alan Harrison, *Ag cruinniú meala: Anthony Raymond (1675-1726), ministéir Protastúnach, agus léann na Gaeilge i mBaile Átha Cliath* (Baile Átha Cliath, 1988), p. 47.

of the sectarianism so evident in Cox's writing. It drew heavily on Keating's defence of the honour of the Irish people, as recorded in their history as a learned, religious, Christian people.[59] Essentially, it imitated the form of *Foras feasa*, but focused on Cox rather than Giraldus as the denigrator to be refuted.[60] MacCurtin was neither an original nor an exceptional scholar, but was unusual in managing to get his English writings into print. This was quite an achievement for one of his background. Just a few years earlier, his contemporary, Seán Ó Gadhra, had lamented the fact that the Irish *seanchas* was not available in print.[61]

It is noteworthy, though not surprising, that MacCurtin chose English as the language in which to publish his defence of the Irish past drawn from Keating's *Foras feasa*. It was among English-speaking audiences that Keating's version of the past was debated; there was no need to defend *Foras feasa* among those who prized the work as the story of the Irish Catholic people. The *Brief discourse* was published by subscription. While it has been noted that most of the subscribers named were of Gaelic extraction, Vincent Morley has argued that the list merely depicts MacCurtin's personal cultural network and should not be used as evidence to suggest that the New English community displayed a lack of interest in history.[62]

William Nicolson's *Irish historical library* (1724) dismissed MacCurtin's book as primarily an abstract of Keating's work.

> There is lately a brief discourse in vindication of the antiquity of Ireland, publish'd by H. Mac Curtin, in two parts; the former whereof gives a short abstract of Keating's larger history of the several adventures of the Gadelians and Milesians, down to the days of St. Patrick. In the second, keeping still close to the matter and method of his master Jeoffry; the author collects the flowers of our following story as low as the year 1171 ... Some genealogies of the great families of this kingdom we are to expect in our historian's third part; unless (what I am somewhat jealous of) the publishing of many such pedigrees, by the late editor[63] of Keating, have already furnish'd us with all that our antiquary had in store upon that head.[64]

Morley has shown that apart from *Foras feasa* the only manuscript sources actually used by MacCurtin were *Caithréim Ceallacháin Caisil* and *Leabhar na gceart*.[65] While he also referred to Peter Walsh's *Prospect of the state of Ireland*, and to O'Flaherty's *Ogygia*, the references were very general, and all his references to Lynch's *Cambrensis eversus* could be found in Walsh's book.[66] The change that had

---

59 *New Hist. Ire.*, iv, p. 467. **60** Morley, *An crann os coill*, pp. 56-7. Morley (pp. 52-4) lists the sources of *Brief discourse* and provides notes detailing the parallels with *Foras feasa*, with Peter Walsh and also with the 1705 edition of Ware's *Antiquities*. **61** Mac Domhnaill (ed.), *Dánta is amhráin Sheáin Uí Ghadhra*, poem 4 (1713). **62** *New Hist. Ire.*, iv, p. 467; Morley, *An crann os coill*, p. 48. **63** Dermo'd O'Connor. **64** William Nicolson, *The Irish historical library* (London, 1724), pp. 49-50. **65** Morley, *An crann os coill*, p. 55. Alan Harrison had suggested (*Ag cruinniú meala*, p. 49) that MacCurtin also used sources not available to Keating, but Morley's evidence indicates that this was not the case. **66** Morley, *An crann os coill*, pp. 52-4.

occurred even since Keating's own day was encapsulated in his comment that 'We have many books of the antient Irish laws exant [*sic*] yet in the kingdom, but we have very few that can read or understand them'.[67]

While MacCurtin's printed book would perhaps have been aimed at those who had also read Cox's work, the book's principal appeal was probably to his fellow Catholics.[68] MacCurtin had other channels of literary and political communication open to him also. He used the medium of satirical poetry to vent his anger at Cox. '*Sgiathlúithreach an Choxaigh*',[69] though anonymous in the manuscripts, was thought by Brian Ó Cuív to be the work of Aodh Buidhe, one of over fifty poems ascribed to this poet. MacCurtin functioned in two cultural worlds, distinguished in part by language, and his writings in either language are best regarded as propaganda rather than history or literature.[70] The texts he turned to as the source of his polemical writings, besides *Foras feasa*, included the political poems '*Tuireamh na hÉireann*' and '*An síogaí Rómhánach*'. These two poems, which represent respectively the Old English and the Ulster Confederate perspectives on mid-seventeenth-century Irish politics, were probably collected for their antiquarian interest rather than their political message.[71] By MacCurtin's day, however, the precise context in which such works had originally been composed had receded from view, and the poems were no longer read in the context of the political environment from which they had originally emerged. Morley has shown that MacCurtin himself often behaved more as an antiquarian than a historian, and the texts he assembled for his own use had no clear focus.[72] While he may have aspired to it, he lacked Keating's understanding of the world of Gaelic historical scholarship. The poems he composed came to be seen instead as generic expressions of regret for a world perceived to have changed, perhaps irrevocably, from the one that had provided the materials for Keating's *Foras feasa ar Éirinn*.

Hugh MacCurtin was a typical 'transitional' figure in language terms, but he was in no doubt at all about his religious allegiance. Though he may have mixed easily with people holding very different views of the Irish past in the course of his professional work as a scribe, and although he may have written with ease in two languages, his work in either language has an intellectual consistency that warns against adopting language as a measure of contemporary political attitudes.

While the use made of Keating's history in the early eighteenth century may have been unimaginative, it is nonetheless apparent that it was continually subject to new readings in the light of the altered perspectives and circumstances of its readers. While it is only to be expected that MacCurtin's reading of *Foras feasa*

67 MacCurtin, *Brief discourse*, p. 312, cited in Harrison, *Ag cruinniú meala*, p. 50.   68 No contemporary evidence has been found to support the notion that MacCurtin was imprisoned on publication on account of his Jacobitism. For a discussion of the traditional story of imprisonment see Harrison, *Ag cruinniú meala*, p. 51.   69 Brian Ó Cuív (ed.), '*Sgiathlúithreach an Choxaigh*', *Éigse*, v (1945-7), pp. 136-8; Donal O'Sullivan, 'A courtly poem for Sir Richard Cox', *Éigse*, iv (1943-4), pp. 284-7.   70 Morley, *An crann os coill*, p. 145; Harrison, *Ag cruinniú meala*, p. 47.   71 Morley, *An crann os coill*, pp. 40-2.   72 See for instance the very miscellaneous material assembled in Maynooth, MS M 86b. Morley, *An crann os coill*, pp. 40-2.

would have been in stark contrast to that of Richard Cox, it is also the case that MacCurtin's approach to *Foras feasa* had little in common with Michael Kearney's earlier interpretation of the same work. The distance between the text and the transmitter had grown, and the close affinity between Kearney's and Keating's views was no longer in evidence among even the keenest advocates of Keating's work by the early eighteenth century. MacCurtin's approach to *Foras feasa* was in truth rather pedantic, bordering on the antiquarian.

V

Even before Keating's history of Ireland was available in print the story it contained was of interest to a wider public than merely antiquarian collectors. Evidence of its wide appeal is found in a work by Sarah Butler intitled *Irish Tales, or instructive histories for the happy conduct of life,* first printed in 1716.[73] This book is an early example of Irish romantic fiction and includes an historical tale evidently drawn from *Foras feasa* and set against the backdrop of events leading to the battle of Clontarf in AD 1014. Though written as fiction, Sarah Butler's work contained footnotes to authorities such as Bede's *History of the English church and people* and Camden's *Britannia*. She also made clear to her readers her familiarity with the writings of Peter Walsh and Edmund Spenser about Ireland,[74] and she drew on Keating's *Foras feasa*. Writing in 1716, she must have used a manuscript version, yet she took for granted that the reader would already be familiar with 'Dr Keating's' work. She informed the reader, in the preface, that her story was drawn from the lives of 'two of the most potent monarchs of the Milesian race in that antient kingdom of Ireland' and the author protested that, despite the novel format, 'I have err'd as little from the truth of history as any perhaps who have undertaken anything of this nature'. Concerning the narrative based on the battle of Clontarf the author asserted that 'it is all historical' and named Keating among the sources on which she had relied for the authenticity of her account.

She readily admitted the distance between her own world and that which was narrated in the tales from Irish history which she chose to popularise. She was aware of the difficulty that arose when she rendered the conversations of her heroes and heroines 'as near as I could to our modern phrase', fearing that such was not the authentic voice of the characters in her story. Critics, she feared, might consider such language 'too passionate and elegant for the Irish, and contrary to the humours, they alledge, of so rude and illiterate a people'.[75] In her preface on 'the learning and politeness of the antient Irish' she insisted that the Irish had not always been rude and illiterate 'although they may seem so now', and she instanced Keating himself as evidence of the university learning of the Irish people of past

---

73 I owe this reference to Raymond Gillespie. The work was first printed with a foreword by the English Deist Charles Gilden, and regularly reprinted. References here are to the Dublin reprint issued posthumously in 1735 (NLI I.6551 Dubl. P.11). 74 Butler, *Irish tales,* 'Preface'. 75 Ibid.

generations. She was concerned to convey the idea that Ireland in earlier times had been a centre of culture, that even institutions like the colleges of the University of Oxford had Irish origins, that learning was the touchstone of civility and that Ireland had a rich heritage of learning and civility. *Foras feasa* itself, together with that history as mediated through the writings of Roderick O'Flaherty and Peter Walsh, were her guarantee of the worthiness of Irish civilisation in past ages.

VI

In the early eighteenth century a network of Dublin-based scribes provided the principal mechanism whereby manuscript copies of the writings of Geoffrey Keating were made available to new patrons. A group of scholars, for whom Tadhg Ó Neachtain may have been the pivotal link between scribes and patrons, had a particular interest in historical manuscripts, and Keating's *Foras feasa* was among the texts available to them. The extant copies of their work indicate that the versions of *Foras feasa* they produced were all in the 'modern' style, but they had access to several different exemplars of *Foras feasa*. They also worked with copies of Keating's theological writings, and occasionally his poetry.[76]

The core group of the Dublin circle of scribes interested in Irish historical manuscripts active in the period 1710-45 included Tadhg Ó Neachtain, Richard Tipper, Seán Mac Solaidh (MacSolly), Stephen Rice and Hugh MacCurtin.[77] Others on the fringes of this group were Dermod O'Connor, William Fannin, William Lynch, and Charles Lynegar (O Luinín).[78] All of these men made transcripts of one or more of Keating's prose works, and some individuals made several copies at different dates. A letter from Sean Mac Solaidh, in Meath, to Richard Tipper in Dublin in 1718, reveals something of the manner in which the scribal network operated, with various exemplars, the tools of their trade, being borrowed from one another. Mac Solaidh reminded Tipper not to forget about a Keating text he had asked for '*Na dearmad Seathrún do chur chugam*'.[79] Both men were so familiar with Keating's work that no further description of the text was considered necessary. Notes made by Tadhg Ó Neachtain of manuscripts he had given on loan to others suggests that he was generous with the texts in his possession. Keating's *Trí bior-ghaoithe an bháis* was among the items on loan. 'Hugh Curtains writing 3 biorghuithe' on the list indicates that Hugh MacCurtin had borrowed an exemplar of the *Trí bior-ghaoithe an bháis* for the purpose of making a copy. A copy of the same text was also given on loan to a person named Roe in

---

76 Richard Tipper was among those who transcribed some of Keating's poetry. RIA, MS 23 L 32; See Hayes, *MSS sources*.   77 Harrison, *Ag cruinniú meala*, p. 47.   78 For an overview see Brian Ó Cuív, 'Irish language and literature 1691-1845' in *New Hist. Ire.*, iv, especially 390-404; for lists of extant manuscripts by these various scribes see Hayes, *MSS Sources*. Also assocated with the group was the young Charles O'Conor of Belanagare.   79 ['Don't forget to send me Geoffrey']; Harrison, *Ag cruinniú meala*, p. 40, from Paul Walsh, *Gleanings from Irish manuscripts* (Dublin, 2nd ed. 1933), pp. 197-204.

Leixlip.[80] Ó Neachtain had himself made a copy of *Trí bior-ghaoithe* in 1717[81] and this may be the manuscript he subsequently lent to others.

Members of the Dublin circle of scribes could supply patrons with copies of a variety of historical texts because they were able to gain access to appropriate exemplars. They catered for the needs of a range of users, both Catholic and Protestant. Among the historial manuscripts available to Tadhg Ó Neachtain were important items such as the fourteenth-century Book of Ballymote, which he referred to as '*Leabhar mór Choláiste Atha Cliath*' indicating its association at that time with Trinity College Dublin.[82] Ó Neachtain had access to the Book of Ballymote through Anthony Raymond as intermediary. A selection of important manuscripts earlier associated with the learned families of Ó Maolchonaire, Mac Eochagáin and Mac Aodhagáin were also available to Ó Neachtain in the early eighteenth century. These evidently included a set of annals known as the *Leabhar Oiris Uí Mhaolchonaire*, a version of the Book of Glendalough, genealogical texts from the Ó Maolchonaire school and the manuscript now known as BL Add. MS 30,512,[83] which may have been the text known to Keating as *Leabhar Ruadh Meic Aodhagáin*.[84] It is clear that Tadhg Ó Neachtain's group also had access to material from the Book of Lecan, and the Book of Uí Maine, the *Réim ríoghraidhe*, *Foras feasa* itself and a history compiled in the 1640s sometimes known as *Leabhar gearr na Pailíse*.[85]

These scribes had access to materials that had been in the hands of traditional learned families in the mid-seventeenth century, and their work no doubt contributed to the preservation of such texts. They provide a vital link to Keating not only by copying his works but also because of their access to the manuscript sources from which he had derived his *Foras feasa*. The Dublin scribes were likewise familiar with the work of the seventeenth-century Irish Franciscans, and among the manuscripts copied by Richard Tipper, for instance, was Ó Cléirigh's genealogies of saints and kings.[86] They were equally familiar with the materials that had been collected by James Ussher, James Ware, Edward Lhuyd and other collectors. The scribes acted as intermediaries between antiquarian collectors of diverse backgrounds and traditional Gaelic families, by copying, translating, explaining and even selling Irish manuscripts.[87] They were interested in the content of the manuscripts themselves, but they were also interested in them as commodities, and were well aware of the commercial possibilities generated by antiquarian scholarship.

---

80 Harrison, *Ag cruinniú meala*, pp. 39-40.   81 Now Maynooth, MS B 9.   82 As mentioned in RIA, MS 24 P 41. The Book of Ballymote is now in the Royal Irish Academy.   83 *BL Cat. Ir. MSS*, ii, p. 483; Harrison, *Ag crunniú meala*, p. 48.   84 See above, ch. 4, for discussion of manuscript sources.   85 NLI, MS G 22. See *NLI Cat. Ir. MSS*, ii, pp. 13-18. This compilation was also known as '*Foras feasa Chloinne Mhíleadh Espaine*', and is usually attributed to Eugene McCarthy, 1648, *RIA Cat. Ir. MSS*, p. 433; *BL Cat. Ir. MSS*, ii, 397; Harrison, *Ag crunniú meala*, p. 48.   86 RIA, MS 23 D 9. This was a composite manuscript, and also included extracts from the Book of Ballymote and BL, Add. MS 30,512. 87 Harrison, *Ag cruinniú meala*, p. 42.

The general outline of *Foras feasa ar Éirinn* was sufficiently flexible to ensure that Keating's work essentially dictated for subsequent generations what the canon of Irish history should be. While James Ussher and other seventeenth-century Protestant historians might have differed fundamentally on matters of interpretation, they did not differ on the matter of sources. By the beginning of the eighteenth century, there had emerged a broad agreement as to what constituted the authoritative sources and acceptable authors of Irish history, and they mostly involved some association with *Foras feasa*. The sources most highly valued were those in the Irish language preserved in ancient manuscripts. These were the sources pursued by antiquarian collectors. They had become more widely known through the medium of Keating's history. Thus, while not all readers agreed that Keating's narrative was the definitive account of early Irish history, most found it to be the most accessible account. Its literary style was undeniable. Its pride in Irish origins was shared by most readers born in Ireland. Its appeal was greatly strengthened by its polemical preface that asserted that it, rather than any foreign history, was the truth about the origins of the kingdom of Ireland and its people. Despite his inclusion of incredible romantic tales, Keating was regarded as a trustworthy and careful scholar in his approach to the primary sources. He had largely succeeded in discrediting Giraldus Cambrensis and Stanihurst and *Foras feasa* had become established as the starting point for subsequent historical enquiry into the Irish past. It became more famous for a time than Cambrensis had ever been. It was little wonder that a variety of plans were being laid for the publication of a printed version of *Foras feasa* in English.

By the early eighteenth century the print medium was being used by the emerging Protestant ascendancy in Ireland as one mechanism to foster new understandings of family origins and national and religious allegiances. A recent analysis by Toby Barnard of the impact of books within this community has argued that 'the contents, look, or mere possession of books helped, both practically and figuratively, to make and define the elites of Protestant Ireland. Owners scarcely cared whether these aids were printed or written in manuscript.'[88] He describes how 'the recently established dynasties of Protestant Ireland copied habits from those whom they had so lately supplanted',[89] and how the appropriation of the Irish past was part of the process of identity formation for this new elite. By the second decade of the eighteenth century, therfore, it was to be expected that plans to make the most accessible general history of Ireland available to new Irish audiences would be taking shape.

Links with an Irish scribal network in the Dublin area, notably Tadhg Ó Neachtain and his circle, made it possible for Anthony Raymond, Church of

---

88 Toby Barnard, 'Learning, the learned and literacy in Ireland, *c.*1660-1760', in Toby Barnard, Dáibhí Ó Cróinín and Katharine Simms (eds), *A miracle of learning* (Aldershot, 1998), p. 225.   89 Barnard, 'Learning', p. 225.

9 Brian Bóroimhe, monarch of Ireland, frontispiece from Dermod O'Connor's 1723
English adaptation of *Foras feasa ar Éirinn*

Ireland vicar of Trim, to advance his interest in the Irish language and its literature. While he claimed that he had learned Irish to communicate with his parishioners who were for the most part monoglot Irish speakers, he also had a particular interest in history.[90] Keating's *Foras feasa* was among the texts in which he had
a particular interest and he sought assistance in the ambitious undertaking of translating the work into English. One of those employed by Raymond to assist his
scholarly endeavours was Dermod O'Connor,[91] son of Tadhg Rua O'Connor of
Limerick,[92] who worked as a scribe in Limerick in the years 1712-16.[93]

He was similarly employed in Dublin in 1719 and 1720, where he was known
to the Dublin scribal circle that included Seán Ó Neachtain and his son Tadhg,
although they did not hold him in high regard. It was in Dublin, too, that he made
the aquaintance of Anthony Raymond. By this time Raymond was already engaged
in research with a view to translating Keating's *Foras feasa*. His knowledge of the
language, however, was probably inadequate and it seems unlikely, even with the
assistance of professional scribes, that he would have achieved his ambition of publishing *Foras feasa* in translation.

Dermod O'Connor moved from Dublin to London in 1720, abandoning
Anthony Raymond's project, but determined to publish his own translation of
Keating's history independently. O'Connor was proved correct in his belief that he
could beat Anthony Raymond into print. He was also correct in his calculation that
such a publishing project could prove lucrative. If marketed correctly, there was
potentially a large English-language readership both in Ireland and in England with
an interest in a general history of the kingdom of Ireland.

O'Connor's translation was published in London at the beginning of 1723 with
a Dublin edition following later in the same year, probably in April.[94] The most
significant difference between the London and Dublin editions was in the content
of the supplementary heraldic and genealogical charts which formed an appendix
to the work. The different editions were customised according to the specific interests of the subscribers on whom O'Connor and his printer relied for financial back-
ing in the venture. There were over 300 subscribers to the London edition while
more than 400 people paid in advance for the Dublin edition. No expense was
spared in the production of the volume, particularly the London edition, which was
printed on higher quality paper than the Dublin edition. In each instance, the publication was clearly aimed at affluent families with Irish connections.

Considerable controversy surrounded the publication, which was attacked by
Thomas O'Sullevane even before it was published, and by Anthony Raymond
immediately afterwards. O'Sullevane criticised the translation because it purported
to be Keating's work when it was not actually a straight translation.

90 On Anthony Raymond see Harrison, *Ag cruinniú meala*. See also, Andrew Carpenter and Alan
Harrison, 'Swift, Raymond, and a legacy', *Swift Studies*, i (Münster, 1986), pp. 57-60.   **91** Diarmaid Ó
Catháin, 'Dermot O'Connor, translator of Keating', *Eighteenth-century Ireland*, ii (1987), pp. 68-87.   **92**
Irish Book Lover, iii (1912), p. 155.   **93** Ó Catháin, 'Dermot O'Connor', p. 71.   **94** Harrison, *Ag cru-
inniú meala*, pp. 93-8.

And it is very strange, it being only to be translated by him, that he would give himself the liberty to add to, or make any variation from the original; (I mean the copy in his hands). But the truth is his [Keating's] name is only made use of for a flourish, or outward show, whilst others behind the curtain are hard at work, in licking this ill-born cub into some shape.[95]

O'Sullevane criticised O'Connor for claiming to have made use of the 'Psalter of Tara' to augment Keating's narrative. O'Sullevane, rightly, cast doubt on the existence of this manuscript, which O'Connor mentioned on the title page of his version of *Foras feasa*.[96]

Anthony Raymond attacked O'Connor's publication accusing him of dishonesty. He rebutted O'Connor's claim that it was he rather than Raymond who had first thought of publishing a translation of *Foras feasa*. In a notice placed in the *Dublin Gazette*, 6 April 1723, Raymond attacked O'Connor and his translation. In a published address to Lord Inchiquin in 1723,[97] Raymond asserted that he was himself working on a history of Ireland and had delayed publication until improvements were made to it. Over 170 potential readers placed orders for copies of Raymond's 'History of Ireland'.[98] However, Raymond complained,

> in the mean time Dermod O Connor, finding I had a considerable offer for the copy of my history, went for London and got the late Mr Toland to publish a translation of Dr Keating's fabulous History of Ireland, in his Name, under the pretended title of Antiquary of Ireland.[99]

Raymond drew attention to some inaccuracies in the depiction of Brian Bóroimhe 'your famous ancestor', particularly in the frontispiece illustration of the ill-fated victor at Clontarf. Raymond concluded that the shortcomings of O'Connor's published text showed 'how little Doctor Keating was acquainted with foreign authors (who have written of this kingdom) when he takes no notice of those honourable accounts recorded of Turlough and Muirtogh O'Bryen by men of the greatest reputation of their age'. Raymond, using Ussher's *Veterum Epistolarum Hibernicarum Sylloge*,[100] as a source, then cited Lanfranc to undermine Keating's material.[101] Concerned to promote his own projected history of Ireland, he challenged the very

---

95 *Clanricarde*, p. cxxiv. The reference to a hidden influence on the text was to John Toland. See David Berman and Alan Harrison, 'John Toland and Keating's history of Ireland (1723)', *Donegal Annual*, no. 36 (1984), pp. 225-9. **96** Keating himself, though mentioning the Psalter of Tara, made no claim to have seen it, or to have used material from it. See above, p. 64. **97** *A letter from Dr Anthony Raymond to my Lord Inchiquin giving some account of the monarchs and ancient state of Ireland* (Dublin, 1723). **98** For the names of the subscribers see Appendix 3 in Harrison, *Ag cruinniú meala*, p. 146. See also Barnard, 'Reading in eighteenth-century Ireland: private and public pleasures', in Bernadette Cunningham and Máire Kennedy (eds), *The experience of reading: Irish historical perspectives* (Dublin, 1999), p. 69. **99** *A letter from Dr Anthony Raymond*, cited in Harrison, *Ag cruinniú meala*, p. 100. **100** James Ussher, *Veterum epistolarum Hibernicarum Sylloge* (Dublin, 1632), p. 71. **101** *A letter from Dr Anthony Raymond*, p. 6.

idea of publishing a translation of *Foras feasa*. 'I would not impose the History upon the Public altho' I had a considerable offer for the copy of my translation'.[102] He had indeed assembled extensive notes, and had attempted his own translation of Keating's history and, like O'Connor, he had publicised his work in advance and had collected subscriptions.[103] He assured Lord Inchiquin that his O'Brien ancestors would not be shortchanged in the history[104] and devoted much of the letter to the idea that Inchiquin could regard himself as the rightful descendant of those O'Briens who had been monarchs of Ireland.

> In the history I am publishing, I shall shew at large that the monarchs of Ireland were as considerable as any princes in Europe of their time, in the mean while, because such a character of a people who have no remains to shew of their former greatness, will not perhaps gain credit without some difficulty, I shall beforehand give a short account of the ancient state of this kingdom.[105]

Despite his criticisms of Keating in connection with the O'Connor translation, it seems clear that Raymond's 'short account of the ancient state of this kingdom' would be derived from *Foras feasa*, if for no other reason than that it was the best available narrative that made the early history of Ireland accessible to a non-expert like Raymond. Neither man would have been capable of using for themselves the medieval manuscript sources on which Keating had based his narrative.

Although he had regular dealings with Dublin scribes, it seems that Raymond was not conscious of any potential readership for the history of Ireland other than an English-speaking one. An indication of Raymond's own perception of the potential readership for Irish history is seen in his proposal for publication of a history of Ireland by John Conry.[106] The fourth section of this work would contain, he asserted,

> A very full account of the progress of the English forces in Ireland from 1169 to 1610 with a Preface. To which the genealogies of many noble English and Welsh families, whose predecessors came hither before, with and after Henry the second to the time of their invasion and also of the most noble old Irish are annexed.

The descendants of the Old English settlers were evidently the primary target audience. The three preceding sections of the history revealed the extent of the influence of the structure that had been adopted in Keating's *Foras feasa*. The proposed history by John Conry was to commence with a section 'Refuting the calum-

102 Anthony Raymond, *An account of Dr Keting's history of Ireland* (Dublin, 1723), p. 18.   103 Harrison, *Ag cruinniú meala*, p. 86; RIA, MSS 24 G 11, 24 G 12, 24 G 13, and 24 G 14 contain many of the working notes he had assembled.   104 *A letter from Dr Anthony Raymond*, pp. 9–10.   105 Ibid. 106 The proposal is cited in detail in Harrison, *Ag cruinniú meala*, pp. 102–3.

nies with which the Irish Nation is aspersed', thus paralleling the preface of *Foras feasa*. The next section was to contain 'the most probable account of the first inhabitants, and a satisfactory one of the Origin, Travels and Voyages of those called Milesians and Gagelians [*sic*], their Conquest of Ireland, and Manner of Government to the year of Christ 432' which mirrored the first book of *Foras feasa*. The third part was to contain 'The most memorable occurrences in Church and state from 432 to 1169', closely following the scope and content of the second book of *Foras feasa*.[107]

The activities of Anthony Raymond, John Conry, Dermod O'Connor and Thomas O'Sullevane all point to the fact that those who wished to produce a history of Ireland in the early eighteenth century thought in terms of a narrative and a structure similar to that found in *Foras feasa*. It further appears that the fame of Geoffrey Keating's history was such that a history of Ireland published in English that purported to be Keating's history was likely to be particularly marketable. None of these individuals had any doubt but that a market existed for an English-language narrative of the history of the kingdom of Ireland. The controversy that arose over the version that was published had as much to do with rival commercial interests as with concern over the merits or otherwise of *Foras feasa* or the lack of Gaelic scholarship displayed in the O'Connor translation.

Something of the depths of the personal squabbling to which the row between O'Connor, Raymond and O'Sullevane descended was recorded in the diary notes of Bodley's librarian, Thomas Hearne.

> Mr Scot told me Mr Oconner's translation of Dr. Keting's History of Ireland is a most horrid silly performance, that Oconner is a most sad blockhead, & wholly ignorant of all learning, that he knows nothing of the old Irish history or language, &, indeed that he is altogether unqualify'd for any such undertaking. He added, that his translation was really done by one Dr. Raymond an Irish clergyman, to whom Oconner was servant and that this Oconner stole it from his master who afterwards came over to England with a design to print all truly at London, but that he died there before he could bring matters about. Oconner, it seems, hath beer in prison, & his nose is eat of with the pox, which he got by having two wives together, both it seems still living. This Oconner, therefore, by what I learn, is an horrid villain.[108]

The dispute between Raymond, O'Connor, and O'Sullevane over the publication of a purported translation of Keating's history is recounted in detail by Alan Harrison in *Ag cruinniú meala*, together with extensive extracts from the published statements by the various parties to the controversy. Raymond and O'Sullevane both considered O'Connor's translation of Keating's work to be inaccurate and

---

107 Harrison, *Ag cruinniú meala*, p. 102. 108 Ibid., p. 115.

exaggerated, and with a deist religious bias because of the alleged involvement of John Toland in the publication scheme. They believed O'Connor's claims to have consulted manuscript sources such as the 'Psalter of Tara' were spurious and they mocked his claim to be the 'antiquary of Ireland'.[109]

Not only was the translation deemed fraudulent in terms of its historical content and critical apparatus, O'Connor was also accused of cheating both the printer and the subscribers to the book.[110] The printer, B. Creake, took his own revenge in 1726 by inserting in the second edition of the book a notice to subscribers, to the effect that he had lost money on the venture, because

> the translator Dermo'd O Connor, who without any thought or Design of paying the Expenses of paper, Print, Engraving, and other accidental charges, before the History could be published, spent and imbezzl'd about the sum of Three Hundred Pounds, in the space of seventeen months, a great Part of it being Subscription Money, which he never brought to Account, nor I never knew of, till Publication of the History.[111]

Despite the underhand dealings of O'Connor with Anthony Raymond, Mr Creake and others, and despite the shortcomings of his scholarship, his 1723 translation of Keating was a commercial success. The second edition of 1726 was followed in 1732 by another printing. A third edition was issued in 1738.

VIII

As commentators writing about Ireland moved away from the local to interpret status and honour on a national scale, *Foras feasa* took on the role of a seminal work that traced the ancestry of the Irish and defended the reputation of the Irish people whatever their current political or religious affiliations. For eighteenth- and nineteenth-century writers, *Foras feasa* had acquired the status that Keating would have attributed to the Psalter of Cashel: it was a compendium that preserved what was important from the distant past.[112]

Thus a mid-eighteenth-century Munster scribe and poet, Seán Ó Murchadha, composed a poem to commemorate having transcribed Keating's work.[113] The composer of '*O's feas gur sgríobhadh an tseanchaidheacht so Chéitinn chlúmhail*' evidently regarded it as a significant achievement to transcribe so important a text.

Those diverse individuals and groups drawn to *Foras feasa* in the eighteenth century to illuminate their past may have differed fundamentally from each other

---

109 Ibid., p. 103.   110 Ibid., pp. 98, 114.   111 *The general history of Ireland, collected by the learned Jeoffry Keating*, (2nd ed., London, 1726).   112 But books and pamphlets continued to be published in London which still relied on Giraldus and not Keating. Such works indicate the ongoing influence of Giraldus, and the lack of awareness of Keating's work outside Ireland before it became available in print in 1723.   113 RIA, MS 23 E 16, f. 61 (Seán Ó Murchadha na Ráithíneach).

in their understanding of what constituted the 'Irish people', but the origin myth provided by Keating could accommodate more than one quest for an historical underpinning of current political aspirations. O'Connor's printed translation consciously tailored the text to non-Catholic audiences, because by the early eighteenth century the market for Keating's history of the kingdom of Ireland included the descendants of New English Protestant settlers who had first come to Ireland during the seventeenth century. By the 1720s they had come to identify with Ireland as their homeland, they were interested in the political idea of Ireland as a distinct kingdom, and they had appropriated the myth of the ancient kingdom of Ireland as part of their own 'Irish' history.

The work of Dermod O'Connor, Anthony Raymond, and earlier translators was more than merely an attempt to transmit Keating's text to different communities as defined by language. Each translation involved adaptation and reinterpretation also. As has been seen, the appropriation of the Irish past through reinterpretations of early history as transmitted in *Foras feasa* was carried out in Irish, English and Latin. In a largely bilingual world people's religious affiliation was a more significant indicator of difference than was language.

By the time Walter Harris reissued *The whole works of Sir James Ware concerning Ireland*, in 1739, it was the translated text of *Foras feasa*, as issued in print in English by O'Connor, rather than the manuscript copies, that was considered most renowned.[114] Harris, however, was severely critical of O'Connor. He had to hand a different English translation of *Foras feasa* in manuscript and drew attention to the discrepancies. However, Harris felt unable to judge which translation was more accurate and had to admit that he had never seen the original Irish text, 'nor, if I had, could I with justice assume the air of having skill enough in the Irish language to compare it with the translations'.[115] Harris's description reveals that for his view of Keating he relied on the published comments of Peter Walsh, Peter Talbot, Sir Richard Cox and Thomas O'Sullevane's 'Dissertation'.[116] Given the nature of Harris's project, it is not surprising that he drew heavily on secondary sources. He was far from alone, however, in lacking 'skill enough' to read Keating in the original Irish. Yet, the language difference was only one indicator of the changes that created barriers to interpretation. The world was no longer the place familiar to the author of *Foras feasa*. By the mid-eighteenth century his history circulated among readers who could no longer be expected to understand the nuances of the political, social and moral issues that had been central to the world of Geoffrey Keating.

---

114 Walter Harris, *The whole works of Sir James Ware concerning Ireland, revised and improved* (3 vols in 2, Dublin, 1739), book i, pp. 105-6.   115 Harris (ed.), *Whole works of Sir James Ware*, book 1, p. 106.   116 Ibid.

12

Conclusion

Keating's story of Ireland, narrated in *Foras feasa ar Eirinn*, was presented to Irish readers as the 'true' history of the kingdom and people of Ireland. It was read by diverse textual communities as a history that asserted the truth about the Irish past in opposition to negative and 'false' histories promulgated by those who would deny Ireland's claims to be an ancient and honourable kingdom. The enormous impact on popular consciousness of the fact that *Foras feasa* alerted readers to the reality of conflicting interpretations of the past should not be underestimated. In a country that hovered between kingdom and colony, readers understood the significance of alternative readings of the past.

The language, the medium and the social and political circumstances in which Keating's writings circulated were all subject to change over time. Similarly the meaning of those writings for the readers who came into contact with them was not constant. At its simplest level the contemporary political and religious communities within which Keating's works first circulated gradually gave way to later controversialists and later still to antiquarians. Centuries later his works became the subject of attention by cultural revivalists and students of the Irish language. Most recently they have attracted attention from students of historiography. Each of these textual communities responded to Keating's work in quite distinct ways. Those responses were dictated, in part, by communal memories and understandings of the world from which Keating's works emanated. Those memories were themselves influenced by the wide dissemination of Keating's writings in earlier generations.

The social and cultural circumstances that allowed Geoffrey Keating become so influential in transmitting the story of the Irish past to later generations have meant that he himself has earned a place in that story. His leading role in shaping the particular combination of myth, religion and history that has defined Irish Catholicism for over three centuries is only now being evaluated. The current generation of historians, acutely conscious of how selective communal as well as personal memory can be, have begun to look anew at how the past is remembered. Keating's version of the past deserves particular attention because of its prolonged and profound influence on perceptions of Irishness. Through his writing Keating sought to interpret for his own people the world they shared, and in doing so strove to be true to himself, to his people, to Ireland, and to God.

Bibliography

GUIDES

Abbott, T.K. and Gwynn, E.J. *Catalogue of the Irish manuscripts in the Library of Trinity College Dublin.* Dublin, 1921.

Allison, A.F. and Rogers, D.M. *A catalogue of Catholic books in English printed abroad or secretly in England, 1558-1640.* Bognor Regis, 1956.

—. *The contemporary printed literature of the Engish Counter-Reformation between 1558 and 1640: an annotated catalogue.* 2 vols, London, 1989-1994.

Baumgarten, Rolf. *Bibliography of Irish linguistics and literature, 1942-1971.* Dublin, 1986.

Best, R.I. *Bibliography of Irish philology and manuscript literature: publications 1913-1941.* Dublin, 1969.

—. *Bibliography of Irish philology and of printed Irish literature, to 1912.* Dublin, 1913.

Bhreathnach, Edel. *Tara: a select bibliography.* Dublin, 1995.

Buttimer, Cornelius G. *Catalogue of Irish manuscripts in the University of Wisconsin-Madison.* Dublin, 1989.

Connolly, S.J. (ed.). *The Oxford companion to Irish history.* Oxford, 1998.

De Brún, Pádraig. *Catalogue of Irish manuscripts in King's Inns Library, Dublin.* Dublin, 1972.

—. *Clár Lámhscríbhinní Gaeilge Choláiste Ollscoile Chorcaí: Cnuasach Thorna.* 2 vols, Cork, 1967.

— and Herbert, Máire. *Catalogue of Irish manuscripts in Cambridge Libraries.* Cambridge, 1986.

Dictionary of national biography, ed. Leslie Stephen et al. 63 vols, London, 1885-1900.

Dillon, Myles, Mooney, Canice, and De Brún, Pádraig. *Catalogue of Irish manuscripts in the Franciscan Library, Killiney.* Dublin, 1969.

Gwynn, Aubrey and Hadcock, R. Neville. *Medieval religious houses: Ireland.* London, 1970; reprint, Dublin, 1988.

Hastings, James (ed.). *Encyclopedia of religion and ethics.* 13 vols, Edinburgh, 1908-26.

Hayes, R.J. (ed.) *Manuscript sources for the history of Irish civilisation.* 11 vols, New York, 1965; *First supplement*, 3 vols, New York, 1979.

Hughes, Kathleen. *Early Christian Ireland: introduction to the sources.* London, 1972.

Keller, John E. *Motif index of medieval Spanish exempla.* Knoxville, 1949.

Kenney, James F. *The sources for the early history of Ireland: ecclesiastical: an introduction and guide.* New York, 1929; reprint Dublin, 1979.

Mackechnie, J. *Catalogue of Gaelic manuscripts in selected libraries in Great Britain and Ireland.* 2 vols, Boston, 1973.

McNeill, Charles (ed.). Reports on the Rawlinson collection of manuscripts preserved in the Bodleian Library, Oxford, classes A-D. *Analecta Hibernica*, no. 1, 1930, 12-178; no. 2. 1931, 1-92.

Moody, T.W., Martin, F.X., and Byrne, F.J (eds). *A new history of Ireland, ix, maps, genealogies, lists*. Oxford, 1984.

Ní Sheaghdha, Nessa. et al. *Catalogue of Irish manuscripts in the National Library of Ireland*, Fascicules I-XIII, 1967-96.

Ó Conchuir, Breandán. *Clár lámhscríbhinní Gaeilge Choláiste Ollscoile Chorcaí: Cnuasach Uí Mhurchú*. Dublin, 1991.

O'Grady, S.H. and FLOWER, Robin. *Catalogue of Irish manuscripts in the British Museum*. 3 vols, London, 1926-1953.

Ó Macháin, Pádraig. *Catalogue of Irish manuscripts in Mount Melleray Abbey, Co. Waterford*. Dublin, 1991.

O'Rahilly, Thomas F., Mulchrone, Kathleen, et al., *Catalogue of Irish manuscripts in the Royal Irish Academy*. Fascicules 1-28. Dublin, 1926-70.

Ó Riain, Pádraig. *Clár na lámhscríbhinní Gaeilge sa Bhreatain Bhig*. Dublin, 1968.

Tubach, F.C. *Index exemplorum: a handbook of medieval religious tales. FF Communications*, no. 204. Helsinki, 1969.

Walsh, Paul and Ó Fiannachta, Pádraig. *Lámhscríbhinní Gaeilge Choláiste Phádraig Má Nuad*. 7 fascicles, Maynooth, 1943-72.

Welch, Robert (ed.). *Oxford companion to Irish literature*, Oxford, 1996.

MANUSCRIPT SOURCES

Manuscripts consulted containing copies of Keating's works (pre-1725)

Aberystwyth: National Library of Wales
413 D: FFÉ
5339 C: TBB, 1704

Armagh: Armagh Public Library
H.III.1: FFÉ, 'A defence' English translation

Belfast: Public Record Office of Northern Ireland
T 2738 (photocopy): FFÉ, early 18th c.

Cambridge: University Library
Add. 4181: FFÉ, 1709 (NLI microfilm P5361)
Add. 4205: TBB etc., 1701 (NLI microfilm P5361)

Cashel: Chapter Library
4729: FFÉ etc., 1714 (NLI microfilm P212)

Cork: University College, NUI Cork
Gaelic 23: ESA, TBB, 1723
Gaelic 62: FFÉ, 1703
Gaelic 92 (Power Collection): FFÉ [1647?]
Gaelic 168: TBB, 1705

Dublin: Franciscan Library, Killiney (now in UCD Archives)
A 14: FFÉ etc. [1636?]
A 15: FFÉ, 1638-41
A 26: ESA, TBB, (also Saltair Mhuire)
A 33: FFÉ, 17th c. (fragments)

Dublin: King's Inns
Gaelic 2: FFÉ, 1657 (NLI photostat)

Dublin: Marsh's Library
Z3.1.7 (76): FFÉ, 1651
Z3.1.17: FFÉ, 'A defence' English translation
Z4.5.6, FFÉ, late 17th c.

Dublin: National Library of Ireland
G 17: FFÉ, 1696
G 49: ESA, 1657
G 54: FFÉ, 1713
G 117: FFÉ, 1693-94
G 192: FFÉ, 1704-06
G 195: ESA, TBB, c.1713? (Comyn MS 14)
G 226: FFÉ, 1722
G 288: FFÉ, 1718, 'A defence' English translation
G 293: FFÉ, 'A defence' English translation
G 361: ESA etc., 1713
G 465: FFÉ, 1710
G 999: FFÉ, 1696
Private copy: FFÉ, 1723 (NLI microfilm P1947)

Dublin: Royal Irish Academy
3 C 2 (937): ESA fragments, [1715?]
3 C 18 (782): ESA, TBB, etc., early 18th c.
23 A 19 (217): TBB, 1716
23 C 1 (371): FFÉ, 1719
23 C 34 (954): FFÉ, 1715
23 E 8 (526): FFÉ, 1721
23 E 17 (957): TBB, early 18th c.
23 E 23 (541): FFÉ, 1702-03
23 F 20 (676): ESA, FFÉ, TBB, 1679-80
23 G 2 (958): TBB, 1704
23 G 3 (678): FFÉ etc, 1715
23 G 9 (784): FFÉ, etc., 1708
23 I 42 (426): FFÉ, c.1701
23 L 25 (107): ESA, c.1697-1701
23 N 18 (707): ESA, extracts from TBB, etc, 1701-02
23 O 10 (143): FFÉ, 1703
23 O 13 (141): TBB, 17th c.
23 O 19 (142): FFÉ, 1643

23 Q 14 (42): FFÉ, 1662
24 G 16 (1136): FFÉ, Michael Kearney's English translation
24 I 5 (1140): FFÉ, John Lynch's Latin translation
24 L 17 (127): ESA, 1698/9
24 L 18 (128): TBB etc, 1724
24 N 3 (483): FFÉ, 1666
24 P 10 (96): ESA etc, 1698
24 P 23 (43): FFÉ, 1641-46
24 P 43 (1406): FFÉ, [1653?]
A iii 2 (735): ESA, 1693
A iii 4 (736): ESA, 17th c.
C iv 1 (540): FFÉ, [c.1650]

Dublin: Trinity College
1325 [H.3.6]: ESA, TBB, etc.
1332 [H.3.13]: FFÉ, 1699-1700
1354 [H.4.13]: FFÉ, 1704
1394 [H.5.22]: FFÉ, 1646
1397 [H.5.26]: FFÉ, 17th c.
1403 [H.5.32]: ESA, FFÉ, TBB, 17th c.
1439 [F.3.21]: FFÉ, 17th c.
1443 [H.2.14]: FFÉ, 1697-99, 'A defence' English translation, adapted

Dublin: University College, NUI Dublin
Gaelic 15: FFÉ, 1698

Edinburgh: National Library of Scotland
Advocates MS 33.4.11: FFÉ, 1695/6
72.1.43 [Gaelic MS XLIII]: FFÉ, late 17th c. (NLI photostat)

Fermoy, Co. Cork: St Colman's College
Gaelic 20: FFÉ, 1721 (UCC, NUI Cork, microfilm 209)
Gaelic 22: FFÉ, 1725 (UCC, NUI Cork, microfilm 209)

London: British Library
Add. 4779: FFÉ, 1694
Add. 4818: FFÉ, 'A defence' English translation (NLI microfilm P17-18)
Add. 18,745: FFÉ etc, 1720
Add. 31,875: TBB, early 18th c. (NLI microfilm P422)
Add. 31,872: FFÉ, 1763
Egerton 107: FFÉ, 1638
Egerton 108: FFÉ, 1707 (NLI microfilm P256)
Egerton 109: FFÉ etc., 1713 (NLI microfilm P256)
Egerton 133: FFÉ etc., 1711-20 (NLI microfilm P413)
Egerton 181: ESA, 1709
Egerton 189: ESA, 1658
Sloane 3806-3807: FFÉ, 1714-15 (NLI microfilm P416-417)

Manchester: John Ryland's Library
Irish 22: TBB, 1710
Irish 123: FFÉ, 1717

Maynooth: Russell Library
B 7: ESA, 1674/5
B 9: TBB etc., 1717
C 2: FFÉ, 17th c.
C 14: ESA etc, 1712-13
Renehan 66: TBB, ESA etc, 1719
Renehan 67: FFÉ, 1707
Renehan 68: FFÉ, 1663

Oxford: Bodleian Library
Fairfax 29: FFÉ, 1643/4
IR.d.1 (31,530): FFÉ, 'A defence' English translation

Paris: Bibliotheque Nationale
Fonds Celtique 66: FFÉ 1644 (NLI microfilm P463)

Stonyhurst College Library
A II.20, vol 2. ESA, TBB, etc 1701-03 (NLI microfilm P471)

Troyes: Bibliotheque Municipale
919: FFÉ John Lynch's Latin translation, 17th c. (NLI microfilm P804)

Washington DC: Woodstock Theological Center Library, Georgetown University
MS 7. FFÉ. John Lynch's Latin translation. 17th c.

Other manuscripts

Cambridge: Fitzwilliam Museum
McClean 187

Chester: Cheshire County Council Record Office
DLT/B/2: Collections touching Ireland, by R. Leycester
DLT/B/76: History of Ireland

Dublin: King's Inns
Gaelic MS 4

Dublin: National Archives
Chancery bills G 351
RC 4/10
RC 5/22

Dublin: National Library of Ireland
G 3
G 22: *Leabhar Gearr na Pailise*
G 292: Thomas Harte adaptation of FFÉ, late 17th c.
GO 35: Genealogies
GO 69: Genealogies

GO 71: Genealogies
GO 159: Genealogies
GO 162: Genealogies
GO 168: Genealogies
GO 176: Genealogies
3,111: Clanricard letters
11,955-11,958: Thomas Harte adaptation of FFÉ, 19th c.

Dublin: Royal Irish Academy
A v 2: Poems on the Dillons
D ii 2: Dinnsheanchas
D iv 2: Dinnsheanchas, prose tales
23 E 16: Poems ascribed to Keating
23 E 26: Genealogical
23 F 21: Poems on the Butlers
23 G 24: Poems ascribed to Keating
23 I 9: Devotional, including *Saltair Mhuire*
23 K 37: *Foras feasa Chloinne Mhileadh Espáine, c.*1714-18
23 N 15: Poems ascribed to Keating
24 G 11-14 (1264-67): Anthony Raymond's collections and translations from Keating
24 G 15 (1135): Thomas Harte adaptation of FFÉ, 17th c.
24 P 13: Historical miscellany, 1621
Ordnance Survey Letters, Co. Tipperary; Co. Londonderry

Dublin: Trinity College
567 (E.3.15): Religious miscellany
1298 (H.2.7): Genealogical and historical fragments
1322 (H.3.3): Dinnsheanchas, 16th c.
1337 (H.3.18): Miscellany, including *Cóir anmann*
1365 (H.4.24): Miscellany

London: British Library
Add. 4777
Add. 19,836: Visitations, 1615 (NLI microfilm P509)
Add. 30,512
Egerton 97
Egerton 106
Egerton 150
Egerton 1782

Manchester: Chetham's Library
A 77: Meredith Hanmer's history, etc.

Maynooth: Russell Library
M 86b

Oxford: Bodleian Library
Carte 62
Laud Misc. 610
Rawlinson MS B 475

PRINTED PRIMARY SOURCES

Annála ríoghachta Éireann: Annals of the kingdom of Ireland by the Four Masters from the earliest period to the year 1616, ed. and trans. John O'Donovan. 7 vols, Dublin, 1851, reprint, New York, 1966.

Annals of Clonmacnoise from the earliest period to A.D. 1408, translated into English by Conell Mageoghagan, A.D. 1627, ed. Denis Murphy. Dublin, 1896.

Annals of Ulster to AD 1131: text and translation, ed. and trans. Seán Mac Airt and Gearóid Mac Niocaill. Dublin, 1983.

Audacht Morainn, ed. Fergus Kelly. Dublin, 1976.

Auraicept na nÉges, ed. Anders Ahlqvist. Helsinki, 1983.

Barclay, John. *Icon animorum*. London, 1614.

Bede. *A history of the English church and people*, trans. Leo Sherley-Price. Revised ed. London, 1968.

Bellarmine, Robert. *Disputationes de controversiis Christianae fidei adversus hujus temporis haereticos*. Ingoldstedt, 1568-9; Venetia 1596, Paris 1608 etc.

Bergin, Osborn (ed.). *Irish bardic poetry*, ed. David Greene and Fergus Kelly. Dublin, 1970.

—. *Sgéalaigheacht Chéitinn, stories from Keating's history of Ireland, edited with notes and glossary*. 3rd ed. Dublin, 1930.

Besse, Pierre de. *Conceptions theologiques sur les quatres fin de l'homme, preschées en un Advant l'an 1605*. Paris, 1606 [BL 846 K 13]; another ed. Paris, 1622 [Bodl. 8° D 307 Linc.]

—. *Conceptions theologiques sur toutes les festes des saincts & autres solemnelles de l'annee, preschees en divers lieux*. 3 vols, Paris, 1618 [BL 848.e.11, lacking vol 2];. another ed. Lyon, 1629 [vol. 1 Bodl. 8° Z 56 Art. Seld.]

—. *Conceptions theologiques sur tous les dimanches de l'annee*. 2 vols. Paris, 1624 [vol. 1 Bodl. 8° D 325 Linc.; vol. 2 8° Z 57 Art. Seld.]

Best, R.I. The Leabhar Oiris or book of chronicles. *Ériu*, i, 1904, 74-112.

Biblia Sacra iuxta Vulgatam Clementinam, ed. Alberto Colunga and Laurentio Turrado (3rd ed. Madrid, 1959).

Boece, Hector. *Scotorum historiae*. Paris, 1526; Lausanne 1574, etc.

Book of Lecan. Leabhar Mór Mhic Fhir Bhisigh Leacain, ed. Kathleen Mulchrone. Dublin, IMC, Facsimile, 1937.

Book of Leinster, formerly Lebar na Núachongbála, ed. R.I. Best, Osborn Bergin, M.A. O'Brien, and Anne O'Sullivan. 6 vols, Dublin, 1954-83.

Buchanan, George. *De rerum Scoticarum Historia*. 1582.

Butler, Sarah. *Irish tales, or instructive histories for the happy conduct of life*. [London, 1716]; Dublin, 1735.

Byrne, Matthew (ed.). *Ireland under Elizabeth, being a portion of the history of Catholic Ireland by Don Philip O'Sullivan Bear* (Dublin, 1903).

Caithréim Cellachain Caisil: the victorious career of Cellachan of Cashel, ed. Alexander Bugge. Oslo, 1905.

Caithréim Conghail Clairinghnigh: martial career of Comghal Clairinghnech, ed. P.M. MacSweeney. London, ITS, 1904.

Calendar of Carew manuscripts preserved in the archiepiscopal library at Lambeth. 6 vols, London, 1926-53.

Calendar of State Papers relating to Ireland, 1509-70. 24 vols, London, 1860-1912.

Camden, William. *Anglica, Hibernica, Normannica, Cambrica, à veteribus scripta*. Frankfurt, 1602.

—. *Britain, or a chorographicall description of the most flourishing kingdomes. England, Scotland and Ireland*, trans. Philemon Holland, London, 1610.

—. *Britannia sive regnorum Angliae, Scotiae, Hiberniae ... descriptio*. London, 1586; 6th ed. 1607.

Canons and decrees of the sacred and ecumenical Council of Trent, trans. Rev. J. Waterworth. London, 1868.

Carney, James (ed.). *Poems on the Butlers*. Dublin, 1945.

Catechism of the Council of Trent, trans. and annotated by John A. McHugh and Charles J. Callan, 2nd ed. New York, 1934.

Clanricarde, Marquis of. *Memoirs of the right honourable the Marquis of Clanricarde, Lord Deputy general of Ireland....* London, 1722. (Preface by Thomas O'Sullevane)

Cogadh Gaedhel re Gallaibh. The war of the Gaedhil with the Gaill. ed. J. H. Todd. London, 1867.

Colgan, John. *Acta sanctorum veteris et maioris Scotiae, seu Hiberniae sanctorum insulae.* Louvain, 1645; fascimile reprint, with foreword by Brendan Jennings. Dublin, 1948.

—. *Triadis thaumaturgae, seu divorum Patricii, Columbae, et Brigidae ... acta.* Louvain, 1647; fascimile reprint, Dublin, 1997.

Comainmnigud Noem hÉrend so sis, ed. Denis T. Brosnan. *Archivium Hibernicum*, i, 1912, 314-65.

A contemporary history of affairs in Ireland from AD 1641 to 1652, ed. J.T. Gilbert. 3 vols, Dublin, 1879.

Cox, E.G. (ed.). A middle-Irish fragment of Bede's ecclesiastical history. In *Studies in language and literature in honour of James Morgan Hart*. London, 1910, pp. 122-8.

Cox, Richard. *Aphorisms relating to the kingdom of Ireland*. London, 1689.

—. *Hibernia Anglicana, or the history of Ireland from the conquest thereof by the English to this present time*. 2 parts. London, 1689-90.

Daniel, Samuel. *The first part of the historie of England*. London, 1613.

Davies, John. *A discovery of the true causes why Ireland was never entirely subdued ... until ... his majesty's happy reign*. London, 1612, reprint, Shannon, 1969.

De Brún, Pádraig, Ó Buachalla, Breandán, and Ó Concheannain, Tomás (eds). *Nua dhuanaire*, i. Baile Átha Cliath, 1975.

Dempster, Thomas. *Scotia illustrior, seu mendicabula repressa, modesta parecbasi Thomae Dempsteri*. [Lyons], 1620.

Durand, William (Durantus, Gulielmus). *Rationale Divinorum Officorum*. Antwerp, 1570; Lyons, 1584.

—. *Gulielmi Duranti Rationale Divinorum Officiorum, i-vi*, eds. A. Davril and T.M. Thibodeau (Corpus Christianorum: Continuatio mediaevalis, 140, 140a). 2 vols, Turholt, 1995-8.

Elias, Chevalier au Cygne. *The Knight of the Swanne. Here begynneth the history of the noble Helyas*, translated out of Frensshe [by R. Coplande]. 1512; 1522, 1560.

Fitzsimon, Henry. *The justification and exposition of the divine sacrifice of the Mass*. [Douai], 1611. [Also available in facsimile, English Recusant Literature (Menston, 1972) vol 108]

French, Nicholas. *The bleeding Iphigenia*. Louvain, 1674.

—. *The historical works of ... Nicholas French*. Dublin, 1846.

Gearnon, Antóin. *Parrthas an Anma*, ed. Anselm Ó Fachtna. Dublin, 1953.

Genealogiae regum et sanctorum Hiberniae, by the Four Masters, edited from the manuscript of Michél Ó Cleirigh with appendices and an index, by Paul Walsh. Maynooth, 1918.

Geoffrey of Monmouth. *History of the kings of Britain*, trans. Sebastian Evans. London, 1912.

—. *The History of the kings of Britain*, trans. Lewis Thorpe. London, 1966.

Gesta Romanorum: entertaining moral stories. trans. Charles Swan. London, 1905.

Gildas, the ruin of Britain, and other documents, ed M. Winterbottom. Chichester, 1978.

Giraldus Cambrensis [Gerald of Wales]. *Expugnatio Hibernica. The conquest of Ireland,* ed. and trans. A.B. Scott and F.X. Martin. Dublin, 1978.

—. *The history and topography of Ireland,* trans. with intro. John J. O'Meara. London, 1982.

Gobius, Johannes. *Scala coeli.* Ulm, 1480.

Grimston, Edward. *The generall historie of Spain.* 1612.

Grosjean, Paul. Édition du *Catalogus praecipuorum sanctorum Hiberniae* de Henri Fitzsimon. In John Ryan (ed.) *Féilsgríbhinn Eóin Mac Néill.* Dublin, 1940, pp. 335-93.

Gwynn, Edward (ed.). *The metrical dindshenchas.* 5 vols, reprint Dublin, 1991.

Gwynn, Lucius. De Maccaib Conaire. *Ériu,* vi, 1911-12, 144-53.

Hakluyt, Richard. *Principal navigations.* 1589.

Harris, Walter (ed.). *The whole works of Sir James Ware concerning Ireland, revised and improved.* 3 vols in 2, Dublin, 1739, 1746.

Heigham, John. *A devout exposition of the holie Mass.* Douai, 1614.

Historical Manuscripts Commission. *Report on Franciscan manuscripts preserved at the Convent, Merchant's Quay, Dublin.* Dublin: HMSO, 1906.

History of the Irish Confederation and the war in Ireland, ed. J. T. Gilbert. 7 vols, Dublin, 1882-91.

Hogan, Edmund (ed.). *Ibernia Ignatiana, seu Ibernorum Societatis Jesu patrum monumenta collecta, 1540-1607.* Dublin, 1880.

Holinshed, Raphael. *The ... chronicles of England, Scotlande and Irelande ....* London, 1577, ed. John Hooker et al., 3 vols, 1587.

Holinshed's Irish chronicle, 1577. ed. Liam Miller and Eileen Power. Dublin, 1979.

Huon, de Bordeaux. *The ancient honorable, famour and delightfull historie of Huon of Bordeaux ... the third time imprinted and the rude English corrected and amended.* T. Purfoot, 1601.

Irish fiants of the Tudor Sovereigns during the reigns of Henry VIII, Edward Vi, Philip & Mary, and Elizabeth I, with a new introduction by Kenneth Nicholls (4 vols, Dublin, Éamonn de Burca, 1994). (Reprinted from *Reports of the Deputy Keeper of the Public Records in Ireland,* 1875-1890).

Jacobus de Voragine, *The golden legend: readings on the saints,* trans. William Granger Ryan, 2 vols, Princeton, 1993.

Jennings, Brendan (ed.). Miscellaneous documents i, 1588-1634. *Archivium Hibernicum,* xii, 1946, 70-200.

—. *Wadding papers, 1614-38.* Dublin, IMC, 1943.

Kearney, Barnabas. *Heliotropium sive conciones tam de Festis quam de Dominicis quae in solari totius anni circulo occurrunt.* Lyons, 1622.

Keating, Geoffrey. *Eochair-sgiath an Aifrinn ... an explanatory defence of the Mass,* ed. Patrick O'Brien. Dublin, 1898.

—. *Foras feasa ar Éirinn: the history of Ireland,* ed. David Comyn and P.S. Dinneen. 4 vols, London, ITS, 1902-14.

—. *Forus Feasa air Éirinn ... History of Ireland,* book i, part i, ed. P.W. Joyce. Dublin, Gaelic Union Publication, 1880.

—. *The history of Ireland from the earliest period to the English invasion,* trans. John O'Mahony. New York, 1857.

—. *The history of the ancient Irish from their reception of Christianity till the invitation of the English in the reign of Henry the second, translated from the original Irish ...with amendments* [by D. O'Connor]. Newry, 1820.

—. *Trí bior-ghaoithe an bháis,* ed. Robert Atkinson. Dublin, 1890.

—. *Trí bior-ghaoithe an bháis: The three shafts of death*, ed. Osborn Bergin. Dublin, 1931.

—. *The general history of Ireland containing 1. a full and impartial account of the first inhabitants of that kingdom ... 6. a relation of the long and bloody wars of the Irish against the Danes ... collected by the learned Jeoffry Keating ... faithfully translated from the Irish ... by Dermo'd O'Connor*. London, 1723; another printing Dublin, 1723; reissued in 1732 without list of subscribers and with an appendix dated 1726.

—. *The general history of Ireland containing 1. a full and impartial account of the first inhabitants of that kingdom ... 6. a relation of the long and bloody wars of the Irish against the Danes ... collected by the learned Jeoffry Keating ... faithfully translated from the Irish ... by Dermo'd O'Connor ... The second edition with an appendix, collected from ... Anthony Raymond*. 2nd ed., London, 1726.

—. *The general history of Ireland containing 1. a full and impartial account of the first inhabitants of that kingdom ... 6. a relation of the long and bloody wars of the Irish against the Danes ... collected by the learned Jeoffry Keating ... faithfully translated from the Irish ... by Dermo'd O'Connor ... The third edition with an appendix ... collected from the remarks of the learned Anthony Raymond*. London, 1738.

King, William. *The state of the protestants of Ireland under the late King James's government* London, 1691.

Laffan, Thomas. *Tipperary's families: being the hearth money records for 1665-66-67*. Dublin, 1911.

Leabhar gabhála: the book of conquests of Ireland: the recension of Micheál Ó Cléirigh. eds. R.A.S. Macalister and J. Mac Neill. Dublin, 1916.

Lebor Bretnach, ed. A.G. Van Hamel. Dublin, ITS, 1932.

Lebor gabála Érenn: the book of the taking of Ireland, ed. R.A.S. Macalister. 5 vols, Dublin, ITS, 1938-56.

Lebor na cert: the book of rights, ed. Myles Dillon. Dublin, ITS, 1962.

Lebor na hUidre: book of the dun cow, ed. R.I. Best and O.J. Bergin. Dublin, 1929.

The life of the glorious bishop St Patricke ... together with the lives of the holy virgin S. Bridgit and of the glorious abbot Saint Columbe. St Omer, 1625.

Lynch, John. *Alithinologia sive veridica responsio ad invectam mendaciis*. [St Malo], 1664; *Supplementum alithinologiae*. [St Malo], 1667.

—. [Gratianus Lucius]. *Cambrensis eversus, seu potius historica fides in rebus hibernicis Giraldo Cambrensis abrogata ....* [?St Malo], 1662.

—. *Cambrensis Eversus, seu potius Historica Fides in Rebus hibernicis Giraldo Cambrensis abrogata ..., ed.* and trans. Matthew Kelly. 3 vols, Dublin, 1848-51.

Mac Aingil, Aodh. *Scathán shacramuinte na h-aithridhe*. Louvain, 1618, ed. Canice Mooney. Dublin, 1952.

Mac an tSaoi, Máire (ed.). *Dhá sgéal Artúraíochta: mar atá Eachtra Mhelóra agus Orlando, agus Céilidhe Losgaide Léithe*. Dublin, 1946.

Mac Cuarta, Brian (ed.). Mathew de Renzy's letters on Irish affairs, 1612-1620. *Analecta Hibernica*, no. 34, 1987, 107-82.

MacCurtin, Hugh. *A brief discourse in vindication of the antiquity of Ireland*. Dublin, 1717.

Mac Domhnaill, [S]. (ed.). *Dánta is amhráin Sheáin Uí Ghadhra*. Baile Átha Cliath, 1955.

Mac Erlean, J.C. (ed.). *Duanaire Dhaibhidh Uí Bhruadair: the poems of David Ó Bruadair*. 3 vols, London, 1910-17.

Mac Firbhisigh, Dubhaltach. Introduction to his book of genealogies. U.C.D. Ms, ed. with trans. Toirdhealbhach Ó Raithbheartaigh in *Genealogical tracts*, i. Dublin, 1932.

Mac Giolla Eáin, Eoin Cathmhaolach (ed.). *Dánta, amhráin is caointe Sheathrúin Chéitinn*. Dublin, 1900.

McKenna, Lambert (ed.). *Aithdioghluim dána*. 2 vols, London, ITS, 1935-40.
—. *Iomarbhágh na bhfileadh: the contention of the bards*. 2 vols, London, ITS, 1918.
Mag Uidhir, Seosamh (ed.). *Pádraig Mac a Liondain: dánta*. Baile Átha Cliath, 1977.
Magnum speculum exemplorum ex plusquam octoginto autoribus pietate, doctrina et antiquitate venerandis, variisque historiis, tractatibus & libellis excerptum... Douai, 1603; 2nd ed. 1605; 3rd ed. Antwerp, 1607; 1611; Cologne, 1618 etc.
Messingham, Thomas. *Florilegium insulae sanctorum, seu vitae et acta sanctorum Hiberniae ....* Paris, 1624.
Meyer, Kuno (ed.). *Rawlinson B. 502: a collection of pieces in prose and verse in the Irish language compiled during the eleventh and twelfth centuries. Facsimile*. Oxford, 1909.
—. *The instructions of King Cormac Mac Airt*. Dublin: Todd Lecture Series, xv, 1909.
Mhag Craith, Cuthbert (ed.). *Dán na mBrathar Mionúr*. 2 vols, Dublin, 1967-80.
Moran, P.F (ed.). *Spicilegium Ossoriense, being a collection of original letters and papers illustrative of the history of the Irish church from the Reformation to the year 1800*. 3 vols, Dublin, 1874-84.
Moryson, Fynes. *An itinerary*. 3 parts, London, 1617.
—. *Shakespeare's Europe: a survey of the condition of Europe at the end of the 16th century: being unpublished chapters of Fynes Moryson's Itinerary*, ed. Charles Hughes. 2nd ed. New York, 1967.
Nennius. *History of the Britons*. trans. A.W. Wade-Evans. London, 1938.
—. *Lebor Bretnach*, ed. A. G. Van Hamel. Dublin, IMC, 1932.
Nicolson, William. *The Irish historical library*. London, 1724.
O'Brien, M.A (ed.). *Corpus genealogiarum Hiberniae*, Volume 1. Dublin, 1962, reprint 1976.
Ó Buachalla, Breandán (ed.). *Cathal Buí: amhráin*. Baile Átha Cliath, 1975.
Ó Coigligh, Ciarán (ed.). *Raiftearaí: amhráin agus dánta*. Baile Átha Cliath, 1987.
O'Connell, F.W. (ed.). *Selections from Keating's Three shafts of death*. Dublin, 1910.
[O'Connor, D.] *Proposals for printing by subscription, the general history of Ireland, translated by D. O'Connor*. London, 1721.
Ó Cuív, Brian (ed.). An eighteenth-century account of Keating and his *Foras feasa ar Éirinn*. *Éigse*, ix, 1958, 263-9. [Extract of preface from *Memoirs.. of the Marquis of Clanricarde*, 1722.]
—. 'Flaithrí Ó Maolchonaire's Catechism of Christian doctrine', *Celtica*, i (1950), pp. 161-98.
—. A seventeenth-century criticism of Keating's *Foras feasa ar Éirinn*. *Éigse*, xi, 1965, 119-40.
—. *Sgiathluithreach an Choxaigh*, Éigse, v (1945-7), pp. 136-8.
—. *Mo thruaighe mar tá Éire*, Éigse, viii, 1956-7, 302-8.
—. *Parliament na mban*. Dublin, 1952.
Ó Fiaich, Tomás (ed.). *Art Mac Cumhaigh: dánta*. Baile Átha Cliath, 1973.
O'Flaherty, Roderick. *A chorographical description of West or h-Iar Connaught, written A.D. 1684*, ed. James Hardiman. Dublin, 1846.
—. *Ogygia, seu rerum Hibernicarum chronologia ...* London, 1685.
—. *Ogygia, seu rerum Hibernicarum chronologia ...*, trans. James Hely. 2 vols, Dublin, 1793.
Ó Gallchóir, Seán (ed.). *Séamas Dall Mac Cuarta: dánta*. Baile Átha Cliath, 1971.
O'Grady, S.H. (ed.) *Silva Gadelica*. 2 vols, London, 1892.
Ó hEodhasa, Bonabhentura. *An Teagasg Críosdaithe*. [Antwerp, 1611]; ed. Fearghal Mac Raghnaill. Dublin, 1976.
Ó Maol Chonaire, Flaithrí [Florence Conry]. *Desidérius, otherwise called sgáthán an chrabaidh*. Louvain, 1616; ed. T.F. O'Rahilly, Dublin, 1941.

Ó Maonaigh, Cainneach (ed.). *Seanmónta Chúige Uladh.* Baile Átha Cliath, 1965.

O'Rahilly, Cecile (ed.). *Five seventeenth-century political poems.* Dublin, 1952.

O'Rahilly, T.F. (ed.). *Measgra dánta. Miscellaneous Irish poems.* 2 vols. Cork, 1927.

Ó Riain, Pádraig (ed.). *Corpus genealogiarum sanctorum Hiberniae.* Dublin, 1985.

O'Sullivan, Donal (ed.). A courtly poem for Sir Richard Cox. *Éigse,* iv, 1944, 284-7.

O'Sullivan Beare, Philip. *Historiae Catholicae Iberniae compendium.* Lisbon, 1921.

—. *Patriciana decas: sive libri decem quibus de diva Patritii vita, purgatorio, miraculis rebusque gestis.* Madrid, 1629.

—. *Zoilomastix,* ed. T.J. O'Donnell. Dublin, IMC, 1960.

Ó Tuama, Seán (ed.). *An duanaire, 1600-1900: poems of the dispossessed,* with translations into English verse by Thomas Kinsella. Dublin, 1981.

Pairlement Chloinne Tomáis, ed. N. J. A. Williams. Dublin, 1981.

Parsons, Robert. *A Christian directory.* [St Omer], 1622.

Paul of St Ubald. *The soul's delight.* Antwerp, 1654.

Pender, Seamus (ed.). *A 'census' of Ireland. c.1659.* Dublin, 1939.

—. The O'Clery book of genealogies. *Analecta Hibernica,* no. 18, 1951, 1-194.

Piers, Henry. *A chorographical description of the county of West-Meath, written, A.D. 1682.* Reprinted from Charles Vallancey (ed.). *Collectanea de rebus Hibernicis,* i, Dublin 1770, Tara, 1981.

Plummer, Charles (ed.). *Bethada naem nÉrenn: lives of Irish saints.* 2 vols, Oxford, 1922.

—. *Miscellanea hagiographica Hibernica.* Brussels, 1925.

—. *Vitae sanctorum Hiberniae.* 2 vols, Oxford, 1910.

Power, Patrick (ed.). *Life of St Declan of Ardmore ... and life of St Mochuda of Lismore.* London, ITS, 1916.

Radner, J. N. (ed.). *Fragmentary annals of Ireland.* Dublin, 1978.

Raymond, Anthony. *An account of Dr Keting's history of Ireland.* Dublin, 1723.

—. *A letter from Dr Anthony Raymond to my Lord Inchiquin giving some account of the monarchs and ancient state of Ireland.* Dublin, 1723.

Richardson, John. *A short history of the attempts that have been made to convert the popish natives of Ireland to the establish'd religion, with a proposal for their conversion.* London, 1712.

Rothe, David. *Analecta sacra, nova, et mira, de rebus Catholicorum in Hibernia.* 1616-19.

—. *Hibernia resurgens.* Cologne, 1621.

Saltair na rann: a collection of early middle Irish poems, ed. Whitley Stokes. Oxford, 1883.

Simington, R.C (ed.). *The civil survey, A.D. 1654-56,* i-ii, *Tipperary.* Dublin, 1931-34.

Spenser, Edmund. *A view of the state of Ireland,* ed. W.L. Renwick. Oxford, 1970.

Stanihurst, Richard. *De rebus in Hibernia gestis.* Antwerp, 1584.

Stapleton, Theobald. *Catechismus, seu Doctrina Christiana Latino-Hibernica. Dublin,* IMC, 1945. Fascimile of 1639 text.

Stokes, Whitley (ed.). Cóir anmann: 'Fitness of names', *Irische Texte mit Ubersetzunger und Worterbuch,* iii. Leipzig, 1897, 285-444, 557.

Stow, John. *A summarie of English chronicles conteyning the true accompt of yeres wherein every Kyng of this Realme ... began theyr reygne.* London, 1565.

—. *A survay of London: contayning the originall, antiquity, increase, modern estate, and description of that citie, written in the year 1598,* ed. Henry Morley. London, 1893.

Suarez, Franciscus. *Defensio fidei Catholicae adversus Anglicanae sectae errores.* Cologne, 1614.

Thomas Aquinas, St. *Summa theologiae: Latin text and English translation.* 61 vols, London, 1964-81.

Thomas, Hibernicus [Thomas Palmer]. *Flores Bibliorum, sive loci communes omnium fere materiarum ex veteri et novo testamento excerpti* .... Antwerp, 1568.

Tiomna Nuadh ar dTighearna agus ar Slanaightheora Iosa Criosd, ar na tarruing go firinneach as Gréigis go gáoidheilg re hUilliam O Domhnuill. Baile Átha Cliath, 1602. [STC 2958]

Toletus. *Summa casuum sive instructio Sacerdotum*. Lyons, 1599.

Uraicecht na Riar, ed. Liam Breatnach. Dublin, 1987.

Ussher, James. *A discourse of the religion anciently professed by the Irish and British*. Dublin, 1631.

—. *Veterum Epistolarum Hibernicarum Sylloge*. [Dublin], 1632.

Vergil, Polydor. *Historia Anglica, ab ipso autore recognita. Novo corollario Anglorum regum chronices epitome aucta per G. Lilium*. Douai, 1603.

—. *The Anglica historia of Polydore Vergil, AD 1485-1537*, ed. Denys Hay. London, Camden Series, lxxiv, 1950.

Walsh, Paul (ed.). A fragment used by Keating. *Archivium Hibernicum*, i, 1912, 1-9.

Walsh, Peter. *A prospect of the state of Ireland from the year of the world, 1576 to the year of Christ 1652*. [London], 1682.

Walsh, T.J. (ed.). Some records of the Irish College, Bordeaux. *Archivium Hibernicum*, xv, 1950, 92-141.

Ware, James. *De scriptoribus Hiberniae libri duo* .... Dublin, 1639; fascimile reprint, Farnborough, Hants, 1966.

—. (ed.). *The historie of Ireland collected by three learned authors, viz. Meredith Hanmer ..., Edmund Campion ..., and Edmund Spenser*. Dublin, 1633; reprinted as *Ancient Irish histories: the workes of Spencer, Campion, Hanmer, and Marleburrough*. 2 vols, Dublin, 1809.

Williams, N.J.A. (ed.). *Dánta Mhuiris mhic Dhaibhí Dhuibh Mhic Gearailt*. Baile Átha Cliath, 1979.

SECONDARY SOURCES

Ahlqvist, Anders. *The early Irish linguist*. Commentationes Humanarum Litterarum, 73. 1982.

Alspach, R.K. *Irish poetry from the English invasion to 1798*. 2nd ed., Philadelphia, 1960.

Anderson, Benedict R O'G. *Imagined communities: reflections on the origin and spread of nationalism*. revised ed. London, 1991.

Armstrong, John A. *Nations before nationalism*. Chapel Hill, 1982.

Barnard, Toby. 'Learning, the learned and literacy in Ireland, c.1660-1760'. In Toby Barnard, Dáibhí Ó Cróinín, and Katharine Simms (eds.), *A miracle of learning: studies in manuscripts and Irish learning*. Aldershot, 1998, 209-35.

—. 'Reading in eighteenth-century Ireland: private and public pleasures'. In Bernadette Cunningham and Máire Kennedy (eds), *The experience of reading: Irish historical perspectives*. Dublin, 1999, 60-77.

Barr, James. Why the world was created in 4004 BC: archbishop Ussher and biblical chronology. *Bulletin of John Rylands University Library, Manchester*, lxviii, no. 2. 1985, 575-608.

Bayley, Peter. *French pulpit oratory, 1598-1650: a study in themes and styles, with a descriptive catalogue of printed texts*. Cambridge, 1980.

Berlioz, Jacques, and Polo de Beaulieu, Marie-Anne. *Les Exempla médiévaux: introduction a la recherches. Suivie des tables critiques de l'Index exemplorum de Frederic C. Tubach*. Carcassonne, 1992.

Berman, David and Harrison, Alan. John Toland and Keating's history of Ireland (1723). *Donegal Annual*, no. 36, 1984, 225-9.

Bertrand, Abbé. *Histoire des seminaires de Bordeaux et de Bazas*. Bordeaux, 1894.

Binchy, D.A. *Celtic and Anglo Saxon kingship*. Oxford, 1970.

—. The fair of Tailtiu and the feast of Tara. *Ériu*, xviii, 1958, 113-38.

Bliss, Alan. *Spoken English in Ireland, 1600-1740*. Dublin, 1979.

Bolster, Evelyn. *A history of the diocese of Cork from the Reformation to the penal era*. Cork, 1982.

Bossy, John. The Counter-Reformation and the people of Catholic Ireland, 1596-1641. In T. Desmond Williams (ed.), *Historical Studies*, viii. Dublin, 1971, 155-69.

—. Essay de sociographie de la messe, 1200-1700. *Annales E. S. C.* xxxvi, 1981, 44-70.

—. Moral arithmetic: seven deadly sins into ten commandments. In Edmund Leites (ed), *Conscience and casuistry in early modern Europe*. Cambridge, 1988, 213-34.

Boucher, David. *Texts in contexts: revisionist methods for studying the history of political ideas*. Dordrecht, 1985.

Boyle, Patrick. *The Irish College in Paris, 1578-1901*. London, 1901.

—. The Irish College at Bordeaux. *Irish Ecclesiastical Record*, 4th series, xxii, 1907, 127-45.

Bradshaw, Brendan. Geoffrey Keating: apologist of Irish Ireland. In Brendan Bradshaw, Andrew Hadfield and Willy Maley (eds), *Representing Ireland: literature and the origins of conflict, 1534-1660*. Cambridge, 1993.

Brady, John. The Irish colleges in Europe and the Counter Reformation. *Proceedings of the Irish Catholic Historical Committee*, 1957, 1-8.

—. The Irish colleges in the Low Countries. *Archivium Hibernicum*, xiv, 1949, 66-91.

—. Father Christopher Cusack and the Irish College of Douai, 1594-1624. In Sylvester O'Brien (ed.), *Measgra Mhichil Ui Chléirigh*. Dublin, 1944, 98-107.

Breatnach, Caoimhín. Rawlinson B 502, Lebar Glinne dá Lacha agus Saltair na Rann. *Éigse*, xxx, 1997, 109-32.

Breatnach, Pádraig A. *Téamaí taighde nua Ghaeilge*. Maigh Nuad, 1997.

—. The chief's poet. *Proceedings of the Royal Irish Academy*, lxxxiii, C, 1983, 37-79.

Bremond, Henri. *Histoire de sentiment religious en France*. 12 vols, Paris, 1916-33.

Brockliss, L.W.B. and Ferté, P. Irish clerics in France in the seventeenth and eighteenth centuries: a statistical study. *Proceedings of the Royal Irish Academy*, lxxxvii, C, 1987, 527-72.

Brownley, Martine Watson. *Clarendon and the rhetoric of historical form*. Philadelphia, 1985.

Bruford, Alan. Gaelic folktales and mediaeval romances. *Béaloideas*, xxxiv, 1966, 1-284.

Burke, Peter. A survey of the popularity of ancient historians, 1450-1700. *History and Theory*, v, 1966, 135-52.

—. *The Renaissance sense of the past*. London, 1969.

Burke, W.P. Geoffry Keating. *Jnl of Waterford and South-East Ireland Archaeological Society*, i, no. 4, 1895, 173-82.

Butler, W.F. An Irish origin legend of the origins of the barons of Cahir. *Jnl of Royal Society of Antiquaries of Ireland*, lv, 1925, 6-14.

Byrne, F. J. *Irish kings and high kings*. London, 1973.

—. *Senchas*: the nature of Gaelic historical tradition: approaches to history. In J.G. Barry (ed.), *Historical Studies*, ix. Belfast, 1974. 137-59.

Caball, Marc. *Pairlement Chloinne Thomáis*, i: a reassessment. *Éigse*, xxvii, 1993, 47-57.

Caerwyn Williams, J.E. and Ford, Patrick K. *The Irish literary tradition*. Cardiff, 1992.

Cairns, David and Richards, Shaun (eds). *Writing Ireland: colonialism, nationalism and culture*. Manchester, 1988.

Campbell, J.L. The tour of Edward Lhuyd in Ireland in 1699 and 1700. *Celtica*, v, 1960, 218-28.

Canny, Nicholas P. Identity formation in Ireland: the emergence of the Anglo-Irish. In N.P. Canny and Anthony Pagden (eds.), *Colonial identity in the Atlantic world, 1500-1800*. Princeton, 1987, 159-212.

—. *The formation of the Old English elite in Ireland*. Dublin, 1975.

—. The formation of the Irish mind: religion, politics and Gaelic Irish literature 1580-1750. *Past & Present*, no. 95, 1982, 91-116.

Carey, John. The ancestry of Fénius Farsaid. *Celtica*, xxi, 1990, 104-12.

—. *The Irish national origin legend: synthetic pseudo-history*. Cambridge, 1994.

—. *A new introduction to Lebor gabhála Érenn*. London, ITS, 1993.

Carney, James. *Studies in Irish literature and history*. Dublin, 1955.

—. *The Irish bardic poet*. Dublin, 1967.

Carpenter, Andrew. Irish and Anglo Irish scholars in the time of Swift: the case of Anthony Raymond. In W. Zach and H. Kosok (eds), *Literary interrelations: Ireland, England and the world*. 3 vols, Tubingen, 1987, i, 11-19.

— and Harrison, Alan. Swift, Raymond and a legacy. *Swift Studies*, I. Münster, 1986, 57-60.

Carrigan, William. *The history and antiquities of the diocese of Ossory*. 4 vols, Dublin, 1905.

Cave, Terence. *Devotional poetry in France, c.1570-1613*. London, 1969.

Chadwick, Owen. *Catholicism and history: the opening of the Vatican Archives*. Cambridge, 1978.

Charles Edwards, Thomas. A contract between king and people in early medieval Ireland: *Crith Gabhlach* on kingship. *Peritia*, viii, 1993, 107-19.

Clanchy, M.T. *From memory to written record: England 1066-1307*. London, 1979.

—. Remembering the past and the good old law. *History*, lv, 1970, 165-76.

Clancy, Thomas H. Spiritual publications of English Jesuits, 1615-1640. *Recusant History*, xix, no. 4, 1989, 426-46.

Clancy, Thomas Owen and Márcus, Gilbert. *Iona, the earliest poetry of a Celtic monastery*. Edinburgh, 1995.

Clarke, Aidan. *The Old English in Ireland, 1625-42*. London, 1966.

—. *The Graces, 1625-41*. Dundalk, 1968.

—. Colonial identity in seventeenth-century Ireland. In T.W. Moody (ed.), *Nationality and the pursuit of national independence, Historical Studies*, xi, Belfast, 1978, 57-71.

Cochrane, Eric. *Historians and historiography in the Italian Renaissance*. Chicago, 1981.

Coláiste Phádraig, Má Nuad. *An Músaem: College Museum*. [Maynooth, 1974?].

Concannon, Helena. *The Blessed Eucharist in Irish history*. Dublin, 1932.

Corboy, J.J. The Jesuit mission to Ireland, 1596-1626. M.A. thesis, UCD, 1941.

Corcoran, T. Early Irish Jesuit educators. *Studies*, xxix, 1940, 545-60; xxx, 1941, 59-74.

Corish, Patrick J. *The Catholic community in the seventeenth and eighteenth centuries*. Dublin, 1981.

—. David Rothe, bishop of Ossory, 1618-50. *Jnl of the Butler Society*, ii, no. 3, 1984, 315-23.

Crane, T.F. *The exempla or illustrative stories from the Sermones Vulgares of Jacques de Vitry*. London, 1890.

Cregan, Donal. The social and cultural background of a Counter-Reformation episcopate, 1618-60. In Art Cosgrove and Donal McCartney (eds), *Studies in Irish history presented to R. Dudley Edwards*. Dublin, 1979, 85-117.

Crick, Julia. *The Historia Regum Britanniae of Geoffrey of Monmouth. IV. Dissemination and reception in the later middle ages.* Cambridge, 1991.

Cronin, Anne. Sources of Keating's *Foras feasa ar Éirinn.* M.A. thesis, UCD, 1933 (author's annotated copy and associated notes in the possession of William O'Sullivan).

—. Printed sources of Keating's *Foras feasa. Éigse,* iv, 1943-4, 235-79.

—. Sources of Keating's *Foras feasa ar Éirinn*: 2, manuscript sources. *Éigse,* v, 1945-7, 122-35.

Cullen, L.M. Patrons, teachers and literacy in Irish, 1700-1850. In Mary Daly and David Dickson (eds), *The origins of popular literacy in Ireland.* Dublin, 1990, 15-44.

Cunningham, Bernadette. Native culture and political change in Ireland, 1580-1640. In Ciaran Brady and Raymond Gillespie (eds), *Natives and newcomers: essays on the making of Irish colonial society, 1534-1641.* Dublin, 1986, 148-70.

—. Seventeenth-century interpretations of the past: the case of Geoffrey Keating. *Irish Historical Studies,* xxv, no. 98, Nov. 1986, 116-28.

—. Geoffrey Keating's *Eochair sgiath an Aifrinn* and the Catholic Reformation in Ireland. In W.J. Sheils and Diana Wood (eds), *The churches, Ireland and the Irish: studies in church history, xxv.* Oxford, 1989, 133-43.

—. The culture and ideology of Irish Franciscan historians at Louvain, 1607-1650. In Ciaran Brady (ed.), *Ideology and the historians: Historical studies, xvii.* Dublin, 1991, 11-30, 223-7.

—. The sources of *Trí bior-ghaoithe an bháis*: another French sermon. *Éigse,* xxxi, 1999, 73-8.

—. Representations of king, parliament and the Irish people in Geoffrey Keating's *Foras feasa ar Éirinn* and John Lynch's *Cambrensis eversus* (1662). In Jane Ohlmeyer (ed.). *Political thought in seventeenth-century Ireland. Forthcoming,* Cambridge, 2000, 131-54.

—. Colonized Catholics: perceptions of honour and history in Michael Kearney's reading of *Foras feasa ar Éirinn.* In V.P. Carey and U. Lotz-Heumann (eds.). *Taking sides? Colonial and confessional mentalités in early modern Ireland: essays in honour of Karl S. Bottigheimer,* Dublin, 2003, 150–64.

— and Gillespie, Raymond. The east Ulster bardic family of Ó Gnímh. *Éigse,* xx, 1984, 106-14.

—. 'Persecution' in seventeenth-century Irish. *Éigse,* xxii, 1987, 21-8.

—. The purposes of patronage: Brian Maguire of Knockninny and his manuscripts. *Clogher Record,* xiii, no. 1, 1988, 38-49.

—. 'The most adaptable of saints': the cult of St Patrick in the seventeenth century. *Archivium Hibernicum,* xlix, 1995, 82-104.

Davies, R.R. et al. (eds). *Welsh society and nationhood.* Cardiff, 1984.

De Jubainville, H. d'Arbois. *The Irish mythological cycle,* trans. R.I. Best. Dublin, 1903.

Dillon, Myles. Laud Misc. 610. *Celtica,* v, 1960, 64-76.

—. The taboos of the kings of Ireland. *Proceedings of the Royal Irish Academy,* liv, C 1951-2, 1-36.

Dobbs, Margaret (ed.). The Ban-shenchus. *Revue Celtique,* xlvii, 1930, 283-339.

Doyle, B.M. Gaelic antiquity and national identity in Enlightenment Ireland and Scotland. *English Historical Review,* cix, 1994, 197-222.

Dumville, David. *Histories and pseudo-histories of the Insular middle ages.* Aldershot, *c.*1990.

Fenning, Hugh. The library of a preacher of Drogheda: John Donnelly, OP, d.1748. *Collectanea Hibernica,* Nos. 18-19, 1976-7, 72-104.

Ferguson, William. *The identity of the Scottish nation: an historic quest.* Edinburgh, 1998.

Firth, Raymond. *Symbols, public and private.* London, 1973.

Foley, R.A. Further lights on Keating. *Waterford and South-East Ireland Archaeol. Soc. Jnl.* ix, 1906, 40-4, 140-2.

Fox, Levi (ed.). *English historical scholarship in the sixteenth and seventeenth centuries.* London, 1956.

Franciscan Fathers. *Father Luke Wadding: commemorative volume.* Dublin, 1957.

Gillespie, Raymond. *The transformation of the Irish economy, 1550-1700.* Dundalk, 1991.

—. *Devoted people: belief and religion in early modern Ireland.* Manchester, 1997.

—. The making of the Montgomery manuscripts. *Familia,* ii, no. 2, 1986, 23-29.

—. The social thought of Richard Bellings. In *Kingdoms in crisis: Ireland in the 1640s: essays in honour of Donal Cregan.* Dublin, 2001, 212-28.

— and Cunningham, Bernadette. Holy Cross Abbey and the Counter-Reformation in Tipperary. *Tipperary Historical Jnl,* 1991, 171-80.

Gillies, William. Arthur in Gaelic tradition, part 1, folktales and ballads. *Cambridge Medieval Celtic Studies,* no. 2, 1981, 47-72; part 2, romances and learned lore. no. 3, 1982, 41-75.

Gleeson, D.F. *The last lords of Ormond.* London, 1938.

Gogan, L.S. Dála Lia Fáil. *Feasta,* iii, no. 2, 1951, 10-12.

Grabowski, K. and Dumville, D. *Chronicles and annals of medieval Ireland and Wales: the Clonmacnoise-group texts.* Woodbridge, 1984.

Grattan Flood, W.H. *History of the diocese of Ferns.* Waterford, 1916.

Haigh, Christopher. *Reformation and resistance in Tudor Lancashire.* Cambridge, 1975.

Hamel, A.G. Van. On Lebor gabála. *Zeitschrift für Celtische Philologie,* x, 1914, 97-197.

Hammerstein, Helga. Aspects of the continental education of Irish students in the reign of Queen Elizabeth I. *Historical Studies,* viii, 1971, 137-54.

Harrison, Alan. *Ag cruinniú meala: Anthony Raymond, 1675-1726, ministéir Protastúnach, agus léann na Gaeilge i mBaile Átha Cliath.* Baile Átha Cliath, 1988.

—. The shower of Hell, *Éigse,* xviii, 1980-1, 304.

—. The story of the Irish language. In Jean Brihault (ed.), *L'Irlande et ses langues.* Rennes, 1992, 11-17.

Hay, Denys. *Polydore Vergil.* Oxford, 1952.

—. *Annalists and historians: western historiography from the eigh.'t to the eighteenth centuries.* London, 1977.

Hayton, David. Anglo-Irish attitudes: changing perceptions oᶠ national identity among the Protestant ascendancy, 1690-1750. *Studies in Eighteenth-century Culture,* xvii, 1987, 145-57.

Henebry, Richard. Geoffrey Keating. *Jnl of the Ivernian Society,* v, 1912-13, 197-202.

Henige, David. *Oral historiography.* London, 1982.

Herbert, Máire. *Iona, Kells and Derry: the history and hagiography of the monastic familia of Columba.* Oxford, 1988.

Higham, N.J. *The English conquest: Gildas and Britain in the fifth century.* Manchester, 1994.

Hill, J.R. Popery and Protestantism, civil and religious liberty: the disputed lessons of Irish history 1690-1812. *Past & Present,* no. 118, 1988, 96-129.

Hogan, Edmund. *Distinguished Irishmen of the sixteenth century.* London, 1894.

Hull, Vernon. Keating, Colgan and *Psaltair na Rann. Zeitschrift für Celtische Philologie,* xvi, 1927, 453-7.

Jackson, Donald. Michael Kearney of Ballylosky: Irish scribe and Butler servant. *Journal of the Butler Society,* ii, no.1, 1980-1, 84-5.

Jennings, Brendan. *Michael O Cleirigh, chief of the Four Masters, and his associates.* Dublin, 1936.

Jungmann, Josef A. *The Mass, an historical, theological and pastoral survey.* Collegeville, 1976.

Kelley, D.R. *Foundations of modern historical scholarship: language, law and history in the French Renaissance.* New York, 1970.

—. History, English law and the Renaissance. *Past & Present*, no. 65, 1974, 24-51.

—. *Versions of history from antiquity to the enlightenment.* New Haven, 1991.

Kemp, Anthony. *The estrangement of the past.* Oxford, 1991.

Kermode, Frank. *The sense of an ending: studies in the theory of fiction.* Oxford, 1966.

Kidd, Colin. *Subverting Scotland's past: Scottish Whig historians and the creation of an Anglo-British identity, 1689-c.1830.* Cambridge, 1993.

—. *British identities before nationalism: ethnicity and nationhood in the Atlantic world, 1600-1800.* Cambridge, 1999.

Killen, J.F. Latin quotations in *Parliament na mBan*. *Éigse*, xvii, 1977-79, 55-60.

Kirk, G.S. *Myth: its meaning and functions in ancient and other cultures.* Cambridge, 1971.

Leerssen, J. Th. *Mere Irish and Fíor-Ghael: studies in the idea of nationality its development and literary expression prior to the nineteenth century.* Amsterdam and Philadelphia, 1986 (2nd ed. Cork, 1996).

—. Archbishop Ussher and Gaelic culture. *Studia Hibernica*, Nos. 22-3, 1982-3, 50-8.

—. *The contention of the bards: Iomarbhágh na bhfileadh and its place in Irish political and literary history.* London, ITS, 1994.

Leith Spencer, H. *English preaching in the late middle ages.* Oxford, 1993.

Lennon, Colm. Richard Stanihurst. 1547-1618 and Old English identity. *Irish Historical Studies*, xxi, no. 82, Sept. 1978, 121-43.

—. *Richard Stanihurst: the Dubliner, 1547-1618.* Dublin, 1981.

—. The Counter-Reformation in Ireland, 1542-1641. In Ciaran Brady and Raymond Gillespie, (eds), *Natives and newcomers: essays on the making of Irish colonial society, 1534-1641.* Dublin, 1986, 75-92.

—. *The Lords of Dublin in the age of Reformation.* Dublin, 1989.

Levy, F.J. *Tudor historical thought.* San Marino, 1967.

Lucas, Peter. *From author to audience: John Capgrave and medieval publication.* Dublin, 1997.

Lynch, M. National identity in Ireland and Scotland, 1500-1640. In C. Bjørn, A. Grant and K.J. Stringer, (eds), *Nations, nationalism and patriotism in the European past.* Copenhagen, 1994, 109-36.

Lyons, John D. *Exemplum: the rhetoric of example in early modern France and Italy.* Princeton, [1989].

McCarthy, Terence Francis. Ulster office, 1552-1800. MA thesis, QUB, 1983.

Mac Craith, Mícheál. Gaelic Ireland and the Renaissance. In Glanmor Williams and Robert Owen Jones (eds), *The Celts and the Renaissance: tradition and innovation: proceedings of the eighth international Congress of Celtic Studies, 1987.* Cardiff, 1990, 57-89.

—. *Lorg an hiasachta ar na dánta grá.* Baile Átha Cliath, 1989.

McCone, Kim. *Pagan past and Christian present in early Irish literature.* Maynooth, 1990.

Mac Cuarta, Brian. A planter's interaction with Gaelic culture: Sir Matthew de Renzy, 1577-1634. *Irish Economic and Social History*, xx, 1993, 1-17.

MacGeoghegan, James. *The history of Ireland ancient and modern.* Trans P. O'Kelly. 3 vols, Dublin, 1831-2.

MacHale, C. *Annals of the Clan Egan. An account of the Mac Egan bardic family of Brehon lawyers.* Enniscrone, 1990.

McKisack, May. *Medieval history in the Tudor age.* Oxford, 1971.

—, Levy, F., and Smith Fussner, F. *The historical revolution: English historical writing and thought, 1580-1640*. London, 1962.

Mac Niocaill, Gearóid. *The medieval Irish annals*. Dublin, 1975.

Magennis, Eoin. A 'beleaguered Protestant'?: Walter Harris and the writing of *Fiction Unmasked* in mid-18th-century Ireland. *Eighteenth-century Ireland*, xiii, 1998, 86-111.

Maniet, Albert. Cath Belaig Duin Bolc. *Éigse*, vii, 1953, 95-111.

Martin, H.J. *The history and power of writing*. Chicago, 1994.

Mason, Roger. Kingship, nobility and Anglo-Scottish union: John Mair's *History of Greater Britain* (1521). *Innes Review*, xli, 1990, 182-222.

—. Chivalry and citizenship: aspects of national identity in Renaissance Scotland. In Roger Mason and Norman Macdougall (eds), *People and power in Scotland: essays in honour of T. C. Smout*. Edinburgh, 1992, 50-73.

Merriman, M.H. Home thoughts from abroad: national consciousness and Scottish exiles in the mid-sixteenth century. In C. Bjørn, A. Grant and K.J. Stringer (eds), *Social and political identities in Western history*. Copenhagen, 1994.

Meyer, Kuno. Mitteilunger aus Irischen Handschriften. *Zeitschrift fur Celtische Philologie*, xii, 1918, 290-95.

Millett, Benignus. *The Irish Franciscans, 1651-1665*. Rome, 1964.

— and Lynch, Anthony (eds). *Dún Mhuire, Killiney, 1945-95: léann agus seanchas*. Dublin, 1995.

Mitchell, Joshua. *Not by reason alone: religion, history and identity in early modern political thought*. Chicago, 1993.

Moody, T.W., Martin, F.X., and Byrne, F.J. (eds). *A New history of Ireland, iii, early modern Ireland*. Oxford, 1976.

Moody, T.W. and Vaughan, W.E. (eds). *A new history of Ireland, iv, eighteenth-century Ireland, 1691-1800*. Oxford, 1986.

Mooney, Canice. Irish Franciscan libraries of the past. *Irish Ecclesiastical Record*, lx, 1942, 215-228,

—. The Irish Church in the sixteenth century. *Irish Ecclesiastical Record*, xcix, 1963, 102-13.

Morley, Vincent. *An crann os coill: Aodh Buí Mac Cruitín, c. 1680-1755*. Baile Átha Cliath, 1995.

Nagy, Joseph Falagy. *A new introduction*, to R.A.S. Macalister (ed.), *Two Irish Arthurian romances*. London, ITS, 1998.

Ní Bhrolcháin, Muireann. A possible source for Keating's *Forus feasa ar Éirinn*. *Éigse*, xix, 1982-3, 61-81.

—. The *Banshenchas* revisited. In Mary O'Dowd and Sabine Wichert (eds), *Chattel, servant or citizen: women's status in church, state and society: historical studies xix*. Belfast, 1995, 70-81.

Ní Chatháin, Próinséas. Bede's ecclesiastical history in Irish. *Peritia*, iii, 1984, 115-20.

Nicholls, K.W. The Irish genealogies: their value and defects. *Irish Genealogist*, v, 1975, 256-61.

Ní Shéaghdha, Nessa. Collectors of Irish manuscripts: motives and methods. *Celtica*, xvii, 1985, 1-28.

Nolan, William and McGrath, Thomas G. (eds). *Tipperary history and society: interdisciplinary essays on the history of an Irish county*. Dublin, 1985.

Ó Broin, T. Lia Fáil: fact and fiction in the tradition. *Celtica*, xxi, 1990, 393-410.

Ó Buachalla, Breandán. An mhesiasacht agus an aisling. In Pádraig de Brún, Séan Ó Coileáin and Pádraig Ó Riain (eds). *Folia Gadelica: essays presented to R. A. Breatnach*. Cork, 1983.

—. *Annála Ríoghachta Éireann agus Foras Feasa ar Éirinn*: an comhtheacs comhaimseartha. *Studia Hibernica*, Nos. 22-3, 1982-3, 59-105.

—. Aodh Eangach and the Irish king-hero. In Donnchadh Ó Corráin, Liam Breatnach and Kim McCone (eds). *Sages, saints and storytellers: celtic studies in honour of Professor James Carney*. Maynooth, 1989, 200-32.

—. Na Stíobhartaigh agus an t-aos léinn: Cing Seamas. *Proceedings of the Royal Irish Academy*, lxxxiii, C, 1983, 81-134.

—. *Foreword*, Geoffrey Keating, *Foras Feasa ar Éirinn*, eds D. Comyn and P.S. Dinneen. London, ITS, 1987 reprint.

—. Cúlra is tabhacht an dáin '*A leabhráin ainmnighthear d'Aodh*'. *Celtica*, xxi, 1990, 410-13.

—. James our true king: the ideology of Irish royalism in the seventeenth century. In D.G. Boyce, Robert Eccleshall, and Vincent Geoghegan (eds), *Political thought in Ireland since the seventeenth century*. London, 1993, 7-35.

—. *Aisling ghéar: na Stíobhartaigh agus an taos léinn, 1603-1788*. Baile Átha Cliath, 1996.

Ó Catháin, Diarmaid. Dermot O'Connor: translator of Keating. *Eighteenth Century Ireland*, ii, 1987, 67-87.

Ó Cathasaigh, Tomás. *The heroic biography of Cormac mac Airt*. Dublin, 1977.

Ó Cathnia, L.P. *Apaloga na bhfili, 1200-1650*. Dublin, 1984.

Ó Ciosáin, Éamon. Les Irlandais en Bretagne, 1603-1780: 'invasion', accueil, integration. In Catherine Laurent and Helen Davis (eds), *Irland et Bretagne: vingt siècles d'histoire*. Rennes: Actes du Colloque de Rennes, 1993, 152-66.

Ó Concheanainn, Tomás. The manuscript tradition of two middle Irish Leinster tales. *Celtica*, xviii, 1986, 13-33.

Ó Corráin, Donnchadh. Caithréim Chellacháin Chaisil: history or propaganda. *Ériu*, xxv, 1974, 1-69.

—. Historical need and literary narrative. In D. Ellis Evans, et al. (eds), *Proceedings of the Seventh International Congress of Celtic Studies, Oxford 1983*. Oxford, 1986, 141-58.

—. Irish origin legends and genealogy: recurrent aetiologies. In T. Nyberg et al. (eds), *History and heroic tale: a symposium*. Odense, 1985, 51-96.

—. Irish regnal succession: a reappraisal. *Studia Hibernica*, no. 11, 1971, 7-39.

—. Legend as critic. In Tom Dunne (ed.). *The writer as witness: literature as historical evidence*. Cork, 1987, 23-38.

—. Seathrún Céitinn. c.1580-c.1644: an cúlra stairiúil. In *Dúchas, 1983, 1984, 1985*. Dublin, 1986, 56-68.

Ó Cuív, Brian. Literary creation and Irish historical tradition. *Proceedings of the British Academy*, xlix, 1963, 233-62.

—. *The Irish bardic duanaire or 'poem-book'*. Dublin, 1974.

O'Curry, Eugene. *Lectures on the manuscript materials of ancient Irish history*. Dublin, 1861.

O'Daly, John. *Kings of the race of Éibhear*. Dublin, 1847.

—. *The poets and poetry of Munster*. Dublin, 1849.

O'Donnell, Terence (ed.). *Father John Colgan, O.F.M.* Dublin, 1959.

Ó Dúshláine, Tadhg. *An Eoraip agus litríocht na Gaeilge, 1600-50*. Dublin, 1987.

—. An tExemplum in 'Trí bior-ghaoithe an bháis'. *Léachtaí Cholm Cille*, xiv, 1983, 90-105.

—. Filíocht pholaitiúil na Gaeilge – a cineál. *Léachtaí Cholm Cille, xiii: Éire Banba Fodla*, 1982, 114-29.

—. 'Ionmholta malairt bhisigh'. *Léachtaí Cholm Cille, viii, Ár ndúchas Creidimh*, 1977, 40-54.

—. More about Keating's use of the simile of the dung-beetle. *Zeitschrift für Celtische Philologie*, xl, 1984, 282-5.

—. Nóta ar cheapadóireacht an Chéitinnigh. *Éigse*, xviii, 1980-81, 87-92.

—. Seathrún Céitinn agus an stíl Bharócach a thug sé go hÉirinn. In *Dúchas, 1983, 1984, 1985*. Dublin, 1986, 43-55.

Ó Fiannachta, Pádraig. Áiteanna sa Bhíobla aistrithe ag Seán Ó Maolchonaire. *Irish Ecclesiastical Record*, xcvii, 1962, 382-8.

—. Dáiví Ó Bruadair. *Léachtaí Cholm Cille, xiii*, 1982, 130-50.

—. Eochair-sgiath an Aifrinn. In *Dúchas, 1983, 1984, 1985*. Dublin, 1986, 33-42.

—. Scéalta ón *Magnum speculum exemplorum*. *Irish Ecclesiastical Record*, xcix, 1963, 177-84.

—. Seán mac Torna Uí Mhaoilchonaire agus 'Eochair-Sciath an Aifrinn'. *Éigse*, X, 1961-3, 198-207.

—. Stair, finnscéal agus annála. *Léachtaí Cholm Cille*, ii, 1971, 5-13.

Ó Fionnagáin, P. Conor O'Mahony, SJ, 1594-1656, separatist. *The O'Mahony Journal*, xvi, 1993, 3-15.

O'Flynn, John. *Two centuries of Catholic bishops of Waterford and Lismore: 1629-1829*. Waterford, 1917.

Ó hEarcáin, Marius. Seathrún Céitinn. *Irisleabhar Manuat*, 1962, 19-25.

Ó hÓgáin, Daithí. *The hero in Irish folk history*. Dublin and New York, 1985.

Ó Laoghaire, Diarmaid. Príomh-fhoinseacha 'Eochair-Sgiath an Aifrinn'. MA thesis, UCD, 1939. (Author's annotated copy in Milltown Institute library)

Ó Maonaigh, Cainneach (Mooney, Canice). Scribhneoirí Gaeilge an seachtú haois deag. *Studia Hibernica*, no. 2, 1962, 182-208.

—. Scríbhneoirí Gaeilge Oird San Froinsias. *Catholic Survey*, i, 1951-53, 54-75.

Ó Muraíle, Nollaig. The autograph manuscript of the Annals of the Four Masters. *Celtica*, xix, 1987, 75-95.

—. *The celebrated antiquary: Dubhaltach Mac Fhirbhisigh, c.1600-71: his lineage, life and learning*. Maynooth, 1996.

—. Aspects of intellectual life in seventeenth-century Galway. In Gerard Moran (ed.), *Galway: history and society*. Dublin, 1996, 149-212.

—. 'Aimsir an chogadh chreidmhigh': An Dubhaltach Mac Fhirbhisigh, a lucht aitheantais agus polaitíocht an seachtú haois deag. In Máirín Ní Dhonnchadha (ed.). *Nua-léamha: gnéithe de chultúr, stair agus polaitíocht na hÉireann, c.1600-c.1900*. Baile Átha Cliath, 1996, 89-117.

O'Nolan, Gerald. *Studies in modern Irish, part iv, being a critical analysis of Keating's prose*. Dublin, 1922.

O'Rahilly, T.F (ed.). Irish poets, historians and judges in English documents, 1538-1615. *Proceedings of the Royal Irish Academy*, xxxvi, C, 1921-4, 86-120.

O'Reilly, P.J. Notes on the coronation stone at Westminster and the Lia Fáil at Tara. *Jnl of the Royal Society of Antiquaries of Ireland*, xxxii, 1902, 77-92.

Ó Riain, Eóin. *Réim ríoghraidhe na h-Éireann, ó aimsir Néill Noíghiallaigh go dtí bás Maelshechnaill Mhic Dhomhnaill, .i. aois an tighearna, 379-1022, maille le na rígthibh go bh-freasabhra ó bhás Mhaelshechnaill Mhic Dhomhnaill go gabhaltas Gall .i. aois an Tighearna, 1022-1169*. Dublin, 1940.

Ó Riain, Pádraig. The Book of Glendalough or Rawlinson B 502. *Éigse*, xviii, 1981, 161-76.

—. *Irish Texts Society: the first hundred years*. London, ITS, 1998.

—. The Psalter of Cashel: a preliminary list of contents. *Éigse*, xxiii, 1989, 107-30.

—. Rawlinson B 502 alias Lebar Glinne Dá Locha: a restatement of the case. *Zeitschrift für Celtische Philologie*, li, 1999, 130-47.

O'Rourke, J. The Lia Fáil or stone of destiny. *Irish Ecclesiastical Record*, 3rd ser, i, 1870, 441-53.

Ó Suilleabhain, Pádraig. Céitinn agus Caesarius Heisterbacensis. *Éigse*, ix, 1960-1, 242.

O'Sullivan, Anne and William. Three notes on Laud Misc 610 (or the Book of Pottlerath). *Celtica*, ix, 1971, 135-71.

—. Edward Lhuyd's collection of Irish manuscripts. *Transactions of the Honourable Society of Cymmrodorion*, 1962, 57-76.

O'Sullivan, William. Correspondence of David Rothe and James Ussher, 1619-23. *Collectanea Hibernica*, Nos. 26-7, 1994-5.

—. Notes on the scripts and make-up of the Book of Leinster. *Celtica*, vii, 1966, 1-31.

Phillips, Henry. *Church and culture in seventeenth-century France*. Cambridge, 1997.

Plomer, H.R. Dermod O'Connor and Keating's 'History'. *Irish Book Lover*, iii, 1912, 125-8.

Polo de Beaulieu, Marie-Anne. Des histoires et des images au service de la prédication: la *Scala Coeli* de Jean Gobi Junior. †1350. In *De l'homélie au sermon: histoire de la prédication médiévale*. Louvain-la-Neuve, 1993, 279-312.

Power, Patrick. *The placenames of Decies*. 2nd ed. Cork, 1952.

—. *Waterford and Lismore: a compendious history of the united dioceses*. Cork, 1937.

Power, Patrick C. *Carrick on Suir and its people*. Dun Laoghaire, 1976.

Quin, E.G. 'Irish studies'. In T. Ó Raifeartaigh (ed.). *The Royal Irish Academy: a bicentennial history, 1785-1985*. Dublin, 1985, 166-87.

R.J.C. *Geoffrey Keating, priest, poet and patriot: his life, times and literary work*. 1913.

Rafroidi, P. The uses of the Irish myth in the nineteenth century. *Studies*, lxii, 1973, 251-6.

Ranum, Orest. *Artisans of glory: writers and historical thought in seventeenth-century France*. Chapel Hill, 1981.

— (ed.). *National consciousness, history and political culture in early modern Europe*. Baltimore, 1975.

Ricard, Robert. Pour une histoire de l'Exemplum dans la littérature religieuse moderne. Recherches sur l'histoire de la predication en Espagne, au Portugal et en France. *Les Lettres Romanes*, no. 8, Louvain, 1954, 199-233.

Risk, May H. Seán Ó Neachtuin: an eighteenth-century Irish writer. *Studia Hibernica*, no. 15, 1975, 47-60.

Robinson, Marian Schouler. Éire and the high kings of Ireland: the concept of flaitheamhnas in Geoffrey Keating's *Foras feasa ar Éirinn*. Ph.D. dissertation, University of California, Berkeley, 1970 (NLI microfilm P7983).

Robinson-Hammerstein, Helga (ed.). *European universities in the age of Reformation and Counter Reformation*. Dublin, 1998.

Rouse, R.H. and Rouse, M.A. *Preachers, Florilegia and sermons: studies on the Manipulus Florum of Thomas of Ireland*. Toronto, 1979.

Royan, Nicola. The *Scotorum historiae* of Hector Boece: a study. D.Phil. thesis, Oxford University, 1996.

Ryan, John. The battle of Clontarf. *Journal of the Royal Society of Antiquaries of Ireland*, lxviii, 1938, 1-50.

—. The historical content of the 'Caithréim Ceallacháin Chaisil'. *Journal of the Royal Society of Antiquaries of Ireland*, lxxi, 1941, 89-100.

—. The mass in the early Irish church. *Studies*, l, 1961, 371-84.

Saunders, J.W. The stigma of print: a note on the social bases of Tudor poetry. *Essays in criticism*, i, 1951, 139-64.

Savage-Armstrong, G.F. *A genealogical history of the Savage family in Ulster*. 1906.

Scowcroft, Mark. Miotas na gabhála in Leabhar gabhála. *Léachtaí Cholm Cille xiii*, 1982, 41-75.

Sharpe, Kevin and Zwicker, Steven N (eds). *Politics of discourse: the literature and history of seventeenth-century England*. Berkeley, 1987.

Sharpe, Richard. *Medieval Irish saints' lives: an introduction to Vitae sanctorum Hiberniae*. Oxford, 1991.

Silke, J.J. *Ireland and Europe, 1559-1607*. Dundalk, 1966.

—. Irish scholarship and the Renaissance, 1580-1673. *Studies in the Renaissance*, xx, 1973, 169-206.

Simms, Katharine. *From kings to warlords: the changing political structure of Gaelic Ireland in the later middle ages*. Woodbridge, 1987.

—. Bards and barons: the Anglo-Irish aristocracy and the native culture. In Robert Bartlett and Angus Mackay (eds), *Medieval frontier societies*. Oxford, 1989, 177-97.

—. Literacy and the Irish bards. In Huw Pryce (ed.). *Literacy in medieval Celtic societies*. Cambridge, 1998, 238-58.

Sims-Williams, Patrick. Some functions of origin stories in early medieval Wales. In T. Nyberg et al. (eds), *History and heroic tale: a symposium*. Odense, 1985.

Smith, Anthony D. *The ethnic origins of nations*. Oxford, 1986.

—. National identity and myths of ethnic descent. *Research in social movements, conflict and change*, vii, 1984, 95-130.

Smyth, William J. Property, patronage and population: reconstructing the human geography of mid-seventeenth century County Tipperary'. In William Nolan and T.G. McGrath (eds), *Tipperary: history and society*. Dublin, 1985, 104-38.

—. Towns and town life in mid-seventeenth century County Tipperary. *Tipperary Historical Journal*, 1991, 163-9.

Sommerville, J.P. James I and the divine right of kings: English politics and continental theory. In Linda Levy Peck (ed.), *The mental world of the Jacobean Court*. Cambridge, 1991, 55-70, 283-9.

—. English and European political ideas in the early seventeenth century: revisionism and the case of absolutism. *Journal of British Studies*, xxxv, no. 2, 1996, 168-94.

Stanford, W.B. *Ireland and the classical tradition*. Dublin, 1976.

Staunton, E. de Lacy. The Ó Maolconaire family: a note. *Journal of the Galway Archaeological and Historical Society*, xx, 1942, 82-8.

Stokes, Whitley. The prose tales in the Rennes Dindsenchas. *Revue Celtique*, xvi (1895), 279-83.

—. The Irish abridgment of the *Expugnatio Hiberniae*. *English Historical Review*, xx, 1905, 77-115.

Stone, Harriet. *The classical model: literature and knowledge in seventeenth-century France*. Ithaca & London, 1996.

Strayer, J. The historical experience of nation-building in Europe. In K.W. Deutsch and W.J. Foltz (eds), *Nation building*. New York, 1963.

Styles, P. James Ussher and his times. *Hermathena*, lxxxviii, 1956, 12-33.

Thomas, Keith. *The perception of the past in early modern England*. [London], 1983.

Tillyard, E.M.W. *Myth and the English mind*. New York, 1962.

Trevor-Roper, H.R. *Queen Elizabeth's first historian: William Camden and the beginnings of English 'civil history'*. Neale Lecture, 1971.

Tubach, F.C. Exempla in the decline. *Traditio*, xviii, 1962, 407-17.

Turville-Petre, Thorlac. *England the nation: language, literature and national identity, 1290-1340*. Oxford, 1996.

Valkenberg, Aibhistín. Pádraigín an Doiminiceach as Caiseal Mumhan. In *Dúchas, 1983, 1984, 1985*. Dublin, 1986, 21-32.

—. Pádraigín Haicéad, O.P., 1604?-1654. *Irisleabhar Mha Nuad*, 1985, 70-87.

Walsh, Paul. Gaelic genealogies of the Plunkets. *Irish Booklover*, xxv, 1937, 50-7.

—. *Gleanings from Irish manuscripts*. 2nd ed. Dublin, 1933.

—. *Irish chiefs and leaders*, ed. Colm Ó Lochlainn. Dublin, 1960.

—. *Irish men of learning*, ed. Colm Ó Lochlainn. Dublin, 1947.

—. Review of Eóin Ó Riain, *Réim ríoghraidhe na h-Éireann*. *Irish Historical Studies*, ii, no. 8, Sept.1941, 444-8.

—. The Book of Lecan in Ormond? *Irish Book Lover*, xxvi, 1938, 62.

—. The dating of the Irish annals. *Irish Historical Studies*, ii, no. 8, Sept. 1941, 355-75.

—. *The Mageoghegans: a lecture ... at Castletown-Geoghegan*. Mullingar, 1938.

Walsh, T.J. The Irish College of Bordeaux. *Journal of the Cork Historical and Archaeological Society*, lii, 1947, 101-15.

—. *The Irish continental college movement: the colleges at Bordeaux, Toulouse and Lille*. Dublin, 1973.

White, John D. *Anthologia Tipperariensis*. Cashel, 1892.

Williams, N.J.A. A note on *Scáthán Shacramuinte na hAithridhe*. *Éigse*, xvii, 1977-9, 436.

—. *Í bprionta í leabhar: na Protastúin agus prós na Gaeilge, 1567-1724*. Baile Átha Cliath, 1986.

Woolf, Daniel. Memory and historical culture in early modern England. *Journal of the Canadian Historical Association*, n.s. ii, 1991, 283-308.

Wormald, Jenny. *Court, kirk and community: Scotland 1470-1625*. London, 1981.

Index

A Bhanba bhog-omh dhona dhuaibhseach, 23,
    81
A Bhanba is feasach dom do scéala, 212
A chóemu críche Cuind chain, 72
Adam, 49, 91, 122-3, 124, 136, 182
Adamnán, St, 94
Adrian IV, pope, 89, 98, 149
adultery, 45, 160, 161
Africa, 124, 139, 192
Aherlow, glen of, Co. Tipperary, 17, 59,
    60, 83
Aimhirgin, 70
Alba, see Scotland
Albion, chronicle of, 87
almsgiving, 163, 168
Ambrose, St, 37, 53
Amhra Choluim Cille, 64, 69, 74-5, 78-9
An síogaí Rómhánach, 214
Anglesea, earl of, see Annesley, Arthur
Anglia, kingdom of, 139
Anglo-Normans, 76, see also conquest;
    Norman invasion; Old English; origins,
    110-12, 127, 148, 150-1, 196; and Irish
    language, 131
Anmann ceathrair ceart ro chin.n, 77
Annála ríoghachta Éireann, 6-7, 83, 105,
    108, 161, 177-8, 187
Annals of Clonmacnoise, 129, 149
Annals of Cluain Eidnech, 63, 79n
Annals of Loch Cé, 105
Annals of the Four Masters, see Annála
    ríoghachta Éireann
Annals of Ulster, 105
annals, 6-7, 70, 72, 77, 83, 105, see also
    individual annals; approved at Tara, 154
Annesley, Arthur, 1st earl of Anglesea,
    202, 203

Anthony, St, 37
antiquarianism, 199, 203-4, 214, 217, 218,
    226
antiquities, 116-17, 118
Ard Macha, 72, see also Armagh
Ardchoill, Co. Clare, 174
Ardfinnan, Co. Tipperary, 17, parish, 19
Armagh, 89, 120; county, 197, see also Ard
    Macha
ars morendi, 49, 57
Arthur, king, 146, 147
Arthurian legends, 147
Asia, 124, 137, 192
Athachthuaith, 134, 141-2, 159, see also
    lower orders
Attila the Hun, 161
Augustine, St, 30, 53, 54-6, 57
Auraicept na nÉces, 64, 130

Babel, tower of, 130, 192
Ballybecan parish, Co. Tipperary, 19
Ballyclerahan parish, Co. Tipperary, 19, 44
Ballycurrene, Co. Tipperary, 44
Ballylomasey, Co. Tipperary, 22
Ballylusky, Co. Tipperary, 24, 176, 183-4
Ballymacooda, Co. Clare, 174
Banbha, 63, 132
Bansheanchas, 64, 69, 72-3
barbarism, 116
Barclay, John, 114-15, 152-3; Icon animo-
    rum, 86
Barrow river, 116
Basil, St, 54
battles, 94, 126, 168-9, 215, see also Cath
Bealtaine, 135-6
Bede, Venerable, 57, 83, 92, 131; Historia
    ecclesiastica gentis Anglorum, 93-4, 215

Beinén, St, 69, 70
Bellarmine, Robert, 30, 32-33, 35, 54, 119;
  De scriptoribus ecclesiasticis, 100;
  *Disputationes de controversiis Christianae
  fidei*, 33, 35
Bellings, Richard, 7, 108
bequests, 163-4
Bernard, St, 53, 54, 78; *Life of Malachy*,
  92
Berthus, 94
Besse, Pierre de, 37, 51, 52-6, 92
Bible, 37, 57; and origin myths, 112, 122-
  40; history, 110-11; parallels with, 75-6,
  144, 161; translation of, 38; use of, 38-
  9, 53-4
bilingualism, 129, 211-5, 225, *see also* lan-
  guage
bishops, 74, 142
Black book of Molaga, 79-80
Boece, Hector, 83, 130-1; *Scotorum histo-
  riae*, 84-5, 98, 108, 112
Bonaventure, St, 30
Book of Ballymote, 67, 217
Book of the Dun Cow, *see Leabhar na
  hUidhre*
Book of Glendalough, 63, 155, 217
Book of Invasions, *see Leabhar Gabhála*
Book of Lecan, 65, 67, 77, 81, 217
Book of Leinster, 79
Book of Uí Maine, 217
Book of rights *see Leabhar na gceart*
books, 128-9, 214, 218; continental, 30, 32-
  40, 49-53, 83; English, 83, 86-97;
  Scottish, 83-6; *see also* publishing, read-
  ers and reading
Bordeaux, 27, 28, 29, 30, 42, 44, 47, 53,
  184; Madeleine University, 29
brehons, 95, 97, 157, *see also* law
Breoghan, (Brigus), 90
Brian Bóroimhe, 62, 68, 69, 126, 145, 149,
  150, 154, 176, 180-1, 192, 219, 221
Brigid, St, 92
Britain, history of, 94; kingdom of, 139
Bruff, Co. Limerick, 19
Buchanan, George, 83, 86; *De rerum
  Scoticarum historia*, 86, 92
Burgat, William, 202
Burgess, Co. Tipperary, 14, 20, 21, 22
Burke, earls of Clanricard, 153, 155
Butler, Éamonn Fionn mac Piarais, 23, 81

Butler, Edmund Mac Richard, 61
Butler, James, 22, 61
Butler, James, 1st duke of Ormond, 202
Butler, James, of Knocktopher, 23
Butler, John, son of 3rd baron Dunboyne,
  23
Butler, Lady Frances, 46
Butler, Margaret, baroness Dunboyne, 24,
  183
Butler, Pierce, son of Edmund, 77
Butler, Richard, of Kilcash, 46
Butler, Sarah, *Irish tales*, 215
Butler, Theobald, 1st baron of Cahir, 18,
  20, 22
Butler, Thomas, 2nd baron of Cahir, 23
Butler, Thomas, 10th earl of Ormond, 22
Butler, Thomas, son of 3rd baron
  Dunboyne, 23
Butlers of Shanballyduff, 23
Butlers of Cahir, 17-18, 19, 20, 22, 24, 25,
  60, 81, 105
Butlers of Dunboyne, 23, 24, 25, 81, 184;
  as patrons, 173, 176-7; links with
  Bordeaux, 184
Butlers of Ormond, 17, 22, 155; marriages,
  153

Caesarius of Heisterbach, 36, 92
Cahir, Co. Tipperary, 17, 18, 19, 25;
  castle, 18, 23; parish, 19, 46; *see also*
  Butlers of Cahir
Caicher the druid, 146
Caimín, St, of Inis Cealltrach, 168
Cairbre Chin Chait, 143, 159
Caithréim Ceallacháin Caisil, 68, 213
Caithréim Conghail Chláiringhnigh, 76
Calvin, John, 5, 32, 114, 119
Cambridge university, 25
Camden, William, 83, 114, 138; *Britannia*,
  94-5, 215; *Anglia*, 96
Campion, Edmund, 86-7, 97, 115, 202, 210
Caomhánach, *see* Kavanagh
Capgrave, John, *Life of Colum Cille*, 92
Caradocus, chronicle of, 87
Carmelites, 46
Carn Conaill, battle of, 79
Carrane, Ellen, 183
Carrick-on-Suir, Co. Tipperary, 17
Cashel, kings of, 69-70
Castlefore, Co. Leitrim, 174

Castlehaven, lord, see Touchet, James
catechesis, 164
Catechism of the Council of Trent, 50
catechisms, 39-40, 128-9, 163
Cath Chrionna, 64
Cath Fionnchoradh, 64
Cath Mhuighe Léana, 64, 75
Cath Mhuighe Muccraimhe, 64, 75
Cath Mhuighe Rath, 64
Cath Mhuighe Tualaing, 64
Cath Ruis na Ríogh, 64
Cathaoir Mór, 124-5
Catholic Confederation, 108, 214
Catholicism and history, 5, 116, 119-21,
    152, 197-8, 209, 213, 226 see also
    Christianity and history
Catholicism and national identity, 9, 120-
    21, 123-7
Cato, Marcus Porcius, 189
Cearbhall mac Muireigéin, 87
Cecil, Sir Robert, 186
Celestinus, pope, 93
Ceasair, daughter of Bioth, 65
chalice, 43-4
Cham (Cam), son of Noah, 124, 192
Charles I, king, 108-9, 126, 147-8, 185-6;
    ancestry of, 147-8
Charles II, king, 195, 202-3
Children of Israel, 118
Christianity and history, 110, 122-3, 137,
    142-3, 145, 167-70, 184, 207, see also
    Catholicism and history
chroniclers, see historians
church institutions, 4, 8, 122-3, 170, 184,
    see also bishops; clergy; monasteries,
    synod; patronage of, 155; role of, 162,
    165
Cian, son of Oilill Ólom, 125
Ciannachta, 125
Ciaran, St, 46, see also Cillín Chiaráin
Cicero, Marcus Tullius, 9
Cillín Chiaráin, Tubbrid, Co, Tipperary,
    14-15, 44, 46, 47, 81n
Civil survey, 18, 183
civility, 215-6
Clangibbon, 17
Clann Mhíleadh, 7, 65, 67, 85, 86, 124-5,
    127, 132-3, 137, 208, 210, 213, 223 see
    also Éibhear, Éireamhón; Stuart kings
    and, 126, 205, 208

Clann Neimhidh, 124, 130, 134, 137, 146
Clanricard, earl of, *see* Burke
Clare, county, 10, 60, 176, 212
clergy, 3, 8, 23, 25, 41-3, 106, 129, 150-1,
    162, 184; as keepers of *seanchas*, 154; as
    owners of mss, 11; as patrons, 199-200;
    as scribes, 198; secular-regular dispute,
    4, 42-43; shortcomings of, 163-4
Clonmel, Co. Tipperary, 17, 20, 29
Clontarf, battle of, 68, 126, 192, 215
Cobhthach Caol, 124
Cody, John, 173n
Cogadh Gaedheal re Gallaibh, 68, 89, 112-
    13
Cóir anmann, 64, 69, 73-4
Colgan, John, 61n; *Acta Sanctorum hiber-
    niae*, 177, 182, 207; *Trias thaumaturgae*,
    196; annotations to *FFÉ*, 181-2
colonisation, 7
colonists, 153, 184
Colpa, son of Míl, 133
Colum Cille, St, 74, 92, 94, 155, 168-70,
    see also *Amhra Choluim Cille*
Columbanus, St, 92
Comeragh mountains, 17
Comerford, Patrick, bishop of Waterford
    and Lismore, 44
Comhghall of Bangor, rule of, 77-8
commonwealth, 4
Comyn, David, 14
Conall Cearnach, 73
Conchubhar mac Fachtna Fáthaigh, 80
Conchubhar mac Neasa, 167
confession, 35, 40, 162-3, 170
Conlaoch, son of Cúchulainn, 80
Connacht, 31, 125, 134; and Wales, 140;
    king of, 150, 160; poets, 196; scribes,
    176
conquest, 99, 131, 193, 204, 208, 223, see
    also invasions, Norman invasion
Conradh na Gaeilge, 14
Conry, Florence, see Ó Maolchonaire,
    Flaithrí
Conry, John, 176, 222-3
contention of the bards, see *Iomarbhágh na
    bhfileadh*
continental colleges, see seminaries, univer-
    sities
contract, with God, 3, 165-7, with king, 5,
    165-7

Cork, city, 26, 29, county, 198, diocese, 28
Corlise, Co. Tipperary, 19, 20
Cormac Conluingeas, 167
Cormac mac Airt, 6, 144, 166; and
  Christianity, 167; *Tecosca Cormaic*, 144
Cormac mac Cuileannáin, 62, 75-6, 87,
  143, 189; death of, 166
Counter Reformation, 3, 4, 47-9
Cox, Richard, 190, 201, 215, 209-11, 225;
  Hibernia Anglicana, 12, 209-11, 212
Cox, Robert, 19
Créacht do dháil me, 195
Creagh, Richard, archbishop of Armagh, 130
Creake, B., publisher, 224
crime, 161, 162
Cromwell, Henry, 193-5
Cromwell, Oliver, 59n, 193-5
Cúil Dreimhne, battle of,168, 169
Cúil Feadha, battle of, 169
Cúil Rathan, battle of, 169
Cumascach, 94
Cúraoi, son of Dáire, 80
Cusack, Mary, 18

Dáire Doimhtheach, 73
Dál Cais, 68, 88, 126, 176
Dallan Forgaill, 74
Daly, John, collector, 183n
Daniel, Samuel, 90, 115
Daniel, William, archbishop of Tuam, 38
Davies, Sir John, 7, 86, 95, 115; *A discov-
  ery of the true causes*, 99-100
de Besse, Pierre, *see* Besse
de Clare, Richard, earl of Pembroke, *see*
  Strongbow
De Maccaib Conaire, 75
de Nógla, Eleanor, 198, 199
death, 31, 45, 48-9, 51, 152, 162, 196
Decies, 16, 24, 140, 149-50, 169
Declan, St, 47
Dempsey family, 124
Dempster, Thomas, 27, 86
Derrygrath parish, Co. Tipperary, 18, 19
Desmond, earls of, *see* Fitzgerald
Diarmait son of Fearghus, king, 168
Dinneen, P. S., 176, 178
Dinnsheanchas, 64, 69, 70-2, 97, 132-6
dioceses, *see* church institutions
divine punishment, 5, 151, 153, 159-64,
  168

divisions of Ireland, 134
Dligheadh gach rí ó rígh Caisil, 69
Dominic, St, 37, 53
Domun duthain a lainde, 70
Doneraile parish, Co. Cork, 199
Donnchadh mac Briain, 149, 154
Donnchadh Mór mac Ceallaigh, 170
Donnelly, John, 188-9
Dooley, James, 177
Douai, 27, 28, 35,
Drangan parish, Co. Tipperary, 183
dress, 155-6, 157
Drogheda, Co. Louth, 29
Dromceat, convention of, 155, 169-70
Druididh suas, a chuaine an chaointe, 23, 81
druids, 95, 146, 159, 165-6, 167
Dublin, capture of, 150
Dublin scribal circle, 212-5, 216-7, 218-9
Duffy, James, 12
Duhy, *see* O'Duffy
Dún Domhnaill, 149
Dunboyne, *see* Butler
Durand (Durantus), William, 32, 34, 54;
  Rationale Divinorum Officorum, 34

Eamhain Mhacha, 72
Easter controversy, 94
Edgar, king of Britain, 87, 115
education, 24, 25-31, 215-6, *see also* semi-
  naries and seminarians; Jesuit teaching;
  universities
Egfrid, king of Northumbria, 87, 115
Egypt, 65, 85, 124, 138
Éibhear, son of Míl, 85, 124, 126, 132-3,
  148, 210
Éire, 132
Éireamhón, son of Míl, 85, 124, 132-3,
  208, 210
Éireannaigh, 9, 106, 109-10, 111, 131, *see
  also* national identity; Old English
England, 138, 139, 187, *see also* Britain;
  histories of, 90; kings of, 150, *see also*
  Arthur; Henry II; James I; Charles I;
  Charles II
English family, 19
English language, 30, 68, 87, 91, 129, 186,
  198, 204, 210, 211, 213, 225
Eochaidh Feidhlioch, 73, 134
Eochaidh, son of Earc, 143

Eochair-sgiath an Aifrinn, 5, 9, 11, 32-40, 46, 52, 56-7, 114, 119, 122n, 142; manuscript copies 174-6, 199
ethnicity, *see* national identity
etymology, 130, 132, 137, 210
Europe, 124, 136, 137, 147, 192; influence of, 3, 6, 25-31, 44, 108, 161-2, 184
Eusebius, 57
evil, *see* good and evil
exempla, 35-7, 50, 52-3
exile, 24, 112, 127-8

fables, 85, 189, 203-4, 207, *see also exempla*, myth
fairs, 17
family history, 113, 191-2, 218
Fannin, William, 216
fasting, 30, 163, 168
Feidhlim Nuachrothach, 73
Feidhlimidh, son of Criomhthann, 70
Féinius Farsaidh, 130
feis of Tara, 154-5, 159
Fenians, 12
Flaithusa Éireann, see *Réim Ríoghraidhe*
Fódla, 132
Foras feasa ar Éirinn, 3-13, 59-101, 168; archaic and modern versions, 178-80; criticisms of, 187-8, 207; date, 59; historical method, 73-5, 136; manuscript copies, 24, 173-200; revisions of, 180; manuscript sources, 60-82; orthography, 178-9; printed sources, 83-101; publication of, 11, 12, 13, 119n, 218-25; style, 13, 76; translations into English, 11, 12, 24, 182-7, 190-2, 200, 204, 207, 210, *see also* Kearney, Michael; O'Connor, Dermod; translations into Latin, 11, 12, 187-90 *see also* Lynch, John
Fiachraidh Suighdhe, 168
Fingal, 153
Fionn Mac Cumhaill, 85
Fir bolg, 7, 65, 96, 130, 137, 146, 210
Fitz Aldelmel, William, 159
Fizgerald, earls of Desmond, 153, 155
Fitzgerald, earls of Kildare, 153
Fitzgerald, Seán Óg, of Decies, 24
Fitzsimon, Henry, SJ, 5, 39, 86n
Flanders, 139
Flann Sionna, king, 166
Florianus del Campo, 87

Forbhais Droma Dámhghaire, 64
foreigners, 142, 146, 150, 153, 160
Formorians, 124
Four Masters, *see Annála ríoghachta Éireann*
France, 24, 26-27, 29, 31, 43, 47, 83, 85, 86, 95,119, 137, 138, 139, 161, 187, 199, 204
Francis de Sales, St, 30
Franciscans, 6-7, 26, 30, 49, 118, 217; hagiography, 169, 177, 182, 196, 207; in Kildare, 177; in Louvain, 6, 10, 39-40, 49-50, 105, 119n, 128-9, 163, 177, 181; in Paris, 30; in Prague, 17; in Rome, 177; scribes, 10, 177-8, 200
French language, 30
Fuaras i Saltair Chaisil, 62-3, 69, 182, 198
funerals, 30-31, 49
Fursey, St, 92

Gaedheal Glas ó dtaid Gaedhil, 90-91
Gaedheal Glas, son of Niúl, 85, 130, 137, 192
Gaedheal, son of Eathór, 130
Gaeil, 85, 110, 112, 115, 126-7, 131, 136, 193, 213; as colonisers, 139; identity, 114; origins, 93, 126-7, 146-7, 151-2, 198, 223, *see also* Gaedheal Glas, Clann Mhíleadh
Gaileanga, 125
gaill, *see* foreigners
Gall, St, 92
Gallamh, *see* Míl of Spain
Galtee mountains, 17
Galway city, 29, 187, 204
Garryroe, Co. Tipperary, 19
genealogies, 6, 8, 22, 23, 60, 62, 67, 72, 111, 112-13, 123-7, 213, 220, 222
gentry, 44-5, 212, *see also* nobles
Geoffrey of Monmouth, 83
geography, 122, 136-40, 159
Germany, 139
giants, 85
Gildas, 115
Giolla Caomháin, 90
Giraldus Cambrensis, 68-9, 94, 96, 106, 114-16, 131, 189, 202, 213, 218; *Topographia Hiberniae*, 89, 96; *Expugnatio Hiberniae*, 96, 112
Glendalough, Co. Wicklow, 154

Glenville, Co. Cork, 199
good and evil, 159-70
Goths, 161
Graces, the, 108-9
Greece, 137, 189
greed, 157
Gregory, St, 53, 54, 57, 161
Grimston, Edward, *Generall historie of Spain*, 90

hagiography, 53, 86, 169, 177, 182, 196, 207, *see also* saints
Hakluyt, Richard, *Principal Navigations*, 89
Ham, son of Noah, *see* Cham
Hanmer, Meredith, 75, 84, 86, 87, 88, 114, 202
Harris, Walter, 225
Harte, Morgan, 206
Harte, Thomas, 201, 206-9
Hearne, Thomas, 223
heaven, 49, 55, 57, 161, 162-3, 165
Hebrew languge, 128
hell, 49, 55, 57, 161, 162-3, 164-5
Henry II, king, 98, 148-52, 198, 210, 222
heraldry, 23, 220
heretics, 39, *see also* Protestants, attitudes to
Herodotus, 138, 189
heroes, 68, 122, 215
hierarchy, 154-8
historians, status of, 95, 97, 142, 157, *see also seanchas*
historical controversy, 8, 202-25, *see also* Catholicism and history; Christianity and history
historical method, 73-5, 108
historical sources, 59-82, 116-19, 136, 154
history, theory of, 8, 99-100, 108-12, 114-21, 207
Holinshed, Raphael, 83; *Chronicles*, 69, 97
Holy Cross, Co. Tipperary, 17, 47
Holy Roman emperor, 147
holy wells, 46
honour, 124, 125, 153, 213; and kingship, 143, 226
hospitality, 115-16
Hyde, Douglas, 14

Iffa and Offa barony, Co. Tipperary, 17, 18, 19

Ignatius Loyola, St, 49
immorality, 160
inauguration, 142-4, 180-1, 210, *see also* kings and kingship; stone, 148, *see also* *Lia Fáil*
incest, 167
Inchiquin, Lord, *see* O'Brien, William
inheritance, 151, 153, 160
Inislounaght parish, Co. Tipperary, 19, 44, 46-7
Inns of Court, London, 25, 97
Instruction for Kings, see *Tecosca Cormaic*
invasions, 65, 137, 146-7, 182, *see also* *Leabhar gabhála*; Norman invasion
Iomarbhágh na bhfileadh, 63, 64, 66, 126
Iona, 74
Ireland, kingdom of, 9, 10, 62, 111-12, 122-3, 138, *see also* kings and kingship; Scoti, Scotia
Irial Fáidh, son of Éireamhón, 133
Irish language, 8, 10, 11, 30, 68, 98, 127-32, 186, 198, 202, 204, 220, 225; and identity, 123, 127-8, 131-2; literacy in, 191, 202, 225; origins of, 123, 130-1; revival of, 14, 226
Irish Texts Society, 13, 14, 180
Is uaigneach duit, a phuirt na bpriomh-fhlaith, 23
Italy, 139, 161

James I, king, 126, 157, 185-6, 205; ancestry of, 147-8, 208; inauguration of, 148
Japheth, son of Noah, 124, 192
Jerome, St, 50, 54, 94
Jesuit teaching, 28, 29, 47, 56-7, 161-2; *see also* universities
John Chrysostom, St, 54
Jonas, 92
justice, 143, 159, 165

Kavanagh (Caomhánach) family, 78, 81, 88, 124
Kearney, Barnabas, SJ, 47-48
Kearney, Michael, translator, 7, 12, 24, 114n, 120, 129, 175, 176-7, 200, 206
Kearney, Patrick, 183
Keating family, 18, 105-6
Keating, Edmund, 19, 20
Keating, Geoffrey; and Cahir, Co. Tipperary, 23, 173; and Moorestown,

Co. Tipperary, 19-21, 28, 44; chalice owned by, 43-4; date of death, 81; family network, 19-21, 22, 105-6; land sold by, 19-20; vestments, 40n; *for other themes see main index entries*

Keating, James fitz Edmund, of Moorestown, 19, 21

Keating, John, 19-20

Keating, John, lord chief justice, 194-5

Keating, Morish, 19

Keating, Nicholas, 19

Keating, Richard, 44

Keating, Richard, of Nicholastown, 18, 19

Keating, Richard, son of James, 19-20

Keating, Richard, son of John, 19-20

Keating, Thomas, 19

Keating, Walter, 19

Kilballynamoney, *see* Moorestown

Kilcomanbegg, Co. Tipperary, 28

Kildare, earls of, *see* Fitzgerald

Kilian, St, 92

Kilkenny city, 29

Killaloe cathedral, 89

Killarney, Co. Kerry, 191

Kilmurray, Co. Tipperary, 19, 20

Kiltoghert, Co. Leitrim, 174

kingdom of God, 58, 123

kings and kingship, 64, 65-7, 69-70, 126, 134, 141-58, 189; and Christianity, 166, 167; and justice, 159, 165; and placelore, 133-7; and sanctity, 163, 170; British, 85, 87, 115; Cashel, 69-70; choice of, 84-5, 142; continuity of, 113-14; death of, 144; fecundity, 145; heredity, 145; high-kingship, 135-6; historiography of, 204-5, 210; inauguration, 142-4, 148, 180-1, 210; military prowess, 145; Munster, 70, 143, 166, 181; Norman, 84-5, 113-14, 142, 155; obedience, 185-6; Saxon, 85; Scottish, 84-5, 205; *see also* Boece, Hector; Stuart, 114, *see also* James I; Charles I; Charles II; subjects, 184-6; succession, 113-14, 142, 145; *see also* contract; Ireland, kingdom of; *Réim ríoghraidhe*; sovereignty

Kinsale, Co. Cork, 209

kinship, 105-6, 112-13, 124, 127, 132, 153 *see also* genealogies

Knocklought, Co. Tipperary, 19

Labhraidh Loingsech, 78-9, 124-5, 139-40

Laffan, Elinor, 44

lamentation, 52-3

landholding, 17-19, 22, 157, *see also* mortgages

landscape, 8, 24-25, 118, 132

Lanfranc, Archbishop, 221

language, 8, 10, 11, 30, 98, 127-32, 186, 210, *see also* bilingualism, *and individual languages*

Latin language, 30, 68, 91, 128, 182, 184, 186, 191, 198, 204, 225

Laudabiliter, papal bull, 149

law, 4, 111-12, 141, 185, 190, 192, 214; and history, 212; and kingship, 143; and parliament, 154-5, 159, 185-6; common law, 185-6; respect for, 116, 152

Leabhar Ard Macha, 63

Leabhar breac Mhic Aodhagáin, 159

Leabhar buidhe Moling, 63

Leabhar Chluana hEidhneach Fionntain, *see* Annals of Cluain Eidnech

Leabhar comhaimseardhachta, 64

Leabhar dubh Molaga, 63

Leabhar gabhála, 7, 8, 64, 65-7, 77, 92, 97, 101, 106, 111-12, 125, 130, 131, 132, 136-9, 145, 187, 210

Leabhar gearr na Pailíse, 217

Leabhar Ghlinne-dá-loch, *see* Book of Glendalough

Leabhar irsi, 70

Leabhar Muimhneach, 22

Leabhar na gceart, 63, 69, 213

Leabhar na gcúigeadh, 64

Leabhar na hUachongmhála (Book of Leinster), 63

Leabhar na hUidhre, 64

Leabhar na nAos, 64

Leabhar oiris Uí Mhaolchonaire, 217

Leabhar ruadh Meic Aodhagain, 77-8, 217

learning, 5, 116, 155, 197, 215

Leath Cuinn, 125

Leinster, 26, 45, 124-5, 134; and France, 139-40; king of, 160

Leitrim, county, 11, 177

Leixlip, Co. Kildare, 217

Lent, 30

Leycester, Peter, 7

Lhuyd, Edward, 191, 199, 205, 217

Lia Fáil, 85, 148, 166, *see also* inauguration

Limerick, county, 195, 199, 220
Lismore, Co. Waterford, 169; diocese, 28,
  31, 41-44
Lissava, Co. Tipperary, 61
literacy, 117-18, 215, 225
Livy (Titus Livius), 189
Loch Garman, see Wexford
Lochlannaigh, 68, 112, 155, 160, 161; in
  England and Scotland, 161
Logan, Patrick, 201
Loghloghry, Co. Tipperary, 19
Louvain, St. Anthony's College, 6, 10, 39,
  105, 128-9, 181, see also Franciscans
lower orders, 8, 152-3, 156, 207, see also
  Athachthuaith
Lughaidh Laighdhe, 73
Lughnasa, 136
Luighne, 125
Luis de Granada, 30
Lurgan, Co. Armagh, 201
Luther, Martin, 5, 32, 114, 119
Lynch, John, 12, 204, 210, 212; as transla-
  tor, 187-90, 200; *Cambrensis eversus*, 187,
  189-90, 196, 202-3, 213
Lynegar, Charles, 216

Mac a Liondain, Pádraig, 197-8
Mac Aingil, Aodh, 36, 49-50, 129, 161, 163
Mac an Bhaird, Domhnall, 22
Mac an Bhaird, Fearghal Óg, 126, 148
Mac an Lega, Uilliam, 77
Mac Aodhagáin family, 23, 217
Mac Aodhagáin, Flann, 174
Mac Ardghuil, Éinrigh, 177
Mac Arthur, Robert, 65
Mac Bheatha, Fearghas, 198
MacBrien family, 17
Mac Bruaideadha family, 23, 181
Mac Bruaideadha, Giolla Brighde, 22
Mac Bruaideadha, Tadhg Mac Daire, 63.
  73
MacCarthy family, 81
MacCarthy, Diarmuid, 27, 28, 79
Mac Carthy mór, 153, 193
Mac Carthy Riabhach, 153
McCaughwell, see Mac Aingil
McCone, Kim, 144
Mac Craith family, 20-23, 60, 76, 81, 106,
  181
Mac Craith, Eoghan Mac Donnchadha, 22

Mac Craith, Flann mac Eoghain, 22
Mac Cruitín, Aindrias, 212
Mac Cruitín, Aodh Buidhe, see MacCurtin,
  Hugh
Mac Cuarta, Séamas Dall, 196-7
MacCurtin, Hugh (Mac Cruitín, Aodh
  Buidhe), 201, 212-5, 216; *Brief discourse
  in vindication of the antiquity of Ireland*,
  12, 212-5
Mac Donnchadha, Donnchadh Óg, 198
Mac Eochagáin family, 23, 76, 81, 181, 217
Mac Eochagáin, Conall, 60, 62, 63, 77,
  129, 178
Mac Fhirbhisigh, Dubhaltach, 60, 65n, 67,
  84, 205; *Leabhar na ngeinealach*, 113
Mac Flannchadha, Cosnamach, 61, 77
Mac Gearailt, Dáibhí, 196-7
Mac Gearailt, Muiris mac Dáibhí Dhuibh,
  196-7
Mac Giolla Eáin, Éoin (McErlean, John),
  81
Mac Giolla Phádraig family, 124-5, 153
Mac Giolla Phadraig, Brian, 157-8
MacMahon family, 88
Mac Murchadha, Diarmait, 149, 160
MacNamara family, 88
MacSheehy family, 88
MacSolly (Mac Solaidh), Seán, 216
MacSweeney family, 88
Magnum speculum exemplorum, 35-36, 37,
  50, 52
Magnus, king of Norway, 89-90
Magog, son of Japheth, 124
Magowry parish, Co. Tipperary, 183
Magrath, Hugh Oge, 23
Maguon, Nicholas, of Loghloghry, 19
Máine son of Corc, 148
Mair (Major), John, 85, 131; *Historia
  Majoris Britanniae*, 85
Mallacht ort, a bháis bhronaigh, 196-7
manuscripts, see also scribes; access to, 76-
  82; in circulation, 10, 11-12, 68; owner-
  ship of, 61, 76-82, 173-4; scribal transmis-
  sion, 10, 11, 12, 13, 119, 173-200, 201;
  Advocates' Library, Edinburgh, 201-2;
  Bibl. de Troyes, MS 919, 187-8; Bibl.
  Nat., Fonds Celtique MS 66, 11, 174n,
  180; BL, Add. MS 30,512, 77, 78, 81,
  217; BL, Egerton MS 107, 174, 180; BL,
  Egerton MS 1782, 78-9, 81; Bodl. Fairfax

MS 29, 59, 176; Bodl. Laud Misc. 610, 61, 62, 81; Cambridge, McClean MS 187, 79-81; FLK, MS A 14, 10, 174n, 177, 180, 181-2; FLK, MS A 15, 10, 180; Maynooth, MS C 2, 176; NLI, MS G 288, 107, 191; NLI, MS G 293, 190; NLI, MS G 293, 209; RIA, MS 23 E 23, 199; RIA, MS 23 Q 14, scribe of, 176; RIA, MS 24 G 16, 175, 182-87; RIA, MS 24 I 5, 188-9; RIA, MS 24 P 23, 71, 179, 180, 181; RIA, MS C iv 1, 176; TCD, MS 1397, 176; TCD, MS 1403, 180; TCD, MS 1443, 190-1; Woodstock Theological Center, MS 7, 187; *see also individual named manuscripts, e.g. Book of Lecan*

Maolseachlainn, 160
Marianus Scotus, 92
markets, 17
marriage, 72, 109, 153
Martin, St, 37, 53, 139
Mass, 5, 11, 29, 30, 31-40, 170,; for the dead, 163-4
Meagher, Conor, 183
Meath, province, 132, 134-6
Mellifont, treaty of, 7
memory, 117-18, 226
Messingham, Thomas, 27; *Florilegium insulae sanctorum*, 27, 83, 86, 92, 93,
Midhe, St, 1678
Mil (Milesius), 65, 124, 137, 148, 196, 208
Milesian origins, *see* Clann Mhíleadh; origin myths
Milis an teanga an Ghaedhealg, 128
Milton, John, 83
missions, 48
Mo bheannacht leat a scríbhinn, 24, 132
Mochua, St, 168
Mochuda, St, 169
Mocler (Moclar) family, 19, 44
Mocler, Henry, 44
Mocler, Jeffrey, 44
Moclerstown, Co. Tipperary, 44
Mogh Nuadha, 74
Mohir, David, 199
monarchy, *see* kings and kingship
monasteries, 151, 154, 170, *see also* church institutions
Moorestown, (Ballynamoney; Kilballynamoney), Co. Tipperary, 19-21, 28, 44

Moors, Spanish, 161
Mór aontrom inse Banba, 23
moral order, 3-4, 9, 116, 151, 159-70
moral reform, 45
moral tales, *see exempla*
mortgages, 19, 28, 45, *see also* landholding
Moryson, Fynes, 115
Moses, 85, 122, 137
Moynihan family, scribes, 190-1
Moynihan, Thomas, 191
Muicinis, 132
Muircheartach, king, 147
Munster, 26, 27, 28, 31, 43, 45, 46, 47-48, 62, 68, 105-6, 126, 127, 132, 134, 140, 156, 193, 194; bias in favour of, 90, 93; kings of, 70, 143, 166, 181; plantation, 17, 106, 140
Múscail do mhisneach, a Bhanbha, 81
Muskerry, 28
myth, 9, 207, 225, *see also* origin myths; and history, 8, 105-6, 111, 135-6

naomhsheanchas, 77, 170
national identity, 9, 111, 113, 114, 120-21, 213, 218; *see also Éireannaigh*, Gaeil, New English, Old English; and language, 127-8, 131-2
neighbours, 161-2
Neimheadh, 65, 137, *see also* Clann Neimhidh
Nennius, 83, 91
Netterville, Patrick, 183
New English, 131, 186, 208-11, 222; historical perspective, 116, 225, *see also* Harte, Thomas; Cox, Richard
Newcastle, Co. Tipperary, 17
Niall Naoighiallach, 136, 138
Nicholastown, Co. Tipperary, 18-19
Nicolson, William, *Irish historical library*, 213
Nile river, 138
Nine years war, 7, 208
Noah, 123-4, 136, 192
nobles, 5, 8, 134, 141, 142, 150, 158, 207, *see also* gentry; and patronage, 154; and pilgrimage, 154; as kingmakers, 154; history of, 115, 153; marriages of, 153; status of, 153
Nore river, 116
Norman invasion, 68-9, 112, 119, 121, 126, 140, 141, 149, 150, 154, 207-8, 212; as

Norman invasion (*cont.*)
Christian conquest, 131; in poetry, 192; *see also* Anglo-Normans; Giraldus Cambrensis
Nubrigensis, Gulielmus, 146

Ó Branaigh, *see* O'Byrne family
Ó Briain, Muirchertach, 68
O'Brien, Caitlín, 199
O'Brien, Sir Donnchadh, of Lemenagh, 212
O'Brien family, 176, 212; kings, 221-2; marriages, 153
O'Brien, John, bishop of Cloyne, 199
O'Brien, Muircheartach, king, 89-90
O'Brien, William, earl of Inchiquin, 221, 222
Ó Bruadair, Dáibhí, 193-6
O'Byrne family, 81, 88, 124
Ó Caoimh, Eoghan, 198-200
O'Carroll family, 125, 153
Ó Cearbhaill, Domhnall, 174
Och mo chreach-sa faisean Chláir Éibhir, 157
Ó Cianáin, Seán, 70n
Ó Cléirigh, Lughaidh, 66, 161
Ó Cléirigh, Micheál, 6, 10, 47, 60, 61n, 65n, 177-8, 181, 196
Ó Clérigh, Muiris, 70n
Ó Colla, Pól, 10-11, 177
Ó Conaill, Seán, 192, 212
Ó Conchobhair, Ruaidhrí, 148, 150, 151, 160, 205
O'Connor family, 125
O'Connor, Dermod, 12, 13, 60, 191, 216, 218-25
O'Connor, Tadhg Rua, 220
Ó Dálaigh family, 23
Ó Dálaigh, Aonghus Fionn, 161
Ó Dálaigh, Giolla Iosa, 22
Ó Diomsaigh *see* Dempsey
Ó Domhnaill, Aodh, 63
Ó Domhnaill, Aodh Ruadh, 161
Ó Domhnaill, Uilliam, *see* Daniel
O'Donnell chiefs, 143
O'Duffy, Eoghan (Duhy, Eugene), 14-15
Ó Duibhgeannáin family, 10, 76, 174
Ó Duibhgeannáin, Fearfeasa, 10, 174
Ó Duibhgeannáin, Flaithrí, 10, 174
Ó Duinn family, 124
O'Dwyer family, 124

Ó Faoláin, Maolseachlainn, 149
O'Flaherty, Roderick, 196, 201, 210, 212, 216; *Ogygia*, 204-5, 213
Ó Gadhra, Seán, 92, 196, 213
O'Gara family, 125
Ó Gnímh, Fear Flatha, 161
O'Grady, S.H., 180, 183
Ó hAnluain, Feidhlim, 197
O'Hara family, 125
O'Harte, Henry, 206
Ó hEodhasa, Bonaventure (Giolla Brighde), 26, 129, 163
Ó hEodhasa, Eochaidh, 148
Oidhidh na gcuradh, 64, 75
Old English, 9, 111-12, 115, 120-21, 151, 188, 193, *see also* Anglo-Normans; history, 209, 214; identity, 109-10, 114-15, 120, *see also* Éireannaigh; origins, 8, 106, 110-12, 126-7; politics 108-9, 119-20, 186
Ó Longáin, Micheál, scribe, 23
Ó Luinín, *see* Lynegar
O'Mahony, John, 12-13
Ó Maolchonaire family, 10, 60, 76, 81, 174, 176, 200, 217
Ó Maolchonaire, Flaithrí (Conry, Florence), 40
Ó Maolchonaire, Iolann mac Torna, 10, 174
Ó Maolchonaire, Muiris Óg mac Muiris, 176
Ó Maolchonaire, Seámus, 174
Ó Maolchonaire, Seán Mac Torna, 78, 79, 140, 174, 176, 199
Om sceol ar ardmhagh Fháil, 156
Ó Maolchonaire, Seán, 10, 176
Ó Maolchonaire, Torna Mac Torna, 77
Ó Murchadha, Seán, 224
Ó Neachtain, Seán, 220
Ó Neachtain, Tadhg, 200n, 212, 216-7, 218-9, 220
O'Neill family, 139-40; marriages, 153
Ó Néill, Flaithbheartach, 154
Ó Nuallain family, 124
oral tradition, 116, 118
Ó Rathaille, Aodhaghán, 192
origin myths, 8, 105, 106, 110-12, 122-40; Biblical parallels, 112, 123, 126; *see also* *Leabhar gabhála*
Ormond, *see* Butler

Ó Rodaigh, Tadhg, 196
Orosius, 92
O'Rourke family, marriages, 153
O's feas gur sgríobhadh an tseanchaidheacht so Chéitinn chlúmhail, 224
O'Sheeran, Thomas, 119n
Ossory, king of, 170
Ó Suilleabháin, Diarmuid, 199
Ó Suilleabháin, Domhnall mac Taidhg Óig, 79
Ó Suilleabháin, Domhnall mac Thomáis, 175, 183
O'Sullevane, Thomas, 20-22, 23, 24, 59-60, 220-1, 223, 225
O'Sullivan Beare, Philip, 27, 161
O'Toole family, 88, 124
outsiders, *see* foreigners, *Leabhar gabhála*
Oxford university, 25, 97, 216

Pairlement Chloinne Tomáis, 45, 129, 156-8, 186, 195
Palladius, 93
Paris, 27, 85 ; Irish Franciscan college, 30; Sorbonne, 177
parliament, 141, 154-5, 156, 159, 185-6, 190, *see also Pairlement Chloinne Tomáis*
Parthalón, 65, 137, 146
Patrick, St, 46, 92, 120-21, 123, 138-9, 142, 192, 207, 213; purgatory, 100
patristic citations, 50-2, 53-7, 164
patrons and patronage, 12, 18, 20, 22, 23, 24, 60, 81, 154, 173, 174, 176-7, 212, 216
Paul of St Ubald, O.Carm., 46
penance, 154, 159, *see also* confession
persecution, 26, 42, 43, 164
Persia, kings, 189
physicians, status of, 95, 97
Picts, 93, 205
Piggott, Colonel Thomas, 18
pilgrimage, 47, 148, 154
placelore, 70-2, 111, 118, 132-40, *see also Dinnsheanchas*, landscape
poetic licence, 88, 115
poetry, 62-3, 64, 66, 126; as historical source, 136, 189; political, 192-8
poets, 20, 22, 26; and Stuart kings, 126, 148; role of, 117; status of, 95, 157
political order, 152-8
Polychronicon, 137

Pomponius Mela, 94
popes, 89, 93, 98, 149, 151, *see also* Rome
Popish Plot, 195
poverty, 152-3
Power family, 19
Power, Rev. Patrick, 173n
Prague, 177
prayer, 163, 168, 170
preacher's handbooks, 35-7, 50, 52, 122
preaching, 3, 9, 40, 43-44, 47, 48-9, 50-4, 57-8, 127, 161, 168, 198
Prendergast family, 19
pride, 160
priests, *see* clergy
printing, *see* books; publishing
Promptuarium exemplorum, 36
prophecy, 146
Protestants, 12, 210; attitudes to, 5, 32, 114, 110, 119, 138
Psalter, *see also Saltair*
Psalter of Cashel, 60, 61-3, 93, 189, 224
Psalter of Tara, 64, 221, 224
publishing, 39-40, 128-9, 213, 218-25; *see also* books, readers and reading; subscription publishing
purgatory, 35, 49, 100, 162-3
Purtil, Edmond, scribe, 173n

Raifteirí, Antoine, 192
Ráth Mór, battle of, 94
Raymond de la gros, 150
Raymond, Anthony, 217, 218-25
readers and reading, 12, 45, 64-5, 101, 117-19, 123, 144, 164, 182, 201-2, 205-7, 211-15, 218, 225, 226; Protestant, 12, 208, 218
Rehill, Co. Tipperary, 20
Réim ríoghraidhe, 64, 65-7, 77, 112, 141, 145, 217
Remonstrance controversy, 202
repentance, 31, 154, 163, 165
Rheims university, 27, 47
Rí na loch in loch-sa theas, 70n
Rice, Stephen, 216
Robert Bellarmine, St, *see* Bellarmine, Robert
Roche, John, bishop of Ferns, 100
Roche, Maurice (Morrish), 28
Rochestown parish, Co. Tipperary, 19
Roman empire, 95, 138-9, 146

Rome, 28, 100, 149, 154, 189, 207; St
    Isidore's college 177
Rothe, David, bishop of Ossory, 27, 61,
    81, 120
Royal Irish Academy, 192, *see also* manu-
    scripts
Ryan family, 124

sacraments, 29-30, 42, 159, 162, 168
sacrifice, 33
saints, 25, 116, 118, 160, 168-70, 207, *see
    also* hagiography; and kings, 169, 210;
    communion of, 162-3
Sallust, 189
Saltair Chaisil, see Psalter of Cashel
Saltair Mhuire, 200n
Saltair na rann, 63, 69
Samhain, 135-6
Scala coeli, 36
Scone, stone of, 148, *see also* inauguration,
    Lia Fáil
Scota, daughter of Pharaoh, 124, 130
Scoti, Scotia, 85, 86, 92, 93, 137, 208;
    kingdom of, 138-9
Scotichronicon, 108
Scotland (Alba), 84-5, 86, 87, 130-1, 137,
    138, 205, 208; kings of, 84-5, 205;
    Lochlannaigh in, 161
scribal transmission, 10, 11, 12, 13, 119,
    173-200, 201
scribes, 10, 23, 60, 176, 177-8, 190-1, 200,
    212, 216-7, 224, *see also* Dublin scribal
    circle; manuscripts
Scythia, 65, 93, 124, 130, 137, 138, 147,
    198, 210
seanchas, 22, 60, 79-81, 91, 130, 154, 213
Seanchas Buitlérach, 113
Seanchas Búrcach, 113
Sean ghaill, *see* Old English
Searc na suadh an chrobhaing chumhra, 194
Sem (Shem), son of Noah, 124, 192
seminaries and seminarians, 25, 27-31, 40,
    44, 46, *see also* universities
Seneca, 50
Serarius, *Life of St Kilian,* 92
sermons, *see* preaching
Sgáthán na sompladha, 35
sin, 3, 45, 157, 159-70; original sin, 5, 48-
    9, 52-3; seven deadly sins, 48-50, 161-2
Slán agaibh, a fhir chumtha, 26
Slanóll, son of Ollamh Fódla, 144

Slieve Bloom mountains, 116
Sligo, 206
social elite, *see* nobles
social mobility, 4, 45, 112, 156-8, 186, 195
social order, 9, 152-8, 165
Solinus, Julius, 94
Sorbonne university, 177
Sourdis, Cardinal de, 28
sovereignty, 134, 141-5, 159-60, 165, 190,
    see also kings and kingship
Spain, 26, 65, 90, 108, 138, 139-40, 161,
    198; king of, 147
Spanish Netherlands, 26, 140
Speed, John, *History of Great Britaine,* 83,
    91
Spenser, Edmund, 86, 114-15, 202, 215;
    View of the present state of Ireland, 87-9
Srú, son of Easrú, 138
St Anthony's College, Louvain, *see*
    Louvain
St Isidore's college, Rome, *see* Rome
St Malo, 27
St Patrick's College, Maynooth, museum,
    40n
St Patrick's stone, 46
St. Eutrope chapel, 30
Stanihurst, Richard, 8, 69, 96, 97-8, 115-
    16, 120, 153, 218; and Irish language,
    131
Stapleton, Theobald, 128, 129
Stow, John, *Chronicle,* 88-9, 91
Strabo, 94
Strongbow, Richard de Clare, earl of
    Pembroke,150, 198, 208
Stuart kings, 7, 8, 126; and poets, 126,
    148; loyalty to, 27, 184-6; origins of,
    126, 204, 208
Suarez, Francisco de (Francis), 32-35, 37,
    54, 119; *Defensio fide Catholicae,* 32, 33-4
subscription publishing, 213, 218-25, *see
    also* publishing
Suir river, 16, 17, 101, 116
synchronisms, 113, 114
synod of Kells, 43, 154
synod of Rathbreasail, 43

Tabhair a lao loinn lachta, 198
Tacitus, Cornelius, 139
Tadhg, son of Cian, 125
Tadhg, son of Lorcán, 154
Tailtiu, 72, 135

Talbot, Peter, archbishop of Dublin, 225
tales, 78-9, *see also* myth
tanistry, 99
Tara, 70, 134-6, 144, 148
Tecosca Cormaic, 144, *see also* Cormac mac
   Airt; kings and kingship
Ten commandments, 49
Thomas a Kempis, St, 30
Thomas Aquinas, St, 54, 56-7, 161-2
Thomas Hibernicus, *Flores*, 39, 50
Thomond, see Clare, county; O'Brien
Thurles, Co. Tipperary, 17
Tipper, Richard, 216, 217
Tipperary, county, 3, 7, 16, 17, 43, 60,
   176-7
Tlachtgha, 135
Tobar Finn, 133
Toland, John, 221, 224
Toletus (Toledo), Francis, 34
Touchet, James, lord Castlehaven, 203
translation, 68, 129, 177, 182-92, 200, 207
   see also Kearney, Michael; Lynch, John
travel, 26-27, 136-40
Trent, Council of, 5, 30, 32, 42-43, 163, 164
Triall gach éinfhir go cúirt Teabóid, 18
Trí bior-ghaoithe an bháis, 3, 4, 9, 13, 35,
   43, 44-5, 48-58, 92, 110, 122, 153, 157,
   161; influence, 196-7; language, 130;
   manuscripts, 174, 176, 199; rhetoric, 53-4
Trí coróna i gcairt Shéamais, 126
Trim, Co. Meath, 220
Trinity College, Dublin, 25, 217, *see also*
   manuscripts
Tuam, Co. Galway, 206
Tuatha Dé Danann, 65, 130, 132, 137,
   146, 166, 210
Tuathal Teachtmhar, 134, 159
Tubbrid, Co. Tipperary, 14-15, 20, 22, 44,
   47
Tuireamh Mhurcha Crúis, 196n
*Tuireamh na Gaeilge agus teastas na hÉire-
ann*, 196
Tuireamh na hÉireann, 192-3, 212, 214
Tuireamh Phádraig Mhic a Liondain, 198
Tullaghmelan parish, Co. Tipperary, 19
Tullamoylin, Co. Tipperary, 176
Turgesius, 155, 165

Ua Faoláin, Tomás, 176
Uch is truagh mo ghuais ón ghleo-bhroid, 23

Ughaine mór, 134
Uidhir Chiaráin, 63
Uisneach, 134-5
Uisneach, sons of, 79
Ulster King at Arms, 23
Ulster plantation, 7
Ulster, 26, 126, 134; Confederates, 214;
   links with Spain, 140; bias against, 68
universities, 25, 27-31, 45, 47, 97, 177,
   216, *see also* education; Bordeaux;
   Cambridge; etc.
upstarts, 112, 156, 186, 195
Uraicheapt, see *Auraicept na nÉces*
Ussher, James, archbishop of Armagh, 61,
   77, 81, 110, 207, 217, 218; *Discourse of
   the religion anciently professed by the Irish
   and British*, 120; *Indice chronologicae*,
   207; *Primordia Ecclesiarum Britannicarum*,
   203; *Veterum epistolarum Hybernicarum
   sylloge*, 119-20, 221

Vallancey, Charles, 199
Vandals, 161
Vikings see Lochlannaigh
Virgil, Polydor, *De rerum inventoribus*, 98-9
Virginia, 210
Voragine, Jacobus de, 37

Wadding, Luke, 100
Wale, Rev. 48
Wales, 138, 140, 205
Walsh, Peter, 201, 211, 212, 215, 216, 225;
   Prospect of the state of Ireland, 12, 202-6,
   213
Ware, Sir James, 81, 86-7, 217, 225;
   Antiquities of Ireland, 196, 203
Waterford diocese, 28, 31, 42
Waterford, 26, 28, 29, 149, city, 42
Waterstown, Co. Tipperary, 19
Wexford (Loch Garman), 26, 93, 132
White Knight, 17
White, James, 44
White, Michael, merchant, 20
While, Michael, scribe, 173n
White, Peter, 97
wills, 45
women, 72-3, 163, *see also Bansheanchas*
Worthington, Thomas, 200n

Yellow Book of Lecan, 79